The Global Third Way Debate

Edited by

Anthony Giddens

Polity

First published in 2001 by Polity Press in association with Blackwell
Publishers Ltd

Editorial office:
Polity Press
65 Bridge Street
Cambridge CB2 1UR, UK

Marketing and production:
Blackwell Publishers Ltd
108 Cowley Road
Oxford OX4 1JF, UK

Published in the USA by
Blackwell Publishers Inc.
350 Main Street
Malden, MA 02148, USA

A catalogue record for this book is available from the British Library.

Library of Congress Cataloging-in-Publication Data

The global third way debate / edited by Anthony Giddens.
    p. cm.
    Includes index.
    ISBN 0-7456-2741-2 – ISBN 0-7456-2742-0 (pbk.)
       1. Post-communism. 2. Mixed economy. 3. Globalization.
  4. Welfare state. 5. Democracy. 6. Right and left (Political science)
I. Giddens, Anthony.
HX73 .G59 2001
337 – dc21

                        00-047849

Typeset in 10 on 12 pt Palatino
by Best-set Typesetter Ltd., Hong Kong
Printed in Great Britain by TJ International, Padstow, Cornwall

This book is printed on acid-free paper.

The Global Third Way Debate

To Michele and Katy

Contents

The Contributors

Michael Allen is a researcher at the Centre for Strategic Trade Union Management at Cranfield University.

Benjamin R. Barber is Director of the Walt Whitman Center for the Culture and Politics of Democracy at Rutgers University, USA.

Luiz Carlos Bresser-Pereira is Professor of Economics at the Getulio Vargas Foundation, São Paulo, Brazil.

Hugh Collins is a Lecturer in Law at the London School of Economics.

Paul Dalziel is Senior Lecturer in Economics at the University of Canterbury, New Zealand.

David Downes is Professor of Social Policy at the London School of Economics.

Stephen Driver is a Lecturer in Social Policy at the Roehampton Institute, University of Surrey.

Ronald Dworkin is Professor of Law at the New York University School of Law.

Michael Edwards is Director of the Program of Governance and Civil Society at the Ford Foundation.

Gøsta Esping-Andersen is Professor of Comparative Social Systems at the University of Trento, Italy and also Visiting Professor in Political Science at the Universitat Pompeu Fabra in Barcelona.

Maurizio Ferrera is Professor of Public Policy and Administration at Pavia University.

William A. Galston is Professor and Director of the Institute for Philosophy and Public Policy at the University of Maryland.

Anthony Giddens is Director of the London School of Economics and Political Science.

Anne-Marie Guillemard is Professor of Sociology at Université de Paris V.

David Held is Graham Wallas Professor of Political Science at the London School of Economics.

Anton Hemerijck is a researcher at the Max Planck Institute for the Studies of Societies in Cologne, Germany and a member of the Department of Public Administration at the Erasmus University of Rotterdam.

Michael Jacobs is Director of the Fabian Society.

Elaine C. Kamarck is Executive Director of Visions of Governance for the Twenty-First Century, a new research programme at the John F. Kennedy School of Government of Harvard University.

Ethan B. Kapstein is Visiting Professor at the INSEAD in Paris and a Visiting Fellow at IFRI, also in Paris.

Mark Latham is the Werriwa MP for the Australian Parliament. He is a member of the Australian Labour Party.

Stephan Leibfried is Professor at the Centre for Social Policy at Bremen University, Germany.

Lutz Leisering is a lecturer and researcher at the Sociology Department of Bielefeld University, Germany.

Luke Martell is Lecturer in Sociology at Sussex University.

Yves Mény is Director of the Robert Schuman Centre at the EUI, Florence and Director of the European Forum.

Wolfgang Merkel is Professor at the Institut für Politische Wissenschaft in the Ruprecht-Karls-Universität Heidelberg, Germany.

Thomas Meyer is Professor at Dortmund University, Germany.

James Midgley is Dean and Specht Professor at the School of Social Welfare from the University of California, Berkeley.

Joseph S. Nye, Jr is Don K. Price Professor of Public Policy and Dean of the J. F. Kennedy School of Government at Harvard University, USA.

Martin Rhodes is Lecturer in Political Science at the EUI, Florence and at the University of Manchester.

Joseph Stiglitz is Senior Fellow at the Brookings Institution.

Simon Szreter is University Lecturer in History, University of Cambridge and Fellow of St John's College, Cambridge and ESRC Research Fellow.

Vito Tanzi is Director of the Department of Public Finances at the International Monetary Fund.

Helen Wilkinson is Senior Research Associate at the think-tank Demos.

Acknowledgements

I should like to thank all those who have helped in the preparation of this book. Boris Holzer worked as my research assistant during an early period when materials were being gathered together. Eunice Goes later took over from Boris and did invaluable work in the preparation of the contributions. David Held read and commented on the Introduction as well as on the suggested list of contributions. I am very grateful to him, and to David Miliband who did likewise. I should like to thank in addition: Anne de Sayrah, Amanda Goodall, Alison Cheevers, Reggie Simpson, John Thompson and Sandra Byatt. I owe a particular debt to Miriam Clarke who worked tirelessly on various versions of the manuscript. Finally, my thanks for her support and encouragement go to Alena Ledeneva.

The publishers gratefully acknowledge the following for permission to reproduce copyright material:

'The Third Way: An Outline' by Mark Latham, from *The Australian Economic Review*, vol. 32, no. 4, pp. 384–98. Copyright © University of Melbourne, Institute of Applied Economic & Social Research. Reprinted with permission of Blackwell Publishers.

'Left, Right and the Third Way' by S. Driver and L. Martell, from *Policy & Politics*, vol. 28, no. 2, pp. 147–61. Reprinted with permission of The Policy Press.

'The Third Ways of Social Democracy' by Wolfgang Merkel. Reprinted with permission of the author.

'From Godesberg to the *Neue Mitte*: The New Social Democracy in Germany' by Thomas Meyer, from *The New European Left* edited by Gavin Kelly, published by the Fabian Society. Reprinted by permission of the Fabian Society.

'A Third Way for New Zealand?', extract from 'Third Way Economics: What Might This Mean in New Zealand?' by Paul Dalziel, from *The New Politics: A Third Way for New Zealand*. Reprinted with permission of Dunmore Press, New Zealand.

'Five Realities That will Shape 21st Century US Politics' by William A. Galston and Elaine C. Kamarck, excerpted with permission from *BLUE-PRINT: Ideas For a New Century*, vol. 1, Fall 1998, published by the Democratic Leadership Council. This magazine is available online at http://www.dlc.org/blueprint

Extract from 'Effective Responses: Policy Mixes and Institutional Reform' from *The Future of Social Europe: Recasting Work and Welfare in the New Economy* by Maurizio Ferrera, Anton Hemerijck and Martin Rhodes © Ministerio do Trabalho e da solidariedade, and the authors, 2000. Reprinted with permission of the authors and CELTA, Portugal.

'A Welfare State for the 21st Century' from *Ageing Societies, Knowledge Based Economies, and the Sustainability of European Welfare States*. Report prepared for the Portuguese Presidency of the European Union, Spring 2000, by Gøsta Esping-Andersen. Reprinted with permission of the author.

Extract from 'Growth, Redistribution and Welfare: Toward Social Investment' by James Midgley, from *Social Service Review*, March 1999, pp. 3–21. Used with permission of The University of Chicago Press.

'Does Equality Matter?' by Ronald Dworkin, published in 'Progressive Governance for the XXI Century: Conference Proceedings' (Florence EUI 1999). Reprinted with permission of the author.

'Taxation and the Future of Social Protection' prepared by Vito Tanzi in January 2000 for 'International Monetary Fund, Fiscal Affairs Dept.'. Reprinted with permission of the author.

Extract from 'Paths out of Poverty: Perspectives on Active Policy' from *Time and Poverty in Western Welfare States* by Lutz Leisering and Stephan Leibfried, published by Cambridge University Press. Reprinted with permission of Cambridge University Press.

Extract from 'The Macho Penal Economy: Mass Incarceration in the US: A European Perspective' by David Downes, published in *Punishment and Society*, January 2001. Reprinted with permission of Sage Publications.

Extract from 'The Family Way: Navigating a Third Way in Family Policy' by Helen Wilkinson, in *Family Business* – Demos Collection, Issue 15. Reprinted with permission of the author.

'Work or Retirement at Career's End? A Third Way Strategy for an Ageing Population' by Anne-Marie Guillemard. Reprinted with permission of the author.

'In Government We Don't Trust' by Joseph S. Nye Jr, from *Foreign Policy*, Fall, 1997. Reprinted with permission of the author.

'Five (Hypo)theses on Democracy and its Future' by Yves Mény, from 'Progressive Governance for the XXI Century', Conference Proceedings (Florence EUI 1999). Reprinted with permission of the author.

'How to Make Society Civil and Democracy Strong' revised for publication from *A Place for Us: Making Society Real* by Benjamin Barber. Copyright © 1999 by Benjamin Barber. Reprinted by permission of Hill and Wang, a division of Farrar Straus and & Giroux, LLC.

'Stakeholding by Any Other Name: A Third Way Business Strategy' by Michael Allen, from *Renewal*, vol. 8, no. 2, Spring 2000. Reprinted with permission of the author and *Renewal*.

'A New Political Economy: The Importance of Social Capital' by Simon Szreter, from *Renewal*, vol. 7, no. 1. Reprined with permission of the author and *Renewal*.

'Is there a Third Way in Labour Law?' by Hugh Collins, from *Labour Law: An Era of Globalisation*, edited by J. Conaghan, R. Fischl and K. Klare, published by Oxford University Press. Reprinted by permission of Oxford University Press.

'The Environment, Modernity and the Third Way', extract from 'Environmental Modernisation: The New Labour Agenda' by Michael Jacobs, published by Fabian Society 1999. Reprinted with permission of the Fabian Society.

'An Agenda for Development for the Twenty-First Century' by Joseph Stiglitz from http://www.worldbank.org/wbi/mdf/mdfl/agenda.htm, slightly edited with approval of the author. Reprinted with permission of Copyright Clearance Center, USA.

'The New Left Viewed from the South' by Luiz Carlos Bresser-Pereira. Reprinted with permission of the author.

'The Third Way and the New International Order', from *Sharing the Wealth: Workers and the World Economy* by Ethan B. Kapstein, © 1999 by Ethan B. Kapstein. Used by permission of W. W. Norton & Company, Inc.

'Humanising Global Capitalism: Which Way Forward?' from *Future Positive: International Co-operation in the 21st Century* by Michael Edwards, published by Earthscan Publications. Reprinted with permission of Kogan Page Publishers.

Extract from 'Regulating Globalization? The Reinvention of Politics' by David Held, from *International Sociology*, vol. 15 (2), June 2000. Reprinted with permission of the author.

Every effort has been made to trace copyright holders, but in some cases this has proved impossible. The publishers would be happy to hear from any copyright holder who has not been acknowledged.

Publisher's Note

An ellipsis [. . .] has been used whenever material from the original has been omitted. Where a paragraph or more has been excluded, a line space appears above and below [. . .].

Apart from the omission of material discussed above, each chapter has been presented as it was originally published. The decision to do this has necessarily entailed inconsistencies of style and spelling between the chapters.

Introduction

Anthony Giddens

The debate about third way politics has moved on a great deal over the past two or three years. So has the advance of third way thinking in the sphere of practical politics. Across the world left of centre governments are attempting to institute third way programmes – whether or not they favour the term itself. Many do – at the time of writing there are self-declared third way parties in power in the UK, New Zealand, Korea, Taiwan, Brazil, Argentina and Chile, among many other countries. Others don't. Thus while the idea of the third way has been intensively debated in continental Europe, by and large the term has not caught on there. Some actively reject it; others substitute different notions, like that of 'the new middle' in German social democracy or the 'purple coalition' in Holland.

We must look behind the terminology, however. There are several reasons why political leaders might want to avoid 'third way'. The term is an old one that has surfaced often before in the history of political thought and political practice, only to disappear again. It has been used by a diversity of political groups in the past, some more from the right than the left. Moreover, 'third way' came back into politics in a rather specific context. It was resurrected by Bill Clinton and the Democratic Leadership Council in the US in the late 1980s, and was then taken up by Tony Blair and New Labour in Britain. Hence some social democrats – inside those countries and elsewhere as well – have come to identify the third way either with the policies adopted by the New Democrats and New Labour, or with the socioeconomic frameworks of the US or UK. From this point of view, it is a product of countries recovering from long periods of neoliberal rule – Reaganism in the US and Thatcherism in Britain. It gives too many concessions to that mixture of market liberalism and moral authoritarianism that is the hallmark of neoliberalism. More generally, the proponents of third way political thinking are seen as advocating Anglo-American society as a desirable model for others to follow.

This interpretation does not provide a useful perspective on the third way debate – and it is not a point of view taken in any of the selections that comprise this book. As understood here, 'third way' refers to a much more generic series of endeavours, common to the majority of left parties and thinkers in Europe and elsewhere, to restructure leftist doctrines. There is a general recognition almost everywhere that the two 'ways' that have dominated political thinking since the Second World War have failed or lost their purchase. Traditional socialist ideas, radical and reformist, were based on the ideas of economic management and planning – a market economy is essentially irrational and refractory to social justice. Even most advocates of a 'mixed economy' accepted markets only grudgingly. But as a theory of the managed economy, socialism barely exists any longer. The 'Keynesian welfare compromise' has been largely dissolved in the West, while countries that retain a nominal attachment to communism, most notably China, have abandoned the economic doctrines for which they once stood.

The 'second way' – neoliberalism, or market fundamentalism – has been discarded even by most of its rightist supporters. The East Asian crisis of 1997–8 showed how unstable, and destabilizing, unregulated world markets, especially financial markets, can be. They do little to help alleviate the extreme inequalities that exist between the poorest and richest countries. Within the developed societies, the electorate has recoiled from neoliberal policies, which suggest it is up to individuals to fend for themselves in a world marked by high levels of technological change and insecurity. The return of left of centre parties to government in so many countries sends a clear signal that people don't want to be left unprotected in the face of the global marketplace.

Leftist parties are being forced to pioneer something new, since the core doctrines of socialism are no longer applicable. Whether or not one uses 'third way' to refer to this attempt at 'something new' doesn't matter. 'Modernizing social democracy', or 'the modernizing left', can be used instead. I continue to use 'third way', however, because it is a useful shorthand term. It refers to the renewal of social democracy in contemporary social conditions. As I interpret the term here, it owes little or nothing to its usage in previous generations. The third way is not to be identified solely with the outlook and policies of the New Democrats, New Labour, or indeed any other specific party, but is a broad ideological stream with several tributaries flowing into it. The doctrinal changes made by left parties or coalitions in the Scandinavian societies, or in Holland, France or Italy since the late 1980s, are as much part of third way politics as those developed in Anglo-Saxon countries.

Some speak of these developments as different 'third ways'.[1] In my view, however, there is an overall political orientation and policy programme emerging, not just in Europe but also in other countries and continents, which can be described as the third way (or updated social democracy). It is still in the process of construction, rather than being a fully rounded system. Different political groups, and different countries, are approaching it from varying historical backgrounds and with differing needs. Because of this, they will not necessarily converge in their specific patterns of development, even while their policy solutions resemble one another.

The backdrop: social change

Third way politics is about how left of centre parties should respond to change – not only to the changing ideological map itself, but to the transformations which stand behind this shift. There are three such transformations which are altering the landscape of politics – globalization, the emergence of the knowledge economy, and profound change in people's everyday lives.

A few years ago, there was some doubt, particularly on the left, about whether globalization was a reality. The unpersuaded would write 'globalization' in inverted commas, to demonstrate their essential scepticism about the idea. This controversy has moved on. Discussion continues about how best to conceptualize globalization, but few would any longer deny its influence – as signalled by the role of global financial markets, new developments in electronic communication and geopolitical transitions, the most far-reaching of which is the ending of the Cold War. Discussion of globalization is no longer concentrated on whether or not it exists, but on what its consequences are. Since the meetings of the World Trade Organization in Seattle in late 1999, these concerns are no longer limited to the sphere of orthodox politics, but call into play various oppositional and counter-cultural groups.

In a somewhat similar way, many on the left were inclined to doubt the existence of the knowledge economy, or at least to downplay its impact. Manufacturing production, they argued, remains central to every modern economy, since physical commodities are essential necessities of life. Moreover, they continued, those who speak of the decline of the working class are making a mistake. Even where people work in service or 'knowledge industries', many jobs come to resemble those in manufacture so far as conditions of work are concerned. Thus the work of a person on the check-out in a supermarket is as routine and monotonous as that of a factory assembly-line operative.

There is still much disagreement about how the knowledge economy should best be understood and what its dynamics are. But there is no longer any doubt that the new economy is real and that its impact is omnipresent. Its origins stretch back some thirty years, to the time when information technology first started to influence production and distribution processes. Technological innovation is the main factor involved in the rapid and progressive shrinking of the manufacturing sector in the advanced economies. In the EU countries, an average of 18 per cent of the labour force works in manufacture, compared to close to 40 per cent a generation ago. Some suggest that within the next fifteen to twenty years, manufacture may follow the path of agriculture. In agriculture, 2 per cent of the labour force produces more than 30 per cent of the workforce in the same sector once did. Perhaps at some future point there will be less than 10 per cent of the labour force in manufacture, producing more goods than seven or eight times as many workers used to do.

The blue-collar working class, the main focus of traditional leftist politics, is disappearing. It isn't true that manufacturing jobs are simply being replaced by routinized service occupations or 'Mcjobs'. It is skilled workers, especially 'symbolic workers', who are in demand in the knowledge economy, not unskilled workers, who are in fact threatened with marginality. Moreover, even low-level service occupations can provide an avenue of mobility into better-paid jobs in a way blue-collar work by and large did not.

The coming of the internet will push these changes even further. No one knows what the full effect of the internet is going to be. Some 80 per cent of internet transactions at the moment are business-to-business and it may be here that its economic influence will be mainly concentrated. Finance and banking are among the areas where internet and intranet technologies have already promoted large-scale restructuring.

The third great source of change in the contemporary world is the rise of individualism. Perhaps not discussed as often as the first two sets of changes, it is at least as important. Many on the left have tended not to grasp this, seeing individualism either as economic selfishness or as consumerism, promoted by the expansion of a market economy. Obviously these traits do exist, but to equate them with individualism as such is highly misleading. Individualism is a structural phenomenon in societies breaking free from the hold of tradition and custom, a transition that is again taking place on a widespread basis. We live our lives in a more open, reflective way than was the case in the past. Among the areas, for instance, where individualism has made itself felt are the family and in gender relations. Women no longer are inevitably 'fated' to lives of domesticity and the rearing of children. They have entered the labour force in large numbers and have acquired many of the freedoms that were for long mainly the freedoms of men – including the right to divorce. These gains have hardly proved unproblematic but there is no going back on them – and they are also becoming global.

The framework of third way politics

In the wake of the collapse of Soviet communism and the wider failures of socialism, some have argued that the division between left and right has lost most or all of its significance. Advocates of third way politics, for example, sometimes characterize it as essentially pragmatic – 'what counts is what works'.

It is true enough that new left of centre thinking places in question dogmas of the past. Thus some ideas and policies once mainly associated with the political right (such as privatization or fiscal discipline) have become commonplace in the programmes of left parties. In a world experiencing such profound changes a certain pragmatism, and a readiness to experiment, are necessary. Yet the division between left and right has not disappeared. It essentially reflects differences in political values. To be on the left is to want a society that is solidary and inclusive, such that no citizen is left outside. It is to have a commitment to equality and a belief that we have an obligation to protect and care for the more vulnerable members of society. As a crucial addition, it involves the belief that the intervention of government is necessary to pursue these objectives. Rightists are liable to deny each of these propositions.

As mentioned earlier, there will not be a single version of third way politics. However, we can identify the key areas of structural reform which a third way approach suggests. All can be described as involving modernization – where that term means adapting to the three big sets of changes discussed earlier:

(1) Reform of government and the state is a first priority. Modernizing social democrats must avoid the traditional leftist strategy of

putting more and more tasks into the hands of the state. It cannot be too strongly emphasized, however, that this is not the same as downgrading public institutions. An overloaded, bureaucratic state is not only unlikely to provide good public services, it is also dysfunctional for economic prosperity. A fundamental theme of third way politics is rediscovering an activist role for government, restoring and refurbishing public institutions. Reforming the state is far from easy in practice, but the aim should be to make government and state agencies transparent, customer-oriented and quick on their feet.

The three sets of changes just described have not only created new conditions which must be confronted, they have injected a new volatility into political attitudes and patterns of voting support. In most industrial countries, levels of expressed trust in politicians and orthodox parliamentary institutions have fallen, as have rates of political participation. The proportion of voters having established loyalties to particular parties has dropped considerably. The largest growing party is what has been called the 'non-party of non-voters' – those disinterested in, or disillusioned with, orthodox political mechanisms.

The growth of political apathy needs to be responded to. When asked why they don't have much interest in politics, most people, particularly the younger generation, tend to mention the self-serving attitudes of politicians and political corruption. Reform processes can help reshape these attitudes, since they reflect real shortcomings in current political systems. Even the most democratic of countries are not democratic enough. Old-boy networks, patronage, backstage deals, open political hypocrisy continue to exist. No doubt none can be got rid of altogether, but progress could certainly be made in minimizing them. Constitutional reform, designed to promote transparency and openness, is a prime means of promoting such goals.

Rooting out corruption is equally important. Some say that corruption has increased in the industrial countries as the sphere of the state has been curtailed. The growth of public–private partnerships, for example, could be seen to offer new opportunities for shady dealings between those involved. However if corruption seems to have become more common than before the main reason is probably that in a world of increasing accessibility of information, previously accepted ways of doing things come to be seen as illegitimate.

(2)   The state should not dominate either markets or civil society, although it needs to regulate and intervene in both. Government and the state have to be strong enough to provide effective steering for the promotion of social development and social justice. A strong state, however, isn't the same as a large state.[2] Where the state is over-

developed, effective government becomes difficult and state power can start to override the wishes and the freedoms of the citizenry.

A similar point can be made about markets. An effective market economy is the best way of promoting prosperity and economic efficiency and has other benefits too. Markets provide for consumer choice and for the free and non-violent exchange of goods across short and long distances. So long as monopoly is effectively controlled, markets provide for open competition in which anyone in principle can join.

However, the role of markets must be kept confined. Where the market is allowed to intrude too far into other spheres of social life, a variety of unacceptable consequences result. Markets create insecurities and inequalities that require government intervention or regulation if they are to be controlled or minimized. Powerful agents within the marketplace can subvert democratic processes. Commercialism can invade areas that should either be the province of government or civil society.

(3) An understanding of the core role of civil society is a crucial feature of new left thinking. Without a developed civil society, there cannot be either well-functioning government or an effective market system. Yet just as in the case of the state and markets, there can be 'too much' of civil society, as well as 'too little'. Important as civic groups, special interest groups, voluntary organizations and so forth are, they do not offer a substitute for democratic government. Interest groups and non-governmental organizations may play a significant role in forcing issues onto the political agenda and ensuring public discussion of them. A society could not be run, however, by an assemblage of such groups, not only because they are unelected, but because governments and the law need to adjudicate between the rival claims they make.

This is one reason why the conservative notion that the state should simply disengage from civil society is wrong. Democracy and the rule of law are necessary controls over the civil sphere. The state both needs to draw sustenance from civil society and also to play an active role in regulating it.

Civil society is not exempt from wider processes of modernization, which it both reflects and to which it contributes. For instance, the internet provides new opportunities for communication and mobilization for a diversity of associations and groups, restructuring them in the process. Government should contribute directly to the modernizing of civil society while maintaining its boundaries from it. Civic entrepreneurship is one quality of a modernized civil society. It is needed if civic groups are to generate creative and energetic strategies to help cope with social problems. Government can lend financial support, or provide other resources for such endeavours. It will profit in its turn, since collaborative projects between government and civil society groups will need those groups to be engaged, determined and competent.

(4)   We need to construct a new social contract linking rights to responsibilities. Most of those who have written on citizenship rights, including T. H. Marshall in his classical analysis, accept that rights also imply duties.[3] But in practice they stress and spell out the rights much more than the responsibilities. The limits of this view are apparent today. Where most people want to be free to pursue their individual life projects, it is logical they should assume responsibility for the consequences of what they do, in respect both of themselves and others. Allocating citizens rights of provision, especially welfare rights, without a spelling out of responsibilities, creates major problems of moral hazard in welfare systems. Welfare systems that aren't integrated with obligations can also produce a culture of deceit – expressed, for example, in high levels of welfare fraud.

The theorem that responsibilities go along with rights has now become widely accepted in some spheres – for instance, it is one of the guiding principles of welfare to work schemes. But it should be seen as a general principle of citizenship, by no means confined to the welfare area. It must apply to all individuals and groups, rich and poor, powerful and less powerful. For elites, 'no rights without responsibilities' means accepting social and moral obligations, including fiscal ones. So far as corporations go, the principle shades over into a more general framework of corporate responsibilities.

(5)   We must not give up on the objective of creating an egalitarian society. It is here that many on the old left express their strongest reservations. In endorsing the essential importance of market mechanisms, aren't modernizing social democrats accepting a society marked by increasing inequalities? In a word, no. The pursuit of equality has to be at the core of third way politics. The recipe 'take from the rich to give to the poor' should remain a cornerstone of centre-left policy. Progressive wealth and income taxes make a direct contribution to social justice, assuming they are deployed effectively. But some of the points made earlier are relevant here. Fiscal policy must be assessed in terms of its contribution to economic efficiency and the overall level of tax revenue it will deliver. All the industrial countries, for example – although in varying degrees – have retreated from the high marginal

income tax rates they used to have. They have done so in recognition that such rates have an impact on incentives and produce high levels of tax avoidance.

Passive economic redistribution, however, has only limited voter support in pluralistic, opportunity-based societies, and has some negative consequences too. It makes sense to put the emphasis upon asset-based egalitarianism, based on investment in skills and capabilities.

As in other areas, tackling inequality cannot be just a case of reacting to insufficiencies of the market. Problems and limitations of the welfare state are involved as well. For instance, child poverty is increasing in a number of EU countries in spite of the fact that welfare spending has grown or remained stable. Some forms of social exclusion, such as those connected with failed social housing, result directly from misapplied welfare provisions.

In addition, there are new sources of inequality which necessitate innovative policy responses. Thus, as noted earlier, the demand for unskilled labour is diminishing as a result of the growth of the knowledge economy. Young men are most directly affected, a phenomenon that connects with wider changes affecting the prospects of men from poorer backgrounds more generally.

Globalization, information technology, and changes in social norms affect elites, not only the less privileged. In considering how best to 'regulate the rich and powerful' we must recognize that new patterns and structures of inequality are involved. However the category be defined, 'the rich' are diverse, ranging from long-established wealthy families to youthful e-millionaires, footballers and pop stars. Few policy initiatives are going to apply to all such groupings. Moreover, some of the key issues involved are not economic – they are to do with how to prevent 'elite opt-out'. Social exclusion at the top – the disengagement of elites from civic involvement – is as important for a society as exclusion linked to poverty.

(6)   The creation of a dynamic, yet full employment economy has returned as a feasible goal in the developed societies – indeed at the time of writing it already exists in the US and in some EU countries too. 'Full employment' of course, means something different today from a generation ago, since it now includes the large-scale employment of women, a growing proportion of part-time jobs, and other changes.

In helping generate and sustain high levels of employment, the role of government is central. Government must provide adequate macro-economic steering and observe fiscal discipline. It must stimulate technological innovation and economic investment. Very substantial investment is required in education and skills training, but not just through conventional mechanisms. New technologies are invading all levels of education and offer major opportunities for educational reform, while lifelong learning is likely to become the norm for the future.

It is not the role of the government to prop up ailing industries. In most cases the social and economic consequences eventually will be worse than if the attempt were not made. This lesson has been driven home by examples from all over the world where well-meaning government intervention has backfired, both in terms of economic efficiency and the social well-being of the workforces concerned. Government can do a great deal, however, to ease processes of economic or technological adaptation. Collaboration between government agencies and civil society agencies, for example, has proved successful in the regeneration of depressed neighbourhoods and regions.

Adaptation to technological change and job creation necessitates the cultivating of flexible labour markets, and here too government has a key part to play. Labour markets that are too rigid, with too high a benefit floor, have perverse effects. They inhibit the development of jobs, particularly in the sheltered service sector, which provide entry into work, especially for younger people. They also create insider/outsider labour markets, where people in jobs may have good social protection, but where others face punitive barriers to entry.

Flexibility in labour markets is not the same as deregulation, as examples from the EU countries show. Countries which have full employment, or close to it, such as Denmark or The Netherlands, have introduced flexibility, but backed it up with human capital guarantees – effective processes of requalification or retraining.

(7)   Social and economic policy must be connected. Here again social democrats have to move away from the emphases of the more traditional left (as well as the neoliberal right). The left used to consider economic and fiscal policy largely from the point of view of redistribution, and thought in terms of rates of taxation rather than the size of the overall tax take. The right saw such issues mainly in terms of economic efficiency, and sought to reduce taxation to as low a level as possible. Most forms of fiscal or economic policy, however, have directly social implications. The same is true in reverse of social policy. The left must acknowledge that social justice isn't always best served by elevating taxes. Tax reductions can in some circumstances both generate a higher tax take, especially where they stimulate job creation, as well as promote social justice. A working families tax credit, for instance, can

help economic efficiency as well as lighten the tax burden on poorer groups.

(8) Reform of the welfare state has already been mentioned. The reasons why established welfare systems almost everywhere need reform are well known. The welfare state developed in an era where neither the risks to be covered, nor the groups most in need, are the same as they are now. To take just one example, with changes in the nature of the family, single parents, particularly single mothers, have become much more numerous. Effective policies must be designed to cope with this change. Welfare reform is also required, however, where the welfare state has created moral hazard or perverse effects. There are some very obvious instances, such as unemployment benefits which lock people out of work when they could be in good jobs, or pensions provisions that inhibit saving.

In practice welfare reform is difficult. The welfare state has created entrenched interest groups, which have come to see benefits as natural rights. Parties elected with a mandate for restructuring welfare systems often shy away once in power. Yet welfare reform in most societies is an absolute necessity if a sustainable welfare state is to be created. For social democrats, of course, the point of reform is not to weaken but to strengthen the welfare state. A safety-net welfare system, as envisaged by the neoliberals, is not an option.

(9) Active policies are needed to combat crime in the here and now, as well as in a longer-term sense. Third way politicians should accept that people's worries about crime are often well founded and that positive strategies have to be instituted to react to them. In the past, some on the left have seen crime as primarily associated with poverty and inequality. Reducing inequality should therefore be the driving force of anti-crime programmes. It is entirely true, of course, that poverty and deprivation create breeding grounds for crime. But research shows clearly that crime has other sources besides inequality – unsurprisingly, because there are many different kinds of crime. Appropriate measures need to be taken to improve the structural conditions that lead to crime, but more immediate policies are at least as important.

Rates of crimes of violence and property crime, at least as reflected in the official statistics, are on the increase in quite a few EU countries, including ones with relatively low levels of economic inequality. This suggests that new approaches to combating crime ought to be tried in

Europe, including some pioneered in the US. 'Broken windows' policies, the saturation policing of areas where public spaces have become
dangerous, the tagging of offenders, reparations to victims and other
strategies should at least be (and are being) experimented with.

(10)   Policies have to be forged to cope with the environmental crisis.
The traditional left found it difficult to integrate the preoccupations of
social democracy with ecological concerns. 'Red–green' coalitions have
mostly proved unstable. Social democratic parties have usually been
pro economic growth, while greens have sought to rein back economic
development. Can these problems be resolved?

It is plausible to suppose that they can. The field of ecological politics has recently been redrawn in several significant ways. It has
become apparent, at least in some areas of industry, that ecological
sophistication, economic growth and job creation can go hand in hand.
The spread of the knowledge economy is a major influence here. Information technology is intrinsically non-polluting. Its application to
industrial production means that less developed countries won't necessarily have to tread the same path followed by the industrial societies in their economic development. Within the affluent economies the
advance of information technology has already contributed to bringing levels of environmental damage down quite substantially.

Ecological issues overlap heavily with wider questions of the management of technological change. The concept and reality of risk must
be central to the new politics. Most ecological problems come down to
assessments of risk, in which lay people are dependent upon the judgements of scientific experts. Environmental risk relates closely to other
risk situations about which political judgements must be made, such
as those involved in GM crops or other areas of biotechnology. These
in turn connect with health risks (and benefits), and even with financial risk. Financial markets are directly involved in most of these areas,
as well as in the insurance mechanisms that play a core part in risk
protection.

Governments must take an interest in all of these fields of risk. Ecological risks plainly cannot be left up to market mechanisms to resolve,
although they do have a part to play. Nor can they be left to the experts,
essential though their judgements are. In most new risk situations,
experts tend to disagree, both about levels of risk and how to react to
them – the controversy over GM foods is a typical example. Most risk
situations have a positive side. There are potential gains involved as
well as losses. Making judgements about these problematic questions
must be a shared responsibility. There must be scientific testing, but
also open public debate about its results.

(11)   We need to establish an effective framework of responsible capitalism. New policies are required for regulating the social and environmental costs that business can impose on the wider community, as well as providing incentives for firms to assume social obligations. The issues involved, of course, are wide-ranging and complex – too much so to deal with adequately here. I shall confine myself to some brief comments.

Shareholder capitalism on the American model at the moment looks to be sweeping all other forms aside. 'Rhineland capitalism', or Japanese capitalism, which only a few years ago were widely held up as examples for others to follow, are under pressure and seemingly in decline. Yet it does not follow that the shareholder model will inevitably triumph. There are powerful influences pushing for greater regulation of corporate behaviour than is feasible in the shareholding model, influences to which social democrats should lend their support. The rise of NGOs, consumer activist groups, and other agencies concerned with monitoring the conduct of corporations, creates constraints that companies ignore at their peril.

Government regulation of corporations will have to be international as well as national. The question of tax havens, for example, should surely be on the agenda for such collaborative action. Offshore companies openly show their indifference to civic concerns. Tax havens not only provide a ground for numerous kinds of doubtful business practices, they also help prop up noxious regimes and various benefits would flow from eliminating or tightly regulating them.[4]

A new European social model?

Most of these points are directly relevant to developments fostered by centre-left governments in the EU. A number of countries around the western and southern edge of the EU are making great strides in terms of economic development. These countries include the erstwhile 'problem economies' – Denmark, Ireland, the UK, Portugal, Spain and Greece. The central continental countries – Germany, France and Italy – have increased growth rates, but remain structurally somewhat frozen, with high levels of unemployment and underemployment.

The societies that are making most progress have introduced flexibility into their labour markets, fostered entrepreneurialism, and invested in technology. They have developed human-capital guarantees and other social protection measures compatible with rapidly changing external economic circumstances. As a result, they have gone some way towards creating a 'virtuous circle' between high employment levels and social spending. All have employment ratios of over 70 per cent. That of the UK, for example, is 76 per cent, and that of Denmark 78 per cent. In contrast, the employment ratios of Italy, France and Germany are 51, 62 and 64 per cent respectively.

A basic question for the near future is, can the central European economies unfreeze themselves sufficiently to create the same 'virtuous circle'? Political policies aren't the only influence needed to make this happen, but they are necessary for it to do so. What could be seen to be happening in the successful economies in Europe is the emergence of a transformed 'European social model' (ESM). It has different national variations, but basically combines flexibility and openness with the maintainance of effective social security.

If it could be further generalized to the other EU countries, the new ESM might confer a range of advantages. It could be more effective in adapting to globalization and the knowledge economy than the current world leader, the United States. European educational systems are on average superior to that of the US. Transport and communications infrastructure is better too. Moreover, 'flexible social protection' ('flexicurity') could be more functional for dealing with rapid technological change than the more deregulated American labour market. Thus people might be more actively willing to change jobs, or take jobs in risky new sectors, if they knew that adequate protective mechanisms were in place to ease the transition, or to provide should things go wrong.

Many neoliberal critics argue that the EU countries must move much closer to the American model if they are to adapt to current changes. But one could make the opposite case. Unless more effective social protection is introduced, and levels of economic inequality brought down in the US, that society will find itself at a competitive disadvantage.

The European Union institutions can contribute to the furtherance of the new ESM. At one time, many on the left believed that old-style social democracy, based on Keynesian demand management and corporatism, could be reinvented at the European level to compensate for its fading influence on the national political scene. That project was doomed to failure. Some of the reforms that are in progress at a national level are also critical to the future of the EU – for instance, further democratization, debureaucratization and devolution. Yet the EU remains a pioneering endeavour, likely to be emulated at some point by countries in other regions of the world. Its importance lies in the fact that it is developing a form of governance above the level of nation, yet where nations keep their identities and much of their autonomy. It is a framework likely to be more adaptable to the global age than anything even the largest of integral nation-states can offer.

The third way and the South

How far are the points listed above of concern to the less developed countries of the world? Many political leaders in those countries describe themselves as third way politicians, but is the third way really only relevant to the industrial countries?

It is certainly not relevant only to those countries. Third way politics has very wide purchase, since parties or governments all over the world have to respond to the fact that the other two 'ways' are no longer applicable. Every one of the eleven points is as germane to the developing as to the developed world. Obviously the contexts in which they apply are sometimes very different, but that doesn't rob them of their importance.

Reform of government and the state is even more necessary – although also more difficult – in countries of the South than in the developed nations. Some Southern societies suffer from inadequately developed state institutions. Most poorer countries, however, have states that are too extensive, bureaucratic and inefficient. Corruption and lack of developed democratic procedures are the norm rather than the exception. State employees may be one of the few groups that are fully unionized, but often the unions block reform rather than facilitate it. Yet effective reform is possible if governments are determined to push it through, as examples from a range of countries (such as Brazil or Mozambique) show.

The importance of civil society to reformist politics in the South is not only well recognized, but some of the main civic initiatives used across the world were initiated in the poorer countries. Microcredit (lending to people who have no money to help them develop business enterprises) originated in Bangladesh, but has since been used in many developed societies too. Community empowerment has become accepted as crucial to development programmes, including those seeking to protect against crime.

Coupling rights to responsibilities goes along closely with these emphases, or should do so. In the poorer countries, many of the social, political and economic rights taken for granted in the richer societies are ill-developed or absent. They need to be put into place, but in fostering them it is important to recognize problems that have arisen in the developed world, some of which can be avoided as they come into being elsewhere. The acceptance of duties and obligations can be crucial in building the civic commitments upon which both a flourishing economy and a solidary society depend. Thus a country building a welfare system can avoid benefit structures that tend to discourage active job search.

Many countries of the South have high unemployment rates and the goal of full employment is almost impossibly remote. The principles of job creation, however, are not so different. Countries which close themselves off from the global economy, and which resist technological innovation, will not prosper. But neither will those which fail to reform some of their basic institutions, including labour markets. Government intervention to increase literacy, and improve education more generally, is crucial, as are sound macroeconomic policies. The imperative of connecting social and economic policy applies just as much to Southern countries as to the richer ones.

Developing societies have at best fragmentary welfare systems: they need to create mechanisms of social protection. In building welfare systems, however, less developed countries can learn from the problems of established welfare states. They can also hope to introduce welfare measures which relate to new economic and technological conditions.

Southern leaders are apt to claim that their countries should not have to observe the same environmental standards as the developed societies, since the richer countries have contributed most to the world's ecological difficulties. Their arguments are to some extent justified. Yet it is in everyone's interest for some of the practices that lead to increasing pollution, or environmental despoliation, to be reduced. Moreover, 'ecological modernization' isn't relevant only to the developed countries. Some of the technologies involved might allow poorer societies to develop more quickly than the more environmentally problematic ones they replace.

Difficult though they may be to cope with in the industrialized world, issues of inequality and exclusion are of an altogether different scale in developing countries. Redistribution, often of land as much as wealth and income, must have a role. But even if redistribution were achieved on a wide basis, it would only have a limited effect on poverty. Tackling poverty in the poorer countries depends upon generating economic development, and upon making sure the underprivileged are included in such development. Neither is easy to bring about. Yet the example of the East Asian countries, even given the problems of the 1998 economic crisis, shows that rapid economic development can be achieved, and that millions of people can be lifted out of poverty in the process.

So far as responsible capitalism is concerned, the North and South have a common interest in creating a framework of governance for the global economy. As globalization intensifies, it makes no sense to suppose that effective responses can be made only on a local or national level. Third way politics must have a global reach. On a world-wide level as well as nationally we have to chart a path which mobilizes the power of states and governments, but avoids the heavy-handed approaches to development that failed so signally in the 1960s and 1970s.

The global problems that have to be faced are huge and by now well documented. Massive amounts of capital flow across the world, but most of this flow is concentrated in the industrial regions and a few other markets in Latin America and Asia. It barely reaches poorer areas, which desperately need capital investment. World economic inequalities are very wide. Some four hundred of the richest individuals in the world have assets greater than the three billion poorest. Levels of global pollution are still increasing and will do so even if the Kyoto targets are met, which seems unlikely. Fundamentalist violence has cropped up in many parts of the world, and looks set to become even more common.

However, for most of the dismal scenarios alternative, more optimistic, examples can be found. Thus Korea in 1970 was poorer than Ghana; it is now richer than Portugal. Health and educational standards globally have improved more over the past fifty years than over the previous five hundred. Some countries (such as Germany) have reduced their energy consumption while still maintaining good growth levels. There may be many horrific local conflicts happening in the world, but perhaps large-scale war between nations is becoming obsolete.

We shall not be able to support these and other more positive trends by adapting an attitude of laissez-faire, much less by seeking to reverse globalization processes. Left of centre governments need to respond collectively, working both within and outside established international institutions. Greater regulation of the world economy, especially with a view to limiting short-term currency speculation; integration of local and global systems of ecological management; boosting international law in respect of human rights; adapting strategies that will prevent local conflicts escalating into war; developing democratic mechanisms above the level of the nation-state – all are needed and all involve active intervention or regulation.

Global governance is best described as a set of prescriptions and conventions that nations agree to follow or be bound by. Most of the existing global institutions, like the United Nations, are international rather than transnational, one reason why they are of only limited effectiveness in today's circumstances. Global governance must still involve these institutions, but has to also involve a mixture of other agencies, public, private and civic.

A century ago there was 'the first age of globalization'. In the late nineteenth century, there was already a good deal of world trade, including trade in currencies, the large-scale migration of populations and the development of new communication systems. Many at that time believed that the twentieth century would be an era of harmonious global co-operation. Instead, there were two world wars and a century of violence. Globalization now is far more intensive than it was then. Some of the old ideologies, like fascism and communism have disappeared. We have more chance of creating effective global governance than was possible a hundred years ago – and our need to achieve it is correspondingly greater.

A resurgence of the right?

We cannot say as yet whether what some have described as the 'magical return' of social democracy will turn out to be transitory. It has important structural roots, since social protection, solidarity and inclusion are vital in a world marked by new divisions and insecurities. Yet voting is more volatile than it used to be, and combating voter apathy is not easy. The left has often in the past fallen from power because of internal conflicts, and the same thing could happen again – for example, as a result of squabbles between the modernizing and the old left. In addition to all of this, the pace of change has become faster than before and the future opaque. It isn't clear that, even when well-equipped and adaptable, governments will be able to guide their citizens through the transitions needed.

Then, of course, there is the challenge from the right, which will come from different sources from the recent past. The neoliberal right is now in retreat in most countries. Attractive to many in the wake of 1989, not least in ex-communist countries, neoliberalism is not a viable political philosophy. The main reason is that it has no effective theory of, or policies relevant to, developing a cohesive and integrated society. Neoliberal conservatives advocate the unfettered rule of market forces, and suppose that the market itself can take care of the problems of insecurity and inequality it itself helps to generate. It can't. The neo-liberals turn to tradition as the means of providing continuity and social solidarity. Yet the unregulated marketplace is one of the main sources of the corrosion of tradition in the contemporary world.

Another main form of conservatism, Christian democracy, is also proving to be a diminishing force. In some countries (like Italy) it has virtually ceased to exist, ceding place to a more disparate array of rightist groups. In other societies the Christian democrats quite often remain an important influence, yet lack a consistent ideology. Most have moved closer to a neoliberal position. But this brings with it the problems just noted.

A significant development within conservatism in recent years is the rise of new parties and groups of the far right. The ideological outlook of the far right has to be understood in terms of the changes that have been the focus of this whole discussion. Like the old left, the far right sees globalization as a destructive influence that has to be resisted. Both look to economic protectionism, or to economic regionalism, as a means of fighting back against it. The far right, however, couples this to cultural protectionism, a defence of the heritage and integrity of the nation. The national inheritance must be shielded from those groups and forces that threaten its values: foreigners, immigrants and the onrush of global cosmopolitan culture. Much the same goes for changes in everyday life. Family values must be shored up, while the advance of women into the labour force, if not halted altogether, should be kept confined.

The far right has made some spectacular gains in Europe. Jörg Haider's freedom party in Austria, for example, achieved 27 per cent of the vote in September 1999. In Switzerland the Democratic Union of the Centre, led by Christoph Blocher, won 22 per cent voting support at about the same time. Wearing the cloak of 'Alpine populism', the far right in southern and central Europe is actively seeking political respectability. Thus the National Alliance entered into coalition with the Berlusconi government in Italy in 1994.[5]

The far right is not in a strong position in all EU or OECD countries. While in Denmark the Popular Party has more than 18 per cent support, in Sweden the like-minded New Democracy Party has faded away, having had twenty-five members of parliament in the early 1990s. In France the National Front is in decline, while in the UK and Germany far right parties have negligible direct political influence. Similarly, Pauline Hanson's version of rightist populism in Australia proved to have little impact; in the US, no comparable figure has surfaced to replace Ross Perot.

Nevertheless the far right is threatening to social democrats, not just because of the views it espouses, but because of its appeal to some categories of social democratic voters. Immigration is a divisive phenomenon in many societies and the centre-left needs to consider carefully how to respond. The theory and practice of social democracy, particularly in Europe, has not been well adapted to the creation of multicultural societies. Those countries which are most egalitarian, such as the Scandinavian countries, or Germany, tend to be ethnically homogeneous. Welfare reform, the avoidance of insider/outsider labour markets, and adopting robust policies towards crime, can all play a part in a left of centre approach to the issues that garner support for the far right.

Support for the wider expansion of education, a core concern of third way politics in any case, is vital for fostering cosmopolitan values. The modernizing left should make a positive case for immigration. The EU countries should seek to learn from the 'best practice' of societies that have successfully absorbed diverse ethnic groups, such as Australia or Canada. Immigration controls need to be strict and non-discriminatory, but once accepted legal immigrants should be welcomed and offered immediate access to social rights, including active labour market schemes.

Limiting or rebuffing the advance of the far right, of course, is only one of the tasks the left faces confronted by newly developing patterns of conservatism. Centrist conservatism, shorn of some of the elements of Christian democracy, might make a comeback. 'Caring conservatism' is not an oxymoron if parties of the centre-right are prepared to accept that there is after all a role for activist government in a globalizing market economy.

The revival of social democracy in electoral terms is still rather tenuous. Social democrats as of early 2000 polled more than 40 per cent of the vote in only two EU countries – Portugal and the UK. In five of the fifteen EU states, social democratic parties had 20 per cent or less. Social democrats were the leading party in only four of the fifteen countries – including France, where Lionel Jospin's socialists held no more than 22 per cent of the vote. Much the same applies in other areas of the world, where left parties or coalitions have rarely got more than small majorities.

A good deal of work still lies ahead, therefore, if we are to make the new century 'a social democratic century'. Third way politics will have to deliver the goods in terms of continuing, preferably expanding, electoral success, and show itself capable of rising to the challenges presented by the changes discussed above.

A note on the contributions

In choosing the contributions included in this volume, I have tried to concentrate upon articles of some substance. Hundreds of articles have been published about the third way debate over the past few years, many of them abstract or philosophical in nature, and many of them critical. I have steered clear of all articles that pose the question, 'Is there a third way?' I have not included any of the sweepingly critical variety either, but have opted for contributions that help flesh out the third way approach and policy orientations.

Notes

1   See Wolfgang Merkel, in this volume.
2   Clause Offe: 'The present historical transformation and some basic design options for societal institutions'. Paper presented at the seminar on 'Society and the reform of the State', São Paulo (26–29 March 1998).
3   T. H. Marshall: *Citizenship and Social Class* (Cambridge: Cambridge University Press, 1949).
4   OECD is actively pushing for the introduction of such measures, and with some initial success.
5   Baudonin Bollaert: 'The rise of "Alpine populism"', *European Affairs*, 1 (Spring 2000).

PART I

One or More Third Ways?

Mark Latham provides an excellent overview of the basic principles involved in the new politics. The information age has different dynamics, structures and systems of belief from the industrial period. It is producing a society marked by the declining hold of traditional beliefs, coupled to a more active orientation to the world on the part of most citizens. Active citizenship and an active welfare state are therefore vital to third way politics, as is an insistence on the recovery of community in the arena of civil society. The third way must provide the means to allow people to come to terms with the knowledge-based economy, but also offer opportunities to those left out. The management of risk, in its negative and positive aspects, is crucial for government and citizenry alike.

These themes are also taken up by Stephen Driver and Luke Martell. Their discussion is situated primarily in the context of New Labour in the UK. As they point out, third way politics is not a finished philosophy, but one in the process of development. The field of third way politics was first defined in a fairly negative fashion, as political thinkers and policy-makers sought to distinguish themselves from pre-existing political perspectives. The third way has now acquired much more substantive content. The authors look in some detail at the values of the contemporary centre-left and consider some of the dilemmas that arise from the goals of the new thinking.

Virtually all left of centre parties in the EU today have restructured their policies in a third way direction. Of course, different institutional backgrounds and constraints mean that the policies developed have not been identical. This is why Wolfgang Merkel speaks of different 'third ways' in the European Union, concentrating on those of the UK, The Netherlands, Sweden and France. He omits Germany, because the German Social Democrats in his view have not as yet reached a coherent political position, something also made clear in the discussion of

Thomas Meyer. Under the leadership of Gerhard Schröder, the Social Democrats (SPD) have preferred the notion of 'new middle' to 'third way'. However there plainly is a great deal of overlap. The key issues that the SPD needs to address, Meyer says, are all third way-type issues – how to respond to globalization, adjust to the new economy, restructure welfare systems and create jobs. It isn't clear as yet, however, whether the SPD will take up one of the positions noted by Merkel or develop an independent stance of its own.

New Zealand has figured prominently in debates about the impact of free market philosophies, because of the policy changes introduced in that country since the mid-1980s. The 'second way' Dalziel shows, has been a failure in New Zealand: economic growth has been relatively low, while inequality and unemployment have increased. A third way framework for New Zealand must find a new role for government and must create innovative policies in the areas of industrial relations, welfare, income distribution and monetary policy.

The contribution from William Galston and Elaine Kamarck comes from the US, but covers many of the social and economic forces to which social democrats elsewhere must adapt. Like Mark Latham, they argue that the information order has produced radical shifts in social and political attitudes, new forms of regionalism, changes in family structure and increasing social diversity. Some on the old left treat the information revolution as radically over-hyped and believe that established industrial production remains much more important. It is impossible to sustain such a view if one looks at the statistics of technological change, however. Wired workers – people who work with computers much of the day – already make up more than half the workforce in California and over 40 per cent of the workforce in the US at large.

The Third Way: An Outline

Mark Latham

[...]

The basis of the third way project is the belief that a strong economy and a strong society are mutually reinforcing. Not only that, but in the values and ideals of the third way, they also make for good politics.

The third way takes the left's lasting principles – concerning the fairness and decency of our society – and applies them to the circumstances of our time: the massive challenges posed to social democracy by globalisation, the information revolution and the changing nature of work, welfare and social solidarity.

Traditional principles – new circumstances – new ideas and policies: this is the modernising role of the third way. It gives contemporary expression to the lasting cause of the left.

- the conviction that a growing market economy can be reconciled with a good society;
- that economic competition can coexist with social cooperation; and
- that the values and policies underpinning this approach make for good electoral politics.

[...]

The third way

Public policy has a habit of running in long cycles. The 1950s and 1960s saw the massive social democratic expansion of public services and Keynesian employment policies. The 1970s and 1980s saw the rise of neoliberalism, through the deregulation of economic markets and the privatisation and corporatisation of government services. The 1990s have seen the advent of third way thinking.

The third way seeks to resolve the core ideological tension of the past two centuries – the clash between socialism and liberalism. It believes that the ethical foundations of socialism – fraternity and equality – can coexist with the freedoms of liberalised markets and liberal democracy. This is why it emphasises a particular set of values – interdependence, responsibility, incentives and devolution:

- *interdependence* – because nations and communities can only meet the challenges of globalisation if they find new ways of working together and supporting each other.
- *responsibility* – because in accepting the rights and benefits of citizenship, people also need to be made responsible for their actions and effort in society.
- *incentives* – because in a world of constant change and uncertainty, people need to be encouraged to save more, to study harder and to work more intelligently.
- *devolution* – because, far from engineering society in the old way, governments now need to push the powers of democracy and public provision closer to civil society.

These values are universal, not sectional. Each and every citizen has a stake in their success. They do not try to break society up into subsets of sectional interest – pitting producers against consumers, managers against workers, well-educated people against the information poor. [. . .]

The third way acknowledges that the collective interest can only ever be built on the things we share in common. Collective action relies on the expression of collective interests and values: a strong economy interdependent with a strong society; rights matched up against responsibilities; government rewarding effort and defunding inactivity; a public sector arising as much from civil society as central government.

These values fit the politics of our time. Voters no longer see their interests in one dimension – either left or right, labour or capital. We have entered an era of multiple points of political identity and interest. In an era of permanent change, universal values are the most effective means by which politicians can unite and inspire the electorate.

[. . .] Whereas the changes brought about by the Industrial Revolution were absorbed over several generations, the information age seems to have arrived in just one generation. Old norms and guarantees appear to be lost forever. We now tend to define society by the way it used to be – hence the growing use of terms such as post-industrial, post-Fordist and post-traditional.

The electorate is now reaching for new social norms – the shared values without which there can be [. . .] no such thing as society. Common values help to glue society together. They give us a collective sense of purpose and normality. [. . .]

This is why the third way sees politics as an exercise in conviction and the teaching of values. [. . .] It denotes a renaissance in the moral foundations of socialism: mutual trust and respect, social cooperation and connectedness, and the social capital of civil society.

[. . .]

Already the way is clear in social policy. A revitalised welfare state has just two purposes – to move people into work or into new skills. Government needs to fund active citizenship, not pander to the inactive. Unless welfare recipients are willing to take responsibility for improving themselves and the society in which they live, they have no right to permanently live off society. The days of open-ended welfare need to end.

Old government was based on passive welfare – transfer payments, bureaucratised services and social engineering. New government needs to generate active well-being – community-based employment, lifelong learning and social devolution. The third way wants to overhaul the postwar welfare state; not to dismantle it, but to rescue it.

A strong society can only come from strengthening the bonds of trust and mutuality between each of its citizens. In a solid society, with its dense networks of respect and cooperation, people are likely to value altruism as much as self-interest. This is why the third way seeks to strengthen civil society through its policies of devolution.

In many cases, this means cashing out entitlements so that people can work together in defining their mutual interests and rebuilding the habits of trust. This does not mean smaller government, just government of a different kind. It reflects a revised role for the state – as a facilitator, as an enabler: still involved in the funding and regulation of services but not necessarily in their provision.

Economic policy

[. . .]

Change is all around us. We now live in a world with fewer economic boundaries and limits on the transfer of information. Global companies have the capacity to produce things anywhere and sell them everywhere. The communications revolution has allowed ideas, information services and cultural values to move seamlessly across national boundaries.

Economic activity is becoming weightless. Its raw materials are becoming less tangible – knowledge, ideas and ingenuity. [. . .]

These changes have radically altered the political economy of Western nations. They demand a new way of reconciling market economies with social fairness. Whereas the old left focused on industry policy and Keynesian economics and the new right set its sights on deregulation and market freedoms, the third way needs to follow a different set of priorities – education, entrepreneurialism and rewards for effort.

It needs to come to terms with the new geography of finance and investment. It needs to make sense of what a knowledge-based economy means for the rules of distribution in society. It needs to find universal appeal in its economic policies, not just pitch at sectional interests.

One commentator has put it this way: 'The Third Way must become the political midwife of this knowledge economy. It must be the political philosophy through which all the tensions and conflicts created by the new economy – over ownership and value, taxation, competition policy and ethics – are resolved.'[1]

This requires a new social contract between the winners and losers from globalisation. If, as some say, the winners – highly skilled, internationally competitive citizens – are increasingly detached from their nation and community, the third way needs to give them a reason to stay close to the public good. Otherwise, it will not be possible to deal with the growing social costs of the new economy.

If, as looks certain, the losers – those without the skills and resources to compete – are no longer able to actively participate in our society, the third way needs to give them a pathway back to social capability. Otherwise, we face the terrible prospect of a permanent underclass in our society.

The stakes are high. The success of the third way project will determine the future of social democracy. It will determine whether the ideals of a good and cohesive society remain viable. This new approach – the political economy of a third way – is likely to rely on five aspects of economic policy.

(i) Strong society/strong economy

Much of our public debate has fallen into a false divide between economy and society. Those with an interest in economic efficiency (so-called 'economic rationalists') are said to be wanting to destroy society. Those committed to a strong society (so-called 'social elites') are said to be opposed to economic growth and productivity. Everywhere the public debate has been infected with this tendency: wet versus dry; left versus right; pro-society versus pro-economy.

This reflects an enormous problem of methodology. The original political economists – like Adam Smith and Adam Ferguson – argued that a strong economy and strong society were closely interdependent. A solid, trusting society would strengthen the market by lowering transaction costs and smoothing the flow of trade. Just as much, market freedoms would be used responsibly in a trusting society, thereby strengthening social opportunity and prosperity. A strong civil society, therefore, was at the heart of both social solidarity and economic growth.

Unfortunately, this linkage was lost last century with the emergence of neoclassical economics. The strength of society was stripped away from the analysis of economic events. As a discipline, economics was reduced to a set of self-contained mathematical formulas and forecasts. Things like civil society – which are very hard to measure and quantify – were deemed to be external to economic modelling.

Over time, society and its economy were interpreted as being in conflict with each other. With the spread of globalisation and resurgence in populism, they are now often perceived as mutually exclusive. Politicians have found it convenient to define themselves by what they are against: either economic reform or social solidarity.

[. . .]

This is why the third way project is so important. It sees the changes of our time – globalisation and the information age – as a unique opportunity to reunite the two disciplines of economy and society. It maintains that economic policy can achieve both goals: strong economy – strong society. [. . .] The third way gives priority to a particular set of public policies:

- *cooperating internationally*: because only by working together – creating new types of economic regulation and governance – can nations make global capital work for their economies and societies.
- *investing in education*: because lifelong learning for all – perhaps alone among public outlays – has the capacity to improve both economic efficiency and social cohesiveness.
- *boosting savings*: because strong private savings not only make the [. . .] economy less vulnerable to shifts in international finance, they also make each of its citizens more secure about their future.

- *investing in infrastructure*: because effective transport and communications links can boost the productivity of the private sector while also assisting the well-being of regional communities.
- *strengthening workplaces*: because an industrial relations system based on collective bargaining in the workplace ensures that a cooperative workplace is also a productive workplace.
- *devolving social services*: because unless governments find a way of tapping the potential of voluntary and mutual associations they will not be able to strengthen civil society – the lynchpin of both a strong economy and a strong society.[2]

(ii) Making markets work

[. . .]

The third way is at ease with the primacy of the market. It has no wish to gut its growth potential by moving closer to a planned economy. It does not see itself as some kind of economic commissar surrounded by five-year industry plans. Without the productivity and prosperity of a market-based economy, it is simply not possible for government – through progressive tax/transfer policies – to redistribute the benefits of abundance.

Indeed, the growth of free trade markets since World War II has been associated with the expansion of the public sector. Across the OECD, the openness of nations to trade is positively correlated with the size of national spending on social programs. Free trade and the growth of the welfare state have been two sides of the same coin.[3]

Nonetheless, the third way recognises that market economies are not without their shortcomings. Many of the inputs to a knowledge economy are public goods which the market either will not provide or will provide inadequately: public goods like research and development, education and training. This gives the public sector its proper role: not as a replacement for market forces; but as a provider of the public goods essential to the success of the new economy. [. . .]

(iii) A new economic geography

The geography of the new economy has split the nation state in two. Finance and investment have become globalised – forcing governments to work at an international level to regulate capital. Yet at the same time, a number of economic problems, such as long-term unemployment, appear to have become localised – forcing governments to take account of regional and even neighbourhood labour markets. National economic policies of the traditional kind – Keynesian pump priming and industry protection – have lost a lot of their relevance.

[. . .]

Most forms of investment have become highly mobile. This foot-loose capital has the capacity to absorb public hand-outs and then subsequently relocate itself to nations offering even more generous forms of business welfare. Bidding wars between nations serve to maximise the advantages and profits of global capital.

This is why nations need to invest in those inputs to the new economy which remain relatively immobile: items of economic value which are not likely to move outside the boundaries of the nation state – like education and infrastructure. This is a critical part of the new economic geography.

The mobility of finance, production and trade has forced a new distinction in the type of economic policies governments might pursue. Public investments which are easily exploited by footloose capital (such as tariffs and bounties) represent a poor choice of policy. Public investments which can not be readily relocated to another country – such as a highly skilled workforce and good transport and communication links – represent a superior strategy. [. . .]

Economic policy needs to bridge the globalised and localised features of the new economy. New regulations and taxes need to be considered at an international level: trade and investment agreements between nations; common currencies and macroeconomic policy; an effective international lender of last resort; the establishment of a transaction or Tobin tax on speculative capital.

[. . .]

These policies need to be complemented by a stronger focus on local and regional labour markets. The new economy is rewriting many of the rules of employment and wage-setting. In many knowledge-based industries, workers now have a bargaining advantage. Other parts of the labour market are dominated by the services sector, in which labour (no matter its cost) can not easily be replaced by capital.

The level of unemployment is now linked to the level of knowledge skills and services spending power in a particular labour market. This is why the third way emphasises spatial solutions to the problems of economic exclusion: labour market adjustment programs; regional education and infrastructure improvements; flexible labour markets underpinned by a decent minimum wage; plus the creation of civil sector employment at a neighbourhood level.[4]

The main concern of the third way is not with the scale of government economic intervention, but the way in which it is directed. In the new economy this means a greater focus on international and local interventions; with a downgrading of the old tools of national policy making.

(iv) Investing in education

Two centuries ago the development of new technology in machines, tools and transport triggered the first major surge in world economic growth. This was the Industrial Revolution. Today our economy is being transformed by another revolution – the emerging possibilities of the information age.

Jobs relying on repetition and muscle power are disappearing. They are being replaced by work in the information and service sectors. Whereas nations once relied on machine power to generate wealth and jobs, they must now harness the brainpower of their people. Everywhere economic activity is becoming less resource-intensive and more knowledge-intensive.

[. . .]

The new economy has a few home truths that none of us can avoid. Well-educated and highly skilled nations succeed in the global economy; poorly skilled nations do not. The new growth theorists have shown how a nation's long-term economic prosperity is linked to its inventiveness, education and research capacity.[5] [. . .]

In many respects, education has become the first domino on the path to full employment. Nations and regions with a strong share of knowledge-based employment are able to generate new sources of income and wealth. The spending power of these high income earners then helps to create new jobs in their local economy, particularly in the service and retail sectors. Hence highly skilled economies follow a virtuous cycle of new growth, new spending power and new jobs – thereby giving semi-skilled workers their best chance of making the transition from old industries to new types of employment.

[. . .]

Smart nations also aim to spread the benefits of education as widely as possible. There can be no greater injustice in an information society than to leave some of its people uneducated: unfair for the uneducated; a deadweight cost on the rest of society.

This is why education needs to be treated as a public good: lifelong learning for all, the universal benefits of a smart nation, and the universal opportunities of a learning society.

[. . .]

(v) Rewarding effort

The renewal of social security requires a broadening of its appeal and relevance. This means ensuring that all citizens find in the welfare system something they can support. The winners out of globalisation need to be exposed to the benefits of collective action. Their appreciation of the public good needs to be kept alive. This is an essential part of a new social contract.

The third way sees advantages in revitalising the universality of welfare, not as a way of lifting government outlays, but to restore the link between contributions and benefits. The experience in Western Europe shows that universal schemes become unsustainable if governments continue to load the funding of benefits onto consolidated revenue. This is why a renewed commitment to universality needs to be based on a system of mixed provision – social insurance funded from private contributions; combined with a publicly funded safety net of minimum benefits.

[. . .]

In the old welfare thinking, government was merely a provider of rights and entitlements. In an era of economic insecurity, however, it needs to be able to help people with the management of economic risk. This means assessing the risks of disadvantage and poverty (based on skill levels, labour market conditions etc.) and then devising the services and reciprocal responsibilities by which each individual might avert these risks. The public sector needs to replicate the success of the financial sector in developing sophisticated systems of risk assessment and risk aversion.

[. . .]

Conclusion

The politics of the industrial age was based on a simple concept – the struggle between capital and labour, between bosses and unions. Political issues and ideologies were framed around a clear dichotomy: right versus left, individualism versus collectivism, freedom versus equality, market forces versus state planning, liberalism versus socialism. Now, however, the certainty and simplicity of this political contest has been lost. Just as the Industrial Revolution turned society on its head, the information age is changing the nature of work, society and politics.

This has become an era of voter dealignment – a time in which party loyalties are weakening and citizens are seeking out new sources of political identity. The global mobility of investment and steady march of economic restructuring, for instance, have given rise to a political divide between economic nationalists and economic internationalists.

So too, the advent of an information-rich society has provided a more diverse set of social values and aspirations. In political terms, this represents a contrast between voters who see themselves as part of a cosmopolitan global village and those who still look inwards on insecure, working class communities.

The pressing challenge for the political system is to respond to the way in which, more than ever, people are working and communicating globally, yet still voting locally. Governments are finding it harder to define and express values and public priorities with universal appeal to their citizens. Globalisation and the information revolution have combined to place new pressures on life's responsibilities and sources of identity. Political interests at a global, national, regional and local level are rubbing up against each other.

[. . .]

A new politics is needed, if only for the purpose of rebuilding public confidence in the institutions of democracy. The electorate is now riddled with cynicism and apathy about the political process. Our democracy is in crisis. Political change needs to be built on a strengthening of political trust.

Ironically, this mass disillusionment with politics has taken place at a time when most political messages represent a recycling of opinion poll messages. This is, in fact, a form of direct democracy, albeit flawed in its motivation and practice. It reflects the way in which political leaders now use the findings of sophisticated opinion polling to mould their own communications with the electorate.

This, in turn, has created a paradox of its own. The more the electorate hears from its politicians the things that they themselves have already told the pollsters, the more cynical they seem to become about the political process. More likely, the public has been able to sense the insincerity of it all: the way in which politicians talk about leadership and principle when, in fact, their methodology is to simply follow public opinion.

The worsening cycle of electoral manipulation and public distrust needs to be broken. The new politics needs to reflect the politics of conviction, rather than manipulation.

[. . .]

The new politics needs [. . .] to deal much more in solutions than images. It needs to express universal values, not sectional deal-making. Hence the relevance of the third way – universal values, radical solutions and a new politics of conviction. It is the way to a stronger democracy and rejuvenated social democracy.

Notes

1 Charles Leadbeater in *The New Statesman*, 8 May 1998, page 33.
2 Rodrik's research has shown how the nations benefiting most from globalisation are those with a strong store of social capital and conflict-resolution mechanisms. Nations with deep social divisions and distrust are disadvantaged by the dislocation costs of economic restructuring. See Rodrik (1998).
3 See Rodrik (1997, pp. 25–6).
4 A more extensive explanation of these issues and policies is provided in M. Latham *Civilising Global Capital*, pages 75–125.
5 See *Civilising Global Capital*, pages 50–6.

References

Latham, M. 1998, *Civilising Global Capital*, Allen & Unwin, Sydney.
Rodrik, D. 1997, 'The sense and nonsense in the globalisation debate', *Foreign Policy*, vol. 107, summer, pp. 25–6.
Rodrik, D. 1998, 'Globalisation, social conflict and economic growth', *World Economy*, vol. 21, no. 2, pp. 143–58.

Left, Right and the Third Way

Stephen Driver and Luke Martell

[. . .]

Our focus in this discussion is on third way ideas in Britain – in particular as articulated by New Labour and commentators who have engaged with Labour modernisers and the policies of the Labour government. Attempts to define a third way fall into two categories. The first begins by stating what the third way is not; the second, what it is or might be – and obviously the first approach can be followed by the second. Clearly it is in the nature of third or middle way politics to rely in part on definitions which are negative or relational in character. A third or middle way must logically stand in some relation to at least two others. What the nature of the relationship is between the elements is significant and cannot be deduced: is it a compromise, a synthesis or just the third of three, for example?

What the third way is not

Within New Labour politics, the third way is defined as 'beyond old left and new right'.[1] The definitions of 'old left' and 'new right' used in third-way thinking are thus significant; as is the meaning of 'beyond'. By 'old left' Labour modernisers have in mind the social democratic Labour politics of the postwar period – in particular, of a post-1960s liberal hue. Generally, by 'old left' (or 'old Labour'), Labour modernisers mean the Keynesian, egalitarian social democrats who tended to favour state and corporatist forms of economic and welfare governance within the context of a mixed economy. Labour modernisers accuse this 'old left' of being too statist; too concerned with the redistribution (and tax-and-spend policies) and not the creation of wealth; too willing to grant rights but not to demand responsibilities; and of being too liberal and individualist in terms of social behaviour and social relationships such as the family. So, if the 'old left' are all of these, then New Labour's third way is concerned to find alternatives to state provision and government control; to promote wealth creation by being fiscally 'prudent'; to match rights with responsibilities; and to foster a culture of duty within 'strong communities'.

By 'new right', Labour modernisers have their sights fixed on Thatcherite Conservatism. New Labour accuses successive Conservative governments – and here they echo significant voices on the right[2] – of being the slave to neoliberal dogma by favouring market solutions in all cases; by having a *laissez-faire* view of the state; by promoting an asocial view of society; and by championing economic individualism which places the value of individual gain above wider social values. So, if New Labour opposes the new right way, as well as the old left way, then a third way could promote wealth creation *and* social justice, the market *and* the community; it could embrace private enterprise but not automatically favour market solutions; it could endorse a positive role for the state – for example, welfare to work – but need not assume that governments provide public services directly: these might be done by the voluntary or private sectors; and it could, above all, offer a communitarian, rather than individualist view of society in which individuals are embedded in social relations which give structure and meaning to people's lives – and that it is the role of governments to promote 'the community' as a way of enriching individual lives.

[. . .]

The advantage to Labour modernisers of this negative or relational approach is to highlight – and exaggerate – the novelty of New Labour. Continuities with the old left – or at least parts of it – are downplayed, as are continuities with Conservative policy making in the 1980s and 1990s – except, of course, where it suits New Labour to appear 'tough', on inflation or trades unions, for example. This is not to suggest that New Labour is simply a more up-to-date version of a postwar Labour government – there are too many important discontinuities – and nor is New Labour simply a continuation of Thatcherism. But it seems reasonable to suggest that if a third way is neither old left or new right, then it – or the political territory where it might be found – can cross the centre ground of politics from left to right: and that a third way politics might embrace not just the centre-left but include more traditional 'one nation' strands of Toryism, as well perhaps as more recent notions of 'compassionate conservatism'.[3]

[. . .]

What the third way is: conditions and values

Tony Blair's attempt to substantiate a third way falls into three parts: first, the general conditions for a third way; second, its values; and third, the means required to achieve the ends given the conditions outlined in the first place.

The general conditions for third way politics rest on the argument that contemporary society is undergoing profound and irreversible changes; and that these 'new times' call into question established political and policy-making frameworks. The central theme here is globalisation. In a speech in South Africa in January 1999, Tony Blair suggested:

> The driving force behind the ideas associated with the third way is glob-alisation because no country is immune from the massive change that globalisation brings . . . what globalisation is doing is bringing in its wake profound economic and social change, economic change rendering all jobs in industry, sometimes even new jobs in new industries, redun-dant overnight and social change that is a change to culture, to lifestyle, to the family, to established patterns of community life.

A third way, then, is required to cope with these 'new times'. For Blair, the old left – postwar social democracy – 'proved steadily less viable' as economic conditions changed as a result of globalisation. In par-ticular, the linchpin of postwar social democracy, Keynesian economic management to achieve full employment, partially repudiated by James Callaghan in the mid-1970s and again under question during Labour's Policy Review in the late 1980s, is seen as redundant in the context of a global economy. The economic liberalism of the new right Thatcher governments, which 'in retrospect' brought about 'necessary acts of modernisation' (in particular, 'exposure of much of the state industrial sector to reform and competition'), ultimately failed because of a political dogmatism which prevented it from dealing with the consequences of globalisation, such as social dislocation and social exclusion, which required more active government.[4]

Third way thinking supports the view that globalisation brings with it greater risk and insecurity, and that it is the role of policy making not to shield individuals from these but to provide the 'social capital' and 'proactive' welfare states which enable them to respond to them and prosper in the global age. And where globalisation is bound up with the new digital information and communication technologies and the 'knowledge economy', individuals need the education and training appropriate to these conditions. Public policy should support business in the creation of 'knowledge-rich products and services' which will be the source of future economic growth. As a result, it is suggested, the competing goals of economic success and social justice/cohesion can be squared. Government promotes economic growth by creating stable macro-economic conditions; and its supply-side social interventions enhance individual opportunity (social justice) and increase non-inflationary growth, which together bring greater social cohesion by reducing social exclusion.

[. . .]

If these, then, are the general conditions for a third way, what about the values that a third way politics might promote? There have been a number of attempts to pin these values down and we shall focus on the four identified by Tony Blair: [. . .] 'equal worth', 'opportunity for all', 'responsibility' and 'community'.

The first, 'equal worth', is the old liberal nostrum that all human beings are equal and should be treated as such and not discriminated against. The second, 'opportunity for all', reflects the New Liberalism in New Labour's third way: that substantive (or positive) freedom requires that individuals have the resources to develop their talents and exercise their liberty – rather than being concerned solely with the legal conditions which support individuals to lead free lives (negative freedom). Equal opportunities do not only go beyond the new right, though. Blair attempts to make a distinction crucial to his third way: that 'opportunity for all' is principally concerned with opportunities and not outcomes:

> The Left . . . has in the past too readily downplayed its duty to promote a wide range of opportunities for individuals to advance themselves and their families. At worst, it has stifled opportunity in the name of abstract equality.[5]

By 'abstract equality' Blair means equality of outcome. While he goes on to suggest that 'the progressive Left must robustly tackle the obstacles to true equality of opportunity', and that these might include 'gross inequalities . . . handed down from generation to generation',

Blair offers a meritocratic understanding of equality – albeit qualified by ideas such as 'lifelong learning'. As we shall suggest later, the debate about equality goes to the very heart of third way politics.

The third of Blair's four values is 'responsibility' and links closely with the fourth, 'community'. 'Responsibility' reflects Blair's ethical turn spelt out in his statement that 'we do not live by economics alone': 'a society which is fragmented and divided, where people feel no sense of shared purpose, is unlikely to produce well-adjusted and responsible citizens'.[6] In a decent society, individuals should not simply claim rights from the state but should also accept their individual responsibilities and duties as citizens, parents and members of communities. A third way should promote the value of 'community' by supporting the structures and institutions of civil society – such as the family and voluntary organisations – which promote individual opportunity and which ground 'responsibility' in meaningful social relationships. [. . .]

There is broad agreement over these values among third way writers,[7] though problems emerge over the interpretation of these values and the extent to which they define a centre-left political project.[8] Meanwhile a key question concerns the means by which centre-left values are put into effect, the third part of a substantive definition of a third way.

[. . .]

The basic framework of third way arguments is that in changing economic and social circumstances, a new politics is required which departs from the major political paradigms of the postwar years: namely social democracy (old left) and Thatcherism (new right). But to what extent does the third way dispense with the traditional divide between left and right, and with the established political categories of liberal, conservative and social democrat? Does it, as Bobbio[9] has asked, transcend and make such categories redundant? Or is it simply a cobbling together of different intellectual positions which may or may not give rise to principles and practices which are contradictory and mutually undermining? There is a degree of ambiguity between and within advocates of a third way on these questions. Blair, for example, argues that 'the third way is not an attempt to split the difference between Right and Left', suggesting not a middle way but something more novel. He then states that the third way offers a new synthesis between liberal and socialist thinking: the third way 'marks a third way *within* the left' (Blair, 1998: 1, italics in original). But some modernisers have their doubts. As Stuart White argues, the third way 'can all too easily be taken to imply that we need, not to modernise, but to exit the social democratic tradition in pursuit of something wholly new and distinctive'.[10]

Beyond left and right?

[. . .]

Some have suggested that contemporary politics is undergoing a 'cultural turn' in which questions of identity have become paramount and that this culturalisation of politics is blurring left/right political distinctions. Anthony Giddens[11] argues that 'emancipatory politics' – concerned principally with questions of political economy; with the distribution of rights and resources – is giving way to 'life politics' – concerned principally with questions of identity and the quality of life. Giddens suggests that these shifts in contemporary political culture blur distinctions between left and right outside the domain of party politics:

> . . . a whole range of other problems and possibilities have come to the
> fore that are not within the reach of the Left/Right scheme. These include
> ecological questions, but also issues to do with the changing nature of
> the family, work and personal and cultural identity.[12]

Left and right concerns cut across these areas and they also sometimes fail to encapsulate differences between points of view on life politics.

Giddens also argues that traditional attachments of left and right to radicalism and conservatism respectively were becoming less and less meaningful after a decade of Thatcherite neoliberal radicalism and in a cultural environment he calls 'post-traditional'. New Labour has since conformed to Giddens' thesis by embracing a brand of social conservatism. For Giddens this makes it seem that old left-right associations do not work any more: particular views are no longer exclusively the property of one or the other. This is reinforced by the fact that popular attitudes do not so easily divide into consistently left or right positions as they used to. On many issues people divide into liberal or communitarian camps, for example, rather than left and right ones.

Such views suggest the moving of politics to areas beyond categories of left and right. But does this mean that left and right are transcended or synthesised or that they merely coexist? Our argument is that the third way involves the combination rather than transcendence of left and right. Principles such as equality, efficiency, autonomy and pluralism, over which the left and right have long been divided, get mixed together rather than left behind. The novelty of the third way lies in this combination of left and right: it is a mixture which is neither exclusively of the left or of the right. In this way, the third way offers a politics which is beyond the closed ideological systems of left and right; but which still combines them both and remains within the tradition of middle way politics which has been a feature of much of 20th-century British politics – most notably New Liberalism, postwar social democracy and one-nation conservatism.

[. . .]

This is what we believe the third way to be essentially about: a more pragmatic political project which is willing to break free from what it sees as the straightjacket of left/right politics.[13] And for this reason, the third way offers a wide and potentially fertile landscape for public policy making, although not one without pitfalls: for example, the internal coherence of public policy when different agendas are in play. [. . .] For if compromises are to be struck and balances are to be found between different values and principles, then it is at the policy coalface that such deals are to be made. Such a political project may actually be in a better position to tackle complex social problems, such as social exclusion, for the very reason that it is relatively light on ideological baggage – or at least willing to make compromises on its contents – and so can approach policy analysis and prescriptions whatever their origins so long as they work.[14] [. . .] It also allows the Labour government to have a more pluralistic approach to policy making, in the sense that certain principles operate in some spheres of policy making and not in others. For example, rights-based liberal individualism in constitutional reform but social conservatism in education and the criminal justice system

We would argue that this more pragmatic and limited notion of politics and public policy, not the more radical and synthetic one, better defines any third way – and in fact what the Labour government is doing in practice. Finding some balance or *modus operandi* between the demands of competing political values; recognising that different values (or combinations of values) may be more suited to different policy areas. These are the approaches which better define a third way and which better encapsulate what the Labour government is doing in practice. While this interpretation of New Labour recognises that reciprocity and mutual dependency between different values and policies is possible in particular circumstances, it is also aware that different interests remain at work and that tensions remain permanent features of the political and policy-making landscape. For example, giving the Bank of England independence to set interest rates *and* establishing a welfare-to-work programme may be a clever mark of third way policy making, balancing the principles of economic efficiency and social justice. But such public policy does not resolve the inherent tensions in any market economy between the inegalitarian outcomes of the market [. . .] and those egalitarian outcomes – 'opportunity for all' – which social justice demands. While a strong economy does support and underpin high rates of employment [. . .] the principle of equality may demand public policies which directly impinge on the inegalitarian dynamics of the market, in particular through higher taxes to pay for social security and public services.

[. . .]

Giddens and Blair: new times and social democracy

Anthony Giddens is often styled as Blair's third way guru. But in terms of the issues to which Giddens sees the third way as being a reaction, on what he says underlies and shapes it, and, consequently, on some of the positive meanings of the third way, there are differences of emphasis between him and Blair. What kind of individualism? What kind of civil society? What kind of politics? What kind of equality? In Blair's and Giddens' answers to these questions there are differences in third ways between old left and new right. Giddens gives different emphases to the social trends he sees as important – globalisation, detraditionalisation, value change in society, changes in social structure and ecological problems. Where they do identify similar significant social changes (for example, globalisation and individualism), Giddens and Blair sometimes define them differently. As we shall see below, Blair sees globalisation and the rise of individualism differently to Giddens and places less emphasis on factors such as the growth of ecological problems. Variations in the positive content of their third ways arise from such underlying differences of emphasis.

While they both stress the role of globalisation, Blair does not put the emphasis that Giddens does on institutions of global governance which might counteract economic globalisation.[15] Blair stresses the need to accept and learn to live with the global market economy. For critics such as Hutton,[16] for example, Blair is too acquiescent to the perceived globalisation of the world economy and to the limits this places on national economic policy making. [. . .] Where Blair does discuss transnational political coordination it is focused mostly on leadership in the European Union and prioritises the need for transparency and democracy in EU institutions rather than the more expansive ideas for global governance that Giddens discusses. Blair's emphasis is more passive and adaptive to globalisation than Giddens', although during the Kosovo crisis Blair did talk of permanent structures for international intervention in humanitarian crises.

The growth of individualism is another phenomenon Giddens and Blair both see as an important influence on politics – but they have different analyses of it. Giddens argues that the sort of individualism that has grown in society is not economic egoism and cannot be attributed to Thatcherism.[17] It is a product of detraditionalisation and increases in choice; and more about moral uncertainty than moral decay. For Giddens, the growth of this sort of individualism requires, as a response, more active responsibility, reflectiveness and democratisation. There are cross-overs here with Blairite ideas of individual responsibility and self-reliance concerning welfare reform, but also key differences. Blair explicitly *does* locate the growth of individualism in, among other things, the right's economic egoism, the left's social individualism and a more general process of moral decay. The active, reflective citizen in a radical democracy is Giddens' model. Blair puts more emphasis, in his response to individualism, on the notion of duty, on moral cohesion and those institutions such as education, family and the welfare state which he believes can and should enforce good behaviour. Giddens' solution is to emphasise active individualism where Blair's is to stress moral responsibilities and standards as an antidote to the individualism he identifies, a more communitarian response. In this respect, third way ideas can be divided between 'post-traditionalists' like Giddens and 'social moralists' like Blair.

Giddens also gives greater emphasis to post-materialist attitudes and quality of life issues expressed in 'life politics' or 'sub-politics'. He is conscious of risk, scientific uncertainty and ecological problems. He does not propose replacing governmental politics with 'sub-politics' but does suggest the latter should have a more important role. Blair's politics are less about quality of life issues beyond conventional economic and social policy concerns: while the Labour government has developed a quality of life index, it remains peripheral to the main body of policy making. The core of New Labour has little interest with active democratising processes for citizens in everyday life outside mainstream politics. To the disappointment of many environmentalists, feminists and others, there is little in Blair's politics which is a direct response to contemporary radical social movements or incorporates their concerns. The democratisation programmes of New Labour are *of* government not *beyond* government. When Blair discusses the need for 'a strong civil society' and 'civic activism', it is not social movement politics he has in mind. His concern is with individuals fulfilling their responsibilities as parents, criminals shouldering individual responsibility and the role of the established institutions of the voluntary sector and the family rather than radical, informal social movements.

Third way values in question: equality and community

Stuart White offers a definition of third way values.[18] These, he suggests, are: 'real opportunity', 'civic responsibility' and 'community'. They tally more or less with those offered by the Labour leader we examined earlier. These values, White suggests, offer a 'general normative framework'. However, unlike Blair, White suggests that they are open to different interpretations, not all of which will fall on the centre-left. This leads him to suggest two lines of division within the third way. The first between 'leftists' and 'centrists' concerns the nature of equality. Like Bobbio[19] he identifies equality as a crucial issue which divides those on the left from those further right. The second line is between liberals and communitarians and concerns the degree of individual freedom in relation to community enforced norms.

There are two points of note which we shall pick up and develop from White. First, the interpretation of third way values is significant and marks out different political positions within the third way. What kind of equality is involved and what kind of community and how much of each? There are divergencies among third ways on such questions. Second, the third way is concerned with means as well as ends. The varying means intended to achieve third way ends – governmental or more voluntaristic, for example – may also lead to a differentiation of third ways.

White's first line of division is between leftist-egalitarian and more centrist-meritocratic third ways. [. . .] Leftists would like to see greater redistribution of income and wealth rather than of just asset-based opportunities; [they] have condemned New Labour's shift from equality of outcome to meritocracy and inclusion as the principal aims of the third way. Differences between Giddens and Blair are evident on this question. Giddens is more egalitarian and launches a stern attack on the inadequacy of meritocracy and equality of opportunity alone:

'Many suggest that the only models of equality today should be equality of opportunity, or meritocracy – that is, the neoliberal model. It is important to be clear why this position is not tenable.'[20] For Giddens equality of opportunity without egalitarian redistribution is self-undermining because it allows inequalities to grow which then prevent more equal opportunities. Inequalities threaten cohesion and send those at the bottom of society the demoralising message that they deserve to be there. Leftist egalitarians might even argue that lower ability (or even lesser effort) should not be a basis for economic inequality. Such a view supports policies such as increased taxes to fund higher public spending on education and health; univeralism in welfare as a basis for common citizenship; and a more directly interventionist state which are to the left of Blair's third way.

[. . .]

A second line of division identified by White is between communitarians and liberals: between those who have a broad understanding of the range of behaviour for which the individual may be held responsible to the community, and for which the state may legitimately intervene, and those who have a much more limited notion. White argues that any third way view must have some commitment to civic responsibility. And it is New Labour's communitarian understanding of civic responsibility – its apparent willingness to set public policy which challenges liberal notions of the private sphere – which is distinctive and which has drawn fire from, among others, the liberal left for being too conservative, too prescriptive, even socially authoritarian. [. . .] Indeed, one of the central Blairite arguments is that the old left were too socially individualist; and that family arrangements, for example, had become too subject to matters of choice and individual fulfilment over and above parents' responsibilities to their children and to the community. On welfare reform, in particular, the 'responsibility' for individuals to find work and to be self-supporting is evidence of the Labour government taking a third way position which is strongly communitarian. This aside, it is important to qualify the degree to which New Labour's third way is, as some have suggested, illiberal. On family policy, for example, where Blair has been accused by some of 'social authoritarianism', the actual policies often support diverse family forms: the Labour government, has proved more neutral on the family than many expected.[21]

This liberal–communitarian distinction conceals further differences in third ways – among liberals and among communitarians. Some who are liberal on social matters, for example, may be left-egalitarian; less interventionist socially but in favour of greater economic interventionism and equality. It is conceivable that some who are liberal on social intervention could be more centrist-meritocrats, although this combination begins to move us to the right rather than left of centre. Similarly those who are sympathetic to Labour's communitarian interventionism on social matters may be leftist-egalitarians or more centrist-meritocrats when it comes to questions of economic equality. So between liberal and communitarian third ways there may be differences and within each yet further third way approaches can be distinguished.

These distinctions leave out a third set of axes to do with the nature of communitarianism along which there is space between old left and new right for third ways to differ. Different sorts of communitarianism can be progressive or conservative, voluntaristic or statist. As we have suggested, criticisms of Labour's communitarianism are often liberal and suspicious of prescriptive moralism. But another line of criticism could come within communitarianism from anyone at odds with its conservative content. This raises issues not of whether community should be promoted but of what sort of community – a 'progressive' community (which promotes modern teaching methods and support for non-nuclear family forms, for instance) or a more 'conservative' sort of community (which emphasises more traditional norms for teaching and the family).

Also glossed over by the liberal–communitarian distinction is a difference between voluntaristic and top-down communitarians. Again, the difference is not over whether greater community or shared moral norms are needed but, in this case, where these come from – state action or more organically. Those who stress the latter can include one-nation or 'compassionate' conservatives or leftist communitarians of more voluntaristic, civil society and social movement traditions, in search of more community but not through state action. Those, like New Labour, who stress the former see governments – through exhortation, symbolic action and legislation – taking the lead in fostering community in society.

This is an example of where third ways diverge on means. How far does the third way involve the initiative of civil society or state? Should welfare be delivered by the state or by greater delegation to the private and voluntary sectors? Can a government committed to strong social objectives deliver on them without the old levers of powers – at least without resorting to new 'cattle prods'?[22] Should welfare be universal or more targeted – and how might a shift to greater targeting impinge upon social democratic values? Does the third way imply global governance or national or local action? To what extent is cooperation between state and other actors, whether governmental or non-governmental, the best path forward? In this way, the third way can diverge on means – and the choice of means in each of these cases will affect the character of the ends reached.

[. . .]

Notes

1   Blair, 1998; see also Blair and Schroeder, 1999.
2   Gilmour, 1992; Gray, 1993; Scruton, 1996.
3   See Dionne, 1999.
4   Blair, 1999: 5–6.
5   Blair, 1998: 3; see also Brown, 1997.
6   Blair, 1995.
7   For example Giddens, 1998; Hargreaves and Christie, 1998; Le Grand, 1998.
8   White, 1998.
9   1996.
10 White, 1998; see also Marquand in Halpern and Mikosz, 1998.
11 1994 and 1998; see also Driver and Martell, 1999.
12 Giddens, 1998: 46.
13 See Powell, 1999.
14 Glennerster, 1999.
15 See also Held, 1998.
16 1998.
17 Giddens, 1998: 34–7.
18 White, 1998.
19 1996.
20 1998: 101; also 1999.
21 Driver and Martell, 2000.
22 See Coote, 1999.

References

Blair, T. (1995) 'The rights we enjoy reflect the duties we owe', *Spectator* Lecture, London.
Blair, T. (1998) *The third way: New politics for the new century*, London: Fabian Society.
Blair, T. (1999) 'Facing the modern challenge: the third way in Britain and South Africa', speech in Capetown, South Africa.
Blair, T. and Schroeder, G. (1999) 'Europe: the third way/Die Neue Mitte', London: Labour Party.
Bobbio, N. (1996) *Left and Right: The significance of a political distinction*, Cambridge: Polity Press.

Brown, G. (1997) The Anthony Crosland Memorial Lecture, 13 February.

Coote, A. (1999) 'The helmsman and the cattle prod', in A. Gamble and T. Wright, *The new social democracy*, Oxford: *Political Quarterly*/Blackwell.

Dionne, E. J. (1999) 'Construction boon: it's no accident that the GOP is being rebuilt by its governors', *Washington Post*, 14 March.

Driver, S. and Martell, L. (1998) *New Labour: Politics after Thatcherism*, Cambridge: Polity Press.

Driver, S. and Martell, L. (1999) 'New Labour: culture and economy', in L. Ray and A. Sayer (eds) *Culture and economy: After the cultural turn*, London: Sage Publications.

Driver, S. and Martell, L. (2000) 'New Labour, work and the family: communitarianisms in conflict?', in H. Wilkinson (ed) *The family business*, London: Demos.

Giddens, A. (1994) *Beyond Left and Right*, Cambridge: Polity Press.

Giddens, A. (1998) *The third way: The renewal of social democracy*, Cambridge: Polity Press.

Giddens, A. (1999) 'Better than warmed-over porridge', *New Statesman*, 12 February.

Gilmour, I. (1992) *Dancing with dogma*, London: Simon and Schuster.

Glennerster, H. (1999) 'A third way?', in H. Dean and R. Woods, *Social Policy Review 11*, Luton: Social Policy Association.

Gray, J. (1993) *Beyond the New Right: Markets, government and the common environment*, London: Routledge.

Halpern, D. and Mikosz, D. (1998) *The third way: Summary of the NEXUS 'on-line' discussion*, London: Nexus.

Hargreaves, I. and Christie, I. (eds) (1998) *Tomorrow's politics: The third way and beyond*, London: Demos.

Held, D. (1998) 'The timid tendency', *Marxism Today*, November/December.

Hutton, W. (1998) *The stakeholder society*, Cambridge: Polity Press.

Le Grand, J. (1998) 'The third way begins with Cora', *New Statesman*, 6 March.

Powell, M. (ed) (1999) *New Labour, new welfare state? The 'third way' in British social policy*, Bristol: The Policy Press.

Scruton, R. (1996) *The Conservative idea of community*, London, Conservative 2000 Foundation.

White, S. (1998) 'Interpreting the third way: not one road, but many', *Renewal*, vol 6, no 2, Spring.

3

The Third Ways of Social Democracy

Wolfgang Merkel

Introduction

A sweeping view of the 20th century reveals a clear trend in social democracy: it moves from the radical rejection of the bourgeois-capitalist order, the abolition of the private ownership of the means of production, the acceptance of a market economy run on welfare state principles and controlled by Keynesian strategies, through to the recognition of societal inequality as a legitimate and functional stratification pattern in highly developed market economies under the conditions of globalised economic transactions. A continual process of political deradicalisation over the past hundred years can thus be identified in European social democracy. From a conspiracy theory perspective this is of course viewed as a downward slope and a betrayal of the 'real' goals of the workers' movement. There has been no lack of such crude findings either from within the movement itself or from scientific circles. Indeed, only the concepts have changed: at the opening of the 21st century the verdict of 'neoliberalism' has emerged replacing that of the betrayal of the labour movement from the beginning of the century.

From a more functionally aware [. . .] perspective, [. . .] deradicalisation can be explained by two [. . .] overlapping factors: the changing opportunities for political action, along with their consequences, which take the form of policy outcomes and in turn influence the structural arenas for action and strategic options of social democratic parties in government. From here the thesis that different contexts demand varying [. . .] 'ways' for successful social democratic government action can be convincingly deduced. [. . .] The impetus for the current debate came, not from within Germany, as at the end of the 19th century, but [was] led from Great Britain by Tony Blair's New Labour Government and Anthony Giddens's (1998) *The Third Way*. At the end of the 20th century the debate about the third way has become the most important reform discourse in the European party landscape.

My reflections on this renewed revisionist debate within social democracy will proceed in three stages:

1   The third way as a theoretical concept.
2   Resources and constraints for social democratic politics at the end of the 20th century.
3   The third ways of social democracy in Western Europe:
    3.1   the market-oriented way: New Labour;
    3.2   the market- and consensus-oriented way: the Dutch 'polder model';
    3.3   the reformed welfare state way: Sweden;
    3.4   the statist way: the Parti Socialiste Français.

I.   The theoretical concept of the 'third way'

The theoretical notion of the 'third way' was definitively formulated by Anthony Giddens. The 'way' was no longer to follow the wide avenue between capitalism and communism, but was rather to take a [. . .] path beyond the radical neoliberalism of the 1980s and the old statist-corporatism of post-war social democracy. From the outset, Giddens and New Labour's new think tanks can be seen as distinct from their own past and from some contemporary social democratic parties on the continent: they no longer view the globalisation of financial markets, the Europeanisation of goods markets and the associated national race for competitiveness simply as an inconvenient constraint on social democratic government policy.

Instead, they see it much more as desirable, serving as a modernising whip on entrenched economic and social structures. Further, globalisation relieves the government of a considerable burden of legitimacy for reforms as far-reaching as they are necessary, particularly where they are directed at strong established interests. However, as a consequence of the globalised money and capital markets, the third way theorists see the scope for national monetary and fiscal policies, as well as for macroeconomic employment and structural intervention, as being much narrower than was the case during the 'golden era' of social democracy (1945–73). The realistic acceptance that globalisation is both a constraint *and* a resource has considerable implications for social democratic politics. The dispassionate view of the new social demo-cratic realists has frequently led to them being given the label of 'neo-liberalism'. It therefore needs to be asked here, to what extent the third way can be differentiated from neoliberalism, so as to then distinguish it from the traditional corporatist-statism of post-war social democracy.

[. . .]

Even a cursory summary of critiques of neoliberalism makes clear the distinction between radical market fundamentalism or the neo-liberal vision of the *minimal state* on the one hand and the concepts of the third way on the other. Labelling it as neoliberal does not make ana-lytical sense and can be seen as having a strategic function in day-to-day political polemic.

Nonetheless, just as clear as the demarcation from neoliberalism is the distancing of the third way from traditional continental social democracy. Third way theorists especially criticise three key stances relating principally to the differing understanding of the structure and function of the welfare state:

- what is argued as the illusion that an increase in social expenditure will automatically lead to a reduction in socio-economic inequality;
- the passive nature of welfare entitlements in the traditional welfare state. Instead of leading to more socially-oriented and individually-responsible citizenship, it leads to privatism, dependency, a loss of discipline and a lack of motivation to adapt oneself to the new edu-cational challenges of the changing labour market;
- the traditional welfare state, rooted primarily in the logic of the classical industrial modernity, has proved too inflexible in the face of post-industrial problems. In part it protects the wrong kinds of social groups, while rarely incorporating new kinds of social risks into its insurance and safety net. Furthermore, welfare payments no longer meet the realistic individual needs and social challenges of the heterogeneous society at the end of the 20th century.

[. . .]

New Labour has abandoned the classical social democratic 'model' of a generous universalist welfare state. Theorists and practitioners of the third way do, however, want to prevent the 'Americanisation' of British society. Social exclusion, societal anomie, rising crime and the emergence of a large underclass are to be prevented in order to enable British people to integrate and again become 'one nation'. Raymond

Plant [. . .] aptly calls the welfare state concept 'supply side citizenship'. In this context supply side citizenship means that the state establishes the framework within which citizens should then realise fair opportunities through individual responsibility. It becomes clear that from such a perspective citizenship is less a conferred right and much more a goal with related duties for which one must constantly strive. It can only be attained through participation in the workforce and the onus is thus on the active state to establish the basic conditions necessary to access the labour market. Each individual is then obliged to responsibly utilise these opportunities. This could be labelled a revamped social democratic 'social contract'. However, the contracting partner and the end result of the contract is no longer the benevolent-paternal welfare state. Rather, it is a state more strongly rooted in liberal (equality of opportunity) and communitarian (protection of the community from the negative effects of individualisation) principles. [. . .] Although Giddens, Plant and others leave no doubt here about the active role of the state, they seem fully prepared to accept greater income inequality as a market and policy outcome. Their acceptance ends only at the point where this leads to voluntary and involuntary exclusion in the higher and lower strata of society.

2.   Resources and constraints of social democratic politics at the end of the 20th century

Theoretical concepts and political programs are not to be automatically transformed into policies. There are usually at least two filters standing between the principles, goals and policy proposals of a party's programme and its realisation. These do not only influence the actual policy decisions (outputs) and policy results (outcomes), but are also frequently taken into consideration when strategies and programmes are designed. The first filter consists of both the resources available to a party for implementing its goals and the constraints restricting it: this can be called the structural filter of political action.

To a large extent this first filter structures the political arena and defines the corridors of action that are open to political actors. This can be viewed both objectively (confining conditions) and subjectively (perception, interpretation). The perception and assessment of this constraint and resource filter marks out the cognitive strategic horizons of political actors. Within these boundaries there is thus a limited number of options open. [. . .] From among these options they make their choices in a second filtering process. This second filtering process is determined by filter 1 and the interaction of strategic and political interests. Normative considerations become often secondary. Beyond the structural constraints and normative considerations the political choices are particularly influenced by competition and co-operation among relevant political actors, particularly government, parties, organisations, business interests and the media. Whereas the first filter represents 'structure', the second filter represents 'choice'.

[. . .]

Which are the specific elements of the filters that impact on social democracy's search for 'third ways' and the 'new centre'? The most significant of these will be outlined here, rather than discussed in detail.

Filter 1: resources and constraints

Resources   The three most important resources for West European social democracies today are:

- Social democratic parties' share of the vote in Europe: as an aggregate number this is no higher [now] than in the post-war decades. But as of 2000 there is a peak of social democratic votes in the core countries, recalling the golden years of the sixties and seventies.
- Governmental power: at the present time, this stands at an historic level. The fact that social democratic parties are governing alone or are dominant coalition partners in 11 EU countries is not so much a trend, but more of an unprecedented coincidence. Whether this 'historic moment of opportunity' consolidates into a medium-term trend depends partly on the credibility and success of the social democratic parties in key policy areas over the next years.
- Decline of conservative and neoliberal parties: of course this is also not an irreversible trend. Rather, it appears to be the temporary exhaustion of a political cycle of about two decades of neoliberal politics, which social democratic parties and governments can exploit.

Constraints   Opposing these resources, located largely in the political arena, are considerable economic and social constraints which restrict social democratic governance. The most important are:

- globalisation (especially of the financial markets);
- Europeanisation of product markets;
- independent European Central Bank with a monetarist statute;
- high national indebtedness narrows the room to move, particularly in high-cost areas such as social policy;
- demographic shifts: the shift in the age pyramid of the society forces changes in old age pension and health policies for reasons of cost;
- diversification of the social structure: the main target group for social democratic policies can no longer primarily be the shrinking male (industrial) workforce or employees;
- individualisation (values, lifestyle etc.) forces a pluralisation of policy content and a change in the hierarchical style of politics;
- compared to the 'Golden Age' (1950–73) the voters of social democratic parties are socio-structurally (primarily industrial workers) and socio-culturally (dense social democratic milieus) less strongly anchored in a core constituency. Rather, they have become more volatile. This means that social democratic parties have to take into consideration an electorate willing to switch allegiances between elections much more than was the case in the immediate post-war decades. The strategic-political boundaries thus become narrower and, despite normative assertions to the contrary, the choices of social democratic governments are more strongly influenced by tactical electoral considerations.

Constraints or resources   Whereas these constraints – albeit with national variations – affect all social democratic governments, there are elements in the structural filter that cannot be classified as restrictions or resources a priori and independently of national political contexts. To this group belong:

- institutional structures of the political system: it makes a significant difference whether the political systems tend to resemble more centralist-majoritarian or more federal-consensus democracies. In the first instance the government's ability to access and organise the political agenda will be greater, more direct and quicker than can ever be the case in consensus democracies where governments are forced to negotiate and reach compromises;
- coalition potential in the party system: single-party government (Greece, Great Britain); left-wing coalition (Germany, France, Italy, Sweden); centre-left coalition (Denmark, the Netherlands); grand coalition (Belgium, Finland, Austria – until January 2000);

- trade unions' strength and willingness to co-operate;
- business interests' strength and willingness to oppose or to co-operate;
- media: in the short term the media allow themselves to be influenced by modern PR. [...] In the medium term, however, their (independent) influence on politics is likely to be stronger than the other way around. This is especially the case in federal systems like Germany where state elections force the federal government continually to justify itself in the public arena shaped largely by the media;
- European Union: for the time being the EU is reducing national governments' powers. These powers can be regained only with difficulty through negotiation and compromise in the interconnected multi-level system of the EU. However, given a corresponding willingness to reach compromise and consensus, new opportunities of policy making, which nation states had lost through the globalisation and Europeanisation of markets, could emerge in particular policy areas;
- politico-cultural traditions and values: content and style of governance are embedded in national political cultures. Dominant societal values and political preferences in the individual countries (such as the stability of the currency in Germany, full employment in Sweden, high levels of welfare in Denmark or freedom with respect to work and leisure time in the Netherlands) can be influenced only in the medium to long term. In the short term, however, they act as important independent contraints on policy formulation.

Filter 2: options and decisions

The second filter is not constituted by structures. Rather, the structures simply represent the 'boundaries' of the political arena. However, within these borders there is a certain range of choices (strategic choices and policy choices as well) for the governments. If this were not the case it would in fact make no difference which party governs, something that is suspected often by voters. [...] In a second filtering process the particular policy options from this 'feasible set' are then transformed into binding decisions through parliamentary majorities and governments. These decisions are thus affected by:

- coalitions and alliances;
- perceptions and interpretations of the options;
- programmatic and policy goals of governments.

With respect to filter 1 all Western European social democratic parties currently face similar external constraints, whereas the internal restrictions and resources vary much more. Just as variable are the political decisions within the second filter. These variations in 'actual policy' are primarily influenced by the differing national resources and constraints, the differing perceptions of the actors and their contrasting programmatic goals. However, the list of constraints indicates that at the end of the 20th century the external restrictions have increased and the political room for manoeuvre, i.e. the 'feasible set' of realistic options, has shrunk. Yet, if we look more closely at the programmes and policies of the governing social democrats, we can identify different styles and contents of social democratic governance, or, metaphorically speaking, different routes followed by the third ways of social democracy.

3.   The various ways of social democracy in Europe[1]

[. . .] In Western Europe at least four different paths can be identified that represent a distinct programmatic, strategic and political profile: the market-oriented way of New Labour, the market and consensus-oriented way of the Dutch polder model, the reformed-welfare state way of the Swedish (and Danish) social democrats, and the statist way of the French socialists.[2] The labelling does not establish any ideal types. Rather, it highlights a characteristic and distinctive feature of the social democratic governments under discussion. These distinctions also reveal my selection criterion in presenting the various third ways – the selective analysis restricts itself to key fiscal, employment and social policy measures.[3] At the end of each section the various 'ways' of the social democratic-led governments are judged by weighing up their respective strengths and weaknesses in light of the social democratic principles of economic efficiency and social justice.

3.1.   The market-oriented way of the New Labour government

Of all the social democratic governments in Europe Tony Blair's Labour Government (1997–) enjoys both the most resources and the fewest constraints in implementing policy. Because of the simple majority electoral system, 43 per cent of votes was sufficient for the party to gain a parliamentary majority of 178 seats and thus to enjoy a comfortable governing majority in parliament. The Labour Government does not have to take into account a coalition partner. The Conservative Party's temporary decline and loss of votes and seats was more sudden and striking in Great Britain than for most conservative parties on the continent. The dramatic weakness of the opposition gave the Labour Government more room to move than is enjoyed by most governing social democrats in Europe. On top of that is the majoritarian institutional structure, which facilitates hierarchical, unilateral governance much more in Britain than in the federal consensus democracies of most continental countries.

[. . .]

Fiscal policy   Like all other current social democratic governments New Labour rejects a classical Keynesian economic policy. Indeed, during election campaigning it committed itself to continuing the conservative fiscal policy of the previous government for at least two years and subjected itself to two general rules:

- all current expenditure is financed only by current revenue. New indebtedness can be entered into only for purposes of investment, not consumption;
- new public debt should be held at a 'stable moderate' level independently of the business cycle; it should not pursue short-term anti-cyclical intervention.

However, the British budgetary policy was no more restrictive than those of most social democratic (and conservative) governments on the continent. Moreover, instead of channelling unexpected tax revenue primarily into debt reduction, under Gordon Brown the Treasury instead used it to finance special education, employment and health programmes.

On the revenue side, New Labour has begun to reorganise the tax system, so that low wage earners will receive either full or significant tax relief. Households in which at least one person works full time will be guaranteed a minimum income of £10,000 through working families income tax credits. Until then household income will be subsidised via a regressive negative income tax, following which the base-level tax rate of 10% will take effect. It is here that the labour market inclusion strategy is evident: first, demand will be stimulated in the low wage employment sector, while, second, such jobs will be made economically viable so as to avoid or at least lessen the American disease of the working poor.[4]

At the same time, company taxes were further reduced and under the Blair Government they are the lowest in the European Union.

Both tax reforms must be seen as supply side measures that have the primary goal of stimulating employment in a sustained manner and thereby preventing the 'involuntary exclusion' at the lower end of the social scale.

Employment policy   Between 1996 and 1999 employment in Great Britain grew at a slower rate (1.03%) than in the EMU area (1.87%). However, this base level employment growth resulted in a considerably higher rate of participation (1997: 76%) than within the EMU area (1997: 65.1%) and the unemployment rate (declining from 8.7% in 1996 to 6.3% in 1998) dropped more quickly than in the EMU countries (1996: 11.6%; 1998: 10.9%). The labour market, which New Labour had left largely deregulated, thus proved more dynamic than most (regulated) labour markets on the European continent. New Labour had better promoted the traditional social democratic goal of inclusion in the labour market (full employment with high rates of participation) than had most social democratic and conservative governments on the continent.

The New Deal is the most notable part of the active labour market policy. Its principal aim is to reduce youth unemployment. The combination of instruments it uses reflect the mixture of incentive and compulsion so characteristic of New Labour: on one hand young people are employed via subsidised positions in the private sector and job creation measures in the public sector. As an alternative, state-financed training programmes are offered. On the other hand, the controls and qualifying criteria guiding the acceptance of employment have been tightened, accompanied by significant cuts in social transfers. These measures aim to eliminate both free riding and those cases of unemployment where accepting employment is not worthwhile because the income is barely about (or even below) the level of welfare benefits. [. . .] In three years of government the Labour administration has succeeded in reducing youth unemployment and halving long-term unemployment. However, even after these three years in office, expenditure on active labour market policy is still visibly beneath the European or even the Scandinavian average. The British figures do improve somewhat if one includes the considerably increased investment in education and training that aims to raise the employability of young people and adapt to the ever-changing qualifications demanded by the labour market.

Social policy   New Labour is selectively reforming social policy according to the principle of 'welfare to work'. Welfare state measures are generally being judged according to how much they increase pressure to enter the labour market. Welfare transfers are intended to act as an incentive (or pressure) to accept employment and certainly should not prevent this. The passive welfare state is thus to be progressively restructured into an active social investment state, with education, health and children the preferred areas for investment. [. . .]

While initial investment and restructuring of the National Health Service has brought modest success, there is no evidence of long-term reform of the old age pension. In contrast, there has been a visible retreat from the social democratic ideal of universalism in social policy. The criteria for assessing need have been tightened [. . .] as a necessary shift in the 'culture of social benefits'. This may indeed prevent abuse of welfare benefits and better target social security to those in real need, yet this may be at the expense of social stigmatisation and a necessarily enlarged bureaucracy when it comes to need assessment. [. . .] New Labour has so far failed to produce either persuasive policy or convincing political action to address the danger that the selective and targeted welfare state will suddenly turn into a marginal one.

The strengths and weaknesses of New Labour's policies

The strengths are:

- the abandonment of protective measures that would hinder economic growth, and thus lead to a loss in economic and social welfare, is more credibly conceived of and put into practice by New Labour than by the other social democratic parties and governments;
- the labour market deregulation inherited from Margaret Thatcher and largely accepted by New Labour reduces the socially unjust discrimination of outsiders (particularly young people and women) in favour of insiders (typically unionised workers). Moreover, the deregulated labour markets facilitate fast structural change from old industries to the knowledge-based service sector;
- the reorientation of a welfare state structurally rooted in the industrial age, and with a socially unjust bias towards the middle classes, to one focusing on those in real need, leads to desired rather than undesirable redistributive effects;
- the particular emphasis placed on education, training and learning recognises the value of human capital and its embedding in social capital (trust, fairness, co-operativeness, team spirit) in its meaning for the individual, the economy and society; the pressure that the

state places on citizens to assume individual responsibility for their own human capital seems socially just from both an individual and a societal perspective.

The weaknesses are:

- by largely abandoning anti-cyclical fiscal and monetary policies, the abdication of political control in favour of the volatile and unpredictable forces of the market has been accelerated;
- giving up the use of the tax system as a powerful means of redistribution will increase social inequality; a high degree of social inequality is detrimental to social cohesion and trust both among citizens and *vis-à-vis* the state;
- the downside of the flexibilisation of the labour market is its discrimination of older workers and the forced horizontal and geographical migration of job-seekers; an additional price of flexibilisation is the weakening of trade unions' bargaining power, which has the probable consequence of lower wages and a further redistribution from earned income to capital;
- the targeting of the welfare state to the really needy, justified from the perspective of social justice, makes the welfare state more vulnerable to demands for its further reduction. That is, if the middle classes no longer benefit from welfare transfers and social services they lose their economic interest in the welfare state and will rationally call for further cuts, as they receive little benefit from the welfare state, yet partly finance it through their taxes.[5] The welfare state will thus lose important allies with an influential political voice. Futher, the danger of a 'two-thirds-society' is very real in Great Britain, as the number of people living below the poverty line is currently already twice as high as in Germany and most continental European states.

3.2   The consensus-oriented way to more market: the Dutch 'polder model'

The political institutions of the British Westminster model, the deregulation carried out during the Thatcher era and the relative weakness of interest groups have so far allowed New Labour to push through its market-oriented political reforms in a largely hierarchical and even statist manner. However, a comparable centralist institutional and political setting does not exist on the European Continent, even in France. The Partij van de Arbeid (PvdA) in the Netherlands is an example of one party and country that comes relatively close to New Labour's market-oriented goals, but which is furthest from New Labour in the strategies and means it has adopted to achieve the goals. While Blair's Labour Government has followed the traditional majoritarian strategy, the Dutch 'polder model' is strongly shaped by consensus: the reforms were agreed upon among both the political parties and the social partners through a democratic negotiation and compromise process. The (traditional and neo-corporatist) socio-economic council and the Wassenaar wage agreement form the institutional framework that has been successfully utilised for economic and social negotiations against the backdrop of increasing social democratic participation in government since 1982 and after 1989.

Because of the consensual way in which they were negotiated, the market reforms turned out to be less radical than in England.[6] In the longer term, however, they may have the advantage of more stable support from those affected by the reforms, as they were included in the decision-making process much more than has been the case in New Labour's hierarchical style of politics. The Dutch case has shown how strongly political institutions, traditions and cultures mould political strategies, force actors to negotiate and co-operate, but nonetheless facilitate innovative employment and social policy reforms. In other words, the British way would not have been possible in the Netherlands and the Dutch way was not necessary to carry out the reforms in Britain. The style of politics and decision-making diverge, while the policy goals and outcomes increasingly converge in key areas (such as the labour market). However, in contrast to Great Britain the 'Dutch miracle' of the nineties is by no means attributable only to the social democrats. Rather, it was engineered by coalition governments in which at various times Christian Democrats, left-liberal and right-liberal parties participated.

Fiscal policy   The PvdA has committed itself to a restrictive budgetary policy that has been pursued during both the 'grand coalition' with the Christian Democrats (1989–94) and the so-called 'purple coalition' from 1994 onwards. Since 1994 the purple coalition has had two priorities in fiscal policy: first, reduction of the budget deficit and gross state indebtedness, and, second, reduction of tax and duties so as to stimulate investment and encourage employment. To achieve the first goal a ceiling was placed on central administration and welfare insurances. In the first four years of government this led to a reduction in expenditure of 0.4% per annum. Growth-induced revenue was used strictly for reduction of the budget deficit. From 1994 to 1998 public expenditure dropped by more than 5% to 42.6% of GDP. Budgetary consolidation was carried out, not least by a reduction in social expenditure, especially the invalid benefit, as generous as it was abused. The social democrats implemented these cuts in the face of opposition from trade unions and parts of their own membership and voter base in the grand coalition. They also pressed on with the policy as part of the purple coalition. There was no neo-Keynesian stimulation of aggregate demand on the expenditure side and only a modest amount on the income side. Income taxes were cut: the top tax bracket from 70% (1989) to 60% (1996) and the base-level tax bracket from 14% (1989) to 6.35% (1996). The latter measure in particular stimulated employment in the lower third of the service industry and also holds up well against social democratic principles from the perspective of distributive politics. The tax cuts were thus aimed less at a general increase in the aggregate effective demand, but rather were much more targeted at the creation of part-time work and low-skilled service jobs.

Employment policy   The employment record of the past two decades in the Netherlands is impressive. Employment growth began in 1983 and lasted until 1992.[7] After a short period of stagnation employment again began to rise at a quicker rate on average than in most OECD states. The Netherlands performed better than most EU states – except Denmark – on almost every indicator of labour market success. [. . .] How exactly did this 'employment miracle' result, whereby the Netherlands came to perform so well on all three central employment indicators of workforce participation, female employment rates and unemployment? Further, what part in this can the Dutch social democrats claim?

The success is essentially the result of three factors: moderate wage increases, the development of labour-intensive service industries, and, above all, the redistribution of work. Wage restraint promoted investment, raised net exports because of comparative cost advantage and meant that more people could remain in employment. [. . .]

Apart from wage restraint and additional social policy measures, these successes were also achieved through moderate labour market deregulation. With respect to patterns of employment, length of employment, and the flexibility and move towards service – sector employment, the Netherlands have moved closer to the Anglo-Saxon labour markets. There are, however, two exceptions to this: on the negative side, even the Netherlands was unable to overcome the Continental affliction of long-term unemployment. On the positive side, the employment dynamic has not led to an income dispersion of American dimensions and the accompanying phenomenon of the working poor. The case of the Netherlands is therefore evidence that,

contrary to traditional union and social democratic thinking, moderate
deregulation of labour markets can lead to more, and to more justly
distributed, employment.[8] That this can occur in a harmonised and
co-operative way, and that it facilitates emancipatory side-effects
(female employment, male part-time work), further weakens future
arguments of those defenders of regulated, but undynamic labour
markets.

Social policy   The Dutch welfare state of the sixties and seventies can
be considered the very model of the passive-compensatory type in the
Continental mould.

[. . .]

The impetus to reform came from the government (the CDA/PvdA
coalition) that at the beginning of the nineties had identified the
extremely low rate of labour market participation as the Achilles' heel
of the welfare state and tax system. The decision to reform the disability benefit (1991) was thus the important prelude to further reforms
aimed at altering the passive-compensatory character of the Dutch
welfare state. As a result of a bonus/penalty incentive system for
employers, a tightening of the criteria for employees, as well as the
obligation for workers to accept 'reasonable', not just 'suitable',
employment, in 1994 the number of those entitled to the disability
benefit dropped for the first time since its introduction. After 1994 the
'purple coalition' pressed on with welfare state reforms under the
leadership of the social democrats. The reform of the sickness and unemployment benefits followed. There were essentially four reforms
that accompanied the shift from passive to active welfare state: the
introduction of financial incentives, limited competition through
the opening up of the system for private insurers, moderation of the
'moral hazard problem' through tightening of entitlement criteria
and controls, as well as stronger state control of the social security
administration.

[. . .]

The strengths and weaknesses of the polder model   Most of the
macroeconomic pro-arguments outlined above in relation to New
Labour also apply to the Dutch Partij van de Arbeid. In addition:

• pressure to enter the labour market has increased, but because of
  the more generous welfare benefits is still weaker and less bound
  up with strong social pressure than in Great Britain;

- the weaker pressure to accept employment is largely compensated for by an intelligent incentive structure that facilitates part-time work without thereby 'punishing' part-time workers in the area of socal security entitlements.
- consensus politics ensures more stable support for the reforms within the population in the longer term; in addition it corresponds to the stated social democratic aim of stronger participatory inclusion of citizens, their organisations and civil associations in policy formulation;
- in contrast to New Labour's policies, citizens enjoy more options and sovereignty with respect to how they manage their working time.

The weaknesses are:

- welfare state free riding has still not been sufficiently restricted, as the high number of disabled benefit recipients – without any parallel internationally – attests to;
- the welfare state is still geared more towards securing a standard of living rather than survival, and thus retains its 'middle-class bias' that discriminates against the truly needy.

3.3   The (reformed) welfare state way: Sweden

In the 1960s and 1970s Sweden was regarded as *the* social democratic model. The Swedish model was characterised by a largely universalist welfare state, full employment, the highest rate of female participation, a harmonised incomes policy that was integrated into economic policy, the strongest trade unions in the Western world, the highest tax burden in a society of astounding tax morals, and the highest level of state expenditure against the backdrop of a rate of economic growth slightly below the OECD average. [. . .] Since the late 1970s several pillars of the Swedish model have [. . .] been considerably damaged: the harmonised incomes policy rooted in solidarity broke down and national debt rose rapidly. Completely new, however, was that the former country of full employment slid into mass unemployment of 9.5% (1993). After reassuming office in 1994 the Swedish social democrats reacted with reforms. [. . .]

Fiscal policy   Contrary to widespread misperception, during the so-called 'golden era' of the 1950s and 1960s the Swedish social democrats were already pursuing supply-oriented policies more strongly than neo-Keynesian fiscal policy. When the Swedish social democrats were re-elected into office in 1994 the minority social democratic government was confronted with a budget deficit of 10%. A Keynesian policy of deficit spending was therefore unlikely not just for reasons of political tradition, but was also precluded by fiscal constraints that could not be ignored. The government therefore reacted in an almost perfectly anti-Keynesian way with a combination of tax increases and expenditure cuts. [. . .] Like almost all social democratic parties in the nineties the Swedish social democratic government declared both its programmatic and actual support for fiscal orthodoxy. Expenditure was now not be used as a way to stimulate demand in an attempt to smooth out the economic cycle.

On the revenue side, supply-oriented components were imposed. The tax burden on businesses was eased and there was a move away from direct income tax and towards indirect consumer taxes. The taxation system that during the sixties and seventies had been the most redistributive in the OECD lost much of its ability to redistribute in the nineties. At least in part because of the less redistributive character of the tax system, income differentials and income dispersion increased in the eighties and nineties. They continue, however, to be some of the lowest internationally.

Employment policy An active labour market policy remains the most striking characteristic of the Swedish employment strategy. At 2.1% of GDP (1997) Sweden still spends more on its active labour market policy than any other country in the OECD. However, in the nineties this was successful to only a limited degree, as was reflected by the fact that unemployment advanced at the same time as expenditure for the active labour market policy increased. At least in practice, in the nineties the Swedish social democrats also moved away from the goal of the highest possible rates of workforce participation. Indeed, the high female employment rate is in decline.[9] [. . .] The period of notice for dismissal in Sweden remains one of the longest in Europe. Despite the reforms mentioned, the Swedish labour market remains highly regulated. [. . .]

A new kind of corporatist consensus, such as exists in the Netherlands, is not yet in sight, neither is the Swedish government able to take radical measures as the British government can. The labour market reform 'jam' in Sweden is unmistakable, and in comparison with Great Britain and the Netherlands, Sweden has fallen behind in the labour market.

Social policy Despite supporting the universalist welfare state in principle, several measures have been passed by the minority social democratic government since 1994 that have begun to change the face of the Swedish welfare state. The most important are:

- moderate cuts in various monetary social transfers (mostly by 5%);
- the introduction of 'waiting days' in cases of sickness chiefly as a way around the worsening abuse of the working days Monday and Friday;
- a ceiling of 75% of the wage has been set for replacement income in cases of sickness; health care continues to be guaranteed free of charge by state health services; [. . .]
- reductions in pensions: basic and additional pensions are increasingly being integrated into one pension that resembles the structure of the German pension system; for the first time employee contributions are being introduced to finance pensions (equal financing via 18.5% of income); the development of a second, privately financed pillar of pensions has begun;
- with 31.9%, Sweden continues to have more than double the rate of public sector employment of Germany, Great Britain and the Netherlands; in this area there are plans for limited reductions in the future, which would primarily affect female workers.

In general the reductions are primarily directed at monetary transfers and to a much lesser extent at the social services. The measures are aimed at strengthening employees' individual responsibility and at cutting down on welfare state free riding. However, the reductions were made from a very high level, and Sweden's welfare benefits must therefore continue to be regarded as the most comprehensive in the Western world. [. . .]

The strengths and weaknesses of the Swedish way   The strengths are:

- Sweden remains one of the most open national economies in the OECD and even during the deep economic crisis of the early nineties did not resort to protectionist measures;
- the supply of investors was improved through tax and social policy measures, so that the outflow of Swedish investment capital was reduced and the inflow of foreign direct investment increased;
- the welfare state has only been tinkered with at the edges; in addition, many of the measures aim to combat parasitic free riding and thus, among other things, also served to improve social justice and strengthen individual responsibility;

- the fight against unemployment remained the political priority; considerable resources were further set aside to fight unemployment;
- the level of tax avoidance and tax erasion by the self-employed and the wealthy is lower in Sweden than in most European Union countries.

The weaknesses are:

- the decline in workforce participation rates, particularly for females, signals something of a shift away from the traditional social democratic goal of full employment with high labour force participation rates;
- the decline in participation rates may lead to further difficulties in financing the heavily tax-based welfare state;
- Sweden continues to have a below average growth rate compared to other OECD countries;
- tariff fronts have been further hardened and no return to a concerted or harmonised incomes policy is in sight.

Restructuring of the Swedish welfare state has certainly begun and has already made considerable progress. Up until now it has proceeded less radically than in Great Britain or even than the Netherlands. While the welfare state continues to reduce poverty and minimise social risks, further labour market reforms must be undertaken if unemployment is not to become entrenched and if the kind of gap in social justice unknown in Sweden's workers' society until the end of the eighties is not to emerge. In addition, failure in the area of employment would in the longer term endanger the financing of the passive-compensatory area of the Swedish welfare state.

3.4   The statist way: the Parti Socialiste Français

Of all the social democratic and socialist parties in Western Europe at the end of the 20th century the Parti Socialiste Français appears to be the most strongly committed to a traditional statist policy. Indeed, the French socialists have remained statist in two senses:

- the institutional structure of France's centralist political system, the weakness of interest groups, the embedding of the party in a left-wing coalition with communists and greens (*gauche plurielle*), and France's statist-republican political culture, all enable the party to retain strong hierarchical state policy control. In France 'parallel governance structures' or institutional veto actors are comparatively weak or do not exist at all.

- the Parti Socialiste promotes the state much more than its sister parties do. This is true for macroeconomic policy, as well as for industry, employment and social policy. This may be interpreted as particular loyalty to traditional social democratic policy goals, but will be paid for [. . .] with a lack of innovation *vis-à-vis* the challenges of economic globalisation and the individualisation of society.

Fiscal policy   Even the French socialists have committed themselves to budgetary consolidation, to which they had turned by the mid-1980s. In the nineties the disciplined budgetary policy helped to force inflation below the EU average. In this sense since 1983 the French socialists have no longer followed the classical Keynesian route. However, since it entered office, differences can be identified between the fiscal policy of the Jospin Government and that of other social democratic governments. The socialist-led government's finance policy stands out from the fiscal priority of budgetary consolidation that is so unmistakable in the rhetoric and practice of the social democratic-led governments in Great Britain, Holland, Sweden and, since Lafontaine's resignation, Germany. In contrast to the rhetoric of austerity [. . .], Jospin talks of a mix of selective consolidation measures, price stability and support for the economic cycle. Indeed, in 1999 the French economy proved itself as one of the economic motors of the European Union with 3% growth in GDP. The French left government strengthened the looming cyclical upturn not with massive demand side programmes, but with measured strengthening of domestic demand: through, for example, the 1997 increase in the minimum wage and the quadrupling of state transfers to families at the beginning of the school year. [. . .]

Divergence from the general trend within the OECD at the end of the nineties is more clearly visible in tax policy. While most countries, with the temporary exception of Sweden, cut tax, the French socialists cautiously and selectively raised certain taxes. This was the case particularly for company tax and for special taxes on income from financial investments. In contrast, those on lower incomes received tax relief. In addition, the French leftist government introduced a financial and social reform component into the tax system that aims to increase the competitiveness of businesses without reducing social benefits. Thus, income-related contributions to health insurance were almost entirely abolished, with the social security deduction from almost all forms of income, CSG (*contribution sociale généralisée*), being correspondingly raised instead. This means, first, a reduction in non-wage labour costs and with it an increase in the competitiveness of businesses, and, second, a partial fiscalisation of social benefits that more fairly incorporate not only wages, but also other forms of income (self-employed, capital income) into the financing of the welfare state.

[. . .]

Employment policy   It is in employment policy that the traditional, statist nature of French socialist politics most clearly comes to the fore. This was evident in the party's plan for reducing youth unemployment. The goal is to create 700,000 jobs that are to be up to 80% state-financed. Of these alone 350,000 will be located in the public sector, a policy that would be unacceptable to New Labour, the Dutch social democrats or the SPD. The remaining 350,000 positions are to be created in the private sector with the help of state income subsidies. Further measures are:

- the labour supply is to be reduced by the subsidising of further early retirement schemes;
- a general law has been passed to allow for the introduction of the 35-hour week, for whose forced implementation state subsidies are to act as an incentive;
- until now scarcely any measures have been implemented to deregulate the labour market, with one modest exception being the easing of termination of fixed-term contracts;

While the first two measures must be seen as traditional social democratic employment policy, the latter has turned out to be a small outlet for flexibilisation in an otherwise highly regulated labour market. However, this deregulated sector of fixed-term, low-paid and rarely socially safeguarded jobs has, particularly in the service industry, proved especially dynamic. If this development is sustained, a dual labour market with a highly regulated but stagnating sector and a deregulated yet dynamic segment with considerable social injustice could emerge, as it has done in Spain.

Social policy   No innovative reforms are yet evident in the French welfare state. Apart from the partial fiscalisation of health insurance, the welfare state continues to be financed primarily through non-wage labour costs, paid overproportionally by employers. However, the socialist French government has cautiously tried to decouple social contributions from income and to finance the welfare state through taxation. Particular emphasis continues to be placed on the welfare state's support of families, though they are now to be assisted in a more differentiated manner based on income and through state supplements. New areas of emphasis are the construction and renovation of apartments, particularly in the ghettos around the large cities. Education, training and schooling receive particular emphasis in government policy, yet, as is the case with the German social democrats, this has not been sufficiently reflected in investment in education.

[. . .]

The strengths and weaknesses of the statist way   The strengths are:

- the basic willingness politically (in a democratically legitimated way) to steer the economy in those areas where the market gives rise to unjustified social hardships is more prominent in the case of the French socialists than of the other social democrat-led governments in Europe;
- the French socialists of the Jospin Government currently show greater readiness than most social democratic governments to compensate for the loss of the ability to control the economy at the nation-state level by achieving better co-ordination of national policies within the EU.[10] This applies especially to employment policy, to the European 'economic government' that should also exercise influence over the monetary policy of a democratically insufficiently legitimated European Central Bank, and to the strengthening of the 'Social Charter' and the 'Social Protocol' of the European Union;
- active labour market policy instead of blind faith that reduction in business, capital and income taxes will bring about long-term job-creating investment.

However, there is a downside to most of these merits, indicating that social democratic politics is not able to adopt certain unified and ideal instruments and policies, but must ponder trade-offs, given its own value preferences.

The weaknesses are:

- the maintenance of the status quo in the welfare state structures is convincing neither in view of its longer term financing and its discrimination of non-familial lifestyles, nor in its passive-compensatory structure that offers too few incentives to accept employment;

- the active labour market policy continues to rely much more strongly on the state subsidisation of work-creation programmes, primarily in the public sector, rather than on negative and positive incentives for individual education and training; individual responsibility to 'invest' in one's own human capital is not sufficiently recognised and encouraged in either its economic or its emancipatory functions;

- protectionist tendencies still exist, particularly in relation to third countries outside the European Union.

The French socialists have so far proved astonishingly resistant to changes in the markets. The current Jospin Government considers this policy to be to a large extent legitimised by the majority support of voters. Backed by this democratic legitimation the French leftist government administers the social and labour market status quo in a traditional manner. However, their recipes offer too few innovative responses to the problems of new at-risk social groups and marginalised classes in post-industrial society. It must be feared that further hesitation in implementing reforms will have to be paid for later with correspondingly stronger cuts to the economic and social prosperity of precisely those weaker classes in society. This would be the classic case of an unintended unsocial consequence of apparently social government action.

[. . .]

Notes

1 I would like to thank my student assistant Christian Henkes for his research, suggestions and criticism in this section.

2 Even after two years in office no comparably clear profile can be identified in the red–green governing coalition in Germany. Constrained by an institutional set up that forces compromise, the New Centre is in many respects still moving along the 'centre path' that has consistently shaped the policies of federal governments in recent decades.

3 Despite its obvious importance, monetary policy is not taken into consideration, because, with the exception of Great Britain and Sweden, it is determined by the European Central Bank for all countries under study.

4 Nevertheless, the number of those living below the poverty line in spite of earning a working wage is considerably higher in Great Britain than in most countries in the European Community.

5 It was always one of the most important strategic arguments in favour of the universalist welfare state in Sweden that as many people as possible should benefit from it so that it would also be in their own interests to retain it.

6 In Great Britain the reforms were mostly implemented by the governments of Margaret Thatcher and John Major and simply accepted by the Blair Government. The Blair Government's reform policies were therefore able to build on a much more deregulated economic and social system than the Dutch social democrats were able to do post-1989.

7 The positive employment record thus began well before the social democrats returned to power (1989), but was extraordinarily successfully continued by them.

8 This more just distribution relates both generally to insiders' and outsiders' opportunities for participation in the labour market and, specifically, to the gender-specific distribution of jobs.

9 Since 1997 Norway (75.6%) has replaced Sweden (74.5%) as the OECD country with the highest rate of female employment. In 1997 Germany had a female employment rate of 61.4% (OECD Employment Outlook, June 1998: 193).

10 This is even more remarkable, given that in the past the 'national' was continually given priority over the 'social' in the French EU policy, even among socialist governments.

4

From Godesberg to the *Neue Mitte*: The New Social Democracy in Germany

Thomas Meyer

The victory of the German Social Democratic Party (SPD) in the 1998 elections opened up a new period in its 135 year history. After the long years of opposition it regained power and formed its first coalition with the Green Party. But it was a victory which was soon to give way to uncertainty. Behind the successful electoral slogan 'Innovation and Social Justice' lay a combination of very general promises to modernise German public life, together with a few concrete pledges to restore most of the cuts in the welfare system introduced by the previous conservative-liberal government. But overall the nature of the promised innovation and social justice remained far from clear.

Since the election the direction of social democratic politics has remained a contentious issue. The resignation of Lafontaine in April 1999 and the issuing of the Blair-Schröder statement in June 1999 triggered an open debate on the nature of the government's policy agenda in relation to social and economic policy. The list of problems which needs to be addressed is extensive and well-rehearsed: a large federal deficit; an unemployment rate of around 10 per cent; the widespread opinion that tax rates are at an unacceptably high level; concerns about the budgetary implications of current welfare commitments (particularly in relation to health and old age pensions); inflexibilities in the labour market and high levels of indirect and direct labour costs; increased inequalities in wage and incomes; and the need for further reforms to promote environmental sustainability. It has become a commonplace on the centre-left that these issues cannot be properly addressed without innovation in social democratic thought and policy.

But the reaction within the SPD to the Blair–Schröder 'third way' programme demonstrates that there is a fine balance to be struck on the terms of policy modernisation. The message is clear: reform is necessary, but the social democratic values of social justice and solidarity should not be the casualties of any modernisation process.

After Godesberg

It is not the first time that debate has occurred within the SPD about the nature of revisionism. The SPD's 1959 Godesberg Programme – which gave Germany a value-based, pragmatic social democratic party – blended key insights from liberalism and socialism. Before this paradigm change the SPD had, for about a century, been characterised by an entrenched dualism between ideological orthodoxy and a half-hearted pragmatism at the level of policy. It was a dualism which created confusion within the party and the wider public in equal measure. Godesberg changed this. It created a new unity between theory and practice which meant that the ideas and ideology used by the party in its programmes and statements were able to guide the day-to-day actions of party representatives grappling with the problems of forming and explaining policy.

The Godesberg reinvention of social democracy emphasised the importance of basic values such as freedom, solidarity and justice, as well as institutional frameworks such as the welfare state. But it was candid in admitting that the precise rules governing the use of private property – together with the mechanisms of social control and market regulation – can only be determined by experience. The adoption of this revisionist interpretation of social democracy in the late 1950s led to the party being accused, not without foundation, of having abandoned many of the defining characteristics of the 'old' social democracy. Following Godesberg it seemed that the ideas of radical revisionism – advanced as early as 1896 by the German social democratic intellectual Edward Bernstein, then in London under the influence of Fabian Socialism – had finally returned home via Scandinavia. The Godesberg Programme finally accepted Bernstein's argument that if social democracy was to be able to cope with the demands of an increasingly complex society, then it had to be a synthesis between the basic values of traditional socialism and some of the institutional ideas of liberalism. This was true in relation to the operation both of the political system and of the economy. Individual rights, pluralist democracy and market co-ordination in a complex economy were argued to be the necessary means of delivering social advancement – as long as they were overseen by a vigilant political authority responsible for guaranteeing that these mechanisms worked to further social demo-cratic values. After Godesberg democratic Marxism, which for three quarters of a century had dominated social democratic thinking, became a minority interest within the SPD supported by only a few intellectuals. Undemocratic Marxism, as represented by the various Communist groups and parties in a number of guises, has not played a role in the party since.

The Godesberg Programme paved the way for the SPD-led govern-ment between 1969 and 1982 to implement a programme of social reform focusing on the democratisation of society, educational reform, and cultural modernisation. In government the SPD faced two major challenges to the Godesberg paradigm. The first came in the form of the new social movements – campaigning on peace, gender and envir-onmental issues – which started to change the political agenda and the electoral behaviour of an increasing part of the German public. They exercised a particularly crucial influence on the left in Germany, includ-ing the bulk of SPD members. In 1980 the Green Party was established, attracting a good deal of the centre-left vote; while the concerns of the new social movements continued to shape debates *within* the SPD. Since then social democrats have had to continue to respond to the new political issues raised by the environmental movement in order to maintain its share of the centre-left vote.

The second major challenge the SPD had to face turned out to be as crucial as the environmental one: it involved the development of a programme suited to the changed social and economic conditions brought about by increasing globalisation. Under pressure from mass unemployment the SPD, in its coalition with the Liberal Party, was driven reluctantly towards austerity policies resulting in cuts in social welfare and the adoption of a supply-side economics agenda. As the SPD was not prepared to continue to make major concessions along these lines the Liberal Party left the coalition government in 1982 and the SPD was sent to the opposition benches for a period which lasted over 16 years.

The Berlin Programme and reunification

These two challenges continued to drive policy debates in the SPD between 1984 and 1989 (presided over by Willy Brandt and subse-quently Oskar Lafontaine and Hans-Jochen Vogel), culminating in the reform package which became known as the Berlin Programme. It represented a step beyond Godesberg precisely because it recast the core social democratic project in a way which registered the need for environmental modernisation and the imperatives of adapting the traditional Keynesian model of economic management. Politically, it was supposed to provide the basis for a broad alliance for reform encompassing the SPD, the new social movements, and parts of the new technocratic elite. Its policy prescriptions were based on a blend of traditional social democratic concerns and the ideas of the new social movements: a security policy based on the termination of the arms race and establishment of internal institutions for peaceful co-operation; social equality in which all women and men have a right to decent employment and equal treatment; scientific and technological advance set within a democratic framework; an emphasis on quality of life issues; and democratic renewal through the encouragement of citizens' initiatives and a vibrant civil society.

It is important to bear in mind that this new party programme was not designed by a group of spin doctors in order to help a handful of party leaders to win elections. Nor was it the product of an elite drafting group. Rather, it was the outcome of a highly inclusive and deliberative process involving a large number of party representatives over a prolonged period of time. It reflected a new party consensus about modern social democratic politics and tried to forge a new electoral settlement.

But 1989 proved to be a watershed. Communist East Germany had come to an end and German re-unification, a very costly project, was looming large. The new policy programme failed to stand the tests of the post-Cold War world order, intensified globalisation, and the political and economic upheavals of re-unification. Far from deriving any benefits from its new image as a modern social environmental reform party, the SPD went on losing electoral support and political credibility.

Instead of presenting itself as a new and forward looking party the SPD rapidly acquired the image of a helpless organisation without a clear vision or effective leadership. This was partly due to the rapid changes at the top of the party: Hans-Jochen Vogel followed Willy Brandt from 1987 to 1991, followed by a brief spell by Johannes Rau in 1993, Rudolf Scharping between 1993 and 1995, and then Oskar Lafontaine from 1995 until Gerhard Schröder assumed control in 1998. Most of the party chairs and candidates for the chancellorship in the federal elections tried to create a particular image of their own, developing selective themes from the Berlin Programme. No clear-cut sense of political identity or continuity was created.

All this occurred at a time when the effects of economic globalisation and re-unification heightened the stress on the welfare state and
increased the numbers of unemployed. In response, new policies were
formulated during the early to mid-1990s to define the SPD's economic
alternative. These included labour market measures which sought to
reduce the indirect costs of labour, in addition to plans for environmental taxes offset by lower employment taxes. There was a renewed
emphasis on active industrial policy, particularly efforts to trigger
industrial innovation in high-tech sectors. Perhaps most significantly
the defence of the core structures of the welfare state was meant to
serve two purposes: the maintenance of minimum standards of social
dignity and security for the 'losers' in the new economy, and the bol-
stering of domestic demand for goods and services in order to stabilise
the economic cycle. Taken together this added up to a mixture of
demand-side and supply-side economics. There was, however, one
over-riding political message: the SPD would stand firm to protect the
welfare state.

The SPD's dilemmas

It didn't last. The recent emergence of the politics of the *neue mitte* (new
centre) represents a significant shift in the SPD's programme. It has
been triggered by a diverse set of factors.

Foremost among these is the SPD's lamentable electoral record. It
was defeated in five consecutive federal elections (though it performed
much more strongly at the state or *Land* level). The rapid turnover of
leading figures at the top of the party; the sweeping dominance of neo-
liberal economic ideologies both in the academic discourse and in the
mass media; and the party's low popular ratings on economic competence, all played a critical role in this failure. Reversing this record
meant coming up with new ways of addressing structural economic
and social changes. The concept of the *neue mitte* developed by
Schröder is, of course, partly an electoral label aimed at eliciting a positive response from the mass media and increasing the reach of the SPD
within the middle classes. But it also reflects the conviction that fresh
ways of approaching deep-rooted political dilemmas had to be found
once in government.

One reason for this derives from the continuing demise of the politics of class. The traditional working class, defined in terms of attitude
and political orientation, is now thought to represent less than five per
cent of the German public. Working class communities with uniform

political preferences have been replaced over the course of recent decades by a large number of political groupings, none of which exhibits an automatic tendency to support social democratic policies. Both the working class and the middle class are now made up of a range of socio-cultural groups with very different attitudes to life, work and politics. They are now classified as 'materialists', 'post-materialists' and 'post-modernists'. It is widely thought that members of these new social groupings are liable to move between different parties depending on their political image and performance. In order to obtain more than forty per cent of the popular vote the SPD has to perform the political somersaults necessary to bind together a number of these different political groupings. In contrast, it is thought that other parties face a much less fragmented core vote.

[. . .]

The most pressing dilemma for the SPD, however, and one which is pivotal in the debate on the *neue mitte*, is that of welfare reform. The glorious welfare record of the SPD seems destined to become an ever greater burden unless the party finds new answers to old questions. The first of these is addressing mass unemployment. But beyond this there is a pressing need to reverse the structural financial crisis of the welfare state: from the intolerable and still increasing costs of the health care system (due to increasingly high levels of medical technology), to the financial stress that demographic change is imposing on the pension system. Beyond the issue of welfare reform there is a continuing need to find political responses to new forms of social risk and the enduring concerns of single issue pressure groups. Themes ranging from the future of nuclear energy to genetic engineering, the deployment of armed forces in US sponsored missions, and the nature of immigration policies have assumed centre-stage in political debate. Neither the traditions of the SPD nor the old centre-left value system provide guidance on these matters. The objective of the politics of the third way should be to provide a coherent framework for addressing these issues.

Schröder and the *neue mitte*

Gerhard Schröder, who in the second half of the nineties gained more and more media prominence, became a promising electoral magnet for the SPD. As chief minister of Lower Saxony he was successful in cultivating his own image as a leading moderniser who was prepared to accept the interests and the ways of thinking of the business community. He strove to find new forms of partnership between politics and business which would help favour the cause of job creation. He also sought to improve the effectiveness of government, both cutting its size and improving its functioning. In order to promote his style of politics he tried to practise a form of communication which diminished the role of the SPD and favoured a more direct and populist relationship with the voters via the mass media. Following his sweeping electoral success in his *Land* in February 1998 there were few within the SPD who doubted his suitability to run as a candidate.

The general election victory of 1998 was the result of an emphasis on four issues during the campaign. First, massive economic innovation and modernisation to enhance Germany's position in a globalised economy; second, maintaining and re-balancing social security and social justice; third, supporting small- and medium-sized enterprises as the motors of economic growth and job creation; and lastly, major tax cuts together with a more just tax formula. Underpinning these themes was a highly professionalised Clinton-style campaign and candidate.

But the post-election euphoria did not last long. The first few months of the SPD-led government were characterised by a remarkable level of tension and confusion on environmental, economic and tax policies. [. . .] The underlying philosophy behind the policies of the 'new centre' still remains elusive. Until the surprising resignation of Oskar Lafontaine as finance minister and party chairman it seemed that the new policy agenda would be defined by the need to find pragmatic ways of reconciling the different positions of Schröder and Lafontaine – a difference which, though oversimplified by the mass media into a straightforward battle between 'traditionalism' and 'modernism', did have some clear dividing lines. Lafontaine put a greater emphasis on the traditional left of centre concerns with social justice, the maintenance of the welfare state and the need for new forms of international economic governance and active macroeconomic management. In contrast, Schröder adopted a Blairite interpretation of the terms on which social democracy should be renewed, talking up the need for welfare reform, a new partnership between business and government, and the need to embrace the reality of globalisation.

Following Lafontaine's resignation it has become clear to most representatives of the party as well as the wider public that a new debate is needed on the nature of modern social democratic politics. An overarching philosophy which binds together those policies which have already been developed (and those which are still in gestation) needs to be articulated. This is not just a matter of political expediency. A clear governing philosophy would provide the basis for a second term SPD-led government, as well as helping to provide answers to the most pressing policy questions facing German society.

The key issues which need to be addressed – all third way-type issues – suggest the need for a further step to be taken beyond Godesberg revisionism. Inevitably, however, the German account of social democratic modernisation will bear its own accent and will in some regards be distinct from the third ways of Clinton or Blair. The SPD's political culture and history, the position of the party in relation to its competitors in the political market place, and the nature of the wider political system, will all help ensure that Germany follows its own path of policy modernisation.

Responding to globalisation

The starting point for both Clinton's and Blair's version of third way renewal is the acceptance of economic globalisation, together with its consequences for economic growth and methods of economic management. Globalisation, however, is a highly ambiguous term: it is multi-dimensional in scope and ambivalent in meaning. Evidently, communication technologies, environmental problems, the spread of disease, cultural trends, and to a certain degree migration, are all transgressing political frontiers – whether individual nations like it or not. This process of internationalisation is increasingly occurring at a global scale. Indeed, financial markets, due to electronic communication and the erosion of legal and political barriers, have been truly global for some time. These represent seismic shifts. But they do not equate with the claims made by supporters of a 'strong' globalisation position who herald the death of the nation state and its governing capabilities. A more balanced analysis reveals that the markets for goods and services, and particularly that for labour, are still very far from being global. Almost all of these markets are in some form transnational, operating at the level of regions rather than at that of the global economy. In the European Union, for instance, more than eighty per cent of the transnational trade of member countries takes place within the single market. Competition is predominantly European, not global.

These issues have great domestic political significance. The meaning and consequences of the term 'globalisation' is a crucial faultline between neo-liberal and social democratic politics. Two issues stand out within contemporary political debate. The first concerns domestic economic policy: for social democrats current levels of globalisation do not render national macroeconomic policies obsolete and should not diminish political responsibility for steering the economy. The second issue concerns the possibility of regaining some of the political influence which may have been eroded at a national level through stronger European political and economic institutions. Beyond this there is considerable scope for more effective transnational and even global forms of governance. The key political question is whether the leading political players have the will to push this agenda. At a European or international level there is potential for more efficient and issue-related forms of political authority, whether it is in relation to environmental standards, the regulation of finance markets, employment policy, or tax harmonisation.

New governance: pluralism and civil society

The need to rethink or even reinvent mechanisms of governance is one of the central themes of public debate in Germany. Changing the relationship between government and the governed must be a central part of the modernisation of left of centre politics. Fortunately, however, the goal of bringing about innovative patterns of governance and a new division of labour between the state and other social actors is one which the traditional German model is well placed to address.

One pressure for reforming existing models of political governance is entirely practical. It is increasingly difficult to rely on top-down methods to steer political and social development within complex societies. Modern governance requires new forms of co-operation, both within the public sector and between the state and civil society. Mechanisms for involving non-governmental groups in decision making have to be created. Some of this is already under way: indeed, government itself is increasingly adopting the role of a social partner brokering, rather than imposing, solutions to social problems. The 'new alliance for jobs', developed by the Schröder government, [...] is a good example of how government can sponsor progressive agreements between relevant economic groups. The political challenge is to encourage these more disparate forms of governance – which often mean government relinquishing power – whilst ensuring that public authorities retain overall responsibility for steering policy development in line with democratically decided guidelines.

The second argument persuading social democrats to champion the transferral of political functions to civil society is a cultural one, based on the need to rebalance rights and obligations in modern societies. This is an argument well-known to communitarians. A re-enforcement of citizens' sense of obligation can strengthen their propensity to try to address social problems without automatically having recourse to government. Restructuring the political division of labour between the state and society should not, however, be mistaken for the neo-liberal agenda of stripping responsibilities from the state and privatising them. Rather, it concerns the effort to make a good deal of state intervention superfluous. Social groupings acting on a voluntary basis, rather than government, can often be more effective in resolving problems by collective action.

Not surprisingly, then, there is a new discussion about communitarianism in the SPD. It seems that this school of thought can be used to supplement social democratic philosophy and politics, but only if it is not used as strategy for legitimising the re-privatisation of public responsibilities. Indeed, the difference between a neo-liberal approach in this regard and the social democratic concept of the 'politicisation of civil society' is a crucial one. For the left of centre, welfare reforms which empower individuals must take place alongside the transferral of greater responsibilities to civil society.

Welfare reform

The German welfare state is badly in need of a reform programme which will make it fiscally sustainable and economically consistent with the wider labour market policy agenda. But this re-engineering of old welfare structures needs to be done in a way which preserves the basic objectives for which the welfare state was invented more than a century ago. With respect to old-age pensions and labour markets, the role of the individual has to be changed; more responsibility and scope for autonomy and choice are needed. In relation to old-age pensions, for instance, there will be a greater onus on the individual to decide how much income to save. But this responsibility will be set against the public security provided by the guarantee of a minimum pension which makes a dignified life in old age possible. With respect to labour markets, current welfare reforms have two key implications. First, legitimate job offers have to be accepted; and second, any job taken by an unemployed person should entitle them to a reasonable increase in income. This adds up to a new division of responsibility and culture of co-operation between individuals, civil society and government.

All this can and must be done. Pragmatism, creativity, and a spirit of innovation are required. But at the heart of modern social democracy must remain the formative belief that every citizen is entitled to a dignified standard of social security when all her own efforts have failed. This guarantee of a decent life is not dependent on economic merit. It is a human right. The welfare state should therefore concentrate its efforts on investing in human and social capital, while also contributing to the creation of new jobs through the creative use of microeconomic initiatives.

Values and crossroads

In the present phase of the new political discourse about the third way and the *neue mitte* it seems likely that the renewal of the German social democracy will continue to embrace many of the challenges articulated by Tony Blair. It will, however, give these its own political inflection, using methods which are suited to the German model to secure change. Though it will have much in common with similar efforts in other countries it will also lead to some distinct positions. 'Social inclusion' will be understood as a minimum precondition for social justice, but not as a basic value in itself. Social justice, the core goal of social democrats, will continue to focus on equality in life chances, the distribution of jobs, tax rates, and the distribution of income and wealth.

Similarly, the new third way emphasis on 'employability' may be an appropriate goal for the new welfare state but it cannot and should not replace government's responsibility for employment. This suggests that growth-enhancing macroeconomic policies, at a national and increasingly transnational level, should remain part of the social democratic armoury. New forms of flexibility and deregulation will, of course, need to be introduced. But the resounding message of the new social democracy should be made clear (and is worth repeating): there should be a guarantee of security and a decent life for all individuals.

Another distinction lies in the approach towards risk and individualisation. It is perhaps ill-advised to emphasise the importance of a 'culture of entrepreneurship' within a social democratic strategy. The very term lends itself to the neo-liberal worldview in which each individual has to stand alone in managing his own fortunes within the global economy. Such an outlook helps to delegitimise the very concept of the welfare state. It is more appropriate for the centre-left to campaign for a new 'culture of social responsibility', which stresses both the responsibility of the individual towards the community and the responsibility of the community towards the individual.

Finally, there is the question of the future role of political parties, particularly the SPD, within the wider political arena. Centre-left parties across Europe are increasingly adopting Clintonesque campaigning techniques and policy styles which downgrade the traditional role of political parties and structures. We forget the importance of political parties at our peril. There remains a crucial political role for parties such as the SPD – both as a large democratic body able through its own actions to help energise civil society, and as a network capable of communicating effectively with the social groups whose members have little time for spin-doctored political messages.

Here then, are some of the distinctive features of the German contribution to the ongoing shared transnational discourse about the renewal of social democracy. The SPD and centre-left intellectuals will continue to give a distinctive German flavour to this debate, seeking to build on the enduring strengths of the German social market. The aim should be, of course, to forge new agreements between national social democratic parties and to use these as the basis for joint political action at a European and global level. But it must be clear that modernisation is about striking a new balance between flexibility and security, and not the ending of the latter.

5

A Third Way for New Zealand?

Paul Dalziel

The 'third way' is one of those phrases like the 'new right' that have been imported into New Zealand from policy debates overseas. The phrase is most closely associated with the New Labour government of Tony Blair in the United Kingdom, although it has also been applied to a number of centre-left governments in Europe and to Bill Clinton's presidency in the United States.[1] Even if this label were not available, however, something like it would have to be invented to define a framework for a centre-left government in New Zealand, given the history of Labour governments in this country.

The first Labour government of Savage and Fraser (1935–49) constructed a framework for economic management based on intense state involvement in policies such as income stabilisation subsidies for farmers, industrial development behind import barriers, large-scale investment in public works and housing construction financed by Reserve Bank loans, universal free access to public education, health care and social security, and a system of industrial relations based on compulsory unionism and arbitration for workers covered by Awards. This approach, which might be called 'the first way' in New Zealand, was not seriously challenged during the Holland (1949–57) and Holyoake (1960–72) years or during the one-term Labour governments of 1957–60 and 1972–75. Indeed, its zenith occurred between 1975 and 1984, when the National government headed by Sir Robert Muldoon introduced a universal taxpayer-funded superannuation scheme, supplementary minimum prices for pastoral farmers, the 'Think Big' energy projects, generally expansive fiscal and monetary policies, and a comprehensive prices and incomes freeze lasting almost two years from June 1982.

This all changed with the election of the fourth Labour government on 14 July 1984. Under the direction of Minister of Finance Roger Douglas, David Lange's government began removing agricultural subsidies, lowering import barriers, reducing spending on public works, corporatising and then privatising government trading departments, deregulating financial and other markets, granting autonomy to the Reserve Bank, cutting back on social security income entitlements and introducing a measure of targeting in New Zealand's universal superannuation scheme. This programme was continued by Jim Bolger's fourth National government as Ruth Richardson and Bill Birch cut social welfare benefits sharply, introduced the Employment Contracts Act, announced the principle that the top third of all income earners should meet most of the cost of their social services (for example, in education and health), and opened up the ACC scheme to private sector competition. Within the framework of economic management produced by these reforms, the major role of the state is to provide a stable macroeconomic environment (that is, price stability and fiscal balance) in order to allow competitive domestic markets to allocate resources efficiently. This framework might be called 'the second way' in New Zealand.

The first part of this discussion presents evidence to show that 'the second way' has failed to deliver higher relative economic growth, lower poverty and reduced unemployment as was promised at its introduction in 1984. Indeed, on all three criteria, New Zealand is clearly much worse off in 1999 than it was fifteen years earlier. This is why a future centre-left government must look for a third way. There is no going back to the first way (which had revealed serious problems leading to its rejection in 1984), and the second way is demonstrably not working.

The economic reforms have failed to deliver

[. . .]

Figure 5.1 compares the real gross domestic product (real GDP) of Australia and New Zealand since 1977 adjusted to a common scale (1984 = 100). Between 1978 and 1984, the two GDP paths were very close, and the annual growth rates of Australia (2.9 per cent) and New Zealand (2.7 per cent) differed by only a small amount during this period immediately before the reforms. After 1984, however, the two series diverged sharply. For eight years New Zealand's output remained virtually

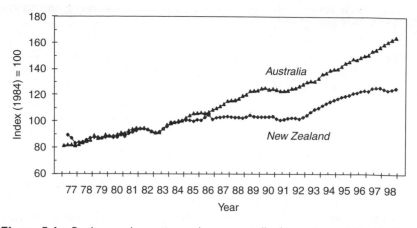

Figure 5.1   Real gross domestic product, seasonally: Australia and New Zealand, 1977–98

static, while Australia continued to grow at 3.0 per cent per annum. New Zealand's annual growth rate then recovered to 3.3 per cent between 1992 and 1998. This was above the pre-reform rate, but was still almost a full percentage point below Australia's annual growth rate of 4.2 per cent.

Consequently, after keeping pace with Australia for the six years before 1984, New Zealand has slipped well behind since. To be more accurate, if New Zealand had continued to grow as fast as Australia after 1984, our GDP in 1998 would have been nearly a third higher than it was. At the current average tax rate, this would have given the government an extra $11 billion in tax revenue, almost equal to its combined budgets for health and education. Over the entire 1984–1998 period, the output gap amounted to $215 billion, equal to more than two years of output in this country. These are huge numbers and represent an enormous sacrifice of lost economic development in New Zealand during the last 15 years.

Further, the major impact of this failure fell most heavily on the low end of New Zealand's income distribution. Community groups have been saying for years that poverty increased dramatically during the reforms, and this claim is now being confirmed in a number of academic studies. Professor Srikanta Chatterjee of Massey University, for example, has undertaken a study of Household Economic Survey data for 1984 and 1996.[2] His research shows that the top ten per cent of New Zealanders increased their share of total income over this period at the expense of the rest of the income distribution. Converting his findings into absolute dollar figures (rather than as income shares), it is possible to say that between 1984 and 1996 the bottom 40 per cent of the income distribution experienced a fall in their spending power of more than three per cent. The cut in spending power for the bottom 10 per cent was a staggering 8.7 per cent. Again, these are very large numbers.

Further, it is clearly understood that an important reason why poverty levels are so high is that the economic reforms did not reduce unemployment. New Zealand's official unemployment series began only in December 1986, but the New Zealand Institute of Economic Research has produced comparable data for earlier years which suggest that in June 1984 the unemployment rate was 3.7 per cent, having peaked at 4.6 per cent in September the previous year. During the transition period of the reforms, the official unemployment rate rose to 10.9 per cent in September 1991, fell back to 6.1 per cent throughout 1996, but rose again to 7.7 per cent by the end of 1998. Thus the unemployment rate was twice as high in 1998 as it was in 1984. Given that the Economic Summit Conference accurately described that 1984 level itself as 'historically high by New Zealand standards', it is clear that once again the reform period has produced a substantial deterioration in a key economic indicator.

[. . .]

A third way for New Zealand

The framework I want to suggest for 'third way' economics in New Zealand is based on a description of the economy as a social system of (i) property rights (ii) specialised production (iii) income distribution and (iv) monetary exchange. In each of these areas there is scope for government involvement that goes beyond the hands-off approach of the second way without returning to the excesses of the first way.

Property rights

The most important piece of legislation governing property rights that requires attention from a centre-left government is the Employment Contracts Act 1991 (ECA). Consistent with the overall framework used to design New Zealand's economic reforms, the preamble of the ECA describes its purpose as 'to promote an efficient labour market'. There is an established school of thought in New Zealand (promoted by the

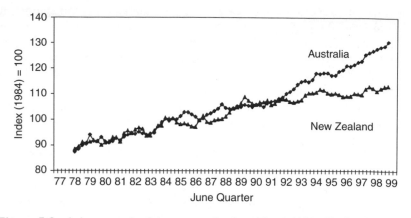

Figure 5.2   Labour productivity, seasonally: Australia and New Zealand, 1978–98

New Zealand Business Roundtable, for example) that labour relations should be treated under normal contract law, with no specialist institutions such as the Employment Court to oversee labour market outcomes. This is a view that a centre-left government must reject. Resistance to the treatment of human labour as no more than a commodity to be trade like any other has always been at the core of the labour movement. Employment contracts involve the very fabric of society – namely, the bodies and minds of its human members – in a way that is not true for any other type of contract. Further, there is often a substantial imbalance of market power between individual employers and employees [. . .] that a civilised society must be willing to address.

There are also sound economic arguments for having a strong industrial relations framework that protects civilised wages and working conditions for employees. In a free market, a firm can seek to undercut the price of its competitors *either* by being more productive *or* by employing workers at lower wage rates. From a macroeconomic perspective, the former is strictly preferred, since productivity improvements are the ultimate source of rising material living standards. In contrast, a weak industrial relations system that encourages wage competition is literally counter-productive, as well as restricting the ability of workers' families to spend.

In this context, consider the data in Figure 5.2 showing average labour productivity for Australia and New Zealand, defined as total real GDP divided by the full-time equivalent employed labour force (that is, full-time employment plus half part-time employment) scaled to equal 100 in the calendar year 1984. The two countries' productivity paths were very similar until 1991 (the year of the Employment Contracts Act), after which New Zealand's average labour productivity growth stagnated while Australia's continued to grow strongly. The graph clearly shows that, contrary to the claims made by its proponents, the ECA was not good for productivity growth in New Zealand.

This does not mean that New Zealand should return to the old system of occupation-based unions with exclusive rights of representation and compulsory membership. International studies consistently show that such a system delivers poorer economic outcomes than systems that are either more centralised (such as the Scandinavian systems with strong peak organisations representing all workers and all employers) or more decentralised (such as in the United States or most Asian countries). This is probably because there is little incentive under New Zealand's old system for each particular union to take into account trends in macroeconomic variables such as unemployment or the terms of trade (that is, the price of exports divided by the price of imports, which reflects New Zealand's international trading conditions).

There appears to be strong electoral support in New Zealand for maintaining a relatively decentralised industrial relations system, which would suggest that policy changes in this area should involve a redesign of the worst features of the ECA rather than its complete replacement by a more centralised system. If this view is correct, there are three aspects that need immediate attention. The first is that the current legislation makes no reference to the unique position of trade unions developed over many decades in the history of the labour movement. Instead, trade unions are treated by implications as just one example of organisations that can offer to act as a worker's bargaining agent. In my view this approach does not work, since trade unions have developed a far wider role in promoting the interests of workers than simply representing individual employees in wage negotiations. Instead, the legislation should explicitly address the powers and responsibilities of trade unions, especially since these must change within a decentralised industrial relations framework compared to under the old Labour Relations Act.

Second, the current legislation has no provision equivalent to the American requirement for employers to bargain in good faith with duly appointed representatives of employees. This severely weakens the position of workers, who must rely on their employers' goodwill to have their views on wages and conditions heard.

Third, although I do not think the electorate would support a return to compulsory union membership at the national level, I do think it is desirable to allow workers at a particular worksite to be allowed to vote by a suitable majority for compulsory union membership at their site (the so-called 'closed shop' provision). The mechanics of such a legislative right need to be carefully thought through (what should be the minimum size of the worksite, for example, and should it be necessary to include all employees or could it cover just one department in a large firm), but such a system reduces free-riding by non-union members on the fixed costs of representation, and also protects current or potential individual workers from being pressured by the employer into undercutting prevailing wages and conditions.

Specialised production

The government itself is an important producer of goods and services in a modern economy, not only through state-owned enterprises, but also in the key areas of law and order, defence, education, health and social services. There has been considerable debate internationally about this role of government, but New Zealand is recognised as adopting a more radical attitude in its reforms than any other OECD country.[3] Many of the government's former trading departments have been privatised and policymakers have sought to separate the funding of services from their supply, especially in housing, for example. Against this background, it is important to emphasise that economic theory supports the idea that there are some goods and services which should be financed and perhaps produced in the public sector. [. . .] It is utterly mistaken to think that there is no place for the specialist role of public sector production in a modern market economy.

More controversial, and worthy of much wider discussion than has taken place in recent years, is what role should the government play in ensuring workers have access to productive employment opportunities.

[. . .]

In current debates about welfare dependency, it is not always appreciated that as recently as March 1985 that were only 140,000 people receiving income-tested social welfare payments in New Zealand. The jump from that level to more than 340,000 people took place between 1985 and 1992 – the period in which the economic reforms were producing large-scale job losses in agriculture, manufacturing and construction. Between 1992 and 1996, the economy recovered to generate 250,000 jobs in four years, but this did not lead to a fall in the number of people on social welfare benefits (which was still 340,000 in June 1996, rising by a further 30,000 during the recession of 1997/8). Figure 5.2 shows that there was also negligible labour productivity growth over the post-1991 period (certainly compared to Australia), so that the new jobs must have been relatively low productivity and low-wage work. The question therefore is whether this laissez-faire outcome should be a matter of concern to the government or whether the current philosophy of leaving job creation to the marketplace is its best option.

In my view, this is a matter where the government ought to intervene, not only because of the poverty implications for individuals trapped in unemployment or low-wage jobs, but also because of the central theme of this chapter – that in an economic system of exchange, it is in everyone's best interest for as many people as possible to be engaged in work that has high rather than low productivity. For this same reason, creating low-skill jobs in the public sector (the railways, for example) or in the private sector behind high tariff barriers (car assembly, for example), which were part of the solution adopted by earlier generations, are not desirable either.

Instead, the question of productive employment opportunities is arguably the most important example of government policy where a 'third way' must be found between the heavy-handed intervention of the first way and the hands-off approach of the second way. I believe the key element to this third way is to be found in *domestic capital production*. Of course there is nothing original in suggesting that in a capitalist economy wealth creation depends critically on producing capital, but this option receives surprisingly little discussion in domestic policy debates about export-led growth, encouraging overseas investment, increasing national saving rates, promoting sunrise industries, and so on. Yet it is *producing* physical, human and social capital that ultimately allows economies to capture the benefits of rising labour productivity.

In advocating a greater involvement of the government in capital production, there are important lessons to learn from the policy disaster of the Think Big energy projects of the early 1980s. Almost everyone accepts that the Think Big programme was far too ambitious in scope and scale, with too little regard to the risks being borne by the taxpayer. Hence, work in this area should begin by taking the time needed to design a robust policy process within the public service to be competent in searching for, evaluating, financing and managing public investment. This could easily take two years of a new government's first term, and perhaps another six months to get up and running, but getting the foundations laid properly is essential for such a policy development to endure.

On the other hand, the failings of Think Big should not blind us to the successful way in which the state contributed to capital formation in New Zealand over many decades. Nor must it be supposed that the only way for the public sector to intervene is by building or manufacturing the capital itself. Often there are opportunities for facilitating private sector investment through judicious government-sponsored coordination, information-gathering, networking and infrastructure development. Such activities are accepted for assisting in the development of international trade opportunities and for encouraging foreign investment; it is a small but important step to extend them to existing and potential domestic producers of productivity-enhancing capital.

Income distribution

Before discussing how a centre-left government might approach the issue of income distribution, it is important to acknowledge that economic models of the labour market tend to show that any government intervention in the distribution of income reduces economic efficiency. In particular, simple supply and demand market diagrams can be used to show that the introduction of a binding minimum wage or the levying of income taxes to fund income support for unemployed workers reduces employment and creates a deadweight social loss compared to a free-market equilibrium. This model was very influential in the decisions to cut social welfare income entitlements in 1991, to exclude beneficiaries from the tax cuts of 1996 and 1998, and to postpone a planned increase in the adult minimum wage in March 1998.

The difficulty with this model is that it is entirely static. That is, the model asks what would be the impact on employment and output of a minimum wage or an income tax *given* pre-existing levels of aggregate demand, capital accumulation and labour productivity. They do not ask the dynamic question of what happens to the future growth of aggregate demand, capital accumulation and labour productivity if competitive forces are allowed to operate unmoderated. Yet it is these three factors, particularly the last, that improve a society's material living standards over time.

The main function of a minimum wage is to define the minimum standard for labour productivity that is acceptable in the domestic economy (since a firm will not employ a worker whose marginal productivity is less than the wage that must be paid). It provides a signal, not only to potential employers, but also to workers about the minimum level of skills needed to find a job. It also sets the floor below which wage competition by firms is not permitted, at which point only productivity competition (for example, through capital investment) is available for increasing market share. In short, the intention of the minimum wage is to prevent some low productivity jobs from being offered and accepted at some point in time (the static model), in order to encourage workers to increase their skill levels and firms to increase the productivity of their worksite over time (the dynamic model).

Thus there is a trade-off involved. A higher minimum wage will lengthen the time a worker can expect to be unemployed while searching for a job, but will raise the average skill level of the labour force and the average productivity of those who are employed. If the minimum wage is set too high, the pool of unemployed workers searching for employment becomes too large to be sustainable, but if it is set too low the economy can get trapped in a low wage, low-productivity growth path such as that shown since 1991 in Figure 5.2.

A fundamental difficulty in a market system of income allocation is that the free market does not make any allowance for the expenditure needs of children. An individual employer is interested only in the productivity of each employee and cannot make any allowance for whether that individual's income is supporting zero, one, two or more children. Market forces produce an outcome where families tend to experience relative poverty compared to households with no children, unless the tax system is used to transfer resources from the latter to the former. New Zealand is very reluctant to make such transfers compared to other OECD countries.[4] In recent years, for example, the universal family benefit has been abolished, income support for families receiving social security payments has been reduced, and the extra financial assistance made available through government programmes (such as the independent family tax credit) has been small and tightly targeted by income.

The 1996 and 1998 tax reductions are a good case study. The rhetoric of these cuts was that they would be targeted to low- and middle-income working families, but in fact, for every dollar of the programme, 40 cents went to non-family households and 31 cents went to families in the top two quintiles of New Zealand's income distribution – only 29 cents in the dollar went to the target group of low- to middle-income families. Thus, even within its own narrowly constructed terms, the programme of tax cuts failed to deliver extra spending power where it is most needed.

This is an issue that a future centre-left government could address very easily. In my view, the principle of providing tax cuts to families is correct, but I do not think there is then any need to target such transfers by household income. Universal family transfers are justifiable because the whole economy benefits if households have access to extra financial resources while children are young. In the short term, such transfers give families greater spending power at a time when earning power is generally low (both because wages and salaries rise with experience and because on average parents are available for fewer employment hours). In the medium term, extra resources spent on young people can forestall the necessity for extra spending on health and law and order when the children become teenagers and young adults. In the long term, investment in the education and health of the rising generation is one of the most important forms of investment society can make in future productivity growth, which is particularly important in the context of demographic trends that will see the ratio of retired to working age people rise sharply in New Zealand over the next two or three decades.

Monetary exchange

If property rights have been justly defined, if workers have access to full and productive employment and if income distribution is rebalanced in favour of family households, then there is very little for the government to do in the monetary exchanges that then take place other than maintaining oversight to ensure markets remain competitive. The great strength of markets is the scope they create for consumer choice and producer efficiency – hence the preference for third way politics to be concerned with the other three components of the economic social system in order to give this relatively free rein.

[. . .]

The central theme of this discussion has been that governments should adopt policies to enhance capital goods production. One of the important factors allowing capital accumulation is the ability of the banking system to extend credit so that firms can finance the construction or manufacture of capital goods in advance of their coming into profitable production. The difficulty is that exactly the same credit-creating ability exists for people who wish to borrow finance not to fund new capital formation, but to purchase already existing real estate or overseas currencies or stockmarket shares in the hope that the price of the chosen asset will rise. If credit for speculative purposes happens on a sufficiently large scale, this itself can be enough to create the expected inflation, at least until the financial bubble bursts (as happened in New Zealand's sharemarket boom and crash in 1985–1986, and in several South-East Asian financial markets in 1996–1997). As a general principle, therefore, policies should aim to restrict the availability of credit for such speculative purposes.

In the past, policymakers approached this problem by regulating financial markets, including promoting the supply of credit towards particular activities (investment in agriculture, for example, or the purchase of a first home). The electronic globalisation of financial markets has made such regulations ineffective. In New Zealand, for example, the foreign exchange market used to be the most tightly regulated in this country. All transactions had to go through the Reserve Bank, which was well placed to enforce all statutory requirements. Nevertheless, when the private sector recognised that the price of overseas currency would almost certainly rise after the 1984 general election, the Bank was powerless to stop speculative forces from draining all its overseas reserves despite entering into substantial forward commitments that eventually cost New Zealand taxpayers billions of dollars in today's prices. Any attempt to curb speculation through regulation is, in my opinion, doomed to failure.

Instead, the most powerful weapon we have against speculation is the existence of a central bank that is committed to increasing interest rates whenever there is any prospect of inflation. This is effective because it immediately increases the cost of credit, and so deters speculators from borrowing in the first place. Thus it is absolutely essential that any proposal for monetary reform must keep intact the institution of an autonomous central bank legally committed to maintaining general price stability. Any weakness of political resolve in this area will only encourage credit-financed speculation, which would require stronger action by the Reserve Bank to offset. The situation where financial market decision-makers think the government *might* allow more inflation but the Reserve Bank maintains its price stability target produces the worst possible outcome for economic activity and employment, and must be scrupulously avoided.

The reason that current monetary policy is an issue (after all, nobody wants inflation for its own sake) is that when the Reserve Bank is obliged to raise interest rates, it has an equally deterrent effect on borrowing credit for productive purposes, and in a small open economy with free international capital flows like New Zealand, it tends to have an amplified impact on the exchange rate to the disadvantage of domestic producers in the tradeable sector. Over the two years between March 1995 and March 1997, for example, New Zealand's trade-weighted exchange rate index rose by 14.5 per cent, and then fell by 17.8 per cent over the next 18 months to September 1998. Such variability in one of the most important prices in a small open economy rightly attracts criticism. It imposes real costs on domestic producers, and was not very efficient in obtaining its objective since the inflationary pressures in New Zealand in 1995 and 1996 arose from the non-tradeable sector (which is relatively immune to short-term movements in the exchange rate).

This last point is the crucial one. The problem with monetary policy in New Zealand is not its objective of 'stability in the general level of prices', but that the instruments available to achieve that objective appear to be inefficient. If so, then progress will come by finding policies that are more effective in targeting speculation in all its various guises without harming real production. The most promising suggestions made by economists so far involve the introduction of special taxes that would make speculation less profitable, either by taxing capital gains or by taxing financial transactions at a rate small enough not to affect long-term lending and borrowing, but large enough to deter frequent short-term buying and selling of financial assets. It would be hard to introduce the latter type of tax in just one country, since this would just drive financial transactions offshore to another country, but there are ongoing discussions about whether the global financial system would be made more efficient if all countries agreed to adopt some sort of policy along these lines.

Conclusion

The end of the twentieth century has seen some remarkable changes in the political economy of countries around the world, such as the collapse of the centrally planned economies of the former Soviet Union, the reunification of West and East Germany; the ending of the apartheid regime in South Africa, the establishment of the North American free-trade agreement, and the creation of a single currency in Europe. Events such as these have given a further impetus to the perennial debate about the proper role of government in a modern market economy. In New Zealand, the immediate context for this debate is the demonstrable failure of the economic reform programme after 1984 to deliver the anticipated improvements in relative economic growth, poverty reduction and high-productivity employment. There is no going back to the old economic management framework, so this analysis has argued the need to find a third way for New Zealand, based on careful government involvement in (i) setting property rights, particularly in labour law (ii) maintaining high-productivity employment opportunities, particularly in capital production (iii) income redistribution, particularly in order to transfer resources to family households and (iv) monetary exchange, particularly by searching for more efficient policies that maintain price stability at least cost to real production.

Notes

1 A good introduction to what the third way means in the United Kingdom is provided by Anthony Giddens' book, *The Third Way: The Renewal of Social Democracy* (Cambridge: Polity Press, 1999). In the United States, Robert Reich's *The Work of Nations* (New York: Vintage Books, 1992) does not use the phrase but is an authoritative presentation of third way assumptions and policies.
2 The paper is co-authored with Nripesh Podder of the University of New South Wales. Its title is 'Sharing the National Cake in Post Reform New Zealand: Income Inequality Trends in terms of Income Sources', and it is available at the WWW address http://econ.massey.ac.nz/inequality.pdf.
3 David Henderson, for example, has written that 'in no other OECD country has there been so systematic an attempt at the same time (1) to redefine and limit the role of government and (2) to make public agencies and their operations more effective, more transparent, and more accountable' (*Economic Reform: New Zealand in an International Perspective*, Wellington: NZBR, 1996: 13).
4 See, for example, Bob Stephens's 'Poverty, Family Finances and Social Security', Chapter 13, in *Redesigning the Welfare State In New Zealand*, edited by J. Boston, P. Dalziel and S. St John (Auckland: Oxford University Press, 1999: 238–59).

6

Five Realities that will Shape 21st Century US Politics

William A. Galston and Elaine C. Kamarck

[. . .]

At the threshold of the 21st century, American politics is unsettled. The New Deal era has ended. But the next political alignment has yet to take hold. High on the list of reasons for this fluidity is that the US is changing – more profoundly and rapidly than most politicians and political institutions have thus far been able to adapt. In the next half-century, America will be reshaped by the growth of the Information Age economy, by the passing of the New Deal generation, by the shifting geography of where we live, by the altered structures of our families, and by the radically increasing diversity of our society. We call these changes the new realities. They are the plate tectonics of our national life, slowly but inexorably transforming the way we earn our living, structure our social bonds, and understand our politics.

[. . .]

Reality number one: the new economy favors a rising learning class over a declining working class

Of the many forces now shifting the ground beneath our feet, probably the most momentous is the advent of a new economy. [. . .]

Today, the industrial era is giving way to an information age characterized by extraordinarily rapid technological change and the globalization of economic activity. New technologies are reducing the cost of information storage and transmission, altering modes of production, forcing shifts in corporate structures, and increasing demand for literacy, numeracy, and problem-solving skills throughout the workforce. Spurred in part by these technological changes, the new global economy is characterized by near-instantaneous flows of information, capital, and productive facilities across national boundaries and by intensifying competition in previously sheltered sectors of national economies.

Understanding the political implications of the new economy is no easy matter. But we are already seeing shifts in the electorate. The old politics was dominated by the class structure of the industrial economy. The concentrations of capital and labor required to compete in the industrial economy generated centralized structures in many aspects of economic, social, and political life. By mid-century, that economy had produced a broad middle class of modest (though rising) levels of income and education that took its cues from large mediating institutions such as big labor, big business, dominant political parties, and a handful of national media outlets.

Today, all that is changing. We can discern the rise of a new learning class of workers who will dominate at least the first half of the 21st century. They will be better educated, more affluent, more mobile, and more self-reliant. They are less likely to be influenced by (let alone submit to) large mediating institutions. Their political outlook and behavior will increasingly defy the class-based divisions of the old economy, and they will be increasingly skeptical of centralized, one-size-fits-all solutions. Rather, they will want a government that helps enable them to succeed, enhances the information to make their own choices, and invests in the most dynamic source of progress and security in the new economy – their own intellectual capital.

The emergence of this new class is evident in several key developments that are already having a major impact.

The hollowing out of the middle class (mostly for the better)

Among these key changes is one of the most widely discussed (and politically charged) aspects of the new economy: the shrinkage of the middle class and widening gap between the wealthy and the poor. Some see these developments as grounds for returning to a [. . .] politics of class warfare; they seek to mobilize lower-income groups for a

new round of interventionist, centralized government that protects
Americans against all forms of economic insecurity.

The tacit assumption behind this line of argument is that the income
gap is growing because of increased downward mobility – that is,
because a substantial portion of the population is being forced out of
the middle class into working poverty. No doubt this is the case for
many lower-skilled workers who have been displaced from secure,
high-paying jobs in the manufacturing and defence sectors. [. . .]

But overall, the assumption of rising poverty and near-poverty is
false. [. . .] The heart of the middle class is shrinking – being hollowed
out – not because poverty is on the march, but because millions of
Americans are surging into the ranks of the upper middle class and
wealthy.

In 1968, only 23 per cent of the population earned $50,000 or more
(in 1996 dollars). By 1996, the proportion of the population earning at
that level had jumped to 34 per cent. During that same period, the heart
of the middle class (families earning $25,000 to $50,000 a year) declined
from 39 per cent to only 30 per cent of the population. Even if we define
the "middle class" more broadly, the results are about the same. From
1968 to 1996, the percentage of American families earning in excess of
$75,000 (in 1996 dollars) rose by almost 10 points, from 6.8 to 16.4, while
the percentage earning $25,000 to $75,000 declined by more than seven
points.

[. . .]

The political consequences of these facts are obvious. On the one
hand, it is a mistake to believe that Democrats can construct majorities
based on a swelling pool of poor and near-poor Americans waiting
to be mobilized by an old-fashioned politics of redistribution; no
such increase has occurred. On the other hand, the tens of millions of
Americans who have seen no increase in their wages over the past
decade need, deserve, and are likely to demand policies that increase
access to education, training, and lifelong learning.

[. . .]

The emergence of wired workers

As traditional unionized workers decline, another group is emerging
that provides a preview of how the politics of the next half-century will
diverge from that of the last.

The Institute for a New California has completed two surveys of
California's population, first in 1996 and again in 1998. These polls

have defined a new category of "wired workers" who regularly use computers on the job, work in self-directed teams rather than top-down hierarchies, and engage in on-the-job problem-solving rather than repetitive routines. Using these criteria, the polls divided Californians into three categories: traditional workers, wired workers, and individuals outside the paid workforce.

Under this definition, wired workers represent an increasingly significant portion of the Californian population. In 1996, these workers constituted 31 per cent of the population and nearly half the working population. Just two years later, wired workers were 37 per cent of the population and more than half the workforce. If these trends continue, these workers will come to dominate California's population [within a few years].

[. . .]

Substantively, wired workers represent a subtle and unpredictable mix of conservative and liberal views. On the one hand, they are very critical of existing public schools (and highly supportive of public charter schools), tend to favor privatization of public services such as mass transit, and are less supportive of affirmative action than are traditional workers. On the other hand, they want government to stay out of lifestyle issues, are more supportive of immigration, and believe in active government protection for the environment, including severe penalties for businesses that pollute.

In short, while wired workers don't want to pull the plug on government, they do want to change the way government operates. They are open to the use of market mechanisms and are broadly tolerant in their social outlook. And for reasons that we do not yet fully understand, they do not feel that their views are adequately represented by either major political party. It seems safe to say that as these new-generation workers become demographically dominant (in California and throughout much of the nation) [. . .] their new interests and outlooks will be major forces reshaping American politics.

[. . .]

Reality number two: the New Deal generation gives way to the skeptical generations

Nothing is more inexorable than generational replacement. The political significance of this process lies in the fact that a generation's formative experiences generate a common understanding of society that shapes political attitudes and behavior throughout a generation's life-cycle. And given the dynamics of generational replacement in contemporary America, a new reality is emerging that is already having a profound effect on our politics. The old politics was dominated by a generation of Americans whose formative experience was a powerful, centralized, and effective federal government. The politics of the next 50 years will be dominated by generations whose experiences have made them more skeptical of centralized government solutions (and of large institutions in general) while remaining receptive to a more modest government that bolsters individual opportunities and protects common goods.

The generation that has dominated national politics for much of the past half century – the New Deal generation – is passing from the scene faster than is generally understood. This generation includes individuals born between 1911 and 1926, who came of age during the Depression or Second World War and were able to cast their first ballots in one of the five presidential elections beginning with Franklin D. Roosevelt's initial win in 1932 and ending with Harry Truman's upset victory in 1948. So defined, the New Dealers constituted nearly 39 per cent of the electorate in 1952 and remained a formidable portion of the electorate until the 1980s. But to understand the scope of the changes at work here, one statistic stands out: In 2000, this same New Deal generation will account for only eight per cent of the voting age population and an even smaller share of the electorate.

[. . .]

The politics of the 21st century must be more selective in the use of federal power and must find new cooperative – not coercive – ways to mobilize support at many levels of government as well as among non-governmental civic associations. Leadership at the national level will, of necessity, require a very different understanding and set of skills than in the command-and-control era that served the New Deal generation so well.

Reality number three: power continues to shift from the cities to the suburbs

[. . .]

As big cities displaced small towns as the center of political life at the turn of the 20th century, so today, suburbs are displacing cities. While most Americans have a general sense of this phenomenon, its dimensions are not fully appreciated – even by political experts. Accordingly, we offer a small sample of statistics that illustrate and dramatize this historic shift.

In the 1960 election, the city of Chicago cast 35 per cent of the statewide vote in Illinois, and it dominated ten of the state's congressional districts. Chicago's suburbs contributed only 20 per cent of the statewide vote and controlled only five congressional districts. By 1996, however, it was the city of Chicago that cast only 20 per cent of the statewide vote and commanded only five congressional districts, while its suburbs doubled their share of the statewide vote to 40 per cent and now control nine congressional seats.

This pattern has been repeated in most states with once-dominant cities. These trends are continuing, pointing to a key shift from the old politics to the new: In the old politics, Democrats could build majorities around their control of large urban centers. In the 21st century, the center of gravity of American politics will be in the suburbs, with cities continuing to play an important role, but one that will have to be coordinated with the dominant concerns of suburban voters.

These trends are already evident at the national level. A quarter of a century ago, there were roughly equal numbers of urban, suburban, and rural districts in the U.S. House of Representatives. Today, suburban districts outnumber urban districts by more than 2 to 1, and rural districts by almost 3 to 1.

[. . .]

This emphasis on the growing power of suburbs does not mean that the politics of the 21st century will be solely suburban based. The new economy hardly renders cities an anachronism. If anything, their role as hubs of commerce, innovation, and culture may turn out to be more important than ever. Democrats will have to build solid coalitions between suburbs and central cities in order to form sustainable national majorities. But there will be a key shift: While in the old politics, the cities served as the center of the Democrats' political universe, in the 21st century that role will shift to the suburbs.

In recent decades, cities and suburbs have often been at odds, divided by racial and ethnic differences as well as by competition for scarce federal resources. Today, new forces point to a convergence of values and interests that hold out hope for a more harmonious relationship. Suburbs are becoming more racially and ethnically diverse, but new suburbanites are concerned with the same quality of life issues that first drove mass suburbanization after World War Two. At the same time, a new breed of forward-looking mayors around the nation has won a mandate to turn around urban centers by addressing the same set of challenges. The potential exists for finding cross-cutting issues such as quality education, public safety, sustainable economic development, and environmental preservation that can form the basis for a 21st century progressive coalition between suburbs and cities.

Reality number four: more children from more diverse backgrounds will be concentrated in a shrinking percentage of households

Few changes in our society over the past half century have been more important than those affecting the American family. Now, one of the most fascinating developments related to families has the potential to create a major new set of challenges for American politics. In the old politics, the electorate was dominated by families with minor children. In the 21st century, a far smaller percentage of households will contain young children and yet the number of young children will reach record highs, greatly complicating the task of maintaining an effective coalition on behalf of children and families.

We know that there has been a massive shift away from marriage and childrearing as the dominant way of life. In 1950, 78 per cent of all U.S. households were married couples, compared to only 54 per cent today. In 1950, married couples with minor children comprised 43 per cent of all households, compared to only 24 per cent today. And there has been an equally significant shift away from marriage as the preferred venue for raising children. In 1950, 93 per cent of all families with minor children were married couples; today, that figure is down to 73 per cent.

[. . .]

Another key trend – the relentless aging of the U.S. population – ensures that the percentage of families with minor children will continue to decline through the first half of the 21st century. Today, about 12 per cent of the population is aged 65 or older. But by 2050, according to Social Security estimates that many regard as conservative, Americans 65 and over will surge to an unprecedented 20.8 per cent of the population.

Meanwhile, the number of children younger than 18 has risen sharply during the past decade and just last year topped the previous record set at the end of the baby boom in 1966. This increase is expected to persist throughout the first half of the 21st century, with the number of children expected to exceed 90 million in 2050, versus just 70 million today. And more than 90 per cent of this increase will come as the result of immigration (principally Hispanic and Asian), so that young people as a group will be even more diverse than the population as a whole.

Taken together, these developments pose a paradox: The needs of children will be increasingly central to the welfare of our society in the 21st century, but the percentage of families with minor children will continue to shrink. A sustainable majority coalition on behalf of children must therefore include more and more households without children, and it must rest on the principle of shared responsibility for all children in our society. The direct appeal to parental self-interest will no longer suffice to support child-friendly policies, as it did during the height of the baby boom.

The alternative to such a broad-based coalition may well be a growing split between an upscale electorate and tens of millions of children – many of them poor, minority, or immigrant – on whom our future will depend, as well as heightened tension between programs directed to children and those that provide income and health security for older Americans. Because an effective 21st century progressive coalition cannot survive such strains, Democrats must begin working now to surmount them.

Reality number five: a new diversity brings the challenge of national identity politics

The challenge of sustaining a coalition for children – and more broadly, of building a 21st century progressive politics – will be complicated by America's changing ethnic makeup. These changes present both dangers and opportunities. The danger is that they could intensify fissures among competing ethnic groups. The opportunity is that grappling with them could spur a new politics of national rather than group identity.

In the old politics, black/white divisions were at the heart of central strategies for both parties, whether it was the Republicans' temptation to practice wedge politics or Democrats' attraction to identity politics. In an increasingly multiethnic politics, these strategies are less likely to succeed and might be replaced by unifying appeals to shared national values and to the opportunities of the new economy.

America's immigration policy is bringing on many of these shifts. In the mid-1920s, the United States adopted highly restrictive immigration laws. During the 40 years that these laws remained in effect, the percentage of foreign-born Americans fell steadily, hitting a historic low of under 5 per cent. Starting in 1965, however, immigration legislation changed dramatically – in the aggregate, with many more immigrants being admitted – and in distribution, with the bulk coming from areas (such as Latin America and Asia) that had been underrepresented in previous flows.

The results of this policy shift are already visible. The percentage of foreign-born Americans has doubled from its low in the mid-1960s; nearly 11 per cent of the population is now Hispanic (versus 12 per cent for African-Americans), while more than 3 per cent is Asian. In New York City, Hispanics now constitute the largest minority group, and more than one-third of the population is foreign-born. In 1997, for the first time ever, the number of Hispanic children surpassed the number of African-American children.

[. . .]

As these transformations unfold, the tendency to use race and ethnicity as wedge issues becomes manifestly counterproductive as the white majority dwindles and, in key states, actually becomes a minority. There are hopeful early signs that Republican candidates in California, Texas, and Florida are rethinking political strategies that have alienated African-American and (more recently) Hispanic voters from their party.

The pressure on the Democratic Party is subtler but, we believe, no less significant. In an increasingly multiethnic democracy, different minority groups will have increasingly diverse interests and demands. [. . .] Asian-Americans may not agree with African-Americans about affirmative action; Hispanics and African-Americans may compete for entry-level jobs. And within individual groups, there will be an increasing diversity of interests – for example, between upwardly mobile middle class African-Americans and others who remain in poverty – that will make appeals to individual groups more complicated than in the past. In the face of these difficulties, the identity politics of the post-sixties Democratic Party will prove no more sustainable than the Republicans' wedge strategy.

This new diversity need not lead to new forms of divisiveness, however. Not only are patriotism and the unifying ideals of the American Dream alive and well; practical politicians will be eager to find ways of maximizing vote counts with broad-based appeals. A new politics of national identity can not only answer the call of principle, but also address practical political problems that old-style wedge and identity politics will be powerless to resolve.

[. . .]

Conclusion

The new political realities we have explored will pose new challenges – political and substantive – for leaders and parties who seek the mandate to govern [. . .] in the [21st] century. How to reconcile the economic interests of two divergent worker classes around a growth agenda that accepts the imperatives of global competition while providing a robust system of economic opportunity and security for all workers? How to honor the values and interests of suburban voters without sacrificing cities to futures of failing schools, crumbling infrastructure, and chronic lack of jobs? How to design coalitions that support investments for children based on a shared commitment to a common future, not direct personal self-interest? And how to build a politics of inclusion and mutual respect that honors every group while advancing the goal of One America around core principles of individual liberty, equal opportunity, and mutual responsibility?

In short, amidst diversity and disagreement, how can we forge a politics of national purpose so that our differences become mutually reinforcing strengths? These are not easy questions. But no leader, no party that seeks to govern our nation in the next century can avoid them.

[. . .]

PART II

The Welfare State, Social Policy and Inequality

All centre-left politicians agree upon the need to reform the welfare state and most governments have initiated policies to this end. While welfare states vary substantially between the different EU countries a similar policy mix, Maurizio Ferrera and his colleagues argue, should apply to all of them – sound macroeconomic steering, wage moderation, employment-friendly tax policy, labour market 'flexicurity', and new ways of coping with social exclusion and poverty. They provide a sketch of what I called earlier a new European social model, a model which might permit a strongly positive adaptation to the new conditions of globalization and the knowledge economy.

Esping-Andersen focuses his discussion on the different types of European welfare system and the possibilities they offer for the future. He emphasizes that challenges on the level of family are just as problematic for welfare systems as those involving the economy. Social protection can't be confined to the welfare state – there is an interplay between state, family and market. A dynamic approach is needed from policy-makers. The same applies to tackling inequality. We have to take a life-chances perspective – what counts is not how many people are poor at any one time but what their chances of mobility are.

The focus of James Midgley's article is upon connecting social and economic policy. The traditional idea of the left is that the resources generated by economic growth should be redistributed to fund social programmes. We need an alternative perspective, which emphasizes that social investments can enhance economic participation and make a positive contribution to development.

Like Esping-Andersen, Ronald Dworkin accepts the inevitability of a shift towards equality of opportunity on the part of the left, but argues that equality of outcome remains vital. A society must find the means of creating decent life conditions for even its most deprived citizens. Two principles, he suggests, should guide our thinking. One is the principle of 'equal importance' – everyone should have the chance to achieve success rather than suffering a wasted life. The other is the principle of 'special responsibility' – individuals themselves should have the opportunity to make choices which determine the paths of their lives. Third way thinking should integrate equality and responsibility.

In my contribution, I argue that social democrats must place more emphasis upon equality of opportunity than in the past. However, equality of opportunity is not feasible without substantial economic redistribution. The formula 'take from the rich to give to the poor' remains central, but its application is more complex and difficult than may appear at first sight.

Vito Tanzi tackles the question of the relation between globalization and taxation systems, particularly as regards public spending. Globalization is creating problems for countries seeking to sustain existing levels of tax revenue. Both individuals and corporations conduct an increasing amount of business outside their home countries, allowing them to evade or under-report taxes. The internet and other forms of electronic transaction are growing enormously; they will be difficult to tax since they so readily operate across borders. Tax havens also add to the difficulties. Nation-states aren't going to be able to cope with these issues acting alone, Tanzi proposes. Governments should consider creating a World Tax Organization which would help co-ordinate tax collection and deal with the many forms of tax avoidance.

Leisering and Leibfried return to the theme of the dynamic nature of inequality. Most students of poverty and inequality have analysed them in a snapshot fashion. But there is a great deal of movement in and out of poverty. Like Esping-Andersen, they argue that social justice must concern the life-course of individuals and not just be understood in a static way. Social policies should draw on people's own capacities for self-help. Rather than just transferring income, social security agencies should help people to help themselves.

David Downes discusses some of the issues involved in new approaches to crime. Crime rates have increased in some European countries with well-developed welfare systems, such as The Netherlands or Germany. The traditional idea that crime rates are low in societies with relatively high rates of economic equality has to be questioned. While rates of crime in some European countries have risen, those in the US have fallen. Does this mean that the European countries should move towards US-style policing and levels of imprisonment? The author concludes that while European countries can learn from the US experience, it is vital to take a different path from the American one.

The family is of key importance in current political debates. Helen Wilkinson proposes a third way in family policy. The right sees changes in family life as reflecting the decay of the traditional family. Re-establishing traditional family forms, rightists say, is the only means of restoring strong family ties. The left, by contrast, has often been unconcerned about changes affecting the family, seeing a plurality of living arrangements as good and desirable. We need to break with each of these views. Some changes in the family are deeply worrying and must be a focus of government response; but returning to the traditional family is not an option.

Anne-Marie Guillemard concentrates on ageing. The proportion of people's lives, particularly men's lives, spent working has decreased considerably in recent years. At the same time, the population as a whole in the industrial countries is getting older – there are far more people over sixty-five than there were a generation ago. In responding to these demographic changes, some of the EU countries have reduced the age of retirement. They have seen such a reduction as protecting older people, and also as a means of dealing with unemployment. But this strategy causes far more problems than it resolves. If the age of retirement is reduced to sixty, firms start to treat workers as more or less redundant to their needs while they are still in their fifties. Even more important, a diminishing labour force is supposed somehow to support large populations of younger and older people who are outside the labour market. The best approach is actually to move the age of retirement up, or abolish it altogether, in order to get more older people into the labour force.

7

The Future of Social Europe: Recasting Work and Welfare in the New Economy

Maurizio Ferrera, Anton Hemerijck and Martin Rhodes

[. . .]

Different welfare states [in Europe] not only confront different problems but they face rather different questions of policy adjustment, given their existing policy mixes and institutional settings. Our argument is not that there is "one best way". It is rather that the requirements for successful policy adjustment can be met by different strategies, as long as these achieve an optimal mix of policy responses, addressing both the general problems of competitiveness and post-industrial change as well as regime-specific endogenous challenges. Below we identify the core requirements for successful adjustment in social and economic regulation and highlight the successful strategies of reform and adjustment by which these requirements have been met in various countries.

As welfare states have become increasingly constrained on the fiscal side they have to increase the efficiency of their welfare programmes, if they are not willing to renege on the core commitments of the post-war welfare state. This effectively means that advanced welfare states have to become more employment-friendly. Below we will catalogue the general requirements of a competitive, employment-friendly and equitable welfare state. The central requirements in terms of the desirable *policy mix* may be summarized as:

- a robust macroeconomic policy;
- wage moderation and flexibility (achieved where possible within broader "social pacts");
- employment-friendly and efficient tax social policy;
- labour market "flexicurity";
- and new methods of tackling poverty and social exclusion.

As far as the *institutional* approach is concerned, those countries seeking to innovate across this range of policies, as well as finding more optimal ways of combining them, must also improve their methods of institutional co-ordination. Thus, for many countries, working their way towards an employment-friendly, welfare-sustaining policy mix has also required building a new system of concertation. In the latter part of this discussion we illustrate how numerous countries have innovated across related policy domains via "social pacts".

Elements of an optimal policy mix

A robust macroeconomic policy

Macroeconomic policy under conditions of liberalized capital markets faces a trade-off among three broad policy aims: Capital mobility, monetary autonomy, and a fixed exchange rate cannot be achieved at the same time. Where financial capital is mobile, national autonomy in interest rate policy can only be reached at the price of an unstable currency, while a fixed exchange rate does not allow national control over interest rates.

Generally, price stability and budgetary discipline have become key elements of any sustainable macroeconomic policy. Persistently high public deficits and inflation rates are undesirable in themselves and incompatible with globalized financial markets. Although the international price competitiveness of a national economy may be restored by strategic devaluations (as Sweden still did in the early 1980s), this strategy nowadays runs the risk of massive capital flight and in any case is ruled out for EMU member states. Moreover, high public deficits increase the debt burden of the state. As a result, the room for fiscal manoeuvre may become seriously constrained as interest payments on public debt rise. Italy and Belgium, which had to pay about 10% of their GDP to service their public debts in the early 1990s, are cases in point. Furthermore, if fiscal imbalances drive up interest rates, this may crowd out investment in the business sector.

Conversely, a strict fiscal policy helps to bring down interest rates, which (over time) may stimulate the economy, reduce the public debt burden, and strengthen the confidence of consumers and potential investors in the economy. Finally, if the structural budget deficit is low on average, there will be some leeway with which to activate the stabilizing function of fiscal policy in periods of low economic growth. The Danish tax reform of 1994 is a case in point, insofar as Denmark's comparatively low structural budget deficit allowed the tax reform to be temporarily under-financed and a low-growth economy to be stimulated. By and large, the perceived role of macroeconomic policy has drastically changed, from nearly omnipotent instrument of full-employment policy to a necessary (but not sufficient) background condition for limited damage control. Employment creation, however, must be pursued by other policy instruments.

As empirical evidence suggests, countries that have been most successful in reconciling the goals of employment and social security, like Denmark and the Netherlands, have pursued a policy of budgetary discipline in recent years. The policy actors in these countries (including the trade unions) also accepted that monetary policy has to be geared primarily towards price stability rather than to full employment. As Denmark (which is not a member of the EMU) also followed a course of macroeconomic stability, there is reason to believe that this recognition basically gained acceptance irrespective of the Maastricht criteria.

Wage moderation and flexibility

The general shift from full employment towards price stability as a primary policy goal in the 1980s meant that macroeconomic policy could no longer serve as a buffer shielding other areas of social and economic regulation from the burden of external adjustment. In the more restrictive international economic environment since the early 1980s, wage restraint remained an important requirement for successful adjustment by facilitating competitiveness, profitability, and as a second-order effect employment. As it lowers wage costs, wage restraint helps to boost competitiveness in the exposed sector.

However, the beggar-my-neighbour argument, which suggests that modest wage increases – given a fixed exchange rate – lower unemployment merely at the expense of trading partner countries, is misguided. A number of economists have argued that sustained wage moderation is harmful to economic progress, because it puts downward pressure on demand, slows down labour market allocation, and, finally, undermines productivity increases through innovation. As the Dutch experience suggests, the employment effects of wage restraint are even stronger in domestic services that were previously priced out of the regular labour market. Thus, there is reason to believe that wage restraint would also be beneficial in a closed economy.

Moreover, if wage restraint leads to higher employment and a concomitant growth in domestic demand, the overall effects of wage restraint on the current account are unclear. Over the last decade, productivity levels in the Netherlands have indeed come down slightly, but this should be explained by the increase in jobs for the low skilled. Finally, in the Netherlands new jobs have mainly been created in the service sector via part-time employment. The rapid expansion of new jobs has led to a concomitant growth in domestic demand.

To the extent that wage developments in the private and public sector are coupled, modest wage increases also lower the public sector wage bill. As a second-order effect, rising employment may contribute to lowering the costs of social security and broaden the revenue basis of the welfare state. Moreover, there is some empirical evidence that wage restraint allows for a smoother interplay among incomes, monetary, and fiscal policies, thus stimulating economic growth while keeping inflation low.

For much of the 1980s there was a strong tendency towards the decentralization of collective wage bargaining, suggesting that national incomes policies would give way to less disciplined combinations of sectoral and company bargaining. More recently, however, we observe a remarkable resurgence of corporatist forms of social pacts and policy co-ordination in a number of countries, notably Ireland, the Netherlands, Denmark, Italy, Finland, Spain, and Portugal – all of which, to one degree or another – have involved income co-ordination. The shift to a hard currency regime in Denmark and the Netherlands during the early 1980s brought the social partners closer together, while the completion of the single market and the EMU entrance exam provided the key impetus for recent social pacts in Ireland, Italy, Portugal, and Spain based on general wage guidelines. It seems that the effects of economic internationalization helped to rekindle the urge to find co-operative, positive-sum solutions to the predicament of adjustment. We return to the importance of such solutions for wider welfare policy reform below.

Employment-friendly and efficient taxation and social protection

Since, as we argue, redistribution through egalitarian wage policy leads to non-market-conforming wages and thus can have negative consequences for employment, the goal of redistribution nowadays is best pursued by social and tax policies. Capacities for expanding welfare spending, however, are severely restricted – by international tax competition, taxpayer resistance and constraints on deficit spending. Although certain countries will be able to enjoy budgetary surpluses, there is now – and will continue to be – greater emphasis on redistributing available public revenues in a more targeted manner while reducing organizational slack. Moreover, making welfare states employment-friendly also means modifying the ways in which taxation and social protection impact on job creation – especially in private sector services. We can differentiate between optimal and sub-optimal policies in this regard by first examining benefits and spending and second modes of finance.

Social spending levels *per se* are no predictor of employment performance. In contrast to the United Kingdom, countries like Denmark and the Netherlands have done well in employment terms without a radical dismantling of the welfare state. It is the structure of financing and spending, rather than the expenditure level that affects the welfare state's impact on economic and employment performance. The Danish mix of intensive spending on social services and active labour market policies is arguably more productive in terms of employment than mere income maintenance programmes concentrating on the aged (such as one finds, above all, in Italy).

By contrast, the continental strategy of labour supply reduction, mainly through early retirement and disability pensions, comes at a high price. They are ineffective in creating new job opportunities for the young (France and Italy have relied heavily on early exit from the labour market, but have very high levels of youth unemployment) and tend to aggravate the financial burden imposed on the active part of the population and further boost labour costs. Strategies that *expand* labour force participation also help to broaden the revenue basis of the welfare state, this is also likely to reduce the financial pressure to cut benefits. Denmark has traditionally high levels of workforce participation and did not, by and large, fall into the continental pattern of workforce shedding. The Netherlands had recently been able to reverse this vicious cycle and increase labour force participation mainly by restricting access to (and curtailing heavy misuse of) their disability schemes. Temporary reductions in labour supply might be necessary during economic crises. However, as empirical evidence suggests, such solutions have a tendency to become permanent. In a period of low economic growth, Denmark's schemes for sabbatical, educational, and parental leave are more appropriate measures for temporary labour supply reduction than is the continental strategy of permanent labour shedding. As in certain other areas, policies aimed to expand the active share of the working age population are likely to be more successful if they are supported by the social partners.

Second, the *financing structure* of the welfare state is equally important in terms of its effects on employment. The financing structure of the welfare state has an immediate impact on employment levels at the lower end of the earnings scale. Social security systems that are financed out of payroll taxes tend to increase labour costs for low-paid employment above the corresponding productivity levels if wages are downwardly sticky. Since Denmark, but also Ireland, mainly finances its welfare state out of general tax revenues, the tax wedge at the lower end of the labour market is relatively low in these countries. The Netherlands, whose welfare state is primarily financed out of payroll taxes, have reduced the tax wedge for low-paid workers by integrating general social insurance contributions into the tax system. This means that the general basic income tax exemption is extended to some branches of the social insurance system. Moreover, a special cut in employer contributions for low-paid workers has been implemented.

The design of systems of social security and taxation also matters in terms of cost efficiency: The welfare state has different redistributive functions, such as reducing poverty, limiting income inequality and providing a certain level of income protection against social risks. While the fulfilment of these goals is severely limited by fiscal constraints, there is a range of policies which effectively moderate this dilemma. Here, again, an analytical distinction between the revenue and the benefit side of the welfare system is helpful. On the revenue side, there are a number of instruments to finance social security which does not increase the overall tax burden on the various factors of production (which tends to hamper employment growth). An option widely used in the Anglo-Saxon welfare states, is the strong reliance on user charges and co-payments for the financing of public social services (health, elderly and child care, as well as education). This does not necessarily impinge on social equity, as economically vulnerable groups might be (partly) exempted from the payment of these fees.

Another financing option, particularly with regard to pensions, which has little detrimental effects on employment, are private mandatory contributions. Ireland, Denmark, and the Netherlands all have made occupational pensions mandatory in recent years (either by the state or via collective agreements). Those countries have thus adopted a combination of a pay-as-you-go-financed basic pension and fully funded and income-related pension on an occupational basis. This mix is superior in two respects: First, this combination allows for a higher degree of risk diversification. Due to their high degree of pre-funding, such pension systems are likely to be comparatively robust against demographic changes. Moreover, the advantage of private and occupational pensions vis-à-vis public pensions lies in the fact that contributions are perceived as part of private consumption rather than as part of the tax wedge and thus are likely to generate fewer work disincentives than contributions to public social insurance schemes. By the same token, pension systems which display an institutional separation between a pay-as-you-go financed basic pension and a fully funded private mandatory insurance, also allow for a more targeted assignment of the various redistributive and insurance functions of the welfare state and are thus less likely to generate distributive conflicts than is the case for pension systems which combine these functions within one tier.

"Flexicurity": secured flexible employment

Growing international competition, technological progress, and changed family patterns have tremendously altered the conditions under which national employment systems operate. Generally, these developments require more flexibility in labour markets with respect to working patterns, wages, and working time. While there is a broad range of possible strategies for increasing labour market flexibility, they are often regarded as counterproductive in terms of equity and social security. Flexibility is often associated with the deregulation of employment protection and social security. The basic challenge for effective employment policy thus lies in reconciling labour market flexibility with measures to counter growing social exclusion and the emergence of a class of working poor. There is no inherent contradiction between these objectives. To the contrary, the general acceptance of flexible arrangements in the labour market is likely to be increased if flexibility is matched by a decent standard of social protection.

Denmark and the Netherlands in particular are telling examples of how both excluding large parts of the workforce from the labour market (a pressing problem in many continental and especially southern welfare states) and marginalizing vulnerable groups within the labour market (typical for Anglo-Saxon welfare states) can be avoided. The successful policy mixes adopted in Denmark and the Netherlands, but also to some extent in Spain, can be subsumed under the label of "flexicurity" a concept developed in the Netherlands.

The Dutch are the pioneers of "flexicurity". In addition to wage moderation, successful policy concertation in the Netherlands has also produced agreements on social security contributions, work sharing and industrial policy, training, job enrichment, low wage levels for low-skilled workers, the development of "entry-level" wages and, most recently, the 1995 "flexicurity" accord in which rights for temporary workers have been strengthened in return for a loosening of dismissal protection for core workers. Low-income workers have been compensated for low wages by targeted tax breaks. Trade unions rescinded their opposition to the creation of part-time and temporary jobs and became the champions of such workers, bridging the gap that usually divides the "insider" from the "outsider" workforce. Hourly wages for such workers have subsequently been bargained to the levels enjoyed by full-time workers: thus, employers can recruit such workers to bolster flexibility, but not as a means of following a low-price production strategy. The 1995–1996 "flexicurity" accords pension and social security benefits to all part-time and temporary employees.

The "flexicurity" debate is inherently related to the feminization of the labour market and the changing status of part-time work in Europe. A new model of employment relations is in the making whereby both men and women share working time, which enable them to keep enough time for catering after their families. If part-time work is recognised as a normal job, supported by access to basic social security and allows for normal career development and basic economic independence, part-time jobs can generate gender equality and active security of working families. In the Netherlands, where part-time work is most widespread, contrary to other countries, it corresponds to female preferences. By and large, Dutch part-time jobs are stable and well paid with access to basic social security.

The generalisation of "flexicurity" as a formula for secured but flexible employment throughout the EU would be linked to a number of different, though mutually reinforcing, policy strategies. There are six dimensions:

- increasing the demand for low-skilled work;
- expanding part-time work and making working hours more flexible;
- labour market desegmentation;
- increasing use of activation policy and tightening eligibility for unemployment benefits;
- reconciling work and family life; and
- the introduction of social drawing rights.

Increasing the demand for low-skilled work   Mainly as a result of technological change, all advanced welfare states have to cope with the problem of declining demand for low-skill work in the industrial sectors. But they differ in the degree to which they have been able to compensate for this development by promoting demand for low-skill jobs in the service sector. Generally, the demand for low-skill work is related to the level of female labour force participation. Higher employment of women typically raises the demand for regular jobs in the areas of care for children and other dependants as well as for consumer-oriented services in general. Thus, demand and supply in service employment are mutually reinforcing. By the same token, it should not come as a surprise that the rapid increase of employment in these service-areas we observe in the Netherlands since the mid-1980s, occurred simultaneously with the quick expansion of female labour force participation.

Increasing demand for low-skilled workers has typically been achieved by forms of wage subsidy, either using tax credits (following the logic of a negative income tax as in Ireland and – to the greatest extent in the UK's "New Contract for Welfare") or, as in the Netherlands, France, and Belgium, by exempting low-skilled workers from social contributions. In the Netherlands, employment subsidy schemes have significantly reduced employers' wage costs, through reductions in taxes and social security contributions, instigating a decline in the tax wedge for employers who hire long-term unemployed. Employment subsidies can add up to as much as 25% of the annual wage.

In Belgium, France and Germany subsidies have also used to promote jobs for the long-term unemployed. The work includes tasks that would otherwise not be done, such as caring for the elderly, gardening, childcare, volunteer work, and the like. In France, social security and tax advantages have also encouraged the development of personal services, whereas in Germany subsidies for recruiting inactive workers is also targeted at the non-business sector. In Spain, subsidies are given to those companies that take on its first employee or makes temporary workers into permanent employees. As a result of the increasing use of employment subsidies of the two kinds outlined above, the number of subsidized jobs has grown dramatically in the European Union. These strategies are, however, of minor importance in mainly tax-financed welfare states such as Denmark, where the tax wedge at the lower end of the income scale is already rather low.

Expanding part-time work and making working hours more flexible
The changing socio-economic environment also requires more flexibil-

ity in worktime patterns. This allows not only for a better use of resources at the level of the firm, but also for a better fit between the firm and employees' needs, which are increasingly deviating from the traditional pattern of lifelong full-time employment. By and large, a voluntary reduction of individual worktime is likely to have fewer negative side-effects than a general reduction in worktime. Uniform, across-the-board, worktime reduction can lead to evasion strategies by employees and firms, thereby expanding the grey economy. Moreover, if general worktime reductions are linked to compensatory hourly wage increases, the resulting jump in unit labour costs might even be counterproductive in terms of employment. (This is basically the same problem that emerges if early retirement and disability pensions are used to reduce the supply of labour.)

In contrast, the expansion of part-time work seems to be a more advantageous strategy. As empirical evidence shows, high levels of employment are usually connected with above-average part-time ratios. The tremendous job growth in the Netherlands we have observed in recent years is partly the product of a rising share of part-time employees. For young people in particular, part-time contracts may serve as a bridge leading to regular employment.

Again, there is no "one best way": an appropriate country-specific policy mix is critically important for setting the right incentive structure so that employers and employees will want to expand both the demand and supply of part-time work. This policy mix can be based on a broad range of instruments: cutting individual worktime is more attractive in those countries that have a basic-pension system and partial individualization of social security entitlements. By contrast, in countries (such as Germany) that combine a system of complete tax splitting between spouses with a strictly earnings-related pension system, part-time employment is punished not only by unfavourable tax treatment but also by more or less proportional cuts in pension entitlements. The propensity for individual working time reduction can be enhanced by lowering the tax burden at the lower end of the labour market to compensate partly for any loss in gross wages. Finally, the standard of social and job protection for part-time workers should not substantially deviate from the level of protection provided for full-time workers. This points to the central importance of labour market "desegmentation"[1] as another essential cornerstone of the "flexicurity" concept.

Labour market desegmentation is geared towards negotiating a relaxation of employment protection for the stable, full-time, core workforce and linking these new standards to increased protection for the peripheral, unstable, part-time, and temporarily employed in the rest of the economy. This helps to contain the growth of precarious jobs, which we have seen, among others, on the French labour market. While a lower standard of protection against dismissal might affect overall employment levels only a little (since a more rapid rise in employment during an economic upswing is likely to be outweighed by a faster cutback in jobs during a downturn), long-term unemployment with its highly undesirable hysteresis effects might well be kept at a more modest level than in countries with high and rigid standards of employment protection. This assumption is also empirically supported by a recent study from the OECD.

As a consequence, systems combining restrictive dismissal protection with meagre unemployment benefits essentially cater to the interests of insiders, whereas systems based on minimal job protection but offering decent standards of social protection for the unemployed bridge the gap between insiders and outsiders more easily. In this respect the Danish strategy is clearly superior to its functional equivalent in the Mediterranean countries. The Netherlands has also followed a strategy of labour market desegmentation, albeit with different means. As already pointed out above, the legal status of part-time workers has been raised. The same is true for employees in temporary job agencies, which experienced a massive boom in recent years. This also meets the interests of employers, whose demand for labour is often subject to considerable fluctuations. Insofar, the increased use of temporary work agencies in the Netherlands is functionally equivalent to low levels of employment protection in Denmark and the Anglo-Saxon countries.

In the Southern group, Spain has also been following a promising strategy of desegmentation in recent years. Since 1997 two new laws allow a reduction of firing costs for certain categories of newly hired workers and for cases of conversion of a temporary contract into a permanent one. In the wake of these provisions, this country has witnessed a remarkable increase of new permanent hirings (from 135,000 in 1997 to 300,000 in 1999). The Spanish solution is regarded with great interest by Italian policy makers, with a view to desegmenting one of the most rigid labour markets of Europe.

Increasing use of activation policy and tightening eligibility for unemployment benefits Ireland, Denmark, the Netherlands, and Portugal have substantially increased spending on active labour market policy in recent years, thereby emphasizing the activation content of labour market policy instead of relying on passive transfers. Finally, as already mentioned, the impact of activation programmes has been strengthened by stronger pressure on the unemployed to accept suitable job offers or participate in education programmes.

Reconciling work and family life is another strategy that has been applied so as to increase labour market flexibility. As quantitative data show, there is considerable cross-country variation in the level of female labour force participation reaching from about 44% in Italy to about 75% in Denmark and Sweden. In the Netherlands, female labour force participation has increased rapidly, displaying a doubling of participation rates since the early 1970s. Clearly, this went in hand with rising part-time opportunities allowing women to combine child raising and participation in the labour market. As a consequence, in many Dutch households the low wage increases that result from long-term wage restraint are compensated (or even overcompensated) for by an additional family income that comes from women's growing job opportunities.

Reconciling work and family life is also the driving force behind the Danish (and Swedish) strategy to massively expand childcare facilities and parental leave arrangements. In Sweden, law stipulates that parental leave, education and training do not interrupt employment. Parents are entitled to a 450-day parental leave and receive a stipend of 75% of their mean salary. Similar but less generous provisions now apply to France and Belgium. In the United Kingdom, by contrast, workers must reach an individual agreement with their employers if they wish to interrupt their career for parental or care leave, except in the case of maternity absence.

Social drawing rights are likely to play an important future role in expanding opportunities for flexible employment across the life cycle in line with individual wishes. Drawing rights are based on the notion of a saving account and autonomous decision by the holder of these drawing rights to make use of their reserve. They are social drawing rights as they are social both in the way they are established (different ways of building up the reserve through the state, the social security or by workers themselves) and in their aims (social usefulness, childrearing, care for elderly family members, training and education). The further advancement of "flexicurity" and social drawing right relies to a great on public policy and receptiveness of key labour market actors. Especially, the trade unions and employers' organizations must open up their organizations to the new realities and new risks and needs of the flexibilization and tertiarization of the labour, especially with respect to the gender and family dimensions of these developments.

New forms of fighting poverty and social exclusion

The global and European market places and the emergence of a knowledge-based economy create new opportunities for economic progress and social inclusion, but also novel risks of poverty and social exclusion. Moreover, endogenous social change reinforces the growing inequalities between dual and single income families, mostly led by women. Recent figures of EUROSTAT, excluding Finland and Sweden, suggest that in the EU 18% of the population, approximately 65 million citizens, live in poverty, defined as the percentage of the population under a low income threshold, set at 60% of the median equivalent income per person in each member state. Official poverty thresholds, as well as the proportion of the population, vary quite markedly across the EU's member states. While in Denmark and the Netherlands income disparities are the smallest and low-income population is only about 10%, in Ireland, Italy, and Spain about 20% of the population live below low-income thresholds.

Dynamics of mobility in and out of poverty also differ by country. Although reliable figures are hard to find, comparative data for the period between 1990 and 1995, reveal that over 80% of the German and Dutch populations never experienced poverty, while this figure amounted to 69% of the British population. While most of the poor in Germany and the Netherlands are poor for only a short period, poverty seems to be more persistent in the UK where the proportion of long-term poverty is 2.5 times higher. The probability of remaining poor after a long spell of poverty is also significantly higher in UK, as compared to Germany and the Netherlands.

Although employment is the best way out of poverty, approximately 12% of the employed live in poverty. While the risk of low income is highest for households without earnings, the working poor still account for a considerable share of low-income individuals. EUROSTAT has calculated that for the EU as a whole, 53% of low-income individuals live in households with some employment.

Tackling poverty effectively requires integrated action across a broad range of policy areas, from social assistance to housing, education, mobility and culture. During the 1990s, fighting social exclusion has become a central priority for many governments. New forms of co-operation and partnerships, including in some cases the socially excluded themselves, are essential. In Ireland, the "Sharing in progress" national anti-poverty strategy (based on a target to bring down long-term poverty in the population from 9 to 15% to less than 5 to 10%) stands out in terms of its strong partnership approach at various levels of decision making and implementation. The Portuguese policy initiatives have been embedded in institutional arenas within which all the relevant stakeholders had a say. French legislation requires public authorities and representatives of the citizens for whom these policies are designed to participate in forums for policy implementation. Meanwhile, in the Netherlands, Belgium and most recently in the United Kingdom, policy makers have launched an integrated approach to social exclusion, to be implemented though specific mechanisms of policy co-ordination and issue linkage across relevant policy areas.

These integrated approaches, based on co-operation and benchmarking, have created the potential for Community action to foster the exchange of national experiences. As poverty and social exclusion are increasingly dynamic phenomena, as material needs and social risks change over time, so there is a clear need for commonly understood data and analysis. This is an area where monitoring and benchmarking at the level of the European Union should take the initiative to make possible this type of problem diagnosis and policy evaluation.

Institutional co-ordination

Finding a new policy mix frequently also requires significant institutional innovation in enhancing the co-ordinated and negotiated character of policymaking and implementation systems. Indeed, this is precisely what has been occurring over the last decade or so in many member states and has underpinned the successful adjustment strategies of countries as diverse as the Netherlands, Ireland, Portugal, Italy and Spain. Their experiences show how reform has been closely related to the forging of new linkages across the policy areas mentioned above.

Among these countries, the Netherlands has proven to be something of a model for advocates of a "third way" between neo-liberal deregulation and the traditional solidaristic European model, both in terms of its institutional rejuvenation and the imaginative reconfiguration of its policy mix. After an interlude of industrial relations strife, the mid-1980s saw a revival of Dutch corporatist policymaking – again with flexible, decentralized bargains within a co-ordinated structure. This has produced something of a model in Ireland, a country which frequently tried but failed to put in place a workable incomes policy in the 1970s [but] has now developed a rather comprehensive social pact. Negotiated in successive phases – in 1987, 1990, 1993 and most recently in 1997 – the Irish social partnership has addressed tax, education, health and social welfare issues in addition to incomes.

The real surprises are Italy, Portugal and Spain where the institutional preconditions for national pacts are particularly weak, and the potential for conflict – over both labour market and social policy reform – especially high. Nevertheless, in all of these countries, incomes policies have been linked in recent years with wider packages of negotiated reform to the labour market, social security and tax systems. In Ireland, Denmark, Italy, the Netherlands, Finland, Spain and Portugal, governments rewarded the willingness of unions to pursue wage restraint by delivering various kinds of side payments ranging from work-time reduction, tax cuts, increased spending for active labour market policy and vocational training. Mandatory contributions to occupational pensions paid by the employers also gained in importance as a module of bi- or tri-partite package deals. Thus, wage bargaining is increasingly about the "social wage" in a broader sense rather than about nominal gross wages. In the Netherlands during the 1980s organized wage restraint was exchanged for work-time reduction first and tax concessions later. In Denmark a basic agreement over paid leave schemes (highly subsidized by the state) helped to dampen the wage demands of the country's relatively well-organized unions.

With respect to the effectiveness of wage bargaining under the economic constraints of the 1980s and 1990s, it is important to underline that the conditions for successful adjustment have changed considerably.

First, the revitalized corporatist bargains in the 1980s and 1990s, first of all, take place in the context of high unemployment, internationalized capital markets, and non-accommodating fiscal and monetary macroeconomic policies. Under these conditions, wage policy not only has to be in line with price stability but also has to allow for profitability and competitiveness. Under high levels of unemployment and increased exit options for employers, the unions have become the weaker partner. Employers only agree to the new deals if they support competitiveness and allow for greater flexibility of working conditions. For their good behaviour unions receive work-time reduction and the promise of jobs and apprenticeship places. However, the unions have had to shelve their earlier drive for a more egalitarian income distribution.

Second, the state is often an important sponsor of these new accords, offering reductions in taxes and social contributions or promising to maintain social benefits in case wage moderation proves effective. The state's capacity to intervene in order to overcome reform blockages remains of crucial importance. The institutional anchoring of price stability and fiscal consolidation by independent central banks and the EMU Stability Pact has empowered the state in this respect, while unions have seen the scope for exercising power reduced. They can no longer expect that excessive wage increases will be accommodated by expansionary macroeconomic policies. As a consequence, expansionary wage policy is likely to backfire and trigger rising unemployment. Under the shadow of this imminent threat, the institutional preconditions of the new social accords are indeed far less demanding than in the case of Keynesian corporatism. Nevertheless, as modern social pacts aim not only at wage restraint but also at structural welfare reforms the co-ordination of reform efforts across various areas of social and economic regulation is crucial.

Third, in the 1990s industrial relations no longer revolved around the dichotomy of centralization or decentralization. Increasingly important is the manner and extent to which the social partners managed to combine decentralized bargaining autonomy with macroeconomic considerations in wage setting. The Danish and Dutch (as well as the Austrian) experiences suggest that two-level wage bargaining systems, placing sectoral or decentralized negotiations within the confines of a broader national framework accord, are comparatively successful in combining macroeconomic objectives with micro-level adjustment. Profitability criteria, as well as the expansion of the service sector have put a premium on wage flexibility at the meso- and micro-levels. Agreements in two-level systems allow sectoral bargainers to strike decentralized deals over productivity, training, and job opportunities for less productive workers within the framework of a longer-term commitment to macroeconomic stability. The Danish and Dutch systems of "organized decentralization" – involving high levels of trust, not only between the social partners at the national level, but even more so between sectoral negotiators and central leadership – provide important lessons for other countries.

In the Dutch case, concertation has been the pre-requisite for innovation in "flexicurity" and labour market de-segmentation. Recent reforms have shelved the differences between the high levels of security for full-time core workers and the lower level of protection for peripheral temporary and part-time workers. This policy promoted part-time work and selective labour market deregulation, which subsequently paved the way for a virtual paradigm shift in Dutch labour market regulation with the adoption of the "flexicurity" law in 1998. Sine 1993 Dutch unions and employers have increasingly come to exchange shorter working hours, an expansion of leave arrangements, the warranty of income stability throughout the year and lower overtime rates against the annualization of working hours and an expansion of work on evenings or on Saturdays. The social partners are also in agreement that employers should honour workers' requests to work part-time unless there are compelling firm-related reasons for rejection.

In Ireland, the social partners hammered out their first tripartite response to the crisis in public finances in 1987 in the form of the Programme for National Recovery (1987–1990). Subsequent agreements renewing and extending that accord have been linked to a centralization of wage bargaining and a growing willingness to address tax, education, health and social welfare issues via central negotiation as well. The emphasis of all four agreements has been on macro-economic stability, greater equity in the tax system, and enhanced social justice. Specific innovations include inflation-proof benefits, job creation (in manufacturing and international services sectors) and the reform of labour legislation in the areas of part-time work, employment equality and unfair dismissal. In the process, Ireland has experienced a remarkable transformation of its industrial relations system over the past ten years or so. It has made a transition from one bearing a strong resemblance to the British adversarial system, to one with strong corporatist elements, capable of delivering low inflation, a high rate of economic growth and widespread innovation in social security, taxation and labour market policy. "Partnership 2000" (1996–7) was negotiated with a larger number of partners, including the Irish National Organisation of the Unemployed and other groups addressing the problems of social exclusion, and includes a National Anti-Poverty Strategy.

In Italy – characterized by extensive industrial relations strife until the 1980s – social pacts since 1993 not only contributed to the fulfilment of EMU entry conditions by effectively taking inflation out of the labour market, but also included agreements on negotiated flexibility and job security. In 1997, the Treu package on labour market reform was adopted, which legalized temporary work agencies (as well as fixed-term and part-time contracts) and simultaneously sought to protect or to improve the rights and entitlements of workers in these kinds of jobs. In addition, improvements were adopted in training programs giving firms a strong voice in training courses. In the process, Italian unions are moving away from their strong defence of rigid labour market regulation at all costs to a policy of more flexible bargaining practices seemingly better able to resolve the threat of deskilling and growing segmentation. Thus, political actors in Italy seem to have recognized that Italy's very strict system of employment protection is the root cause for the strong insider–outsider cleavage on the labour market.

Meanwhile, in Portugal, the period until the mid-1980s saw attempts at incomes policy and concertation but an inadequate institutional framework undermined them. Particularly problematic – as in the Italian case – was the absence of strong authority on the part of the trade unions and the need for a strengthened role for the state, making it a more reliable and consistent bargaining partner. Also as in Italy, it was the commitment to eventual EMU membership after 1990 (under an enlarged-majority PSD government) that led to an emphasis on an anti-inflation, lower public debt strategy. At the same time there developed a broad consensus on the need for a new distributional coalition linked to the country's aspiration for full EMU membership.

Reflecting this consensus – and regardless of the continuing fragility of trade union structures – there have been five tripartite pacts since 1987 – the latest was signed in 1996 – focusing on incomes and social policy and labour market measures. They have been presented from the outset as critical for improving the competitiveness of the Portuguese economy and for integration into EMU. The agreements have been very wide-ranging, covering pay rise ceilings, levels of minimum wages, easing regulations on the organization of work (rest, overtime and shift work) – i.e., internal flexibility – and on the termination of employment (external flexibility) and the regulation of working hours.

Under the 1996 short-term agreement (consolidated by a Strategic Social Pact in 1997), income tax for those on low incomes has been reduced, a more favourable tax treatment has been made of a variety of health and education benefits, and old age pensions. In mid-1998 the levels of state retirement and contributory pensions were raised, requiring significant changes in the way the system is financed.

Recent developments in Spain reflect a general shift away from the pacts based on the protection of insider rights that emerged from the Franco period, towards a more broadly based pact mirroring those struck in Portugal and Ireland. This reflects a commitment on the part of the state to reform in the labour market, demands from employers for greater flexibility and the need of unions to strengthen their own organizational base. Given low membership and a correspondingly low level of financial resources, and their need for the legitimacy that bargaining with the state can confer on them, the incentives for union involvement are high. Innovations in wage bargaining have also been important. As in the Italian case, these reflect a recognition by employers, unions and government that a new wage bargaining structure – containing decentralized flexibility within a national framework – is essential for containing inflationary pressures under EMU.

The 1994 "Toledo Pact" included a focus on the rationalization and consolidation of the public social security systems. The pact has facilitated subsequent deals on labour market flexibility and pensions, as well as – more recently – the first sectoral agreements on reduced working hours (in savings banks) and talks on incentives to encourage part-time working. The pensions reform deal, struck between the government and the social partners in October 1996, made major innovations. These included the reduction in the number of special regimes (an equity increasing measure); an increase in the proportionality between contributions and benefits; the financing of health care and social services through taxes; and the reduction of employers' contributions in order to foster job creation. The labour market reform of April 1997 was also extensive, and saw the first major concession by Spanish unions to labour market outsiders when they agreed to a decrease in high redundancy payments in exchange for a reduction of insecurity for those working on temporary contracts. Bolstered by such progress, Spain too appears to be working its way towards an institutionalized pact, although the coalitional supports in this case remain rather weak.

Conclusion

In sum, an effective redesign of social security systems is required to prevent implicit or explicit disentitlement in relation to two groups in particular: women workers (who are often discriminated against by male breadwinner-oriented social security systems); and those not in permanent, full-time employment. At the same time new forms of active social security systems have to guarantee access to skill acquisition and social services at any point during the life cycle. In terms of labour regulation, a shift away from legislated or rule-governed labour market regulation to negotiated labour market regulation is to be preferred. A shift away from adversarial industrial relations towards a more consensual model also at the enterprise level, together with the joint implementation of training mechanisms and priorities, is also desirable.

Finally, innovating across policy areas requires a long-term investment in negotiated structures of governance. So far, such experimentation has focused on the traditional bargaining partners – the state and the representatives of employers and employees. There is a pressing need, however, for the stimulation of the so-called "civic" dialogue, with the extension of concertation on welfare reform to other concerned groups, including third sector organizations and representatives of the unemployed and the anti-poverty lobby. The case of Ireland – where such broader experimentation has been conducted – could provide useful lessons (of both how and how not to proceed) in this respect.

Note

1 The concept of labour market desegmentation has been suggested to us by Jonathan Zeitlin.

8

A Welfare State for the 21st Century

Gøsta Esping-Andersen

[. . .]

What I present here is [. . .] an attempt to construct a welfare edifice that is in [. . .] harmony with the kind of economy, employment, and family that is in the making. [. . .] The challenge is immense because the revolutions in both employment and family structure are creating massive new opportunities but also new social risks and needs. Changing technologies, intensified global integration, and our capacity to adapt, occupy center-stage as far as competitiveness is concerned; the service sector will over-determine as far as employment is concerned. Although it is evident that high-end services will dominate job-trends, both the new family needs and a full employment scenario will imply a sizeable share of low-end, low-productivity jobs in social and personal services. It will, accordingly, be difficult to avoid new dualisms. A knowledge-intensive economy will produce new skill-based cleavages with, possibly, polarization. How to deal with the losers is one major challenge. A knowledge-intensive economy necessitates not just expertise among producers, but also among consumers. Therefore, unless we succeed in broadly strengthening the cognitive capacities and resource base of citizens, the long-term scenario might very well be a smattering of 'knowledge islands' in a great sea of marginalized outsiders. This poses the first-order challenge of how to democratize skills. [. . .] And it poses the second-order challenge of how to redesign social policy. The most simple-minded 'third way' promoters believe that the population, via education, can be adapted to the market economy and that the social problem will, hence, disappear. This is a dangerous fallacy. Education, training or life-long learning cannot be enough. A skill-intensive economy will breed new inqualities; a full-employment service economy will reinforce these. And if we are unwilling to accept low-end services, it will be difficult to avoid widespread unemployment. In any case, education cannot undo differences in people's social capital.

The new family and life course pose an equally formidable challenge. Greater instability and the rise of 'a-typical' households mean also potential polarization. At one end, divorce, separations, and single parenthood create severe risks of poverty. At the other end, the trend towards dual-earner households strengthens families' resource base. We must assume strong marital homogamy, and therefore a widening gap between strong and weak households.

The standard male breadwinner model that once guaranteed adequate welfare and high fertility is declining both numerically and in its capacity to effectively prevent child poverty. Indeed, the conventional family may increasingly constitute an obstacle to flexibility and adaptation since too many citizens' welfare depends on the job and income security of one person. And with family revolution is emerging new life course patterns, much less linear, homogeneous, and predictable. The upshot is that new risks and resource needs are bundling heavily among youth and in child families. The challenge, again, is to redefine social policy so that it nurtures strong and viable families and protects those most at risk. If those most at risk happen to be children and youth, the urgency of reform is so much greater because it is today's children that will be tomorrow's productive base – or, in the case of failure to reform, tomorrow's expensive social problems.

As was always the case, access to paid work is families' single best welfare guarantee. The difference today is that emerging family types face new and severe tradeoffs between employment and family obligations; tradeoffs that are better resolved by access to services than traditional income maintenance. Postwar 'welfare capitalism' functioned well because labor markets and families themselves were the principal source of welfare for most citizens, most of their lives. Presently, both labor markets and families create widespread insecurity, precariousness, and often social exclusion and this means obviously added burdens on public social protection schemes. The single greatest challenge we face today is how to rethink social policy so that, once again, labor markets and families are welfare optimizers and a good guarantee that tomorrow's adult workers will be as productive and resourceful as possible.

The emerging risk and needs structure is in stark contrast with the existing, highly aged-biased, emphasis of most contemporary European welfare states. Our social policy challenge implies a rethinking of the life cycle, of the balance between income transfers and services and, more generally of the guiding principles of social justice and equality. If Europe aims to maximize its competitive position in the World economy and, at the same time, commit itself to full employment, new inequalities will be difficult to avoid. The burning question is, what do we do about them? The most fundamental conclusion that emerges is that we must re-think the concept of social rights. The existing principle of guaranteeing maximum welfare and equality 'for-all-here-and-now' cannot be consistent with the emerging economic imperatives. If relatively low incomes, bad jobs, or precarious employment cannot be avoided (and might arguably even merit encouragement), there is the issue of how to soften their welfare effects in the short-run. However, the core welfare issue must focus on long-run dynamics, on citizens' life chances. Low wages or bad jobs are not a threat to individuals' welfare if the experience is temporary; they are if individuals become trapped. In brief, the core principle of social rights should be redefined as effective guarantees against entrapment, as the right to a 'second chance'; in short, as a basic set of *life chance guarantees*.

The diversity of European welfare regimes

These challenges to social protection are not equally severe across all European welfare systems. We must avoid two errors. One is to ignore the great diversity of European welfare systems. A second is to remain too narrowly preoccupied with just the welfare state. Society's total welfare package combines inputs from the welfare state proper, markets (and especially labor markets), and families. Many view the welfare state as overburdened, inefficient, threatened or, simply, malfunctioning. Some advocate that it be radically slimmed, others that it be strengthened, and still others that it be overhauled. Whatever opinions are put forth, there is an implicit view of what, alternatively, ought to be the role of markets and families. Those who advocate 'decentralization' basically suggest a greater responsibility to families and the 'local community'; those who champion privatization assign welfare to the cash-nexus but, in practice, the result would also be a greater burden on many families. To capture the interplay of state, family, and market, it is useful to cast our analysis in terms of *welfare regimes*.

Turn the clock back to the postwar decades, and we would identify two distinct European welfare regimes. The Nordic-cum-British was largely general revenue financed, stressing universal, flat-rate benefits. The other, prevalent in Continental Europe, emphasized contribution financed and employment-based social insurance. As social protection systems evolved and matured by the 1970s, differences emerged much more clearly. The Nordic countries branched out into a unique model, first by adding an earnings-related component to flat-rate 'citizens' benefits and, secondly, by shifting the emphasis from income transfers towards servicing families, stressing employment-activating policies and, above all, women's integration in the labor market. The Nordic model may be famous for its generosity and universalism, but what really stands out is its employment-bias and its 'de-familialization' of welfare responsibilities. Britain, in contrast, gradually moved towards more targeting and income testing, assigning more welfare responsibilities to the market – thus converging with North America. The hallmark of most Continental European countries is how little has changed. They remain firmly wedded to employment-based, contributory social insurance but have extended coverage to residual groups via ad hoc income-tested programs (like the RMI in France or the pensione sociale in Italy). A second defining feature of Continental European, and especially Mediterranean, social protection systems is their strong *familialism*, i.e. the idea that families hold the principal welfare responsibility for their members, be it in terms of sharing incomes or in terms of care needs. Hence, these countries are uniquely committed to protecting the male breadwinner (via insurance and job protection), highly reliant on social contributions for financing, and comparatively very under-developed in social services.

Such differences mean that we cannot forge general strategies for social reform at an abstract pan-European level. It also follows that we shall err terribly if we limit our attention solely to *governments'* welfare role. I believe it is futile to discuss whether we should reduce public social commitments without considering what effects such might have on family and market welfare delivery. A strategy of 'de-centralizing' welfare to community and family may sound appealing to many, but how will it affect women's double role as workers and care-givers? Alternatively, a scenario of more markets may appear more efficient, but if this means that large populations will be priced out of the welfare market, do potential efficiency gains clearly outweigh potential welfare losses? Reforming European welfare commitments for the coming century implies *regime change*, that is reordering the welfare contributions of markets, families and state so that the mix corresponds better to the overall goals we may have for a more equitable and efficient social system.

The transformation of the social risk and needs structure

Most European social protection systems were constructed in an era with a very different distribution and intensity of risks and needs than exists today. With the main exception of Scandinavia (and Britain), the allocation of welfare responsibilities between state, market, and families has not changed dramatically over the past 50 years. What has changed, however, is the capacity of households and labor markets to furnish those basic welfare guarantees that once were assumed. Indeed, both now generate new risks and, equally importantly, also new needs.

The postwar model could rely on strong families and well-performing labor markets to furnish the lion's share of welfare for most people, most of their lives. Until the 1970s, the norm was stable, male breadwinner-based families. With few interruptions, the male could count on secure employment, steady real earnings growth, and long careers – followed by a few years in retirement after age 65. Women would typically cease to work at first birth, and were thus the main societal provider of social care for children and the frail elderly. Unemployment and poverty were limited among prime-age households, and the main social risks were concentrated at the two 'passive' tail-ends of the life cycle: in large child families, and among the aged. Hence, besides health care, European welfare states came to prioritize income maintenance and, *par excellence*, pensions.

The problem behind the new risk configuration is that it stems primarily from weakened families and poorly functioning labor markets. As a consequence, the welfare state is burdened with responsibilities for which it was not designed. A well-functioning welfare state for the future must, accordingly, be re-calibrated so that labor markets and families function more optimally.

Family risks

Families today have far fewer children, yet child poverty is rising. Ongoing changes in labor markets and families affect young households most severely. The reasons are well-documented: Firstly, unemployment and insecurity are concentrated among youth and the low-educated (males in particular). The incidence of 'no-work households' is sometimes alarmingly high, and this is one symptom of an emerging new polarization: Homogamy means that unemployment, precariousness, and poverty 'comes in couples'. Youth often face serious delays in 'getting started', in making a smooth transition from school to careers, or in forming independent families; Southern European youth can often anticipate three years' unemployment and this, obviously, is one cause of falling birth rates. The consequences of youth precariousness vary nonetheless depending on social policy approach. The unemployed – particularly youth – face severe revenue problems in many EU countries. Southern Europe's 'familialism' implies that most unemployment is absorbed by parents, but this is not the case in Northern Europe. Where, as in Denmark, unemployed youth are typically entitled to social benefits, poverty is modest; where, as elsewhere, they rely primarily on assistance, poverty is widespread.

The new risks are also a function of the rise of 'non-standard' households. [. . .] Two types have, in particular, become prominent: the 'no work-income' and the single parent household. Both run high risks of income poverty. No-work households are generally transfer-dependent, often relying on social assistance. Except in Scandinavia, child poverty is alarmingly high in lone parent families. Yet, across all kinds of child families – in two-adult families as well as in single parent households – the strikingly best safeguard against poverty is that mothers work. The low levels of single-parenthood poverty in the Nordic countries are, in fact, less due to generous social transfers than to adequate work incomes made possible by child care. Simply put, mothers' employment is a very effective antidote to the risks that come with family instability and labor market precariousness. If this is the case, the single most pressing social policy issue has less to do with income maintenance and much more to do with servicing working mothers.

The new distribution of life cycle risks is most evident when we contrast younger and older households. The economic well-being of child families has been eroding while, concomitantly, it has improved among the elderly. High incomes have allowed the elderly to live independently and, coupled to rising longevity, this implies that the chief needs among the aged have shifted towards caring services. And herein lies one of the key epochal transformations: the main welfare needs within young and aged households have less to do with improved income transfers and more to do with access to services. Among the ultra-aged in particular, the pressing need is for home-help services and care centers. Within child families, poverty can best be stemmed by enhancing parents' labor market prospects and earnings capacity.

Notwithstanding, most European welfare states remain uniquely biased in favor of the aged rather than youth; in favor of income maintenance rather than services. The Nordic countries are an exception as far as servicing is concerned; and with Ireland, they remain the exception in prioritizing young families.[1] Put differently, society may be overspending on passive maintenance and under-investing in the kinds of resources that strengthen citizens' capacities.

Services can, besides government, be provided by the market or families themselves. In Europe, however, marketed family services, such as private day care, are generally priced out of the market.[2] In brief, where government provision (or subsidization) is absent, as in most Continental and especially Southern Europe, families themselves must shoulder most of the caring burden of children and the elderly. The upshot of familialism is of course to worsen women's incompatibility between family responsibilities and paid work and, indirectly, to weaken families' capacity to autonomously combat poverty. But since, in effect, young cohort women today do work, traditional familialism mainly provokes another perverse result, namely a *de facto* low-fertility equilibrium!

Welfare asymmetries across generations and the life course

We should be careful to avoid a simple zero-sum trade-off between the welfare of the aged and the young. There exists, of course, some evidence that the rising welfare of retirees occurs at the expense of youth and children, at least in countries (like the U.S. or Italy) where improvements in aged welfare have not been accompanied by an upgrading of family policies. Also, it is clear that income distribution trends in most countries favor the aged. The median retired household can usually count on a disposable income of at least 80 per cent of the national median.[3]

Certainly there remain pockets of poverty among the aged, typically concentrated among widows and persons with problematic contribution histories. Old-age poverty tends to be higher in countries which, until recently, had large rural populations (Greece, Italy, and Spain, for example). It is also well-known that retirement income declines somewhat with age. Nonetheless, all indications are that the large mass of pensioners in most countries have sufficient (and sometimes perhaps 'excess') incomes, especially in light of reduced consumption and household capital expenditures, and because an often very large proportion (the EU average is 75 per cent) of the elderly own their home outright. What is more, in many countries retirees enjoy preferential tax treatment and are generally exempt from social contributions.

The economic well-being of today's elderly is the result of a unique combination of factors that produced high retirement income and life-time asset accumulation.[4] [. . .] The average household at age 65 possesses wealth that equals 4–5 times its annual income stream. And, although we have only scattered nation-specific evidence, there are indications of pension over-provision in some countries. My own analyses of Italian family expenditure data indicate a 30 percentage point excess of income over expenditure in the average retiree household. A recent study by Kohli on intra-family money streams indicates a huge dominance of transfers from the aged (70+) to their children and grandchildren: 24 per cent of income is transferred to their children; almost 15 per cent to their grandchildren.[5]

Such downward intra-family redistribution surely varies by income decile and by nation. Moreover, excess revenues reflect not just pension generosity but also home ownership, private assets, and lower consumption needs. Still, where it exists the redistributive effect must be considered perverse if the welfare of youth is becoming a function of the riches of their retired forebears. Indeed, it is doubly perverse in the sense that pay-as-you-go pensions are financed by the working age population. The welfare state was presumably built in order to even the playing field, but here is a case where it helps re-establish inherited privilege.

Any debate on reforming pensions must consider the life course specificities of past, current and *especially* future retiring cohorts. If current retirement cohorts are generally well-off it is because they are the main beneficiaries of Golden Age capitalism. Firstly, most of their careers spanned decades of strong productivity and earnings growth with low unemployment among prime-age males. Secondly, with the regulation of seniority rights and the emergence of efficiency wage systems, the age-wage profile was de-coupled from productivity – hence rising earnings even when productivity declines with age.[6] Thirdly, today's pensioners are the chief beneficiaries of pension-upgrading in the 1960s and 1970s. Fourthly, although there has been a decline in real earnings growth in recent decades, the financial returns on investments have risen.

A major reform of present pension systems confronts the dilemma that future retirement cohorts are unlikely to amass similar life-time assets, either through individual initiative (work and savings) or through the redistributive mechanisms of public pension schemes. Or, more likely, future retirement cohorts will, if uncorrected, become far more dualistic, possibly even polarized in terms of life chances. Today's youth often face serious delays in passing to stable employment: besides longer schooling, a large proportion can anticipate protracted and maybe frequent unemployment combined with more precarious employment. This correlates with skills and education. Secondly, as de-regulation weakens the security of the prime-age 'insider' work force, career interruptions and redundancies are increasingly likely, among the less skilled in particular.[7] Thirdly, today's young cohorts are un-likely to benefit from decades of powerful real earnings growth and, if productivity bargaining becomes increasingly decentralized, seniority-based wage systems may weaken. Again, there is a clear trend towards more inequality in skills-based earnings power. Fourthly, these are the cohorts which will fully experience the impact of ongoing pension reform in EU member countries, with the shift towards more individualized and actuarially based entitlement calculations. And, yet once again, this will favor the strongest workers in the labor market.

If *de facto* retirement age will remain at 59–60, today's young cohorts will be hard put to cumulate a minimum of, say, 35 contribution years towards the basic pension. There cohort-specific disadvantages are, nonetheless, offset by three key factors: One, their higher educational attainment and superior cognitive skills imply greater adaptability and ability for retraining across their careers. As they age, an investment in retraining may appear more logical than, simply, early retirement. The stronger is the skills and educational base of young workers today, the greater will be the pay-off when they eventually age. Two, each new retirement cohort shows sharp improvements in health and longevity, and all indications are that this will continue. Already today, the typical 65-year-old male can expect another 8–10 disability-free years. Those who are young now will be able to count on many more disability-free years. Three, the ongoing growth of women's life-time employment implies that future retirement households will be able to double up pension savings or, in the case of divorce, women will increasingly have independent pension entitlements.

A strategy of resolving the looming pension crisis by radically re-ducing pension entitlements today would be counter-productive in the long run if, as is very possible, future retirees will look more like their forebears in the 1940s or 1960s. If, now, pensioner households have too much income, it would be a more equitable, and certainly more prudent, policy to simply tax away the excess.[8] If, then, a major reduc-tion of public pensions is a sub-optimal long-run strategy, our atten-tion must shift to an alternative policy. As virtually all agree, the key to long-term sustainability lies in population growth and, more realis-tically, in raising participation rates.[9]

[. . .]

The link to labor markets

The new welfare policy priorities that emerge from the preceding analysis boil down to one basic issue, namely that social policy must maximize citizens' productive resources and life chances. It is important to recognize that any 'work-friendly' policy must align itself to the dynamics of a services-led economy.

The service economy is tendentially dualistic, combining knowledge-intensive professional and technical jobs with low-end, low value-added, and labor intensive, servicing. The former are concentrated in business and some social services (teachers, doctors); the latter in sales, consumer, and also some social services (restaurant workers, home helpers, nursing assistants). Europe, like North America, is very dynamic as far as business services are concerned. Europe's development of social services is, excepting Scandinavia, sluggish. And European private consumer services are stagnant if not actually in decline.

Contrary to popular belief, services are *everywhere* biased in favor of skilled and good jobs. The dilemma, nonetheless, is that a significant amelioration of mass unemployment means stimulating also low-productivity services, and this means that we must rely also on personal consumer services and social services. The good news is that these are sheltered from international trade competition; the bad news is that they compete directly with unpaid household 'self-servicing'. The problem is that many services are extremely price sensitive. They will grow if, as in the United States, wages and costs are relatively low, and thus affordable or if, as in Scandinavia, they are subsidized by government.[10]

Herein lies the great European policy dilemma. The task of forging a more equitable and efficient social protection system, as outlined above, pales in comparison to the trade-offs involved in stimulating employment-intensive services. *Yet, no solution exists unless we realize that social protection and service employment are directly linked.* The gist of the problem is simple, namely that strong service growth implies more taxation if we emphasize public services or, alternatively, more wage inequality (and lower fixed labor costs) if we emphasize market services.

Most European welfare states and industrial relations systems have committed themselves for decades to a degree of security for the prime age (male) worker, and a degree of earnings and income equality, that is not compatible with a large, low-end service economy. Moreover, the existing financial pressures on most European welfare states today make it difficult to replicate the Nordic countries' social service expansion twenty years ago.

This dilemma is now well-recognized within EU member states. Witness the extension of targeted wage subsidies (usually aimed at youth and contingent on training), and recent EU-level proposals to stimulate labor intensive services through a reduction of the VAT.[11] There is virtually universal agreement that strong wage compression, a high tax wedge (especially through mandatory contributions) and, perhaps, overly rigid employment regulation block lower-end services. The great dilemma, though, is that the kind of *tout court*, American-style, deregulation that would fuel such jobs is unacceptable to European policy makers.[12]

The stagnation of low-end services in Europe is directly linked to the nexus between families and social protection. On one hand, employment-based social insurance systems impose very high fixed labor costs whose marginal effect is especially strong in low-wage, low-productivity jobs: a high tax-wedge *de facto* prices them out of the market. On the other hand, the lion's share of such service jobs compete with households' own internal servicing capacity. So, where women's employment rate is low, households service themselves; where most women work, households' demand for outservicing increases. In brief, the double earner family externalizes its servicing needs and creates jobs.[13]

As discussed above, dual earner families require services to begin with and herein lies the gist of a win-win policy scenario, namely that more social care services are a key instrument in combating poverty *and* a potentially very effective employment multiplier. Markets cannot generally guarantee affordable, high-quality care for small children or the aged, and high-quality day care is crucial if our aim is to optimize the life chances of children. In other words, public subsidies or direct public delivery is basically a first precondition. Here, in other words, is a prime rationale for shifting welfare priorities in favor of servicing families. An investment in women's ability to work is also an investment in family welfare and in job creation.

Since the traditional welfare state defined its obligations primarily in terms of income maintenance for those unable to work, social protection has been viewed as 'unproductive' consumption and problematic redistribution. This 'income maintenance' philosophy has, by and large, been carried over in address to contemporary social problems. Yet, I have tried to make a strong case that servicing families is the single most effective policy against poverty, welfare dependency, and also an investment in human resources at the same time. In brief, family services should be regarded not as merely 'passive consumption', but also as active investments which yield a long-run return.

[. . .]

The social advantages of a low-end, labor market are clear: it provides easy-entry jobs for youth, immigrants, low-skilled workers, and returning women. Whereas in much of Europe now, the transition from school to work can last for years, and where immigrant workers have difficulty integrating themselves into the official economy, and where low-skilled workers are increasingly condemned to unemployment, low-end services could play a very positive function *if*, that is, they do not become life-long traps. A brief spell of low earnings and un-rewarding work will not, by definition, harm people's life chances – to the contrary, if they provide bridges into the labor market or help supplement income. The criteria by which we must judge the costs and benefits of low-end jobs cannot be based on snapshot notions of equality for all, here-and-now. The only reasonable benchmark is life course dynamics.

[. . .]

A low-end labor market need not be incompatible with a new welfare state scenario. Indeed, one might restate the point in this way: *no win-win welfare model for Europe will be possible unless we accept a different notion of equality*. We have become accustomed to an overly static, here-and-now, concept of redistributive justice: the welfare state must assure that all citizens are protected always. A far more realistic principle would be that our future welfare state accepts, perhaps even sanctions, inequalities here-and-now in order to maximize better life chances for all. If the 'knowledge society' and the modern family create inequalities, the most effective social policy would be one that guarantees that citizens will not become trapped into social exclusion, poverty, or marginality across their life course.

A European welfare state for the 21st century

[. . .]

The issue before us has to do with the long term, with the kind of society that our children will live in. And if this means redefining welfare priorities, we cannot escape the need for some common, basic criterion of what is desirable, given known constraints. What are the common goals to be reached? What do we seek to accomplish? What are the first principles that must guide policy-making? What, in brief, can be our common yardstick of justice, of equality, of collective guarantees and individual responsibility? And, once agreed upon, how can our commitments to equity be best put to use in order to maximize efficiency?

Basic criteria for policy choice

We must probably assume that most EU countries have reached their maximum limits of public expenditure and taxation. In fact, convergence towards the Maastricht criteria compels expenditure reductions, not bold and expensive reform vistas. The need for restrictive policy already limits the degree to which nations can promote the knowledge society, be it investments in infrastructure, education, training, or in improved social welfare.

The resource dilemma worsens considerably when we take into account the new inequalities and social risks that knowledge-based economies inevitable provoke. The evidence is by now clear that the social opportunity structure, rewards, and life chances create new winners and losers and, most likely, a deepening gulf between those with skills and those without. The new service economy can create jobs, but it *cannot* guarantee good wages and jobs for all. The fabric of our social protection systems will therefore be put to a severe test in terms of nurturing efficiency while securing social cohesion, welfare and equity. We must probably accept two ground rules for policy making. We are compelled to re-prioritize the allocation of our existing welfare package. One, we cannot pursue too one-dimensionally a 'learning society', a human capital-based strategy in the belief that a tide of education will lift all boats. Such a strategy inevitably leaves the less-endowed behind and, equally importantly, it requires that we redistribute resources and welfare to families and, especially, to children. The modern family is an integral part of the new economic scenario, and its welfare risks are mounting. Children's ability to make the best out of schooling depends not just on the quality of schools, but also on the social conditions in their families; women are today often more educated than males but will have difficulty putting this to maximum use without generous leave programs and care services.

The second ground rule is that new social policy challenges cannot be met by additional taxation or spending as a percent of GDP. We must accordingly concentrate on how to improve upon the status quo. Entitlement conflicts and equity issues are easily subdued when the total pie grows. When, instead, we must divide the pie up differently, a clash of interests is hard to avoid.

[. . .]

Principles of reform: towards a social investment bias

Contemporary policy slogans such as work-friendly or women-friendly benefits, life-long learning and social investment strategies, or the popular distinction between active and passive measures, all have in common an implicit distinction between policies that somehow enhance or diminish citizens' self-reliance and capacities, economies' efficiency and productivity. Such slogans reflect a growing unease with the existing bias of compensating the losers of economic change with passive income maintenance, of reducing labor supply, or of parking surplus workers on public benefits. The new policy vocabulary mirrors a growing consensus that social policy must become 'productivist', to coin an expression traditionally used in Swedish policy making. That is, social policy should actively mobilize and maximize the productive potential of the population so as to minimize its need for, and dependence on, government benefits. [. . .]

Some policies can be regarded as an investment in human resources, capabilities and self-reliance; others, while welfare enhancing, are clearly passive income maintenance. Obviously, such a distinction is – and must be – ambiguous. Unemployment benefits appear 'passive', but they *do* aid workers in their search for new employment, and they do improve the labor-matching process. Similarly, child allowances add to families' consumption power but they do also diminish poverty and thus enhance children's future life chances. *The important point to stress here is that contemporary policy fashion tends to stress far too narrowly the wonders of 'activation' policies while ignoring income maintenance.* The need for 'passive' measures will not disappear even in the best designed, productivist welfare state: there will always be people and groups that must depend primarily on redistribution, and activating citizens' productive potential often necessitates income subsidies. Regardless, a first principle of any win-win strategy must be that it prioritizes social investment over passive maintenance.[14] A second, derivative principle, is that highest priority should go to social investments in children – who are our future productive potential.

Towards a new welfare state design

[. . .] The preceding analysis points to a set of concrete policy priorities:

- *maximizing mothers' ability to harmonize employment and children*
- *encouraging older workers to delay retirement*
- *socializing the cost of children mainly by prioritizing investments in children and youth*
- *redefining the mix of work and leisure across the life cycle*
- *reconceptualizing 'equality' and basic social rights as being primarily a question of life chance guarantees*

This will, in the most general terms, imply a greater emphasis on protecting young households, and a stronger emphasis on servicing families.

The limits of a learning strategy

Accelerating the pace towards a knowledge- and skill-intensive economy implies heavy investments in education, training and cognitive abilities. Those with low human and social capital will inevitably fall behind and find themselves marginalized in the job and career structure. The problem is a double one because such an economy requires not only highly skilled producers, but also users, of knowledge. It is accordingly tantamount that educational investments be as broad-based as possible. As so much recent research has shown, concrete expertise may be less salient than possessing the essential cognitive abilities required to learn, adapt and be trainable in the first place. Activation measures, such as training or retraining, will have a low payoff if workers' initial cognitive capacities are low. They are much more likely to pay off if they are designed around a more comprehensive and individualized 'activation package'.

One pervasive problem across Europe today is that the stock of low-educated and low-skilled 'excess' workers can be very high – in part because of delayed agricultural decline, in part because of heavy job losses in traditional, low-skill industries, and in part because of an often wide gulf in education between generations of workers. A massive investment in learning will probably reap most of its benefits among younger cohort workers. The dilemma, then, is how to manage the present stock of mostly older, low-skilled males. Early retirement has, so far, been the leading policy and it may have been the only realistic policy so far. Life-long education is an attractive alternative, but may be overly costly and ineffective if the main clientele are older, low-skilled workers. A third policy would be to de-regulate job protection and seniority wage systems so as to align wages closer to productivity differentials – as is generally American pratice. This would cause the incomes of youth and older workers to decline, possibly sharply so.

There exists no ready-made formula for a win-win policy in this regard – largely because the problem varies dramatically from country-to-country. An obvious first step is to assure that future generation workers will have a sufficient skill and cognitive base so that the dilemma eventually evaporates. The problem is the second step, namely what to do with the existing stock. If we are assured that early retirement in the past decades has succeeded in managing what was a transitory glut of elderly low-skilled workers, the dilemma resolves itself and the process of curtailing early retirement can be accelerated. If not, we are left with a mix of continued early retirement, possibly retraining, or downward wage adjustments (or re-employment). The social partners are clearly unwilling to accept across-the-board de-regulation of job security and wages, but it might be an efficiency gain to prolong the employability of older workers by subsidizing part of their wage bill. This is especially the case if, as often occurs, retired workers return to work in the undeclared shadow economy. Just like in the case of youth workers, very high fixed labor costs help price them out of the market.

An effective life-long learning strategy can be effective when the basic cognitive skills are already present, and this means that we need to assure that coming generations have the resources required to benefit from investments in training and education across their lifetime. In many EU countries, the existing generational gap is enormous and it is, therefore, tantamount, that this is not reproduced in the future.

Equitable retirement

The principal problem in today's overly aged-biased welfare systems is that they provide incentives with inequitable results. Workers easily collude with employers to retire early because they will gain little or nothing by postponing exit. At the same time, the pay-as-you-go nature of pension schemes means that retirement at high benefits is heavily financed by the active workforce. Reinstating actuarial incentives to delay retirement would clearly be more equitable and efficient, and it would vastly improve upon the transparency of costs involved in retiring out older workers.

Since workers can expect to be disability-free until age 75, raising and flexibilizing retirement age to 65 in the medium-term, and possibly 70 in the long-term, via incentives can be positive for individual workers and also for welfare state finances. Abolishing mandatory retirement age and developing flexible mechanisms of gradual exit could be pursued immediately. Longevity implies that the share of ultra-aged (80+) just about doubles every two decades. And this means costly and intensive servicing and care needs. If, as I have suggested, retirement households often enjoy 'excess' income and wealth which, if *not* taxed, generates perverse redistribution, an incentive-neutral and far more equitable policy would be to earmark taxation of pensioners to their own collective caring needs. Such a taxation mechanism, even if highly progressive, is also likely to be distributionally neutral across pensioner households (the rich generally live longer).

Altering the welfare and work nexus among the aged cannot be an end in itself, but is primarily a means to achieve more intergenerational equity and a more efficient utilization of public resources. [. . .] There are really only two genuinely effective policies to combat the long-term financial consequences of aging: sharply reducing pension entitlements, or raising participation levels. Reducing entitlements means stimulating private pension plans for large parts of the population. The problem with a private-dominated pension mix is that it replicates life course inequalities, and the more that private plans grow, the more is it likely that we shall see downward pressures on public benefits targeted to low-income households. Even if a system dominated by private schemes augments national savings rates (and thus 'efficiency'), they will possibly lead to non-Paretian outcomes: the weakest may end up worse off. Identifiable trends in labor markets also threaten the viability of a predominantly private pension structure since declining job security and more intense inequalities will negatively affect workers' capacity to accumulate individual savings.

Harmonizing family welfare and labor markets

Postindustrial, service-dominated labor markets cannot avoid producing new inequalities. One source of dualisms comes from systems of strong protection of stably employed 'insiders' with a possibly growing clientele of 'outsiders', such as precariously employed temporary workers or the unemployed. Insider–outsider cleavages tend to affect youth and women workers most negatively. A second source of new inequalities comes from the rising relative wage premium of skills. And a third will emerge if, and once, labor-intensive consumer services grow. The standard trade-off between jobs and inequality, epitomized by the US–Europe comparison, is far too simplistic, but it is difficult to imagine a return to full employment in Europe unless also low-paid and often low-quality service jobs are encouraged.

European industrial relations systems and welfare policy are generally premised on a commitment to wage equality and job security. Hence wage minima, contractual regulations, and high fixed labor costs are difficult to touch. There are two prevailing arguments against a 'low-wage labor market' through de-regulation. The first, and most convincing, is that US-style de-regulation not only creates huge inequalities, but also that it threatens the basic fabric of trust and co-operation built into European models of social partnership. Europe's tradition of broadly negotiated 'efficiency wage' arrangements is, to a great degree, its comparative advantage. The second, and far less convincing, argument is that a low-wage service economy poses a direct threat to families. The defence of existing regulatory practice is often premised on the traditional assumption that families' welfare depends almost exclusively on the wages, job security, and accumulated entitlements of the male breadwinner.

This family model is in rapid extinction. Unfortunately, some of its latter-day successors, like single parent households, are at high risk but much less so if the parent is able to work. Two-income families enlarge the tax-base and minimize the welfare lacunae that prevail when wives' entitlements are derived from the husband. And the dual-earner family is the single best strategy to minimize child poverty. Two earners is moreover an effective household buffer in the eventuality of employment interruptions. It follows that a knowledge-society strategy premised on investments in education *must* be coupled to a recast family policy, the cornerstones of which must be guarantees against child poverty. Such guarantees must center on affordable child and aged care, on adequate child benefits, and on maternity and parental leave arrangements that minimize mothers' employment disruption and maximize their incentive to have children. In the long run, therefore, the most persuasive 'win-win' strategy is to re-direct resources to child families if our goal is to sustain our long-term welfare obligations towards the aged while effectively combating social exclusion.

Whether the externalization of family care is placed in the market or directly furnished by public agencies is unimportant, as long as standards and affordability are guaranteed. [. . .] There [is] a strong case for prioritizing high standard child care services to the weakest families since optimal quality care may offset inequalities that stem from uneven social capital within families.

Life chance guarantees rather than here-and-now equality for all

Any assessment of the pros and cons of heightened labor market inequalities must be premised on a dynamic, life chances perspective and not, as is typically the case, on a static view of fairness and equality. Low-end, low-paid jobs, even at near-poverty wages, are not by definition a welfare problem. The acid test of egalitarianism and justice is not whether such jobs exist or what share of a population is, at any given moment, low-paid. Low-end employment would be compatible with '*Rawlsian*' optimization if it does not affect negatively people's life chances. The issue here is entrapment and mobility chances.

On this score, unfortunately, research has not yet provided much undisputable evidence. We do know that a sizable minority of low-wage workers in the USA remain trapped for many years (a higher rate than is the case in Europe where, comparably, low-wage jobs are much rarer). And those most likely to become trapped are the low-skilled. We also have fairly good evidence that, net of family origins, skills and education constitute the single best guarantee of mobility. Hence, expanding low-wage service jobs in tandem with heavy investment in skills would, for the majority, constitute a win-win policy. The problem lies in the risks of entrapment among the minority which, perhaps, is 'untrainable' or, for various other reasons excluded from mobility. It is precisely for this reason that a 'learning strategy' needs to be accompanied with a basic income guarantee strategy.[15] Nonetheless, the problem of inequality would disappear if the welfare state extends a basic life chances guarantee to citizens: a guarantee of job mobility via education or, alternatively, a guarantee that condemnation to a life of low wages does not imply income poverty throughout the life course.[16]

At the risk of repetition, the greater is the investment in social resources among children, the greater will be the later pay-off in terms of life-long learning abilities and readjustment, and the smaller will be the burden of compensating the 'losers'.

Leisure and work

The kind of 'win-win' scenario presented above appears heavily biased towards work. Notwithstanding sluggish growth, European GDP *per capita* is now 50 percent greater than before the 1970s Oil Shocks. And such wealth ought to translate into more leisure time. [. . .]

Contemporary European political debate is dominated by the controversy over the 35-hour week, promoted for its purported positive effects on job-creation. If, indeed, its main goal is to stimulate employment, the strategy is at best controversial and, at worst, self-defeating. If the goal is to extend leisure time, the question that few have posed is, why focus on weekly or monthly, rather than on life-time distributions of leisure and work?

The irony is that the call for a shorter work-week follows several decades of significant work-time reductions on a yearly and a life-cycle basis. The typical EU member country's annual working hours is now down to 1600–1700 hours, mainly attributable to the spread of part-time work, vacations, holidays, and paid leave arrangements, and – unfortunately – also to unemployment and exclusion from the labor market. Much more dramatic are reductions in life-time employment. The average (male) worker in 1960 would work for roughly 45 years; his contemporary equivalent will work perhaps 35 years. It is not altogether clear to what extent more leisure is voluntary and desired, and to what extent it reflects inability to attain gainful employment. In the case of women, most leisure is often unpaid housework.

Should we favor more leisure on all accounts? Fewer weekly hours, annual hours *and* life-time hours? If so, do we agree on the associated economic opportunity cost? Is it equitable if the cost of leisure for some is shifted onto the shoulders of others? Do our leisure-time arrangements adequately maximize our productive potential? Can we envision alternative, more equitable and efficient, distributions between leisure and work? These are questions that almost no one raises in the current social policy debate, but they are crucial for any consideration of a new welfare order.

To some extent, the prevailing leisure–work mix is due to intended policy effects, like maternity or parental leave. But, to a large extent, it is also due to unintended consequences of policies designed to (or unable to) solve completely different problems. Early retirement and unemployment are obvious examples. Leaving aside 'unwanted' leisure, do we in fact have an adequate understanding of what would be citizens' optimal leisure–work preferences? I think not. Early retirees may be individually content to exit prematurely, given constraints and incentives. But if these incentives are societally harmful and were thus removed, would the desire to exit remain? Would Italian women's employment rates follow Holland's if restrictions against part-time work were eliminated? Or would Dutch women's working hours approach full-time if, as in Scandinavia, affordable day-care were available?

The chief problem is that past policy has resulted in overly rigid leisure–work arrangements that permit individual workers little choice as to how to optimize their own mix. At the same time, work-leisure incentives for some groups are gained at the cost to others. Basically, existing practice reflects a social order that is no longer dominant. We have, so far, bundled free time within the working week, within stip-ulated vacations and holidays, and at the tail end of our lives. If our goal is to optimize life chances in a dynamic sense, such an order may not be compatible with the exigencies of an evolving knowledge society.

Emerging trends in family and labor market behavior suggest that citizens' demand for leisure and work may be spaced out across the life cycle in a radically different manner than so far. The case of paid maternity and parental leave is one of the few examples of policy that seeks to address emerging incompatibilities. A full-fledged 'life-long learning' model will require similar arrangements, namely paid edu-cation or training leaves. There is a strong case to be made in favor of the idea floated within Nordic social democracy in the 1970s [. . .] to re-think the work–leisure mix in terms of life-time 'leisure accounts', that citizens (after a minimum number of contribution years) can draw upon their retirement savings accounts at will, be it for purposes of education, family care-giving, or pure vacation. There is, in principle, no reason why retirement should be concentrated in older ages. A radical version of the win-win scenarios developed above would, in fact, call for the abolition of retirement as we know it and redefine it as an issue of pacing individuals' life course. If some are more risk adverse, they will opt for educational leaves or minimal career inter-ruptions; if some are more induced towards leisure, they will favor interruptions. The bottom line is that citizens have much greater indi-vidual command over how to design their own life course, over how to mix work, education, family, and free time. If the financial con-sequences are transparent, an individual will be able to rationally decide whether the choice of time off at age 35 against one less year of retirement is advantageous or not.

[. . .]

Notes

1   Social transfers account for only 1/3rd of working single mothers' total income in Scandinavia.

2   My own estimates suggest that due to high fixed labor costs and wage compression, full-time, full-year day care in countries such as Germany or Italy costs about half of what an average full-time employed mother can expect to earn. A significant reduction of relative servicing costs can only realistically occur on the backdrop of a radical de-regulation of wages and reduction of fixed labor costs.

3   We usually define the poverty line as less than 50 per cent of median (adjusted) disposable income.

4   Public transfers account for the lion's share of total disposable income in countries like France, Germany and Sweden (70–90 per cent), but far less in others (such as the UK or the USA, where private pension plans and accumulated savings play an important role). Earnings (often undeclared) can play an important role in pensioner income packages. This may be especially pronounced in cases, such as Italy, where early retirement is prevalent and where there exist strong incentives to supply and demand workers who do not need to pay fixed labor costs. Pension schemes are, in some cases, clearly subsidizing the informal economy.

5   In some countries, young families' access to housing depends heavily on inter-generational capital transfers of this kind. M. Kohli: 'Private and public transfers between generations', *European Societies*, vol. 1, 1999, pp. 81–104.

6   To illustrate the point, workers at age (ca) 60 earn 100 per cent of average wage in Denmark and the UK, a full 140% in France, but only 80 per cent in the USA:

Estimated Age–Wage Relativities for Males. 1990. Average = 100

	at age ca. 20–25	at age ca. 50	at age ca. 60
Denmark	85	105	100
France	70	120	140
UK	80	125	100
USA	65	105	80

Source: OECD.

7   The OECD estimates that workers with less than secondary education can expect 5–7 years of unemployment over their lifetime in the UK, Finland and Spain, and between 3 and 5 years in Ireland, Germany, Sweden, France, Belgium, Denmark, and Canada.

8   The same argument holds for privatizing pensions. Just like public insurance schemes, private plans work well for workers with long stable and well-paid careers. Coverage is low among employees in atypical (such as part-time or temporary) employment, and traditional employer occupational pension plans are eroding as a result of the decline of large firms. Encouraging private pensions for the top half of the labor market and limiting public pension commitments to the bottom half of the population is certainly one possible long-term scenario. I assume, however, that such a scenario is not on the political agenda in the large majority of EU countries. Targeting public pensions only to the poor would reduce the public expenditure burden dramatically, but to put it bluntly: why should we construct inequalities in the future when it is not necessary?

Privatization will never qualify as a Paretian welfare improvement. As far as taxing retirement income is concerned, one should clearly avoid too much taxation since this may produce negative savings incentives among pre-retirement workers. If there is inequity in the distribution of resources between the aged and the young, a system of taxing excess incomes among the aged would be acceptable (and more incentive-neutral) if it were earmarked to cover other risks among the elderly (such as disabilities and intensive care needs).

9   Forecast simulations suggest that a move to strictly targeted public pensions (covering the bottom third only) would bring most countries' pension finances into balance by 2050.

10 In the Nordic countries, up to a third of total employment is in the public sector, fueled by social service growth. There, like across the European continent, private consumer services are generally 'priced out of the market' – indeed, they have been declining over the past decades.

11 Individual countries, like Denmark, have experimented with alternative subsidization schemes to induce more consumption of service labor. Often such subsidies are an attempt to avoid that lower-end services end up in the black economy.

12 And, that such deregulation would almost surely have adverse consequences across the entire labor market, not to mention that it would by necessity imply a major roll-back of existing welfare guarantees.

13 Hence, women's average weekly hours of unpaid domestic labor is almost twice as high in Spain as in Denmark.

14 Contemporary national accounts systems are unable to distinguish between social expenditures that play an 'investment role' and those that do not. Parallel to the distinction between capital and consumption accounts, some social expenditures arguably enhance a nation's capital stock and reap a dividend. The actual task is daunting and full of ambiguities, but this is also the case in conventional national economic accounts (should a tank or a jeep for the military be classified as investment or consumption?).

15 Whether such an income guarantee be designed around the Anglo-Saxon formula of work-conditional income supplements or along more traditional social assistance lines is left open.

16 It is very important to distinguish this 'life chances' guarantee from conventional 'guaranteed citizen income' plans that many advocate. Above all, the life chances guarantee is meant to be premised on work and not, like the latter, on the assumption that there will not be sufficient work available. Indeed, the main principle here is to reward the incentive to work. This is not the place to discuss the practical design of such life chance guarantees. Clearly, active training and learning policies will come to play a core role. One might consider a variant of the American 'earned income credit' subsidy, or similar 'negative income tax' models, as a means to guarantee welfare for those who end up trapped in inferior employment.

9

Growth, Redistribution, and Welfare: Toward Social Investment

James Midgley

[. . .]

It is widely accepted today that social welfare and economic development are antithetical notions. Although economic development is about growth, profits, and accumulation, social welfare is about altruism, social rights, and redistribution. Economic development is viewed as a dynamic process that creates wealth and raises standards of living. Social welfare is regarded as a mechanism for redistributing this wealth to fund social services for the poor and the oppressed.

The belief that the purpose of social welfare is to redistribute resources through social policies and programs was widely accepted in the 1950s and 1960s, but it has now been vigorously challenged by the claim that redistributive social expenditures have impeded economic development. Critics of social welfare argue that the resources transferred from the productive economy into unproductive social expenditures are inimical to economic prosperity. They contend that substantial cuts in social expenditures are needed if economic growth is to be sustained. They claim that retrenchments in social welfare will shift the emphasis from consumption to production, mobilize capital for further development, create employment, increase incomes, and raise levels of prosperity.

Advocates of the redistributive welfare model have been thrown into disarray by these arguments. Although they have produced empirical evidence to show that social programs do not, in fact, impede economic growth, their claims have been ignored. Many now recognize that conventional redistributive arguments based on conceptions of need, altruism, and social rights have lost credibility. New ideas that offer a plausible alternative rationale for social welfare, enhance economic development, and have wide electoral appeal are urgently needed.

The social development approach offers a promising opportunity to meet this challenge. This approach seeks to harmonize social policy with economic development and to identify and implement social programs that make a positive contribution to economic growth. By identifying and implementing social programs of this kind, arguments about the deleterious effects of social welfare on the economy become moot, and the case for social welfare becomes compelling. Social development also offers a new rationale for redistribution by advocating the allocation of collective resources for social investments that return resources back to the economy.

[. . .]

Social development: productivism and social investment

As an approach for promoting social welfare, social development seeks specifically to end the bifurcation of social welfare and economic development and to formulate a conception of social policy as productivist and investment oriented, rather than redistributive and consumption oriented.[1] As will be shown, this does not obviate the need for state intervention in social welfare but seeks instead to foster a new conception of redistribution as social investment that generates positive rates of return and continuously feeds resources back into the economy.

The social development approach not only emphasizes productivist social policies and programs but links them to broader attempts to harness the power of economic growth for social ends. Advocates of this approach believe that economic development is a powerful dynamic for progress. However, they also believe that if left alone, economic growth results in conditions of distorted development marked by conspicuous contrasts between wealth and poverty, and the exclusion of substantial numbers of people from participating in the productive economy.[2] For this reason, they advocate interventionist strategies that create employment, raise incomes, and contribute positively to improved standards of living.

Attempts by social development advocates to direct economic development toward social ends are accompanied by attempts to shift the emphasis in social welfare from consumption and maintenance-oriented social programs to those that invest in people and enhance their capacity to participate in the productive economy.[3] Although they recognize that some social welfare clients will never be economically active, they believe that many of those who are currently dependent on social benefits can be brought into the productive economy through appropriate interventions. They also believe that most of those who are currently maintained in dependency, stigmatized, and relegated to the status of second-class citizens would prefer to participate in the productive economy. However, instead of exhortations to find employment and threats of punitive sanctions, advocates argue that efforts are better spent allocating resources that will inculcate the skills needed to become economically active. Creating employment opportunities and providing supports that ensure economic integration are also necessary.[4]

Social development is concerned not only with increasing labor-market participation but with promoting human capital formation, accumulating assets, mobilizing social capital in poor communities, and developing microenterprises. It is also concerned with enhancing the efficiency of social programs to minimize waste and assure cost effectiveness. At a broader level, social development seeks to remove impediments to economic participation, such as racial and gender discrimination, and to create a climate conducive to economic development.[5]

The following examples are intended to illustrate some of the ways in which the notion of productivism and social investment can be implemented in social welfare. These examples are not intended to be an inclusive or definitive list but are designed, rather, to stimulate further debate on how social welfare can be revitalized by adopting an inclusive developmental perspective that ends the compartmentalization of social welfare and economic development. They are listed as discreet examples, but they can obviously be combined to create a comprehensive strategy for promoting social welfare.

Increasing cost effectiveness in social welfare

Like many other public-sector programs, the social services have often been accused of waste, bureaucratic inefficiency, and mismanagement. It is also claimed that they function to fulfill political agendas and serve the interests of bureaucrats. Because these programs are not subjected to the discipline of the market, critics claim that they continue to operate even if they are wasteful and do not attain their stated goals.

These arguments have obvious implications for economic development. The transfer of resources from the productive economy to maintain wasteful social programs is hardly conducive to economic growth, particularly if the volume of resources is large. Although reliable data to support allegations of inefficiency are scarce, many people believe that a substantial proportion of the national product is being spent on wasteful social programs. This belief is being used by the detractors of social welfare to justify both the retrenchment and privatization of these programs.[6]

Although these assertions are often exaggerated, social administrators cannot in all honesty claim that efficiency is an overriding consideration in social welfare. New social programs are often established because of their political appeal or in response to the activities of interest groups, and often they are introduced without the research and the careful design, testing, and experimentation that characterize projects in many other fields. Social data on which to base decisions are frequently disregarded. Evaluation research in social welfare is now well developed, yet relatively few social programs are properly evaluated, and when they are, their findings are often neglected.[7] Because the expertise and technologies needed to ensure efficiency are now available, they should be more widely used. Where they are effectively used, they can make a major difference. For example, studies on the cost effectiveness of probation as an efficient, low-cost alternative to imprisonment demonstrate that it is possible to increase value for money in the social services.[8] All social programs should be evaluated, and attempts to assess their rates of return, as well as contribution to economic development, should be given priority.

Applying cost-effectiveness technologies to social programs is an essential ingredient of the social development approach; however, the political dimension cannot be ignored. Programs are often modified to reduce costs for political purposes even though the longer term costs of these reductions may be very high. Deinstitutionalization undoubtedly saved money by closing expensive mental hospitals, but underfunding community mental health services has exacerbated the problems of neglect, poverty, and homelessness among people suffering from mental illness. A similar scenario is likely in the recent welfare reform initiative, in which political and fiscal considerations have played a much more prominent role in shaping policy than has scientific information about the most effective ways of helping poor clients to become self-sufficient. For these reasons, changes should not be based solely on cost savings, but on the premise that program changes will produce greater returns to investments.

Enhancing human capital investments

Social development advocates believe strongly in social programs that invest in human capital. They have been inspired by economic studies showing that investments in education produce high rates of return not only to individuals but to the economy and greater society.[9] Econometric research on the social rates of return of educational investments is now extensive, and it is generally accepted that economic development requires human capital investments of this kind.[10] Human capital research has also been extended into the fields of health and nutrition, where it is widely believed that these investments promote economic development.[11]

The human capital argument has also been applied to social welfare, particularly in child welfare and services to people with disabilities. For example, many developing countries in Asia have augmented and even replaced conventional remedial child-welfare services with programs that emphasize human investments and community prevention. Abandoning high-cost residential care and other remedial services, social workers use community day-care centers as a focal point for service delivery. These centers educate children and improve their nutrition and health. They also offer opportunities for maternal health education, family planning, and other programs that enhance the status of women. By involving the entire community in child development and maternal health care, these programs invest in human beings and at the same time encourage community involvement in the prevention of child neglect.[12]

Attempts to cater to people with disabilities have also emphasized human capital investments in the form of skills training in vocational and related subjects. Intended to promote economic participation and self-sufficiency, these programs have not always been realistic in preparing people for the job market, and they have often required extensive subsidies. Nor have they always been used effectively. There is a tendency in the industrial countries to underuse programs of this kind and to maintain clients on income support programs. In many developing countries, expensive training workshops that cater only to a small proportion of those in need have been created in urban areas, well away from rural communities where many people with disabilities reside. Often, clients are trained in skills not in demand in the local job market. The need for more appropriate interventions that prepare people for self-employment or cooperative enterprises is now being emphasized. Despite these shortcomings, it is widely accepted that human capital investment programs produce positive rates of return. Future resource allocations should be increasingly committed to social investment programs of this kind.

Promoting social capital formation

Proponents of social development also favor programs that promote social capital. The concept of social capital is still poorly defined, but it is currently being used in civil society analysis to refer to the volume and intensity of cooperative social relationships in communities.[13] Research in the field indicates that enhanced community integration can promote local economic development. In a widely cited book, Robert Putnam and his colleagues found that regions in Italy with well-developed civic traditions have higher rates of economic development than do regions in which social integration is low.[14] This finding suggests that high levels of social capital are positively associated with high rates of economic growth. It also suggests that programs that promote social integration have a positive effect on economic development.

Social workers have long been engaged in community practice with low-income communities, but they have generally focused on social and political activities, neglecting local economic development projects.[15] Although social and political activities are obviously important, community practice must pay more attention to projects that raise incomes and address people's material needs. This does not mean that the conventional roles of community workers need to be abandoned, but rather that traditional community organization skills be focused toward economic development projects. As Michelle Livermore and I suggested, this involves both creating social capital and directing it toward productive activities.[16] We recommend that community workers collaborate more closely with planners and local economic development specialists to create new enterprises (particularly among women and low-income clients), encourage communities to support local enterprises, assist in creating local community development agencies, help establish networks for employment referral, and attract external investment for local economic development.

Social development advocates believe that creating social capital and directing it toward local economic development should form an integral part of all community social work practice. Community activists, who have traditionally sought resources from public agencies for local social programs, should place more emphasis on programs that build networks and stimulate activities that promote economic growth. In the current ideological climate, resources are more likely to be allocated to community projects if they demonstrate a rate of economic return rather than serve political objectives.

Developing individual and community assets

There has been a growing interest in recent years in the role of asset development in social welfare. Inspired by the work of Michael Sherraden, the asset approach promotes personal savings among low-income people through what are known as Individual Development Accounts (IDAs).[17] As an added incentive to save, savings deposited in these accounts are matched by the government. Accumulations can be used for socially approved purposes such as education or housing. Sherraden and other advocates of this approach believe that programs that encourage the poor to save are much more useful than income support programs that simply maintain poor people at basic consumption levels. An asset development approach generates the material resources people need to escape poverty. It also changes attitudes and behavior so that participants gain confidence and a determination to be successful.[18]

Although Sherraden's work has emphasized individual asset development, he recognizes that asset development can also be promoted at the community level. For example, the creation of social infrastructure is a viable form of community asset development.[19] Community development in Africa and other parts of the developing world has historically emphasized projects that combine the efforts of local people with those of public agencies to build local roads, bridges, irrigation and drinking water systems, clinics, schools, and other facilities. Community-held assets are important in that they provide the economic and social base on which development effort depends. They should be integrated with individual asset development programs to form an integral part of a wider social investment strategy.

Facilitating economic participation through productive employment and self-employment

Social programs can also contribute to economic development by assisting low-income people and welfare clients to find productive employment or self-employment. Rather than using scarce resources to maintain needy people on income transfers, the social development approach favors programs that help them to find employment or become self-employed. In this way, they not only earn money but become self-respecting citizens who work, pay taxes, and contribute to economic development.

Programs of this kind have been advocated for many years, but it is only in relatively recent times that they have been widely promoted and implemented. Job training and placement services for people receiving income support were first introduced in the 1960s, but they were underfunded and given little prominence. Employment was given greater emphasis with the enactment of the 1988 Family Support Act, and it has since become a primary element in the recent changes introduced by the Clinton administration. Evaluations of employment programs for welfare recipients show modest improvements in economic participation.[20] Similar programs designed to increase labor market participation among people with disabilities have existed for many years, but studies show that much more needs to be done to enhance client involvement and program effectiveness. This is particularly true of programs for people suffering from mental illness, where the difficulties of placing clients in remunerative employment are particularly challenging.[21]

The use of the tax system to subsidize through tax credits the incomes of those in poorly paid occupations has received widespread bipartisan support and today, many low-income families benefit from these provisions. However, as Joel Handler points out, tax credits are primarily designed to assist the working poor and have not been effectively used to promote employment among the recipients of income support programs.[22] Although the problem [was] addressed by the Clinton administration, which significantly expanded the program to allow AFDC recipients to receive benefits and obtain credits against earned income, further changes to the tax system could encourage more welfare recipients to enter productive employment.

In addition to placing clients in employment in the open labor market, efforts have also been made to create jobs for those in need. Sometimes this has been done in partnership with the private sector, but often, new employment opportunities have been established within the public sector. In some cases, jobs that were previously open have now been set aside for welfare recipients and, in others, welfare recipients have been required to work in voluntary agencies and similar settings in exchange for benefits. Sheltered employment has also been used for those who are unlikely to cope with the demands of the open labor market.

Recently, there is growing interest in the role of microenterprise development as a means of enhancing the economic participation of social service clients. Social workers are playing an increasingly important role in promoting such programs, particularly in Asian countries such as the Philippines, where the government replaced its conventional social assistance program with a microenterprise program for special-needs clients.[23] Similar programs have been introduced in other developing countries and more recently in the United States. Coupled with micro-credit programs, they offer an alternative to conventional income maintenance approaches.[24]

However, it is seldom recognized that these employment and self-employment components of productivist social welfare require substantial investments. Programs that create employment, provide placement and support services, and inculcate the knowledge and skills clients need to participate effectively in the labor market cost money. In addition, supports are needed to ensure long-term success. As is now generally recognized, poorly skilled individuals are not likely to earn incomes that are adequate to meet living costs, child care, transportation, health, and other basic needs. These challenges must be addressed, and welfare-to-work programs must be adequately funded. It is not acceptable that poor clients be exhorted to find work or subjected to coercive threats without adequate investments that can help them to be productive citizens.

Removing barriers to economic participation

If social development is to enhance the participation of social welfare clients in the productive economy, it must also seek to remove the impediments that block economic participation. The poor and social welfare's traditional clients face numerous barriers to economic participation, which must be addressed. As was noted earlier, it is a question of not only having the skills and abilities to find a job but of traveling to work, securing child care, and overcoming numerous other obstacles that impede economic participation.

In addition to these everyday difficulties, more serious and entrenched obstacles to economic participation must also be addressed. These include the institutionalized problems of discrimination based on race and ethnicity, gender, nationality, disability, age, and other factors. Unless these challenges are met, the effectiveness of skills development, job placement, and employment-support programs will continue to be impeded.

Although the United States has probably led the world in developing antidiscriminatory and affirmative action policies, much more needs to be done if barriers to employment are to be eradicated. The recent rise of an anti-affirmative action sentiment is disturbing because it reflects a deeper, underlying belief among many Americans that people who are different from themselves are being unduly favored. These attitudes are particularly troubling with regard to immigrants, who once again face the prospect of being openly discriminated against. Because immigrants have traditionally played a vital role in the American economy, removing barriers to their participation is urgently needed.

Creating a social climate conducive to development

As many economists recognize, economic development does not only depend on conventional economic inputs such as capital, labor, and human skills, but on the wider social and political context in which development takes place. It is obvious that political instability, civil conflict, and institutionalized corruption have been a major cause of economic stagnation in many parts of the world.[25] Many economies have been devastated by conflict. Once prosperous cities such as Beirut have been reduced to ruin by the violence accompanying social fragmentation. Economically viable regions of the former Yugoslavia have been desolated and reduced to poverty by social disintegration. Local economies in many urban areas of the United States have been devastated by the crime and violence arising from poverty and social disorganization.[26]

The extraordinary degree of crime and violence in America is expensive in both human and economic terms. The costs of the wasted human resources associated with crime, drug abuse, violence, and the other manifestations of distorted development that characterize the country's economic growth is huge and a major threat to sustained long-term progress. In addition, the exclusion of a sizable minority of the population from participating in economic development limits productive capacity as well as the ability of the population to consume. Similarly, unemployment not only carries high social costs but reduces consumption among the unemployed that in turn depresses demand with resulting wider negative economic effects. The need for a strategy that reduces these costs and enhances economic participation is only too obvious. By promoting sustained economic development and encouraging participation in the productive economy among all sections of the population, social development seeks to minimize these costs.[27]

Redistribution through social investment

Dwindling electoral support for a redistributive conception of social welfare based on notions of need, altruism, and social rights poses what is arguably the greatest challenge to social policy today. In the absence of an effective alternative rationale, the campaign for abolishing state welfare is likely to gather momentum. The recent so-called welfare reform legislation has seriously undermined the nation's social safety net for poor women and their children, for low-income elderly immigrants, and for children with disabilities. Other social programs are also under attack, and the crusade to privatize Social Security is well underway.

Rather than seeking to defend an unworkable redistributive conception of social welfare, social policy advocates should consider the merits of the social development approach that calls for harmonizing social policy and economic development and offers a conception of redistribution based on investments in people and communities. This approach is not antithetical to traditional social welfare values and ideals but, rather, reframes them in ways that fit current economic, social, and political realities. Social development enhances social rights by increasing economic participation and, by promoting economic participation, it reduces the wide disparities that exist between those who participate in the productive economy and those who do not. [. . .] Social development's attempts to address the obstacles to economic participation are also highly consonant with wider efforts to promote social justice. As shown earlier, social development is concerned with social investments that require resources and inevitably involve redistribution. Conventional social policy approaches advocate redistributive measures for purposes of consumption and maintenance, while social development proponents argue for redistributive measures that promote social investments. Traditional rationales for redistribution based on altruism and social rights have lost their resonance. It remains to be seen whether a redistributive rationale based on social development will have greater appeal.

Notes

This article is a revised version of the Allen T. Burns lecture given at the University of Chicago in October 1997. I am grateful to Jeanne Marsh and the faculty of the School of Social Service Administration for inviting me to give the Burns lecture and to share my ideas with them. Special thanks also to Neil Gilbert, Eileen

Gambrill, Meredith Minkler, Michelle Livermore, and Will Rainford for their helpful comments on earlier drafts of this article.

1   For a detailed account of the social development approach and its history, see James Midgley, *Social Development: The Developmental Perspective in Social Welfare* (Thousand Oaks, Calif.: Sage, 1995). Midgley stresses the Third World origins of the social development approach, pointing out that the term was introduced during colonial times to emphasize the need for social interventions that would support national economic development. The promotion of these programs and the wider linking between economic and social policy has since exerted considerable influence in Third World development circles, particularly in the policies and programs of international development agencies. The view that it is possible to promote economic growth and simultaneously redistribute economic resources in ways that do not impede further growth has been expounded in the literature on Third World development, but especially in Hollis Chenery, Montek Ahluwalia, Clive Bell, John H. Duloy, and Richard Jolly, *Redistribution with Growth* (Oxford: Oxford University Press, 1974).

2   See Midgley (n. 1 above). See also Denny Braun, *The Rich Get Richer: The Rise of Income Inequality in the United States and the World* (Chicago: Nelson-Hall, 1997); Sheldon Danziger and Peter Gottschalk, *America Unequal* (Cambridge, Mass.: Harvard University Press, 1995); Brian Nolan and Christopher T. Whelan, *Resources, Deprivation and Poverty* (Oxford: Clarendon, 1996); Vic George and Irving Howards, *Poverty Amidst Affluence: Britain and the United States* (Aldershot: Edward Elgar, 1991). The concept of social exclusion, which is closely associated with that of distorted development, is being more widely used in European social policy circles today. See Jos Berghman, "The Resurgence of Poverty and the Struggle against Exclusion: A New Challenge for Social Security in Europe," *International Social Security Review* 50, no. 1 (1997): 3–21.

3   This poses a major challenge for social work, which has traditionally been concerned with remediation and maintenance. The challenge is outlined in James Midgley, "Social Work and Social Development: Challenge to the Profession," *Journal of Applied Social Science* 21, no. 1 (1996): 7–14.

4   This approach differs significantly from that of Lawrence Mead, *The New Politics of Poverty: The Non-Working Poor in America* (New York: Basic, 1992), who insists that adequate employment opportunities are available to absorb the poor. It is not a lack of opportunities but rather of an institutionalized culture of indolence that perpetuates an underclass of nonworking people in the United States. Mead advocates using compulsion to insure their integration into the labor market.

5   Social development's productivist focus is more compatible with current economic global realities than conventional social policy approaches. The growing impact of economic globalization and the advent of postindustrial forms of economic organization based on post-Fordist systems of production have significantly altered the economic basis for conventional approaches to social policy. The coming of postindustrial society is said to require the dismantling of the welfare state. However, it can be argued that these economic realities are best accommodated not by retrenchments but by social investments that reduce the numbers of low-skilled people in society and enhance their ability to function effectively in an increasingly competitive economy. For a more detailed dis-

cussion, see Robert Reisch, *The Work of Nations: Preparing Ourselves for 21st Century Capitalism* (New York: Knopf, 1991); Lester Thurow, *Head to Head: The Coming Economic Battle among Japan, Europe and America* (New York: Morrow, 1992), and *The Future of Capitalism: How Today's Economic Forces Shape Tomorrow's World* (New York: Morrow, 1996); Jeremy Rifkin, *The End of Work* (New York: Putnam, 1995).

6 For a discussion, see David Stoesz and James Midgley, "The Radical Right and the Welfare State," in *The Radical Right and the Welfare State* (Savage, Md.: Barnes & Noble, 1991).

7 See Richard A. Berk and Peter H. Rossi, *Thinking about Program Evaluation* (Newbury Park, Calif.: Sage, 1990); Emil J. Posavac and Raymond C. Carey, *Program Evaluation: Methods and Case Studies* (Englewood Cliffs, N.J.: Prentice-Hall, 1989); David Royse, *Program Evaluation: An Introduction* (Chicago: Nelson Hall, 1992); Frederick W. Seidl, "Program Evaluation," in *Encyclopedia of Social Work*, ed. Richard L. Edwards et al., 19th ed. (Washington, D.C.: NASW Press, 1995), pp. 1927–32.

8 David Macarov, *Social Welfare: Structure and Practice* (Thousand Oaks, Calif.: Sage, 1995).

9 As the World Bank notes (*World Development Report, 1991: The Challenge of Development* [Washington, D.C.: 1991]), the economic success of East Asian countries such as Japan, Korea, Singapore, and Taiwan has depended on the population having the skills and knowledge to engage in productive economic activities. Similarly, education increases innovation, entrepreneurship, and productivity. Leading exponents of human capital theory with reference to education include Gary S. Becker, *Human Capital: A Theoretical and Empirical Analysis with Special Reference to Education* (New York: Columbia University Press, 1964); Frederick H. Harbison, *Human Resources as the Wealth of Nations* (London: Oxford University Press, 1973); George Psacharopoulos, *Returns to Education: An International Comparison* (Amsterdam: Elsevier, 1973); Theodore W. Schultz, *The Economic Value of Education* (New York: Columbia University Press, 1963), and *Investing in People: The Economics of Population Quality* (Berkeley and Los Angeles: University of California Press, 1981).

10 Econometric calculations have shown that increases in the numbers of years children attend school add incrementally to both national output and to personal incomes. See George Psacharopoulos (n. 9 above). See also George Psacharopoulos, *Returns to Investment in Education: A Global Update* (Washington, D.C.: World Bank, 1992).

11 Brian Abel-Smith and Alcira Leiserson, *Poverty, Development, and Health Policy* (Geneva: World Health Organization, 1978); World Bank, *World Development Report, 1993: Investing in Health* (Washington, D.C., 1993). The role of public health in boosting agricultural production had already been demonstrated in the 1960s with reference to malaria eradication campaigns in Asia. See Robin Barlow, "The Economic Effects of Malaria Eradication," *American Economic Review* 57, no. 2 (1967): 130–48.

12 Midgley, "Social Work and Social Development" (n. 3 above).

13 James Coleman, "Social Capital in the Creation of Human Capital," *American Journal of Sociology* 94, no. 2 (1988): S95–S120; Robert Putnam, "Bowling Alone: America's Declining Social Capital," *Journal of Democracy* 6, no. 1 (1995): 65–78.

14   Robert D. Putnam, with Roberto Leonardi and Raffaella Y. Nanetti, *Making Democracy Work: Civic Traditions in Modern Italy* (Princeton, N.J.: Princeton University Press, 1993).

15   This is not true of many African countries, where community development has historically focused on economic projects. As James Midgley and Peter Simbi suggest in "Promoting a Development Focus in the Community Organization Curriculum: Relevance of the African Experience" (*Journal of Social Work Education* 29, no. 3 [1993]: 269–78), community workers in the United States have much to learn from African colleagues in promoting social economic development.

16   James Midgley and Michelle Livermore, "Social Capital and Local Economic Development: Implications for Community Social Work Practice," *Journal of Community Practice* 5, no. 1/2 (1998): 29–40.

17   Michael Sherraden, *Assets and the Poor: A New American Welfare Policy* (Armonk, N.Y.: M. E. Sharpe, 1991).

18   Ibid. See also Guatam N. Yadama and Michael Sherraden, "Effects of Assets on Attitudes and Behaviors: Advance Test of a Social Policy Proposal," *Social Work Research* 20, no. 1 (1996): 3–11.

19   Midgley, *Social Development* (n. 1 above).

20   Numerous evaluations of employment training and placement programs for recipients of income support have been undertaken. For an overview, see Daniel Friedlander and Gary Burtless, *Five Years After: The Long-Term Effects of Welfare-to-Work Programs* (New York: Russell Sage Foundation, 1995). A major impediment to greater success is the persistence of a culture of eligibility compliance within social service agencies rather than one designed to support clients to attain self-sufficiency. For a discussion see Mary Jo Bane and David Ellwood, *Welfare Realities: From Rhetoric to Reform* (Cambridge, Mass.: Harvard University Press, 1994).

21   Studies by the U.S. General Accounting Office show that employment training and placement programs are still underused primarily because of the emphasis placed on eligibility determination rather than on rehabilitation. See, e.g., General Accounting Office, *People with Disabilities: Federal Programs Could Work Together More Efficiently to Promote Employment* (Washington, D.C.: U.S. Government Printing Office, 1996), and *Social Security: Disability Programs Lag in Promoting Return to Work* (Washington, D.C.: U.S. Government Printing Office, 1997). The recent Personal Responsibility and Work Opportunity Reconciliation Act of 1996 (PL 104–193) places enormous emphasis on employment, but it is doubtful that sufficient resources will be made available to train or place recipients in employment. For a discussion, see Martha Ozawa and Stuart Kirk, "Welfare Reform," *Social Work Research* 20, no. 4 (1996): 194–95; and Dennis Poole, "Welfare Reform: The Bad, the Ugly, and the Maybe Not So Awful," *Health and Social Work* 21, no. 4 (1996): 243–46.

22   Joel F. Handler, *The Poverty of Welfare Reform* (New Haven, Conn.: Yale University Press, 1995). The problem is vividly described by Kathryn Edin and Laura Lein, *Making Ends Meet: How Single Mothers Survive Welfare and Low Wage Work* (New York: Russell Sage Foundation, 1997). They found that many of the welfare recipients they interviewed did not report income from employment because punitive benefit reductions would reduce them to destitution.

23   Angela Reidy, "Welfarists in the Market," *International Social Work* 24, no. 2 (1981): 36–46.

24   Steven Balkin, *Self Employment for Low-Income People* (New York: Praeger, 1989); John F. Else and Salome Raheim, "AFDC Clients as Entrepreneurs: Self-Employment Offers an Important Option," *Public Welfare* 50, no. 4 (1992): 36–41; Michelle Livermore, "Social Work, Social Development, and Microenterprises: Techniques and Issues for Implementation," *Journal of Applied Social Sciences* 21, no. 1 (1996): 37–46.

25   The World Bank, *World Development Report, 1997: The State in a Changing World* (Washington, D.C.: World Bank, 1997) emphasizes the role of the state in dealing with crime and violence and creating stable conditions for economic development. See also Edward N. Muller, "Income Inequality, Regime Repressiveness and Political Violence," *American Sociological Review* 50, no. 1 (1985): 47–61.

26   Conditions in many urban areas have been captured by the imagery associated with the concept of the underclass, which has gained currency in sociological and popular circles. See William Julius Wilson, *The Truly Disadvantaged: The Inner City, the Underclass, and Public Policy* (Chicago: University of Chicago Press, 1987), and William Julius Wilson, ed., *The Ghetto Underclass* (Thousand Oaks, Calif.: Sage, 1993); William Kelso, *Poverty and the Underclass* (New York: New York University Press, 1994). See also Judith R. Blau and Peter M. Blau, "The Costs of Inequality: Metropolitan Structure and Violent Crime," *American Sociological Review* 47, no. 1 (1982): 114–29; Steven F. Messner, "Economic Discrimination and Societal Homicide Rates: Further Evidence on the Costs of Inequality," *American Sociological Review* 54, no. 4 (1989): 597–611.

27   Drawing on the earlier work of A. C. Pigou, Richard Titmuss (*Social Policy: An Introduction* [London: Allen & Unwin, 1974]), argued that social policy should redress the social costs associated with economic development. These include the costs of pollution, of injuries sustained during employment, and the costs of unemployment. Titmuss showed that the burden of letting these costs lie where they fall are very high. More recent studies have echoed this finding. In their study of mortality rates in 30 U.S. cities, Mary Merva and Richard Fowles established a clear link between health conditions and adverse economic conditions. They revealed that rising unemployment between 1990 and 1992 was responsible for significant increases in morbidity and mortality, which were harmful in not only human but economic terms. See Mary Merva and Richard Fowles, *Effects of Diminished Economic Opportunity on Social Stress* (Washington, D.C.: Economic Policy Institute, 1992).

10

Does Equality Matter?

Ronald Dworkin

Equality is the endangered species of political ideals. A few decades ago any politician who claimed to be liberal, or even centrist, endorsed the ideal of a truly egalitarian society, at least as a utopian goal. But now even self-described left-of-center politicians reject the very idea of equality. They say they represent a "new" liberalism or a "third way" of government, and though they emphatically reject the "old" right's creed of callousness, which leaves people's fates to the verdict of an often cruel market, they also reject what they call the "old" left's stubborn assumption that citizens should share equally in their nation's wealth.

This "new" doctrine declares, against the "old" right, that society should ensure that every citizen who is willing to work if he can has adequate nutrition, housing, education and medical care for himself and his dependents. The community, they insist, must achieve that "sufficiency" for everyone. But it also declares, against the "old" left, that equality is a false goal, because once those minimal standards are met, government has no further obligation to make people equal in anything. It is not the fault of government, on this view, when some people grow rich while others remain at the basic level sufficient for a decent if frugal life.

Does a political community owe only "sufficiency" and not equality to its members? That might seem a pointless or at least premature question, because even the prosperous democracies are very far from providing a decent minimal life for every member. Should we not concentrate on that lesser requirement, ignoring, at least for the foreseeable future, the more demanding one of strict equality? But that strategy might well be self-defeating. Once it is conceded that the comfortable members of a community do not owe the uncomfortable equality, but only some decent minimum standard of living, then too much turns on the essentially unanswerable question of how minimum a standard is decent, and the comfortable are unlikely to give too demanding an answer. Replacing "equality" with "sufficiency", in the rhetoric of long-term political aims, is likely to put paid to any genuine attempt even to secure the latter.

So it is not premature to challenge the growing orthodoxy against equality. Why has that virtue suddenly attracted a bad name? The answer lies in the popularity, in the middle of the last century, of a confused account of what equality means: much of today's hostility to equality is actually hostility to a misunderstood version of it. Some parties of the left, and some academic socialists and liberals, did seem to suppose that genuine equality means that everyone must have the same wealth, at every moment in his life, no matter whether he chooses to work or what work he chooses – that government must constantly take from the ants and give to the grasshoppers. That flat, indiscriminate, version of equality is easily mocked and easily rejected. There is nothing to be said for a world in which those who choose leisure, though they could work, are rewarded with the produce of the industrious.

But if genuine equality does not mean that everyone has the same wealth, no matter what, then what does it mean? There is no straightforward or uncontroversial answer to that question. Equality is a contested concept: people who praise or disparage it disagree about what it is they are praising or disparaging. The correct account of equality is itself a difficult philosophical issue: philosophers have defended a variety of answers. Would it not be wise, then, to follow the new fashion, and abandon equality as an abstract ideal, just for that reason? If we cannot agree whether true equality means equality of opportunity, for example, or of outcome, or something altogether different, then why should we continue to puzzle about what it is? Why not just ask, directly, whether a decent society should aim that its citizens have the same wealth, or that they have the same opportunities, or only that they have "sufficient" wealth to meet minimal needs? Why not forget about equality in the abstract, and focus instead on these apparently more precise and tractable issues?

We cannot forget about equality. We cannot abandon the abstract ideal because the most fundamental commitment of a legitimate political community – a commitment on which its legitimacy depends – is itself an abstract egalitarian commitment. No government is legitimate that does not show equal concern for the fate of all the people over whom it claims dominion and from whom it claims allegiance, and it is imperative that we consider together, as theorists and as citizens, the practical implications of that undeniable political responsibility. We must explore and debate, for example, what distribution of a community's resources and opportunities is consistent or inconsistent with its equal concern for all.

For the distribution of property and liberty among the citizens of a political community is the product of a legal order. That distribution massively depends on which laws the community has enacted – not only its laws governing ownership, theft, contract and tort, but its tax law, labor law, civil rights law, environmental regulation law, and laws of practically everything else – and also depends on how those laws are enforced by the executive departments of government and interpreted by the judicial departments. When government enacts or sustains one set of such laws rather than another, or when it enforces or interprets those laws in one way rather than another, or when it declines to change the laws in place or the standing enforcement or interpretation of these, it fixes, to a considerable extent, the opportunities that different citizens have to lead the lives they want. On any such occasion it is not only predictable that the government's action or inaction will improve the position of some citizens and worsen that of others, but even, to a considerable degree, which citizens' positions will be improved or worsened. In the prosperous democracies it is generally predictable, for example, whenever government curtails welfare programs, that its decision will make the bleak lives of poor people bleaker still. We must be prepared to explain, to those who suffer in that way, how they have nevertheless been treated with the equal concern to which they are entitled. If we cannot – if we must concede that they have not been treated with equal concern – then we must try to identify what changes would erase that unforgivable stain on the legitimacy of our community, and work toward those changes.

That is why we worry – and need to worry – about what equality is, and how it can be secured. Of course, we need not use the word "equality" to name our concern: we might invent a different term to name the ideal we are trying to explore. But there seems no point in that: we might as well use the right name, if only to emphasize that sufficiency is not equality. If some political community really did succeed in guaranteeing the material means for a decent life to even its poorest citizens, but allowed some citizens to become rich, and to have the opportunity not just for a minimally decent life but for a fascinating one, the question would remain whether that result was consistent with equal concern for all.

What policies of a twenty-first century mature democracy would meet the requirements of equal concern? Of course, a full answer would be unmanageably complex, because a full answer would require a description of thousands of laws and policies, and these would be different for each distinct political community because each has its own particular history, traditions, and economic, political and other circumstances. But we can hope intelligibly to describe the central features of a theory of equality, and usefully to illustrate and elaborate those central features through a discussion of the concrete and divisive issues that now occupy a particular political community.

That large project has two parts. We must pursue it in political philosophy, because we must be able to state, with the rigor required in the discipline, a coherent account of our ideal. But we must also be ready, indeed anxious, to test our theories against actual political problems and controversies, including the great national debates over health care provision, welfare programs, electoral reform, affirmative action, and genetic experimentation. We must, that is, work not only outside-in, from general philosophy to more detailed theories, but also inside-out, from concrete political issues toward the theoretical structures we need responsibly to confront those issues.

I emphasize this interdependence of theory and practical controversy because I believe it important that political philosophy responds to politics. I do not mean that political philosophers should avoid theoretical complexity. We should not hesitate to follow an argument that begins in practical politics into whatever more abstract arenas of political philosophy, or even philosophy in its more general parts, that we are driven to explore before we can achieve what strikes us as a satisfactory intellectual resolution, or at least as satisfactory a resolution as we feel able to reach. But it is important that the argument that ends in general philosophy should have begun in our life and experience, because only then is it likely to have the right shape, not only finally to help us, but also finally to satisfy us that the problems we have followed into the clouds are, even intellectually, genuine not spurious.

I emphasize the need for inside-out thinking for a further reason as well: to introduce another, yet more abstract, level of argument: we must aim to show how the central themes of a theory of equality can be located in a more general account of the humane values of ethics and morality, of the status and integrity of value, and the character and possibility of objective truth. We should hope for a plausible theory of the central political values – of democracy, liberty, and civil society as well as of equality – that shows each of these growing out of and reflected in all of the others, an account that conceives equality not only as compatible with liberty but as a value someone who prized liberty would also therefore prize, and that takes liberty to be what someone who is egalitarian in the responsibility-protecting way would want it to be. We should hope, moreover, for theories of all these that show them to respect even more basic commitments about the value of a human life and about each person's responsibility to realize that value in his own life. These aims, I know, are contrary in spirit to two of the most powerful contemporary influences on liberal theory: the political liberalism of John Rawls and the value pluralism of Isaiah Berlin. They nevertheless seem to me to describe the most appropriate next program for contemporary political morality.

Two humanist principles (which I have called the principles of ethical individualism) seem to me fundamental to any such comprehensive liberal theory, and though I cannot discuss these principles, or their impact on such a theory, in any detail here, it may be helpful briefly to describe them and to suggest how, together, they shape and support an appealing account of equality. The first of these is the principle of equal importance: from an objective point of view, it is important that human lives be successful rather than wasted, and equally important for each human life. The second is the principle of special responsibility: though we must all recognize the equal objective importance of the success of a human life, one person has a special and final responsibility for that success, namely the person whose life it is.

The principle of equal importance does not claim that human beings are the same or equal in anything: not that they are equally rational, or good, or that the lives they create are equally valuable. The equality in question attaches not to any property of people but to the importance of their lives coming to something rather than being wasted. The consequences of that importance for the rightness or wrongness of anyone's behavior is a further question, moreover. If I accept the principle of equal importance, I cannot say, as a reason why my children or neighborhood or race should receive special advantage or treatment, that it is objectively more important that they or we prosper than that others do. I cannot even offer that proposition as a reason why I should pay more attention to my daughter's welfare than to yours. But of course I may have other reasons that explain why I should: for example, that she is my daughter. In some circumstances, however, the principle of equal importance has a very strong implication for conduct. The most important of these is the political context: a democratic government must take the objective point of view towards the fate of its own citizens, and the principle that from that perspective each citizen's fate is a matter of equal importance is the most important source of the political requirement of equal concern that I mentioned earlier.

The principle of special responsibility is neither metaphysical nor sociological. It does not deny that psychology or biology can provide causal explanations of why different people choose to live as they do choose, or that such choices are influenced by culture or education or material circumstance. The principle is rather relational: it insists that so far as choices are to be made about what would count as a successful life for a particular person, within whatever range of choice is permitted by resource and culture, he is responsible for making those choices himself. The principle does not endorse any choice of ethical value. It does not condemn a life that is traditional and unexciting, or one that is novel and eccentric, so long as that life has not been forced upon someone by the judgment of others that it is the right life for him to lead.

The general theory of equality that we need would respect both those principles. The first principle demands that people's fate be, so far as government can achieve this, insensitive to who they are – their backgrounds, gender, race or particular sets of skills and handicaps. The second principle demands that their fate be, again so far as government can achieve this, sensitive to the choices they have made. I make no assumption that people choose their convictions or preferences, or their personality more generally, any more than they choose their race or physical or mental abilities. But I do suppose – as almost all of us in our own lives do suppose – that we are ethically responsible for the consequences of the choices we make out of those convictions or preferences or personality.

I said earlier that many politicians are now anxious to endorse what they call a "new" liberalism, or a "third" way between the old rigidities of right and left. These descriptions are often criticized as merely slogans lacking substance. The criticism is often justified, but the appeal of the slogans nevertheless suggests something important. The old egalitarians insisted that a political community has a collective responsibility to show equal concern for all its citizens, but they defined that equal concern in a way that ignored those citizens' personal responsibilities. Conservatives – new and old – have insisted on that personal responsibility, but they defined it so as to ignore that collective responsibility. We need not choose between these two mistakes. We can achieve a unified account of equality and responsibility that not only respects both values, but explains each in terms of the other. If that is the third way, then it should be our way.

11

The Question of Inequality

Anthony Giddens

Social democrats must revise not only their approach to, but also their concept of, equality in the wake of the decline of socialism. On the face of things, nothing would seem more obvious, yet many on the more traditional left seem to accept this only grudgingly. There is no future for the 'egalitarianism at all costs' that absorbed leftists for so long. Michael Walzer has put the point very well:

> Simple equality of that sort is the bad utopianism of the old left . . . politi-
> cal conflict and the competition for leadership always make for power
> inequalities and entrepreneurial activity always makes for economic
> inequalities . . . None of this can be prevented without endless tyran-
> nical interventions in ordinary life. It was an historical mistake of large
> proportions, for which we [on the left] have paid heavily. . . .[1]

The contemporary left needs to develop a dynamic, life-chances approach to equality, placing the prime stress upon equality of opportunity. Modernizing social democrats also have to find an approach that reconciles equality with pluralism and lifestyle diversity, recognizing that the clashes between freedom and equality to which classical liberals have always pointed are real. Equality of opportunity, of course, has long been a theme of the left and has been widely enshrined in policy, especially in the field of education. Yet many on the left have found it difficult to accept its correlates – that incentives are necessary to encourage those of talent to progress and that equality of opportunity typically creates higher rather than lower inequalities of outcome. Equality of opportunity also tends to produce high levels of social and cultural diversity, since individuals and groups have the chance to develop their lives as they see fit.

Rather than seeking to suppress these consequences we should accept them. Social democrats should be happy to acknowledge that this position brings them closer to ethical liberalism than many used to think. [. . .]

T. H. Green, Leonard Hobhouse, and others who thought like them distanced themselves from socialism and took an affirmative attitude towards market mechanisms. Economic competition is desirable, Hobhouse argued, but it presumes community and cooperation, which must have an ethical base. Government and the state shouldn't 'feed, house, or clothe' its citizens, but should 'secure conditions upon which its citizens are able to win by their own efforts all that is necessary to a full civic efficiency'.[2] There are reciprocal obligations, Hobhouse emphasized, between the individual and government; public and private concerns have to be in balance.

The ethical liberals insisted that the state should not undermine personal autonomy. Arnold Toynbee stressed that voluntary organizations – such as Toynbee Hall – should be developed so as to cultivate people's personal capabilities. Education, understood in a broad sense rather than purely vocationally, was to be the main instrument in cultivating initiative and responsibility.

These ideas have a clear affinity with some of the themes of contemporary third way politics. Yet the third way isn't, and can't be, just a reversion to ethical liberalism. The ethical liberals wrote before, or during, the rise of socialism as a major political force, whereas we are living after its demise. We have to construct policies of social justice that respond to the causes of that demise, which have created quite different exigencies from those of the past.

Here more recent authors are more instructive than the ethical liberals. Amartya Sen's concept of 'social capability' makes an appropriate starting-point.[3] Equality and inequality don't just refer to the availability of social and material goods – individuals must have the capability to make effective use of them. Policies designed to promote equality should be focused upon what Sen calls the 'capability set' – the overall freedom a person has to pursue his or her well-being. Disadvantage should similarly be defined as 'capability failure' – not only loss of resources, but loss of freedom to achieve.

Freedom defined as social capability isn't close to the self-seeking agent presumed in neoliberal economic theory. Individuals, as the communitarians say, exercise freedom precisely through their membership of groups, communities and cultures. It is not only individual choice that is at the core of pluralism, but also the diversity of cultures and groups to which individuals belong.

Equality and inequality revolve around self-realization. Apart from where people lack even the minimal requirements for physical survival, the same is true of poverty. What matters isn't economic deprivation as such, but the consequences of such deprivation for individuals' well-being. People who choose to live frugally are in quite a different position from those whose existence is blighted by unwanted poverty. A similar principle applies in terms of the life cycle. A person who is temporarily impoverished, but who, for whatever reason, is able to break free from poverty, is in a different situation from those mired in poverty in the long term.

A further example is unemployment. An individual who is unemployed might be living in a society that pays high levels of social security. Although economically in the same position as someone in work, or close to it, that person might be worse off in terms of well-being, because enforced unemployment is widely associated with lack of self-esteem and with the 'oppression of surplus time'.

An emphasis on equality of opportunity, it should be made clear, still presumes redistribution of wealth and income. There are several reasons why, but two are worth mentioning in particular.[4] One is that since equality of opportunity produces inequality of outcome, redistribution is necessary because life-chances must be reallocated across the generations. Without such redistribution, 'one generation's inequality of outcome is the next generation's inequality of opportunity'.[5] A second is that there will always be people for whom opportunities will necessarily be limited, or who are left behind when others do well. They should not be denied the chance to lead fulfilling lives.

With these various points in mind, we can move to look briefly at the basic statistics of inequality in contemporary societies.

Comparing inequalities

It is generally accepted that inequalities of income and wealth declined in most industrial countries over the period from 1950 to 1970. Since the early 1970s they have risen again in the majority of developed societies, although not in all. As measured by the official statistics at least, the developed countries differ considerably in terms of inequality. Those having the highest levels of income equality include the Nordic countries, Belgium and Japan. In the middle are societies such as the UK, France, the Netherlands and Germany. Countries with the highest degree of income inequality, as measured by official statistics, are the US, Israel, Italy and Australia.

The US appears as the most unequal of all industrial countries in terms of income distribution. The proportion of income taken by the top 1% has increased substantially over the past two or three decades, while those at the bottom have seen their average incomes stagnate or decline. Defined as 50% or less of median income, poverty in the US in the early 1990s was five times as great as in Norway or Sweden – 20% for the US, as compared to 4% for the other two countries. The incidence of poverty in Canada and Australia is also high, at 14% and 13% respectively.

Although the average level of income inequality in the European Union countries is lower than in the US, poverty is widespread in the EU according to official figures and measures. Using the criterion of half or less of median income, 57 million people were living in poverty in the EU nations in 1998. About two-thirds of these were in the largest societies: France, Italy, the UK and Germany.

Economic inequality, by and large, has been on the increase, but it would be misleading just to say bluntly, as some do, that the industrial countries have become more unequal than they once were. In some countries – Italy is one example – inequality has gone down, as measured by the usual statistics. Moreover, since 1996 the trend towards increasing income inequality in the US has been reversed. The numbers living below the poverty line have also dropped. In 1998 there were nearly 5 million fewer people in poverty than in 1992. The incomes of blacks and Hispanics in the US rose by 15% over that period.

There are other changes that run counter to increasing inequality. For example, in economic as well as social and cultural terms women have become much more equal to men than they used to be. 'Social egalitarianism', as measured in opinion surveys, has also increased. As one observer puts it: 'In my perception, people now care more rather than less about equality. They are more insistent on their standing as equals (what makes him think he is better than I? What makes her think she can tell me what to do?), less prepared to accept a subordinate position or believe everything the authorities say.'[6] In most industrial countries socially stigmatized groups, such as gays, or the disabled, have made progress towards full social acceptance.

The consequences of such changes are complex. The fact that children and women are now over-represented among the poor, for instance, partly reflects the wider gains that women as a whole have made. There are more single mothers than before, and single mothers on average have lower incomes than their married or coupled counterparts. At least one of the reasons for the rise in numbers of single-parent households is the increasing autonomy of women. Women actively leave unsatisfactory marriages more often than they were able to do before; and the number of never-married women with children has climbed.

The orthodox statistics about inequality and poverty are collected in the aggregate from year to year, and provide no data on shifts in individuals' economic circumstances across the life cycle. Until recently, we simply didn't know much about such shifts. Most approaches have assumed that poverty is a long-term condition. Even researches involving in-depth studies of individuals have nearly all been concerned with movement into poverty, rather than out of it. Only those currently in poverty are usually interviewed or studied. In addition, a good deal of research has concentrated upon groups unrepresentative of the poor as a whole, such as people living in inner-city ghetto areas – where poverty is often of long duration.

Recent research has suggested we should alter our way of thinking about poverty and the policies aimed at reducing it. Data from a number of countries show that, for the majority who experience it, poverty is not a permanent condition demanding long-term social assistance programmes. A surprising number of people escape from poverty – but a greater number than used to be thought also experience poverty at some point in their lives. Using the definition of 50% or under of median equivalent income, researchers in Germany found that over 30% of West Germans were poor for at least one year between 1984 and 1994. This figure is three times the maximum number of poor in any one year.[7] Those who moved out of poverty mostly did not become stuck just above the poverty line. They reached a level of two-thirds of the national average when they were not poor. However, more than half returned to poverty during at least one year over the ten-year period.

A study carried out in the UK interviewed a national sample of adults each year from 1991 to 1996, to investigate shifts in income. The researchers found a great deal of income mobility, most of it short-range. Just over a third became poor for at least one year over the period.[8] 'Time is not simply the medium in which poverty occurs', one contributor observes, 'it forges its very nature.'[9] Research carried out by the Organization for Economic Cooperation and Development compared the US, UK, Germany and Canada.[10] The results showed that 20–40% of the population were in poverty for at least one year over a six-year period. Most were poor only for short spells. 2–6% remained poor over the whole period. However, because of their long stay in poverty, they made up fully a third of the total time all individuals spent below the poverty line. Contrary to the 'static statistics', the research showed that a higher percentage of people experienced poverty in Germany than in the other countries.

Disentangling the causes of increasing economic inequality is not easy. Only a few studies have investigated the issue in a detailed and systematic way, most of them coming from the United States. The results, however, are interesting and important. According to such research, in spite of the forcefulness with which the argument is sometimes pressed, free trade seems the least important influence. Skilled workers in the industrial countries are supposedly at an increasing disadvantage when compared to their counterparts elsewhere, who will work for much lower wages. Hence wages are driven down in the developed economies, and job opportunities become fewer. However, disparities of income have not grown only, or even primarily, in industries where trade is important, suggesting other factors are at work. Moreover, if the thesis were correct, the share of world commodity trade held by the industrial countries should have declined significantly over the past two decades. In fact, this hasn't happened. The proportion taken by the most developed countries has grown rather than shrunk. Ireland, Portugal and Austria, among others, have greatly increased their share. Even those which have lost out in relative terms, such as the UK, Sweden, or France, are exporting as much as they did twenty years ago.

The same applies to industrial output. The proportion held by the affluent countries, at 80%, has declined only slightly since 1980. Over this period, production for the world as a whole has doubled, while the Asian countries, particularly China, have vastly increased their output. Since the world economy as a whole has expanded, the continued share held by the industrial countries has proved compatible with increased production elsewhere. The East Asian successes have not happened at the expense of Western industrial workers. The West exports more to them than they do in return, as is true of the relation between Western manufacture and Third World countries as a whole.

Technological change is more important than global free trade. The spread of information technology leads to a declining demand for unqualified workers, whose job opportunities and wages therefore also decline. At the same time, those with skills or a strong educational background are able to increase their productivity and their earning power, pulling further away. One of the most in-depth studies we have suggests that technological change also accounts for part, but only part, of the increased income inequality observable in the US over the period 1990–6.[11] Most of that increase, the research concludes, is due to the other factors – demographic trends, changing work patterns in families and growing inequalities coming from non-labour sources, particularly capital assets. Less than 30% of the overall rise in inequality in the US between 1969 and 1992 is accounted for by earnings inequality among men in work. There are increasingly affluent members of two-earner families plus childless people who are economically successful. Houses, shares and pension funds, rising in value over the period, have added to their prosperity.

Taxation and redistribution

Social democracy traditionally has a straightforward and morally compelling solution to inequality: take from the rich and give to the poor. Can such a formula still be applied today? The answer is that it can and should be. Modernizing social democrats should accept the core importance of progressive taxation as a means of economic redistribution.

Taking from the rich to give to the poor, however, isn't the simple and sovereign solution it seems to be on the surface. A diversity of problems has to be confronted.

1   We first have to decide who 'the rich' are. In the case of Bill Gates and other billionaires this doesn't cause too many difficulties. So far as income tax is concerned, however, the category of 'the rich' has to include large numbers of the merely affluent if it is to generate significant revenue and have a substantial redistributive effect. We also have to consider the factor of upward mobility. Bill Gates made his money from nothing. The possibility of becoming very wealthy is presumably not something that should be denied to people, since it may motivate exceptional talent. Moreover, even taking a good deal of Gates's wealth away from him wouldn't help others very much. The extent of his earnings partly reflects the greatly enlarged size of modern economies. A magnate like J. P. Morgan held a level of wealth that meant something in the US economy. At one point he had sufficient liquid capital to finance all the capital needs in America for four months. He owned less than a third of the assets Bill Gates has. Yet Bill Gates's money could finance the current American economy for only part of a single day.

2   It is no longer feasible, or desirable, to have very steeply graduated income tax of the sort that existed in many countries up to thirty or so years ago. All countries have pulled back from such a practice, although some have done so more radically than others. To some extent, this change has been enforced – the better-off sections of the electorate have become resistant to paying very high tax rates. High rates of income tax hence increase levels of tax evasion, a phenomenon

pointed to in the celebrated Laffer curve. Lowering taxes in some contexts can lead to an increase in tax revenue. One certainly cannot
assume that higher tax rates always result in higher tax revenues. A
luxury tax on boats introduced in 1991 in the US resulted in a dramatic
fall in revenues as the entire luxury boat industry nearly disappeared.
Just as important as these considerations is the fact that steeply
graduated income tax can act as a disincentive, penalizing effort and
therefore job creation and economic prosperity.

3   Social democrats should therefore rid themselves of the idea that
most social problems can be resolved through increasing taxes to the
greatest extent possible. In some situations the reverse theorem applies
– tax cuts can both make economic sense and contribute to social
justice. If carefully applied, tax cuts can increase supply-side investment, creating more profit and more disposable income. A bigger tax
base is thereby created in the economy as a whole. Other tax-cutting
strategies, such as the Earned Income Tax Credit pioneered by the New
Democrats in the US, can also be brought into play.

4   Fiscal policy has become inseparable from processes of reform of
government and the state. Governments can no longer 'take' taxes from
their citizens without ensuring that the revenue is spent effectively, in
a framework of transparency. Research shows that in most EU countries as well as in the US, a majority of the population feels that the
government 'wastes a great deal of taxpayers' money'. This is one of
the reasons many give for being prepared to engage in tax evasion. In
a survey in Germany, 70% said they would consider 'a major violation'
of the tax laws if the opportunity was there, on the grounds that the
government squanders the revenues it derives from taxation.[12]

5   We have to decide exactly how best to help the poor and the less
privileged. There is a general relation between economic equality and
levels of spending on the welfare state. The Scandinavian countries,
which spend more than most others, are the most egalitarian. Yet it does
not follow that spending more on existing welfare systems will help to
alleviate inequality. The Scandinavian welfare state has its own specific
difficulties. As Gøsta Esping-Andersen says of Sweden, 'from left to
right, most analysts of the Swedish model now concur that the
extremely egalitarian wage structure gives disincentives to work additional hours, or to augment skills and education. The marginal wage
gain is simply too low.'[13] Sweden does not do well in international statistics in terms of its average levels of schooling and educational attainment. As mentioned earlier, it is also one of the very few Western
countries to have suffered an absolute decline in terms of net jobs
created over the past twenty years.

Assessing and comparing different taxation systems, especially in terms of their redistributive effects, is a complex task. Some general conclusions relevant to policy, however, can be drawn. Comparison of Western countries shows that in all of them the tax and transfer system does have redistributive effects. Sweden stands at the top: its tax and transfer system reduces inequality by 50% from market income to disposable net income. The US is lowest, with a reduction of 20%. The UK and Australia have reductions of around 25%, Finland 30%, Denmark and Germany 40%.

Taxes and transfers combine in various permutations to produce these consequences. One study looked at two aspects of income tax in this respect – level of taxation and progressiveness.[14] For example, the Australian income tax system in the mid-1980s was steeply progressive, but had relatively low overall levels of taxation. The Swedish tax system, by contrast, had considerably higher taxation levels, but a low degree of progressiveness. Much the same was true of Denmark. The Nordic welfare states, together with Germany, have a more universal social transfer system, with high benefit levels. The researchers concluded that levels of taxation, coupled to social transfers, are more important sources of redistribution than the degree of progressiveness of income tax. The Nordic welfare states create a significant transfer of income to households with low market incomes, but also to those with higher incomes too. Australia and the UK are the only two countries where the income tax system is more important than the social transfer system in reducing economic inequality.

The implications of all this are fairly clear, although not easy to implement. Social democrats in all countries need to sustain a substantial tax base, if public and welfare policies are to be funded and economic inequality kept under control. They need to do so in the context of the reform and further democratization of the state itself. Progressive income tax needs to play a role in reducing inequalities, but it is neither sensible nor necessary to try to return to the steeply progressive systems of the past. In general, social democrats should continue to move away from heavy reliance on taxes that might inhibit effort or enterprise, including income and corporate taxes. Seeking to build up the tax base through policies designed to maximize employment possibilities is a sensible approach – indeed, it is a key emphasis of third way politics.

Obviously taxes that discourage the production of 'bads', most notably green taxes, should be relied upon as much as is feasible. It is not clear as yet how much income can be raised through eco-taxation, but the possibilities seem considerable. Shifting taxation onto energy, waste and transport, and away from labour or environmentally friendly business activities can be achieved in a number of ways. Terry Barker simulated a number of ecological reform packages for the British economy. For instance, carbon/energy taxes could be increased over a five-year period. The extra revenue generated would be used to reduce employers' national insurance contributions, and fund a domestic energy-saving programme to protect the poor. The projected results were compared with a scenario in which the economy carried on as before. Over a ten-year period, the changes would generate 0.1% more economic growth and create 278,000 extra jobs.[15]

In general, moving taxation towards consumption, as virtually all the industrial countries have done, makes political and economic sense. If consumption were taxed progressively, rather than only income, the incentive to save would be higher. Saving and investment are major engines of longer-term economic growth. Collecting such taxes need not be more complicated than collecting income tax. Receipts wouldn't have to be kept for every purchase; taxable value could be calculated on the difference between current income and current savings. Having a large standard deduction would obviate the need to make some consumption categories exempt.

We should insist that wealth taxes stay on the agenda, particularly so far as inheritance is concerned. Equality of opportunity is not compatible with the unfettered transmission of wealth from generation to generation. Bill Gates's rise to extreme wealth is one thing; allowing such economic privilege to carry on across the generations is not. As in other areas, tax incentives can be mixed with other forms of regulation. Positive incentives for philanthropy, for example, can have as significant a role as taxes on the direct transmission of wealth.

Finally, governments need to work together – as to some extent they already do – to coordinate tax-gathering from multinational companies. Many multinationals engage in tax arbitrage and transfer pricing to limit their international exposure to taxation. Transfer pricing is a critical issue for nation states. Over 80% of multinationals in one study admitted to facing a transfer pricing inquiry from local or foreign tax authorities at some point. The international tax transfer pricing regime that exists at the moment should be tightened up. The existing system is slow, cumbersome and hit and miss.[16]

Will these sources of taxation generate sufficient income for public institutions? No one knows for sure. The problem of securing adequate taxation is unlikely to go away. Citizens will be increasingly reluctant to pay taxes where the revenues aren't being used to their satisfaction, even in those countries that currently sustain higher taxation income than is the norm. The spread of internet business activities, and of e-money, could further exacerbate these problems. Social democrats need to continue to think creatively about taxation, and to connect such thinking with the structural reforms of government and the state mentioned earlier.

[. . .]

Notes

1   M. Walzer, 'Pluralism and social democracy.' *Dissent* (Winter 1998): 47–53, 50.
2   L. T. Hobhouse, *Liberalism*. London: Williams & Norgate, 1911, pp. 148 and 152.
3   Amartya Sen, *Inequality Reexamined*. Oxford: Clarendon Press, 1992.
4   Giddens, *The Third Way*. Cambridge: Polity Press, 1998, pp. 101–4.
5   James Tobin, 'A liberal agenda.' In *The New Inequality*, ed. Richard B. Freeman. Boston: Beacon, 1999, pp. 58–61.
6   Anne Phillips, *Which Equalities Matter?* Cambridge: Polity Press, 1999, pp. 130–1.
7   Lutz Leisering and Stephan Leibfried, *Time and Poverty in Western Welfare States*. Cambridge: Cambridge University Press, 1999. (See chapter 13 in this volume).
8   Stephen P. Jenkins, 'Income dynamics in Britain, 1991–6.' In *Persistent Poverty and Lifetime Inequality*, ed. John Hills. London: CASE, 1999, pp. 3–8.
9   Robert Walker, 'Lifetime poverty dynamics.' In *Persistent Poverty and Lifetime Inequality*, ed. Hills, pp. 9–16.
10 Howard Oxley: 'Poverty dynamics in four OECD countries.' In *Persistent Poverty and Lifetime Inequality*, ed. Hills, pp. 22–7.
11 Gary Burtless, 'Technological change and international trade: how well do they explain the rise in US income inequality?' In *The Inequality Paradox*, ed. James A. Auerbach and Richard S. Belous. Washington: National Policy Association, 1998, p. 29.
12 Bodo Hombach, *A New Awakening: The Politics of the New Centre in Germany*. Cambridge: Polity Press, 2000.
13 Gøsta Esping-Andersen, *The Three Worlds of Welfare Capitalism*. Cambridge: Polity Press, 1990.
14 Rune Ervik, 'The Redistributive Aim of Social Policy.' Syracuse: Maxwell School of Citizenship and Public Policy, 1998.
15 Terry Barker, 'Taxing pollution instead of employment.' *Energy and Environment* 6 (1993).
16 Lorraine Eden, *Taxing Multinationals*. Toronto: University of Toronto Press, 1998, p. 635.

12

Taxation and the Future of Social Protection

Vito Tanzi

It is a general perception that in recent years the world has been changing rapidly and that it is likely to keep changing in future years. In the introduction to his latest book, Bill Gates predicts that: "Business is going to change more in the next ten years than in the last fifty."[1] He adds that "These changes will occur because of a disarmingly simple idea: the flow of digital information." Kenichi Ohmae has called attention to the globalization of the four Is, namely Investment, Industry, Information, and Individuals. As he points out, investment is no longer limited by geography; industry has gone global with the growing role of the multinationals and with the distribution of their productive capacities in several countries; information is more easily available through the internet and can be and is transferred cheaply and in real time from one part of the globe to another part; and individuals are less and less confined to the place where they were born and raised.[2] The cost of travel, especially when expressed in terms of a person's income, has fallen dramatically thus encouraging many to visit other countries.

It can be argued that the present wave of globalization is nothing new. There have been periods in the past when trade and capital flows were growing rapidly and, as shares of GDP, for some countries, were as high as they are now; and when technological change and the fall in the obstacles to international transactions, such as transportation costs and the speed at which information could be transferred, provided a great stimulus to globalization. And there were periods when large masses of immigrants moved across countries or continents. Yet, the important change at the present time is what Gates mentions in the above quotation, namely the trade in information and knowledge made possible by the information revolution and by the increasing market value of knowledge. This change has convinced many that we are experiencing a "new economy" characterized by much faster productivity gains. As it happened after the introduction of the railroad or of electricity, the information revolution might bring to the world a period of high and sustained growth.

Modern economies are much more knowledge based than past economies which were much more resource based. The capacity to access information and to transfer it cheaply and instantaneously to individuals who put a high value on that information and are willing to pay for it makes this period distinctive and opens many possibilities and some problems for the future. Some of the ongoing changes will subject the existing institutions, created under a different environment, and especially the tax systems and the systems of social protection, to significant stress. There is no question that these institutions will need to adjust to the new environment. Whether the adjustment will be smooth or difficult remains to be seen. It will depend largely on the vision and on the technical and political skills of those who make policy decisions.

The changes that are occurring and that are likely to continue to occur in future years, as new technologies develop and as the available technologies and the existing trends spread to incorporate more and more countries and more and more people, will affect relative prices, jobs, income distributions, tax revenues, government expenditures, regulations, and other areas.

Because of the total impact of globalization:

The prices of some products will fall significantly while the prices of others will increase. These changes in relative prices will hurt some activities, some industries and some countries while they will help others.[3] As an example, it is unlikely that, in the absence of globalization, Finland would have benefited as much as it did from the development and the production of high quality cellular phones. At the same time, traditional industries will see jobs disappear thus leading to the kind of antagonism against globalization that was in evidence in Seattle during the 1999 meeting of the World Trade Organization.

Some groups of workers, and especially those with high technical aptitudes and skills, who can more easily adapt to new technologies, are likely to benefit. Just think of those who went to work for Microsoft or for Nokia two decades ago; or the workers in India doing computer programming for American companies![4] On the other hand, low skilled workers, unable to adjust to the new world, will be negatively affected.[5] Some writers and some labor union leaders have argued that globalization destroys jobs and is, thus, directly responsible for the growth in unemployment experienced by several countries and especially by European countries. Thus, they argue that all workers are likely to lose. See for example, Forrester (1999) for an emotional and articulate, though not convincing, statement of this thesis. These individuals do not recognize the job creating impact of globalization and the impact on productivity of the information revolution.[6]

Closely linked to the issue of the impact of globalization on relative wages, is its impact on income distribution within countries and across countries. Evidence reported by various sources indicates that the income distribution of many countries has become more uneven in recent years and some economists have tried to establish links between this statistical trend and globalization. To the extent that globalization is a factor in the worsening of the income distribution of countries, and as long as one of the fundamental roles of the government is an improvement in the income distribution, a potential problem arises if globalization increases the need for governmental intervention while, at the same time, it reduces its capacity to intervene. The problem raised by a worsening of the income distribution across countries is even more difficult to solve in the absence of a world government and because of falling transfers to poor countries.

There is now a growing literature that points to the fragility of the existing tax systems in the face of the developing trends. While the evidence of the quantitative impact of globalization on tax revenue is still limited, that evidence may not tell much about the future. It is likely that, as time passes, the impact of globalization on tax revenue will accelerate and will become quantitatively evident. The reasons for this statement will be discussed later. If globalization reduces tax revenue and the governments' ability to have tax systems that are progressive and equitable, the governments will lose a major instrument for promoting social protection. For sure, their ability to finance present levels of social spending will be reduced.

[. . .]

The impact of globalization on the welfare state may come from various channels, some more general than others. It may come from the increasing competition that globalization brings about and thus from the need for more efficiency.[7] It may come from the increasing mobility of factors of production, especially financial capital and individuals with great ability. It may come from international pressures to level the regulatory playing field or to introduce uniform standards or codes of conduct. These channels are likely to become more important with the passing of time. Thus, effects that are barely noticeable now will become more visible later.

Globalization tends to raise the share of trade in gross domestic products and, as a consequence, to expose inefficient sectors or industries to greater foreign competition. Enterprises or workers that have operated behind the protection offered by high tariffs or by other protective policies may find themselves without such cover. This applies especially to public enterprises engaged in industrial protection. For some of the countries belonging to the European Union, the help that occasional devaluation had offered in the past is no longer available. In this swim or sink environment the need to become more efficient becomes obvious. But efficiency depends, in part, on the actions of the enterprises and of the workers themselves and in part on policies. A country that imposes high taxes or other constraints (say a very short work week) on its enterprises and workers puts them at a potential competitive disadvantage vis-à-vis enterprises that operate in different environments.

With globalization financial capital and high skilled or high talented individuals become much more mobile because their options expand to other countries. High taxes or too constraining regulations create strong incentives for them to move elsewhere. The loss of highly talented individuals and the outflow of financial capital can have a negative effect on the growth rate and on the tax revenue of a country. In an open world where foreign competitors face lower taxes and fewer constraining regulations, it becomes more difficult and more costly for a country to maintain high taxes and more regulations.

Globalization brings strong pressures on the international community to level the international field in which individuals and enterprises operate. Thus, existing rules about foreign trade, about the environment, about cultural and health related protection, about the operation of financial sectors, about transparency in fiscal accounts and in accounting standards in general, may need to be changed. The current ongoing discussion about remaking the architecture of the international financial system is, in a sense, a movement toward the leveling of the international playing field. In this environment it will become progressively more difficult for some countries to maintain the tax burdens necessary to sustain high levels of spending, or to continue to use regulations and tax expenditures to promote, through them, the current levels of social protection.

While globalization may affect the existing welfare states in many different ways, the most direct and powerful impact will probably come through its effect on tax systems. There is now a growing literature on globalization and tax systems so that there is no need to repeat the arguments presented in that literature. See Tanzi (1995 and 1996). For the time being there is little, if any, evidence that the tax systems of the industrial countries are collapsing. On the contrary, for the majority of these countries the level of taxation is at a historical high. However, in most countries in recent years, the tax level has stopped growing and, in a few, there has actually been some decline. Furthermore, some finance ministers have been complaining about the effect of tax competition on the revenue of their countries and the OECD and the European Community have been concerned about various aspects of tax competition.

While the fiscal house is still standing and looks solid, one can visualize many fiscal termites that are busily gnawing at its foundations. These include:

a. *Increased travel by individuals* which allows them to shop, especially for expensive items, in places where sales taxes are lower. This creates incentives, especially for small countries, to reduce excises and other sales taxes on luxury products in order to attract foreign buyers.[8] This form of tax exporting and of tax competition will progressively reduce the degrees of freedom that countries have in imposing excise taxes on many high-priced products. In fact, revenue from excise taxes, especially if gasoline and tobacco products are excluded, has been falling rapidly in recent years;[9]

b. *Increased activities* on the part of some highly skilled individuals conducted *outside of their countries* which allows them to underreport or not to report at all their foreign earnings; at the same time, more and more individuals are now investing their savings abroad in ways that allows them to underreport or even evade taxes. This has been a major concern on the part of the European Commission that has been advocating the use of minimum taxes on incomes from financial assets.

c. *A growing use of electronic commerce and electronic transactions in general* largely taking place outside of the tax system. Electronic commerce has been growing at very high rates and is expected to reach very high volumes within a few years. A large share of the world commerce, and especially that among enterprises, could soon be channeled through the Internet.

Electronic commerce is going to be a nightmare for the tax authorities.[10] This commerce is bringing with it some important changes.

The first change is that from real transactions, requiring papers which leave various traces for the tax authorities to follow, to virtual transactions which leave much less identifiable traces. If origin-based taxation should prevail, sales establishments would choose to locate themselves in places where there are low or no sales taxes. But destination-based taxation may be very difficult to implement especially in a world set to facilitate foreign trade.[11]

The second is the increasingly important change from the production and sale of *physical* to *digital* products. Many products which have been traditionally sold in shops, and in a format that gave them some physical content, will lose their physical characteristics and as a consequence the territoriality of the sales outlets will be more difficult to determine. Music, writing, photos, engineering plans, movies, medical advice, educational services, and so on can now be downloaded directly over the Net. Furthermore, the downloading can be done from almost anywhere in the world.

In the circumstances described above, the meaning of tax jurisdiction becomes vague. Who should pay the tax and who should collect the money? And how should this be done? In the brave new world of the future, the importance of physical products will continue to fall, while that of products made up of pure knowledge, and thus not having physical characteristics, which can be sold from anywhere in the planet will increase. Newspapers, books, records, and many other "products" will disappear as "products."[12] The full implications of these changes are still barely understood.

d.   The growing importance of *off-shores and tax havens* as conduits for financial investments that to a large extent has been stimulated by the flow of digital information that allows money and knowledge to be moved easily and cheaply in real time. Estimates of these deposits are in the range of US$5 trillion. It is unlikely that many of those who earn incomes on these deposits report them to their national tax authorites.[13]

There is now growing interest on the part of the authorities of some large industrial countries to deal with this problem and the G-7 countries have been paying some attention to it. The United Nations has also been trying to attract attention to this problem. But the solutions are politically and technically very difficult. Thus, it remains to be seen whether this problem will continue to grow or some way will be found to contain it.

e.   The growth of new financial instruments and agents for channeling savings, such as *derivatives and hedge funds*. Many hedge funds operate from off-shore centers and are not, or are little, regulated. Furthermore, the same problems mentioned with electronic commerce appear in even greater extent with electronic investments. There are huge problems of identification of individuals, of transactions, of incomes, and of jurisdictions where the individuals live or where the incomes are generated.[14] In many cases, unless or until these incomes are repatriated and declared as incomes, their taxation will remain problematic.

f.   The growing importance of *trade* that takes place *within multinationals*, among their different parts situated in different countries. This intra multinational trade now accounts for a large and growing share of total world trade. It creates enormous problems for the national tax authorities deriving from the use of "transfer prices" by the multinationals and from the likelihood that some of these enterprises manipulate these transfer prices to move profits to the jurisdictions where taxes are low. Under present tax arrangements this problem is likely to grow. The tax authorities of many countries are now worried about this trend but are often at a loss on what to do about it.

g.   The growing *inability* of countries *to tax*, especially with high rates, *financial capital* and also incomes derived by individuals with highly tradable skills. High tax rates on financial capital or on highly mobile individuals provide strong incentives to the taxpayers to move the capital abroad to jurisdictions that tax it lightly or to take residence in low tax countries. The taxation of incomes from financial capital has become a major issue within the European Union and has been forcing countries either to lower marginal tax rates on incomes or to introduce dual income taxes.

h.   The possibility that real money may begin to be *substituted by electronic money* in the normal transactions of individuals. In this case, the money accounts of individuals could be embedded in the chips of electronic cards which could be used to make payments and settle accounts. This trend would surely increase the difficulties of the tax authorities as well as those of the monetary authorities.

These are examples of the brave new world we are entering and of the fiscal termites that I mentioned above. It is possible that the world community might be able to develop ways of dealing with some of them or of introducing new taxes. For example, off-shore centers and tax havens could be driven out of existence by strong, punitive actions on the part of the industrial countries. Countries might agree to unlimited exchange of information on taxpayers facilitated by computer technology.[15] Hedge funds might be subjected to closer scrutiny and strong regulations. Governments might learn to deal with transfer pricing or introduce new ways of taxing multinationals. And they might develop ways to monitor electronic commerce and electronic money or introduce new taxes such as "bit taxes," "Tobin taxes" or others. They may even create a World Tax Organization which would help in discussing the problems and in developing and coordinating solutions. However, it is unlikely that all these actions will be taken or that they will succeed in killing all the fiscal termites. Thus, the conclusion must be that it would be prudent for many countries and especially for the welfare states to begin preparing themselves for what could prove to be significant falls in tax levels in future years.

The fall in revenue might come at the same time when governments experience the need for more spending in particular areas, either as a consequence of the aging problem or of globalization itself. Under current policies the ongoing demographic changes will create strong pressures on governments to spend more for health and for pensions. These effects will become particularly pronounced, in many countries, in about a decade from now when the baby boomers will begin to retire. But by that time the effects of globalization on the tax systems could become particularly strong.

Globalization may create pressures for increased spending for education, training, research and development, the environment, infrastructures, and for institutional changes partly to increase efficiency and partly to comply with international agreements. These expenditures are consistent with the traditional or basic role of the state in its allocation function. Thus, expenditure for social protection, which is a newcomer in the role of the state, could be squeezed between falling revenue and increasing needs for more traditional types of spending. In such a situation, the state will need to rethink its role in the economy. [. . .]

Until 1960, in most industrial countries, public spending was less than 30 percent of GDP. After 1960 there was a large increase in public spending in many countries to increase social welfare. However, it is not easy to prove that this large increase in spending actually contributed correspondingly to an increase in social welfare.

Assume, for example, that between 1960 and the present time per capita income had increased at the same rate as it did;[16] but assume that public spending *as a share of GDP* had remained at the 1960 level. Does it necessarily follow that the welfare of society would have been necessarily lower? Individuals would have had more disposable income, because of lower taxes. Alternative ways of protection against various kinds of risks would have been developed by the market or by the individuals themselves. The governments could have focused their attention more directly towards those truly in need of social assistance and towards their more basic objectives rather than creating programs that involved the whole population. Perhaps this may happen over future years. The governments may progressively disengage themselves from many activities and may exploit alternative ways of achieving these objectives with less direct financing. There are already many alternatives available from the experiences of various countries and a concentrated search for alternatives would undoubtedly generate other options to ensure essential or basic social protection will lower tax burdens.[17] But in such a world the power of the state to *effectively* and *efficiently* regulate relevant private activities would need to be enhanced. Without a stronger and more efficient regulatory activity on the part of the state and without much imagination on the part of policymakers the suggested change may not produce desirable results.

Notes

1 See Gates (1999) p. XIV.
2 See Ohmae (1995).
3 For a discussion of who gains and who loses from globalization see the papers by Lal and by Bhagwati in Horst Siebert, editor (1999).
4 The lists of the world richest individuals published annually by Forbes magazine now include many individuals, some very young, who made their fortunes from these technological breakthroughs.
5 There is now a large literature on this issue. Inter alias see the papers by Leamer and by Burda and Dluhosch in Siebert, editor, op. cit.
6 Interestingly, the country that is the leader in the introduction of these new technologies, the United States, has seen its unemployment rate fall to the lowest level in several decades.
7 Globalization and especially the internet provide much more timely information of prices and other relevant variables thus increasing competition.
8 Some airports have become huge shopping centers.
9 See OECD, *Revenue Statistics* (1999).
10 Governor Gilmore of the State of Virginia, who heads the U.S. Advisory Commission on Electronic Commerce, has been arguing that such commerce should be tax free.
11 A recent article in the *New York Times*, January 10, 2000, p. 1, entitled, "Online Sales Spur Illegal Importing of Medicine to U.S." gives a sense of the problem. The article cites the commissioner of the Customs Service that: "The Internet has given us a lot more work. We have been deluged with prescription drugs coming in from overseas. It is a major challenge to deal with this large increase in volume."
12 The phenomenal growth in the value of internet stocks in the past couple years is an indication of things to come.

13 One reason is that some of this money represents laundered money. Additionally, it is very difficult, under existing rules, for national authorities to identify the owners of these accounts.
14 Often it is difficult to distinguish regular incomes from capital gains and many countries do not tax capital gains.
15 However, legal restrictions and national interests are likely to prevent this from happening. See on this issue Tanzi (1995) and Tanzi and Zee (1999).
16 In fact, many would argue that the growth of per capita income would have been higher if the tax and spending increase had not occurred because lower taxes and lower social spending would have created less distortions and less disincentive effects.
17 The forthcoming book by Tanzi and Schuknecht (2000) includes several chapters that discuss some of these alternatives.

References

Bhagwati, Jagdish, 1997, "Globalization: Who Gains, Who Loses?" in Siebert, editor, op. cit., pp. 225–36.
Burda, Michael C. and Barbara Dluhosch, 1999, "Globalization and European Labor Markets," in Siebert, editor, op. cit., pp. 181–207.
Forrester, Viviane, 1999, *The Economic Horror* (Cambridge, Polity).
Gates, Bill, 1999, *Business at the Speed of Thought* (Warner Books).
Lal, Deepak, 1999, "Globalization: What Does It Mean for Developing and Developed Countries?" in Siebert, editor, op. cit., pp. 211–224.
Leamer, Edward E., 1999, "Competition in Tradables as a Driving Force of Rising Income Inequality," in Siebert, editor, op. cit., pp. 119–152.
Ohmae, Kenichi, 1995, *The End of the Nation State – The Rise of Regional Economies* (The Free Press).
Siebert, Horst (editor), 1999, *Globalization and Labor* (Tübingen: Mohr Siebeck).
Tanzi, Vito, 1995, *Taxation in an Integrating World*, (Washington, D.C.: Brookings).
——, 1996, "Globalization, Tax Competition and the Future of Tax Systems," in *Steuersysteme der Zukunft*, edited by Gerold Krause-Junk (Berlin: Duncker & Humblot) pp. 11–27.
Tanzi, Vito, and Ludger Schuknecht, 2000, *Public Spending in the 20th Century: A Global Perspective* (Cambridge: Cambridge University Press).
Tanzi, Vito, and Howell Zee, 1999, "Taxation in a Borderless World: The Role of Information Exchange," in *International Studies in Taxation*, edited by Bertil Wiman (The Netherlands: Kluwer Law International).

13

Paths out of Poverty: Perspectives on Active Policy

Lutz Leisering and Stephan Leibfried

[. . .]

Research suggests four new policy orientations to [poverty and social exclusion]:

The time dimension of poverty and Social Assistance ('temporalisation') suggests the need to reconceptualise anti-poverty policy as *life-course policy*.

The action potential of the poor, which is the driving force behind the dynamics of poverty, implies the need for – and the feasibility of – an *enabling approach*, focusing on paths out of Social Assistance, rather than just administering cases and paying benefits.

When poverty spreads beyond traditional marginal groups ('democratisation'), then the barriers between 'policies for the poor' and 'policies for workers' or 'policies for citizens', between the lower and the higher tiers of the welfare state (which are particularly pronounced in comprehensive European welfare states of the conservative and social-democratic variety) lose their meaning. An *integrated social policy* is thus called for.

Dynamic research, which evaluates the impact of Social Assistance on people's lives, is itself part of a new *reflexive social policy*. The latter relies on continual social reporting as well as the monitoring of its own effects, quite unlike traditional Social Assistance.

Life-course policy

[. . .]

Until the end of the 1980s, German Social Assistance evinced hardly any policy differentiation. The official statistics of course distinguished various categories of claimants, but they did not give rise to measures geared to these groups' specific needs. In the more general social policy arena [. . .] there is a common way of differentiating policies, notably by identifying *'problem groups'* or *'target groups'*, such as 'the unemployed', 'the elderly' or 'the homeless', and to devote policy measures to them. This approach is of limited use.

The first problematic issue is that the people in these groups experience such wide differences in the *duration* of poverty and other problems that a uniform policy can scarcely hope to offer solutions to the whole group. In fact, the dynamic approach seems to suggest that anti-poverty policies ought to be differentiated according to the duration of poverty – whether it is short or long term in the simplest case. In a study of relative income poverty among children in the USA, Robert Walker argued for distinct policies for groups according to duration. For example, he proposed state loans for the temporarily poor and for those with repeated short-term spells. A provision of this kind would lift 35 per cent of poor US children out of poverty. For those who repeatedly experienced longer spells of poverty he proposed a package of conventional social policy measures, including the support of employment opportunities and health insurance coverage. By contrast, only structural reform of the socio-economic system could promise relief to the long-term poor.

Closer examination shows, however, that the temporal structure of poverty cannot be easily translated into a meaningful and effective policy design: the members of a given group interpret their experience of poverty differently. The second problematic issue in differentiating policies, therefore, is that objective, chronological time ('how long does poverty last') is modified by *subjective* and *biographical time*. It is politically difficult to identify and influence these dimensions of time. The efficacy of policy measures depends to a great extent on how those targeted react to the policies and actively participate in them – and thus on their subjective orientations of action. The complexity of these problematic situations exceeds the precision of the measures normally available for policy use.

A policy perspective which uses life-course theory to temporally distinguish different life situations does not escape the underlying dilemma of target group policies. Faced with the amorphous mass of problems among the general population, political strategies to combat poverty cannot avoid selecting certain groups for action, identifying them and targeting their measures on them, even though these groups are very heterogeneous in composition and the intended beneficiaries may possibly be missed. The groups which are identified in practice are chiefly marginalised groups in the lower social strata and socio-structurally defined 'problem groups' in the core population. The temporal analyses have offered a new cross-cutting dimension, which shows how changeable the life circumstances of the members of such groups can be. This increases the dilemma of social policy between universal measures based on standardised services intended for large social groups, and selective measures aimed at smaller sections or even designed for individual circumstances.

The third problematic issue is, then, that even when aimed at small groups, social policy can take temporal aspects into account only in a way amenable to the administration. We might call this *administrative time*. A Social Assistance official cannot normally predict if a new claimant will be long or short term. Unlike the hindsight of social science analysis, prognostic tools would be required to identify potential long-term claimants – or, equally, short-term claimants. In order to be practicable, such predictive measures would have to be restricted to basic socio-demographic indicators such as being female, young or a single parent, each of which identifies a target group.

Furthermore, it is not only hard to determine how long poverty will last, both objectively and subjectively, and how duration can be handled by the administration, but – the fourth problematic issue – we have to clarify how long Social Assistance ought to last. This involves normative questions about the legitimate duration of receiving Social Assistance or other social benefits, which have to be answered in the democratic process. For instance, should long-term claims be totally prohibited, as in the Clinton Reform Act of 1996, and, if so, for which groups? Which sections of the population should be allowed to have time out at the expense of the state, that is the taxpayers, and in what circumstances and for how long? This is a question of how legitimate certain lifestyles are, and such questions go far beyond those who are poor. While the subjective and the administrative dimensions of time tend to show the limits of policy, this normative dimension suggests scope for political action to shape living time – to define *political time* with regard to individual life courses. This is life-course policy.

[. . .]

By putting a premium on particular life-course patterns, Social Assistance and other social security systems presuppose fundamental political decisions about models of life in our society. In reforming Social Assistance, society has to decide: what patterns of life does it want to open up for – or impose on – women and men, families and lone parents, the low-paid and the well-off, children and old people? Does it want to perpetuate the [. . .] model of the 'male breadwinner' and consequently discriminate against women in the pension system – and therefore, if the breadwinner is absent, force them into the safety net of Social Assistance? Does it want to continue to pursue the ideal of the two-parent family at the cost of allowing the children of lone parents to spend their first formative years in poverty? Should the fiction of male life-long full-time employment be maintained, and should the unemployed be punished by unfavourable social policies? These issues demand nothing less than a new definition of living time, comparable and intertwined with similar debates in industrial relations about new patterns of spreading working hours over the week, over the year and in the life span. Fundamental social arrangements have to be rethought: the relationship between the sexes, the extension of the concept of productive work beyond paid work in the market, and the relationship between the generations, as manifested in questions of poverty among children or the reduction in social services for the increasing proportion of elderly people.

[. . .]

An enabling approach

A key issue of reform is the action potential of the poor. In sociology, especially in the study of marginal groups, the agency of the poor has often been denied. Social policy makers have either equally denied agency, sometimes blaming its extinction on ill-designed social security systems, or they have emphasised the negative side of it – scrounging, abuse of benefits, pursuit of hedonistic or deviant ends – to justify repression, social control and cuts in benefits. However, the dynamic approach to poverty and on-going social assistance reforms in several countries during the second half of the 1990s have converged in vindicating the poor as agents: active claimants require active, enabling policies, poverty dynamics require 'dynamic policies'. Dynamic research has revealed a degree of agency among the poor which conventional poverty policies have not fully exploited. Although longitudinal analyses do not support the notion of social assistance making claimants passive and dependent, improved assistance could even further their activity.

The finding that claimants are generally more active than widely believed and that most of them manage either to terminate claiming or to cope while claiming, might tempt politicians to save money by reducing support, because 'claimants are able to help themselves'. On closer examination our findings suggest the contrary: investing in claimants pays, because most of them are both able and determined to make use of support to become independent or in order to secure a decent living if they are unable to become independent. This would make a case for maintaining and extending support services and limiting control measures. Enabling policies are in fact being introduced, even if driven by fiscal pressure.

The current transnational political emphasis on 'getting people off welfare' should, however, be put into perspective. Many claimants cannot terminate claiming within a given period or are not expected to do so by cultural norms specific to each country, because they are sick, old, young (children) or objectively have no chance of returning to work or because society does not expect them to work, as in Germany in the case of lone parents with younger children. [. . .]

In 1996 and 1997 new approaches to social assistance reform emerged in Germany, Britain and the USA that went beyond a mere readjustment of the levels of wages and benefits or of controls. These new departures aim to exploit the claimants' potential for action by offering active support rather than merely creating incentives by making work pay. This diverse set of measures is multi-faceted: some include coercion, deterrence and a reduction of entitlements, others provide new real routes to independence, and many blend coercion and support.

In Britain, even before Tony Blair took office, the Job Seekers' Allowance was introduced in 1996 to supersede both Unemployment Benefit and Income Support for the unemployed. This includes compulsory re-training and participation in work schemes. After his landslide electoral victory in May 1997, Blair appointed Frank Field Minister for Welfare Reform. Field tried to design policies that incite people to get off assistance, embedded, though, in a moral crusade against 'dependence' and 'abuse' of benefits. While Field's hopes of recasting the welfare state in general and even solving the problems of unemployment and lone parenthood on this basis seem elusive (he quit after a year of office), we may realistically expect to see more people leaving social assistance than before, possibly an extra 10 per cent or even 20 per cent of the clientele. More could only be achieved if benefits were curtailed and access further restricted. This, however, would be a different story altogether: not an active policy forging imaginative links between benefit and labour market but simply a value-based decision against the social rights of certain groups, like lone mothers whose benefits were cut in Britain in 1998.

In Germany, too, Social Assistance has traditionally only 'administered', not empowered the poor so that we could speak of 'passive institutionalisation'. But from the mid 1990s a minor revolution has been taking place in major municipalities. Driven by budgetary pressures the move towards modernising public administration has eventually reached Social Assistance, that marginal component of the welfare state. For the first time, the prime objective of Social Assistance, to 'help claimants help themselves', is being taken seriously and the effectiveness of measures is being evaluated. Computerised processing of file records, New Control Models to rationalise the administration and new instruments for supporting claimants are being introduced to boost efficiency and effectiveness. Above all, getting claimants off benefit has become a primary goal.

Ideally such measures can reduce costs as well as help the poor. Clients, staff and local employers are mobilised to avert long-term claims. While conventional work schemes within and without Social Assistance led to a 'secondary labour market' propped up by the government, some of the new initiatives aim at the 'real' primary labour market. The city of Hamburg, for example, has charged a private Dutch company *Burean Maatwerk* (Dutch for 'work to measure') to get long-term unemployed claimants of Social Assistance back to work. The method operates on precise knowledge of the characteristics of each unemployed person and of the needs of individual local employers. On this basis many people found a job, even new jobs were created and millions of DMs were saved. Conventional labour exchanges do not normally collect and use knowledge to this extent.

[. . .]

Integrated social policy

Social policy and social administration in the field of poverty in Germany suffer from a modernisation lag. This also applies to the dominant images of poverty and to the basic assumptions about how to combat poverty in politics. Poverty has traditionally been pushed to the margins in the political system, it has been effectively re-sidualised. Poverty issues are not treated as a significant element in strategic social-policy planning, but instead they are concentrated into a separate system (Social Assistance) outside the regular social security system. Social Assistance did not assume a more central po-sition in politics until fiscal and labour-market pressure mounted in the 1990s. The poor are seen as a negligible residual category of modern society. The finding that poverty transcends traditional social boundaries and reaches into the middle classes fundamentally calls such residualising assumptions and institutionalisations into question. Instead, it demands modernisation, a differentiation and normalisation of poverty policies and images appropriate to the new kinds of poverty.

In considering poverty policy, developments in Social Assistance must be distinguished from developments in higher-tier social security systems. The German social security system has a dual structure: a central core, composed chiefly of Social Insurance schemes, and a peripheral field of social services at the heart of which lies Social Assist-ance. The core programmes are not intended to address poverty risks; for example, as a matter of principle, there is no minimum pension. Entitlements are based on the individual employment record and on marriage. Nor does family policy recognise the minimum needs of chil-dren or of divorced women. [. . .]

The dualistic model has always presupposed and tolerated that the core institutions would allow a certain amount of poverty which then had to be dealt with at the periphery. Problems arose when this 'state-produced poverty' began to increase faster than expected, as it did at the end of the 1970s. By contrast with the 'poverty approach' of the Anglo-Saxon welfare states, the principal aim of the German system is to secure a person's achieved standard of living by means of earnings-related benefits. This benefits the middle classes most, thus creating strong political support for the welfare state. Conversely, means-tested benefits are claimed by only a small section of the population. Under these circumstances, Social Assistance plays a much smaller role in the debate about the future of the welfare state than it does for instance in the USA.

[. . .]

The position of Social Assistance in Germany's dual system of social security must be rethought. The more that poverty is recognised as transcending social boundaries, the less difference can be seen between

the claimants of Social Insurance programmes and those of Social
Assistance, in spite of the total policy separation between these two
tiers maintained by administrative structures. The widespread criticism that Social Assistance has degenerated to a pension-like benefit
for relevant social groups instead of being a marginal system of last
resort for 'atypical cases', cannot be supported on the basis of the duration of claims. It is, however, true that Social Assistance extends to specific groups in society and not just to atypical individuals.

[. . .]

[An] 'integrated' social policy [. . .] would make poverty policy an
integral part of general social policy for the first time in Germany. But
even an integrated policy would have its limits. It is doubtful whether
it would make the welfare state 'poverty proof' in a social sense,
since legal and administrative integration of the poor would not do
away with social differentiation. As long as benefits for 'the poor' are
restricted to minimum standards, 'policy for workers' and 'policy for
the poor' will remain distinct, even if they are jointly provided within
the framework of the Social Insurance system, Child Benefit and so on.
To that extent, the negative status of the poor is maintained as those
who have no valid claims other than their need, and thus [. . .] will
receive nothing more than minimum subsistence benefits.

Minimum benefits for the unemployed, for example, if integrated
into the general Unemployment Benefit scheme, would probably not
differ much from Social Assistance as regards the level of benefits,
means-testing and the stigma attached. Higher levels of benefit in
pursuit of wider social policy goals can normally be justified politically
only on the basis of criteria of demonstrable merit. This leads to fundamental questions of values and choices. Benefit entitlements could
be based on a wide range of positively evaluated 'life-time contributions', such as bringing up children, acting as a care-giver or other
socially valued work. Obviously, this would involve positive and
negative discriminations and create new inequalities.

Reflexive policy

Reflexive poverty policies take conscious account of the consequences
of their own operations. Eligibility for Social Assistance is often a result of the failure of prior income maintenance systems such as social
insurance or family benefits (the concept of 'welfare-state produced

poverty'). Efforts must be increased to report statistically on social conditions and poverty and to monitor the effects of policies.

[. . .]

Conventional cross-sectional counts of the number of Social Assistance claimants still remain useful for fiscal purposes from an accountancy perspective. They reflect the actual case-load of the Social Assistance agency. But longitudinal and other temporal data are often indispensable even for resource planning purposes. [For] example in the United Kingdom it was planned to transfer resources from the elderly to families, based on the greater susceptibility of families to being poor. But it was also observed that families were on average poor for a much shorter period than the elderly were, and thus each family cost the welfare state less.

To meet its objectives a report on social conditions must give information on the following topics: the extent of poverty measured both cross-sectionally and longitudinally, that is the 'incidence' as well as the 'prevalence' of poverty, the duration and patterns of poverty measured in terms of objective chronological time; the subjective perceptions of time of those affected by poverty and the biographical significance of poverty; and finally poverty careers as defined and propelled by public institutions, above all Social Assistance. The latter point increases the welfare state's own knowledge of itself. [. . .]

Just as the welfare state's regulation systems and welfare-state produced poverty have increased in complexity, so the state must concern itself more with inspecting and monitoring its operations.

[. . .]

We can distinguish three types of failure of prior systems which correspond to [. . .] three kinds of poverty caused by the welfare state [. . .]:

administrative delay and *inefficiency* in delivering insurance benefits to the unemployed and old, who therefore have to wait for benefits which will eventually be paid;
the structural *ineffectiveness* of the insurance system showing inadequate benefits to people whose work records fall below the norm, for instance pensioners whose level and amount of contributions are not up to standard;
poor coordination between the social security systems themselves, and between them and other fields of policy or law. Notable examples

include tax policy and the problem of coordination between the tax threshold and the minimum subsistence level according to Social Assistance law; policies applying to foreigners and asylum seekers and the prohibition of taking paid work; legal policy and the co-ordination of minimum income levels protected against attachment and the Social Assistance scales; and the question of benefits for released prisoners.

In the 1990s [in Gemany and some other EU countries] the question of insufficient coordination has, however, been tackled in some fields, for example the prohibition of employment by asylum seekers has been relaxed, and the minimum subsistence income level has been declared tax-free according to a high court ruling. But no improvement in the effectiveness of income maintenance policies has been apparent. In order to test if a system achieves its goal of ensuring a given income replacement level for the standard citizen, one must discover how far reality deviates from the ideal of the 'standard pensioner' (*Eckrentner*; defined as a person with 45 years of full employment and average income). No such monitoring of the effectiveness of Social Insurance has yet been institutionalised. One policy conclusion which could be drawn is that the abolition of poverty or at least its minimisation should be firmly established as a goal of the Social Insurance system. Standards would have to be laid down to define the boundaries at which deviations from the 'normal' work record would be treated as problematic. For the first time this would offer criteria for identifying the poverty-relevant consequences of Social Insurance, and thus help to derive ideas for reform.

The effects of Social Assistance, the second field in which poverty policies can be monitored, also demand attention. [. . .] The most notable gap in the official analysis of the effects of the Federal Social Assistance Act is the absence of any information on 'latent poverty' or 'the hidden numbers in poverty': people who fail to claim Assistance although they are entitled to it. The total failure of politics to confront the problem of latent poverty stands in stark contrast to the fundamental significance of the state's guarantee of a minimum subsistence income for all citizens. The welfare state actually contributes to latent poverty through its 'passive institutionalisation' of Social Assistance, that is, the authorities make no outreach-effort to offer help to those who need it but who, out of ignorance or shame, avoid claiming. Outreach-efforts are [. . .] more pronounced in Anglo-Saxon countries, especially when new programmes are legislated, like Supplemental Security Income (SSI) in the USA which aimed at the elderly and the disabled. The problem has hardly been taken up by the social sciences.

Studies were mainly confined to the 1970s and 1980s, and suggest hidden poverty figures of around 50 per cent of those entitled. One might assume that the numbers of the hidden would have tended to fall considerably, since those eligible for Social Assistance increasingly see it as their right. However, there are no recent empirical studies of the problem.

Active anti-poverty policies must expose not only the extent but also the causes of the failure to claim, if they are to identify the critical points for locating countermeasures. [. . .]

Regular reports on poverty and social conditions together with systematic monitoring would add up to what we termed 'reflexive policy'. [. . .] In this way, the [. . .] welfare state's institutional and cultural division into a core indifferent to poverty and a neglected and marginalised poverty sector could be overcome. This would be a step in the direction of integrating anti-poverty policy with social policy as a whole.

[. . .]

14

The Macho Penal Economy: Mass Incarceration in the US: A European Perspective

David Downes

Introduction

American exceptionalism in deviance and control, for most of the 20th century, consisted of exceptionally high rates of serious crime, notably homicide, robbery, hard drug dealing and gang violence in both its juvenile and organised crime forms. Theorising about crime [. . .] has been massively influenced by this major contrast with the general run of European experience. So there has been a certain experience of cognitive dissonance as, over the past two decades, crime rates in the USA have levelled off and recently fallen, whilst those in some European countries have risen, in the case of serious property crimes, to surpass the US rates. Moreover, these trends have occurred despite a sharpening of the contrasts between the USA and Europe in the alleged root causes of crime: the extent of inequalities of wealth and income, poverty and the apotheosis of the winner/loser culture. An aetiological crisis, due to crime trends spinning out of alignment with predictions drawn from the major social theories, was avoided only by the phenomenal growth of the US prison population. Even powerful causes can be over-ridden by so devastating a penal response, though there are the awkward facts that state by state increases in imprisonment correlate only weakly with crime rate fluctuations, especially crimes of violence.

[. . .]

No comparable democratic society has embraced what Leon Radzi-nowicz[1] termed 'penal regression' with remotely equivalent fervour. Of the other high imprisonment societies, China remains pre-democratic, and Russia, the former Soviet bloc countries and South Africa, are – for very different reasons – in transition from massively oppressive regimes. In the 1980s, by contrast, a new right Britain did the opposite, to everyone's surprise. It was only in the 1990s, clearly influenced by the American example, that the appeal of a 'prison works' strategy was seen as ideologically more palatable, politically advantageous and also cheaper than crime reduction bought by substantial increases in employment and welfare services. And in The Netherlands, a high-cost welfare society, imprisonment also came to be seen as the only resort where welfare and lesser punishments had failed. The Netherlands too has quintupled its prison population over the past two decades, albeit from a far lower base and, as yet, to no more than the European average.

There are, however, several examples of resistance to this trend. The Scandinavian countries have maintained very high welfare spending with relatively low and, in the case of Finland, striking falls in impris-onment levels. France and Germany have maintained a steady state despite rising crime rates. Closest to home, Canada has preserved roughly stable crime and imprisonment levels for two decades, an achievement that is rarely mentioned in Anglo-American debate on penal policy. And, of course, there are some states within the USA which have bucked the trend in significant respects.

A great deal rides on whether or not, and the extent to which, the USA is an exceptionalist outlier in the penal sphere or both a prefigur-ation and a driver of things to come. If the era of global capitalism is both highly criminogenic *and* punitive [. . .] and if [. . .] the more devel-oped societies resort heavily to penal innovations in periods of rapid changes in their political economy – as in the late 16th, late 18th and now late or post 20th Centuries – then we can expect the latter course to be followed.

[. . .]

A comparative perspective on penal futures

In their comparative analyses of incarceration trends, both Tonry and Kuhn rightly stress the unique scale of US incarceration and the extent to which it 'dwarfs' that in comparable European societies.[2] [. . .] The challenge is to assess how far the recipe for the US mass incarceration is in embryo in European and other societies. In addition, having gone this route alone, the US is actively exporting it, and key groups in comparable societies are eager to adopt it. It may be more, not less, difficult for other societies to resist its appeal when the USA is both its role model and its advocate, both in the 'law and order' and in other political and economic respects.

1.   Crime is not the problem?

[. . .] Crime rates in the USA, with the signal exception of lethal violence, are now relatively normal compared with several European societies. It is a peculiar irony of American exceptionalist mythologizing that the right to bear arms, which harbour the potential for instant lethal violence, is regarded as sacrosanct, whilst the right to bear drugs, whose potential is rarely so, is regarded as taboo. Hence 'crime is not the problem' as a cause of US mass incarceration, as only a quarter of admissions to prisons are for violence.[3] But the fact that European crime rates have reached US proportions, whilst it may be reassuring from an American perspective, is disquieting from a European vantage-point. Signs of relative normalcy to the one may portend the advent of pathology to the other. Burglary and car theft may be non-lethal offences but they are still profoundly unsettling, especially when experienced as repeat victimisations. [. . .]

The most damaging crime phenomena are those periods in which a quantum leap in crime rates coincides with allied sequences of events yielding a virulent symbolism of social breakdown. Thus, the mid-1960s to the mid-1970s in the US combined steep rises in crime with a doubling of the homicide rate; the assassinations of John and Robert Kennedy, Martin Luther King and Malcolm X; major urban riots, both racial and anti-war; and extremist political violence. There were elements of 'la grande peur' of revolutionary France in the atmosphere of the times. In Britain, the 1980s saw a doubling of the crime rate and, especially in 1989–92, when the crime rate rose by 50 per cent, in a context of rioting and high unemployment following deindustrialisation, the sense of a breakdown of social order was very strong. The murder of a 2 year old boy, James Bulger, by two older boys, provided the climax to a decade of growing fear of crime that symbolised a sense of social changes spinning out of control. In The Netherlands, the rising crime rate 1979–84 resembled a cliff face compared with earlier trends. Combined with fears about hard drug use and drug-related crime, it provided conditions ripe for a toughening of criminal justice and penal policy. In all three countries, but to very different degrees, the scene was set for prison populations rising to unprecedented heights.

The definition of the problem, heavily influenced by political and media agendas, seems crucial in explaining whether structural or punitive measures are deployed in response. In the USA and to a lesser extent in Britain, the most influential explanation imputed rising crime and riots to a newly jobless marauding underclass. In The Netherlands, 'depillarisation', the erosion of the institutionalised bases of informal social control in the family, denominational groupings, the school and the community, was seen as the principal cause in the influential 'Society and Crime' Report. This explanation probably did more to arouse anxieties than to allay them, and the publication of the first International Victim Survey in 1987, showing The Netherlands to be apparently the most crime-prone nation surveyed, compounded such fears. Other Western European countries to have experienced such trends have avoided or resisted so penal a response, though several – e.g. Italy, Spain, Portugal – have raised their prison populations markedly. In others, – e.g. Austria, France – politically fascistic parties have gained ground.

Crime thus holds the potential to symbolise social breakdown in ways which mobilise popular and elite support for punitive formal controls to be stepped up to previously impermissible heights and lengths. Seismic shifts can occur in the regulatory character not only of the criminal justice field but across the entire culture of control. As a result, even when crime has ceased to be *the* problem, changes have been set in motion which are immensely difficult to modify and may be impossible to reverse. In this welter of disturbing change, imprisonment offers one touchstone of secure social order. Prisons are the guarantee that *ultimately* law and order will be enforced or restored. Modes of punishment are profoundly expressive, and the symbolic potency of imprisonment in particular offers politicians endless dramaturgical possibilities, conveying multiple messages to different audiences. It is *the* sign that governments are prepared to do whatever it takes to wage war on crime. In some penal climates it attains a kind of fiscal benefit of clergy, as an experiment that cannot fail – if crime goes down, prisons gain the credit; but if they go up, we clearly need more of the same medicine whatever the cost.

2. The politics of law and order

With some allowance for time-lags, Tonry rightly sees much common experience between the USA and European societies on this front. In

Britain, crime control emerged as a partisan issue only in the 1970 General Election, then even more resoundingly in 1979. In the USA, it first surfaced with Goldwater in 1964, in The Netherlands 20 years later. In France, Germany, and the Scandinavian countries, it remains much less prominent, despite highly visible episodes of youthful disorder and growing drug use. Though variation persists, two trajectories are discernible. The first is that, once embarked on a course of 'governing through crime', with the heightened emotionalism and bidding-up of punitive measures that this entails, no society has managed to find a way of extricating itself from that upwards spiral. Part of that pattern is at least *some* convergence between the USA and Europe at the ideological level. It may well be that Americans have given less weight than Europeans to social and economic factors in offending behaviour, but rehabilitation also connotes self-improvement aided by counselling and treatment, a long established if now marginalized American practice. At the European end, "analogous to the conversion of the welfare state since the 1980s into . . . a 'market economy', diminishing the responsibility of the state to its citizens and heavily emphasising individual responsibility, causes of criminal behaviour are no longer seen as lying in the criminal's social background, life situation and the circumstances of the offence, but in the moral fault of the actor resulting in acts of free will for which he is fully responsible."[4] The second is that economic growth in the richest countries has in part depended on inflows of migrant workers, has fostered immigration from former colonies, and prompted refugees to seek haven on a scale not easily accommodated without conflict. The problems involved in integrating diverse culturally distinctive groups into highly unequal societies can all too readily be translated into crime control terms.

In Britain, only since 1992 have both major parties engaged in 'populist punitiveness.' The Tories had long contrived to cast Labour as a party neglectful of the police, 'soft' on crime and tolerant of public disorder born of industrial militancy. Labour had pursued the alternative case that rising crime was largely due to social and economic inequalities. [. . .] From 1989–1992, Britain experienced a major recession, with male unemployment rising to 15%; a prison population falling from 50,000 to 42,000; and a crime rate that rose by almost 50%. For the first time in over 30 years, the Conservative lead over Labour as the party best able to guarantee law and order vanished. Labour pressed home their advantage, not by emphasising the links between economic factors and rising crime but by stressing the leniency of sentencing. Tony Blair's celebrated sound-bite on the need to be 'tough on crime, tough on the causes of crime' nicely allowed for both, but the sub-text, being 'tough on criminals', was what emerged in policy terms. This strategy owed much to the American Democratic Party's approach to avoiding a repetition of the Dukakis debacle of 1988. Clinton was 'smart' as well as 'tough' on crime. To neutralise Michael Howard's 'Prison Works' policy, Jack Straw, both in opposition and in government, formulated policies (some enacted in the 1998 Crime and Disorder Act, some either still forthcoming or meeting resistance) which Labour would hardly have countenanced before 1992. These include:

- activating minimum mandatory penalties for burglary, drug-dealing and violence (authorized by a statute passed by the outgoing Conservative Government);
- the creation of Anti-Social Behaviour Orders which, *inter alia*, blur the distinction between criminal and civil law burdens of proof;
- local authority powers to impose curfews for juveniles;
- re-naming the Probation and After Care Service the 'Community Punishment and Rehabilitation Service' (a measure to which 85% of Chief Probation Officers are opposed);
- reducing the threshold for returning probationers to court from three breaches to two (a breach being such conduct as failing to attend a meeting with the officer at the agreed time); and automatic withdrawal of social security benefits for up to 6 months for a second breach.
- the extension of privatised prison management from 3 prisons to 14;
- the ending of *doli incapax* (the presumption of lack of offending awareness) for offenders under the age of 14;
- the replacement of Social Security payments by subsistence vouchers for asylum seekers;
- the prosecution of 'squeegee merchants' and beggars;
- drug testing of arrestees at police stations;
- extending disclosure to employers of previous convictions to all offences.

Much of this catalogue is inspired by the American example of 'zero tolerance' policing and prosecution. The effect is that both major parties have engaged in raising the punitive stakes, and the prison population in England and Wales rose from 42,000 to 65,000 in six years.

There are, it must be said, compensating liberal components to offset the generally punitive drift of these measures. For example:

- Labour have embarked on a generously funded programme of 'restorative justice' and community crime reduction projects for disaffected youth, stressing reparation, mediation and mentoring for young offenders and those at risk of crime;

- Jack Straw took the brave decision to mount a public enquiry into the Stephen Lawrence case, in which the hugely bungled investigation by the Metropolitan Police of the murder of a black teenager by local white youths was defined as 'institutional racism' by the resulting Report;
- The UK, a long-term but reluctant signatory to the European Convention on Human Rights, has now incorporated its provisions into domestic law;
- the age of consent for homosexual relations should be reduced to 16, to match that for heterosexual relations.

[. . .]

The second common trajectory crucial to the politics of law and order is that "the concern with crime and fear of victimisation has grown out of all proportion to the actual increases in criminality; fear which typically is most focused on traditional 'street crimes' and crimes allegedly committed by powerless minority groups . . . Across Europe and in the US, increasing proportions of the prison population consist of 'minorities' and foreigners."[5] In Europe, contradictory impulses are at work. On the one hand, the shared political aspiration is for a Europe *sans frontières*, with freedom of trade and movement, upheld by the European Court, the Convention on Human Rights, etc. On the other hand, the inflows of refugees, migrant workers and immigrants from both former communist and colonial societies provokes resentments that have [. . .] fed into the politics of far right ethnocentrism. One attempt at resolution is to legislate for equal opportunities but also to step up penalties for the offences in which the most discriminated against ethnic minorities are disproportionately involved. The over-representation of Afro-Caribbean compared to white prisoners in Britain is much the same as in the US. In The Netherlands, the proportion of non-Dutch prisoners rose from 12% in 1981 to 26% in 1992; and a growing proportion are from second-generation ethnic minorities. While much controversy surrounds the view that such minorities are disproportionately involved in crime, the perception has grown that they are unusually disaffected, resistant to welfare measures and recalcitrant. In this situation, even liberal elites are prone to disillusioned acceptance of exclusionary measures: in England, black children are permanently excluded from school at three times the rate of white children; and the scale of expulsions overall rose greatly during the 1990s to 12,668 in 1996/97 (10,400 in 1998/9) (Department for Education and Employment, 10 May 2000). These trends all hold potential for penal expansion.

3. Risk and security

More common ground between Europe and the USA can be found in the combination of a heightened awareness of victimization by crime and greater expectations of personal security and public safety. Expectations about safety and security have increased hugely in the post-war period. The Social Democratic ideal of cradle-to-grave work and welfare; immense improvements in medical care and surgery; the post-war settlement that, despite the nuclear threat, held out the prospect of peaceful international relations; and the makings of a system of world governance promised future stability. In the lives of most people in the democracies of the West, and with the signal exception of the Vietnam war, victimisation by crime was the principal source of risk that could not be personally controlled or ameliorated. Oral histories tend to confirm this sense of crime as an increasingly unwarranted scourge. It has fuelled the growth of such movements as victim rights and victim support and the vast and growing investment in situational crime prevention: mass electronic surveillance, target hardening, security checks and gated communities are now so pervasive that the crime rate might well be termed the displacement rate. Cars left un-alarmed, property left unguarded and houses only minimally secured are now bad insurance risks, with the worst-hit communities becoming uninsurable. The more repressive the controls, the more regressive becomes the crime, with poorer areas – notoriously the de-industrialised wastelands – plagued by multiple victimization. The promise of situational control was that the contested terrain of 'root causes' could be ignored. But while such controls may have helped contain crime rates, they have hardly been reduced at all substantially. Insofar as crime rates persist at a high level or even increase despite such measures – which have immense implications for the exclusion and control of deviant groups and individuals – the potential for yet further resort to imprisonment is ever-present.

Among the more potent images of risk and insecurity are the mentally ill, decanted from dwindling institutions to insubstantial community care. What gets noticed in the community are the visibly distressed and deviant, whose often-unkempt appearance, verbal aggression and odd behaviour disturb harassed commuters and busy shoppers. Though it is no comfort to victims, their contribution to lethal violence is minute, but what there is has fuelled demands for 'some-

thing to be done' about the most dangerous, severely disordered per-
sonalities. The current British Home Office proposal is that indefinite
detention should be the provision, even in the absence of offending
behaviour. Given the difficulties of diagnosis, this is a recipe for
expanding incarceration to a fresh target group of uncertain
dimensions.

The *macho* economy

[. . .]

International commentary often takes the USA to be some kind of ultra-
capitalist lost cause in terms of welfare spending. But this is a travesty.
In 1993, even after a decade of Reaganomic tax cuts for the rich and
welfare cuts for the poor, US spending on public welfare services still
amounted to some 21% of GDP, compared to 26% in the UK and 29%
in Germany. The UK and Germany are, on this measure, closer to the
US than to Scandinavian countries, where over 40% of GDP is devoted
to public sector welfare. On health, the US spent a slightly *higher*
proportion of GDP on its public health sector than the British spent
on the National Health Service, and over twice as much if private
health spending is included. On education and social security they are
roughly the same, though the US system favours the better off much
more than in Britain; really big differences only obtain in housing. What
this implies is the underlying strength of constituencies within the USA
for a substantial mixed economy of welfare, rather than an absolute
difference between the USA and Europe.

For the past two decades, however, the pressures towards privatisation and a reduction of public spending have gathered pace. The
impact of different interpretations of the third way will be crucial in
determining how far this tendency will be pushed. The debate is
increasingly couched in terms of the greater success of deregulated
market economies, most notably the US, by comparison with the more
'corporatist' economies of Europe, with the UK occupying an intermediate position following the partial continuation of New Right pri-
vatisations by New Labour. At stake is the continuing commitment to
far more substantial public sector investment in the lead countries of
Scandinavia, The Netherlands, Belgium, France, Germany and Italy.

The sheer size of the US prison population has now become an important factor in this macroeconomic matrix as never before. As Beckett
and Western (1997) have clearly spelled out, the US prison population
now amounts to some 2% of the male labour force. As a result of pris-

oners being excluded from the labour force count, a convention which merits re-examination, this factor alone has reduced the official figure for male unemployment by some 30–40% since the early 1990s.

[. . .]

It may be, therefore, that mass imprisonment in the US will make its impact on Europe less by the direct export of its components, such as privatisation, and mandatory and tougher sentencing, and more by its masked impact on macroeconomic policy, encouraging a retreat from substantial welfare services, from the involvement of trade unions in economic regulation and from employment safeguards.

[. . .]

There are at least four other respects in which the US penal phenomenon feeds into important debates in a distorting fashion. First, it is associated with both a successive stabilisation and actual reductions in the US crime rate *and* with an unprecedentedly long period of economic growth. Both factors combine to lend mass incarceration an aura of hard-won success, of benefits outweighing costs, which may prove influential in other countries. It hallows the export of private prison systems by Wackenhut and Correctional Corporation of America. The fact that the economic growth is despite, not because of, the prison explosion may be swamped in the rush to buy into its apparent success.

Secondly, as Beckett and Western argue, imprisonment damages employment prospects after release and heightens risks of recidivism. The criminogenic effects of custody are met in circular fashion by yet more incarceration. This helps explain why the US prison population has risen so incessantly beyond all seeming limits, and suggests that the US is now locked into a penal economy which is both self-replicating and subject to a multiplier effect due to progressively steepening mandatory sentences.

Thirdly, and paradoxically, the tight labour market created in part by mass imprisonment *may* be one reason for the falls in crimes against property, as a consequence of rising prosperity and even low wage employment. It is, however, the imprisonment and not the employment that gains popular credit.

Fourthly, there is a *macho* quality to the long US boom that may be heightened by mass incarceration. High prison populations hold inflationary implications, due to the tight labour markets on which they exert a concealed effect, and due also to the huge, largely unproductive nature of the investment involved. These are currently masked by the low inflation achieved in the US partly by productivity gains from information technology, but partly from high levels of foreign investment. A certain *machismo* inheres, however, in the steep disparity between Stock Market valuations and company profits; the size of the current account deficit; and high levels of consumer debt. When the downturn comes, it could be that mass incarceration will exert a Keynesian, stabilising effect, to be sustained for economic reasons. But a recession will fall most damagingly on those ex-offenders and ex-prisoners who have been employed, if at all, in the most precarious and least protected jobs, and whose employability has been most eroded by custody. These pressures predictably heighten their risk of recidivism and re-imprisonment. The interaction between these two trends could spell the even greater expansion of the prison population to well above the two million mark.

It is also the case that a *macho* economy produces a *macho* society. When economic strength and cut-throat profitability are the drivers of conduct, when job stability and decent wages are a folk memory; when skilled professionals can be told to clear their desks within the hour; when you are only as good as your last deal; and when secrecy in takeovers, asset stripping and head-hunting are conducted with sublime disregard for ethics, then the basis for some sort of Kantian respect for persons in social relationships can hardly be said to exist. The *machismo* of the street, in drug dealing, hustling and physical intimidation, with its lack of eye contact, demand for 'respect' and contempt for weakness, is [. . .] a poor basis for primary labour market employment. It is, however, a good preparation for street crime and survival in prison. The *machismo* of the powerless is a symmetrical parody of that of the powerful in a winner/loser culture.

Conclusions

'Europe has to withstand the American "example"! . . . It is improbable that it will become like the US in the future. The latter has given them too bad an example of what a failure can look like.'[6] One can only hope that this is indeed to be the case. But the burden of this analysis is that the components of a steep rise in imprisonment in Europe, especially in Britain, have been assembled. At the macroeconomic level, the case against more regulated economies is strengthened by fallacies about low unemployment fostered by mass incarceration itself. And Europe does not have to *match* the US rate of imprisonment for Europe to experience the makings of a social and political disaster: even to reach half the US level, or 330 per 100,000, would mean tripling current rates of imprisonment in Europe. The off-the-scale character of US imprisonment may even induce complacency elsewhere that their prison populations are so much lower that even steep rises in their terms would be comparatively negligible.

It is certainly the case that Europe and other societies should resist the US example on the penal front. But what are the prospects for resistance within the USA itself? Here there is much common ground with Europe. 'We think of the US as a nation dedicated to private enterprise. Yet [unlike in Britain] its water supply remains in public hands, as do some important rail lines; and there are no plans to privatise the federal mails.'[7] And, as noted above, education, health and social security remain major public services, despite the huge inroads of the grossly enlarged criminal justice and penal systems. In other words, there is a basis for interpretations of American exceptionalism to be reclaimed from the new right by the constituencies which created the New Deal and the Great Society programmes. It may be that those constituencies have been fragmented by deindustrialisation and suburbanisation, but the potential for their reassembly surely lies in the need for security against the hazards of the 'risk society' that can only be collectively provided.

The crime form most unique to American society, lethal violence, presents awesome problems of regulation, but Zimring and Hawkins have documented the links with lack of gun control to provide a case which can be tirelessly put for far greater restrictions, even if they are dubious about its prospects. On racial discrimination and drug law enforcement, we should heed William Julius Wilson's prescription on joblessness and inequality: that although they affect young black men most adversely, they are transracial problems that are best dealt with as needing common solutions.

Taken together, these three strands provide a front on which to contest the case for mass incarceration. Otherwise, the country which invented the juvenile court but is now executing juveniles, and in which no presidential candidate opposes capital punishment, will carry on, and seek to carry others with it, as if it had no alternative.

Notes

1   Leon Radzinowicz, 'Penal regressions', *Cambridge Law Journal*, Vol. 50, 1991.
2   M. Tonry, *Malign Neglect: Crime, Race and Punishment*, New York: Oxford University Press; A. Kuhn, 'Incarceration rates around the world', *Overcrowded Times*, Vol. 10, 1999.

3 Against this view, Matthews (1999) argues, citing Lynch (1988) and the work of
   Farrington, Langan and Wikstrom (1992, 1994 a and b), that the US is not especially punitive once the more serious character of crime in America is taken into
   account: 'The differences between the USA and England and Wales are largely
   a product of different rates of crime rather than major differences in sentencing
   practice . . . However, the USA tends to impose longer prison sentences for those
   convicted' (p. 99). This conclusion seriously understates substantial differences
   between the two societies, and between the US and other Western European
   countries, in sentences for non-violent crimes and drug offences, the fastest
   growing component of US incarceration rates. Even Lynch (1995), who is also
   keen to challenge the image of the USA as relatively punitive, summarises
   Farrington and Langan's (1992) data as follows: 'The probability of incarceration following conviction was not radically different across nations for violent
   crimes, but it was substantially different for property crimes . . . A person found
   guilty of burglary in the United States had a .74 probability of a custodial sen-
   tence but only a .40 chance in England and Wales . . . The large differences in
   time served between the United States and the other countries occurs for property crimes – burglary and larceny' (Lynch, 1995, pp. 33–4). For burglary, the
   same source gives the US average of time served as 10.6 months compared with
   6.8 months in England and 5.3 in Canada. For larceny, the mean time served is
   7 months in the US compared with 4.65 in England and 2 months in Canada.
   For drug offences, the differences are even more substantial. And, as Currie
   notes, these figures are mostly based on mid-1980s data, so that 'after nearly a
   decade and a half of relentlessly stiffening sentences [in the US], . . . our comparative severity has increased substantially' (Currie, 1998, p. 19). Moreover,
   while within offence differences, such as carrying weaponry, may account for
   steeper sentences for robbery, this factor is far less likely to apply to burglary
   and larceny (see Zimring and Hawkins, 1997, pp. 44–6). Matthew's argument is,
   however, a timely reminder that we lack up-to-date, close grained analyses of
   comparative sentencing practice.
      The urge to normalise American punitiveness also encourages playing down,
   or ignoring, what is happening at the extremes of the sentencing spectrum, as
   distinct from its middle range. Thus 'it is curious that those who argue that the
   US is not especially punitive generally fail to mention that we are the only industrial democracy that still makes significant use of the death penalty for homicide' (Currie, p. 17). And for the least serious offences, the US has pioneered, or
   reactivated, an array of 'quality of life' crimes, for whose violation the risks of
   arrest, detention and subsequent imprisonment are now greatly increased
   (Parenti, 1999, Ch. 4).
4 Junger-Tas, J. (1998) 'Dutch penal policies changing direction', *Overcrowded
   Times*, Vol. 9, 5 October.
5 I. Marshall, 'How exceptional is the United States? Crime trends in Europe
   and the US', *European Journal on Criminal Policy and Research*, Vol. 4, 1996,
   p. 31.
6 A. Kuhn, 'Incarceration rates: Europe versus USA', *European Journal on Criminal
   Policy and Research*, Vol. 4, 1996, p. 49.
7 R. Blackburn, 'How to bring back collectivism', *New Statesman*, 17 January 2000,
   p. 25.

References

Beckett K and Western B (1997) "The penal system as labor market institution: jobs and jails, 1980–95" *Overcrowded Times*, 8, 6.

Blackburn R (2000) "How to bring back collectivism" *New Statesman*, 17.1.00.

Currie E (1998) *Crime and Punishment in America*, New York: Holt.

Department for Education and Employment (2000) *Permanent Exclusions from Schools and Exclusion Appeals, England 1998/9 (provisional)*, London: Government Statistical Service.

Farrington D and Langan P (1992) "Changes in crime and punishment in England and America in the 1980s" *Justice Quarterly* 9: 5–46.

Farrington D, Langan P and Wikstrom P (1994a) "Changes in crime and punishment in England, America and Sweden in the 1980s and 1990s" *Studies in Crime and Crime Prevention*, 104–31.

Farrington D, Langan P and Wikstrom P (1994b) "Changes in crime and punishment in England and America in the 1980s" *Justice Quarterly* 9, 1, 5–31.

Home Office (1999) *Managing Dangerous People With Severe Personality Disorder: Proposals for Policy Development* London: Home Office (July).

Kuhn A (1996) "Incarceration rates: Europe versus USA" *European Journal on Criminal Policy and Research (Developments in the Use of Prisons)* 4, 3, 46–73.

Kuhn A (1999) "Incarceration rates around the world" *Overcrowded Times*, 10, 2, April.

Lynch J (1988) "A comparison of prison use in England, Canada, West Germany and the United States" *Journal of Criminal Law and Criminology* 79, 108–217.

Lynch J (1995) "Crime in international perspective" in Wilson J and Petersilia J (Eds.) *Crime* San Francisco: ICS Press.

Marshall I (1996) "How exceptional is the United States? Crime trends in Europe and the US" *European Journal on Criminal Policy and Research (Europe Meets U.S. in Crime and Policy)* 4, 2, 7–35.

Matthews R (1999) *Doing Time: An Introduction to the Sociology of Imprisonment* London: Macmillan.

Radzinowicz L (1991) "Penal regressions" *Cambridge Law Journal*, 50, 422–44.

Society and Crime: A Policy Plan for the Future (1985) The Hague: Ministry of Justice.

Tonry M (1995) *Malign Neglect: Race, Crime and Punishment* New York: Oxford University Press.

Tonry M (1996) "The effects of American drug policy on black Americans, 1980–1996" *European Journal of Criminal Policy and Research (Europe Meets U.S. in Crime and Policy)* 4, 2, 36–62.

Tonry M (1999) "Why are U.S. incarceration rates so high?" *Overcrowded Times*, 10, 3 (June).

Zimring F and Hawkins G (1997) *Crime Is Not The Problem: Lethal Violence in America*, New York: Oxford University Press.

15

The Family Way: Navigating a Third Way in Family Policy

Helen Wilkinson

[. . .]

Many families today experience huge strain. Relationships are breaking down at a rapid rate; more and more children are growing up in disrupted families; birth rates are in decline; and there is a serious tension for many between the demands placed on them to be good parents and spouses and to be high achievers in an increasingly competitive workplace. Our very notion of family itself appears to be threatened. The long-term trends suggest that we are not only living in a 'post divorce' society (in which divorce is commonplace), we are rapidly moving to a 'post marriage' one where marriage itself is increasingly redundant. (The first-time marriage rate is at its lowest possible level since 1889 and cohabitation is a cultural norm.)

There is a direct public policy interest here. Finance is a major factor. Weakened families cost the state money both directly and indirectly. In this context the state has a public interest in strengthening families, regardless of their structure. But political interest in families goes deeper. Families are the foundation of civil society, where we first learn moral values. Families generate social capital – the trust and relationship skills which enable individuals to cooperate. Family breakdown is a major factor in declining social capital and wider social dysfunction. The state has an interest and a role in preventing this.

But there is also a broader argument. The future growth of the economy, the vibrancy of our community life and culture, and the well-being of tomorrow's retirees – all depend on how well families manage to raise the children who will become the citizens and workers of tomorrow. In short, the state has an interest in the capacity of our nation's children to thrive.

A tired debate

In spite of this critical role (or indeed perhaps because of it) debates about family life have a 'manic depressive' quality. On the one hand, conservatives lament the trends in family life. On the other, liberals celebrate the greater freedom that has accompanied these changes. Discussions about enhancing the well-being of our children and about strengthening families get lost in the fruitlessly polarised arguments between these positions.

Neither perspective fully comprehends the dynamics of change. Liberals downplay the costs of social change, while traditionalists misread lessons from history. In reality, the story is of decline and progress. Family change has brought greater freedom and autonomy but this process has not been without costs, and these have been borne most clearly by children.

There has been an unhealthy polarisation between liberals who affirm individualism and tend to take a relativist view of family values and structures, and between conservatives who talk a lot about values but neglect household economics. The result? A policy impasse. Yet we have been presented with a false choice. The problems being experienced by families today are rooted both in economic stress (whether of time or money) and in family disintegration. Any progressive family policy must address both these issues or it will fail.

We are just beginning to understand the full range of costs that society bears when families raise children less effectively than they can. The time is ripe for a progressive child-centred family policy which acknowledges the new realities and affirms enduring values. The challenge for government in the twenty-first century will be to find ways of stabilising families in an era of globalisation and enhancing their child-rearing capacity, without imposing severe burdens on taxpayers and the state.

[. . .]

Frontiers of family policy

There are two large-scale and interwoven problems which need to be addressed if we are fully to understand the way in which families are changing as we move into the twenty-first century. The first is the need to strengthen intact families to help minimise the risk of break-ups and dysfunction. The second problem is family disintegration caused by divorce and relationship breakdown. This trend needs to be tackled directly because family breakdown carries with it a public health cost for all concerned. This is exacerbated by the culture of exclusion in the most deprived urban areas, where families are at high risk of fracturing or not cohering in the first place. Strengthening fragile families will be critical if we are to grapple with the causes of social exclusion and stand a chance of stopping the transmission of poverty and insecure attachment from one generation to the next.

Politicians should try to strengthen intact families in various ways. The emphasis should be on ensuring that working families benefit from high quality subsidised child care, from varieties of paid parental leave, and from a 'family-friendly' tax and benefits system. Government will look to employers to play more of a role in facilitating changes in the culture of workplaces. Public–private partnerships will become commonplace as government seeks to place a share of financial responsibility for family life on taxpayers and employers in recognition of the fact that individual parents have paid too high a price in recent decades in foregoing income and advancement at work to take on the role of child-rearing.

The public health perspective requires that we make investments now in child care in order to reap benefits over the long term in reduced incidence of family breakdown, delinquency and exclusion, and increased levels of work satisfaction and performance, family cohesion and educational attainment. Welfare-to-work strategies need to be combined with schemes of paid parental leave, enabling parents to spend time with their family in the early years (critical for child health and family bonding) while at the same time giving unemployed individuals the opportunity to move into the labour market. In areas of social exclusion, where the numbers of people forming traditional intact families are in most serious decline, targeted welfare-to-work policies will be a vital means of giving individuals the economic stability to think about family formation.

Such economic measures should be combined with voluntary relationship and parenting programmes. The American experience suggests that the most innovative programmes have been rooted in the communities they serve, administered and designed by local community agencies which can foster the necessary trust and commitment with their clientele to make such schemes successful.

To date, welfare reform has been framed with adults' needs in mind. Tomorrow's welfare reform agenda will need to be 'child-friendly'. Just as working parents should benefit from genuine choices between high quality child care or parental leave, so too unemployed parents should benefit from welfare reform which recognises the value of family cohesion. The parental care credit advocated by [some] as an adjunct to government welfare-to-work strategies for single parents should be integrated into the next generation of [welfare-to-work] options, driven by notions of equity and choice, and by public awareness of the importance of parental involvement in the early years of a child's life.

Attention will focus increasingly on enhancing fathers' role in family life, not just in providing for the family, but also in caring for children. Paid parental leave schemes will be one step in the right direction, but we should also anticipate innovations such as the establishment of a fatherhood task-force (modelled on task-forces and 'fatherhood commissions' in some American states) in imaginative efforts to raise public awareness about fathers' responsibilities as nurturers. Such a task-force's remit would be to review family policy across the board to assess how far specific measures and bureaucratic cultures help raise the profile of fatherhood and contribute to positive outcomes.

[A new] politics of the family should aim to strengthen families disrupted by divorce or other breakdown, with children's well-being at the heart of policy. Recent reforms have been based on the view that whilst marriage may no longer be for life, parenthood is, and that so far as possible children should not suffer for their parents' mistakes. This emphasis on parental responsibility and managing the 'good break-up' is a pragmatic response to the new realities. It means starting with families as they are, rather than with how we wish them to be. Family policies should not be seen as a zero-sum game between two competing ways of living.

This approach should continue. Its success should be measured in terms of its impact on family health: its capacity to minimise conflict during and after relationship breakdown; the extent to which it facilitates father involvement; its impact on child well-being and so on. Informed by an awareness of the health impact on adults and children affected by family breakdown, policy-makers should focus on identifying effective ways of resolving unsatisfactory relationships as well as maintaining healthy attachments between parents and the child, regardless of the relationship between the adults.

Pressures to reform the system of child support will mount because of awareness in the policy-making community of the costs incurred (financial and emotional) when fathers are not present in the lives of their children, perhaps especially of boys. Measures aimed at strengthening the ties that bind non-resident fathers to the lives of their children will rise to the top of the domestic policy agenda. Typically women have been the 'gatekeepers' to family life and because they have frequently had negative experiences with these men, they are reluctant to allow them back into their lives. However, American experience suggests that it is possible to forge a new consensus. Innovative 'team parenting' initiatives have achieved some degree of success in involving fathers and mothers as stakeholders in their children's future and could be tried out in Britain.

Effort should be focused on low-income non-resident fathers via welfare-to-work schemes which integrate personal and social skills training. Evidence to date from various innovative schemes in American states suggests that such programmes have wide appeal both for their employment and educational component, provided that participation is not forced on fathers. (Such an approach is not incompatible with tougher more rigorous enforcement of child support enforcement for the genuine 'deadbeat dads', the fathers who can pay but won't.)

Complementing such experiments could be attempts to develop a single point of access for dealing with the public consequences of the break-up of a household – finance, access and visitation issues – regardless of the marital status of the couple concerned. A number of innovative US states are experimenting with such approaches.

If the American experience is anything to go by, the makers of future family policy will bring fathers into the equation in unprecedented ways. The whole direction of family policy, which has historically marginalised fathers and focused on the mother/child dyad, should be reframed. The emphasis should be as much on shifting attitudes to family life and fatherhood within the bureaucracies and community at large, as on specific policies for supporting families.

Family policies will also need to grapple with three secular trends: the shift to the *post-divorce society* (in which divorce is commonplace); the shift to the *post-marriage society* (where the role and function of marriage is increasingly called into question) and the *growth in child-free families* (witnessed by the declining birth rate). In pursuing a public health strategy in family policy, we may need to seek ways to slow down, or even reverse, these movements.

These are grand goals demanding long-term strategy. But how are they to be achieved? What role should government play in promoting marriage, reducing resort to divorce and dealing with parenting issues?

Just as tomorrow's adults need the skills and competencies required to cope in an increasingly flexible and competitive economy, so too they need a more robust set of interpersonal and communication skills to cope with more demanding and fluid personal relationships. The challenge will be to create opportunities to learn – rather than programmes relying in vain on coercion or moral exhortation. Classroom education, soap opera wisdom, counselling and advice services will all play a part.

Tomorrow's family should be a learning family and lifelong learning about relationships will be key. As we graduate from the classroom into adult life, we should be encouraged to seek advice and help where possible through local community agencies which provide advice and information about relationships and parenting. These should be part-financed by government, but independent of it.

In policy terms the focus should be more on preventive strategies. We need to spend more now on the basis that we will save later. This means investing in relationship and parenting skills together, given that the single most important determinant of successful childrearing is lack of conflict between parents. We also need to concentrate our energies on making successful long-term relationships more likely, not on making divorce harder.

Critics might argue that governments should not involve themselves in affairs of the heart: that relationships are private and should remain so. Preventive strategies in family policy recognise that the fall-out from broken homes imposes wider social costs, and that it is worth trying to reduce these through more holistic policies. This is why we have a collective responsibility to enhance our capacities to sustain stable and intimate relationships, and why government has a role in trying to improve citizens' chances of success in long-term relationships, without interfering unacceptably in private life.

The second major goal should be to foster a marriage culture. Here policy-makers must feel that they are swimming against the tide. Marriage rates are in decline and the first-time marriage rate is at its lowest level ever. Yet, in the early decades of [this new] century, the promotion of marriage could rise up the agenda in policy circles, as the public health argument in favour of marriage becomes better understood and the research evidence more widely known.

[. . .]

For successful and stable marriages do not just enhance the well-being of children, they benefit the adults concerned, generate good health and at their very best enhance the social and cultural capital of the individual concerned. People in successful marriages are on balance healthier and happier than those who are single or unmarried. They also tend to be better off, and to have a denser network of connections to the community.

In this sense, marriage helps build and sustain social capital. As an institution, it can generate trust, a sense of belonging and the strong and secure attachments required to nurture individuals who can thrive throughout life. It follows that policy-makers should be concerned to include gay couples within their remit and to offer them the same rights to legal marriage as heterosexual couples, on the basis that commitment and trust between individuals should be encouraged and fostered regardless of sexual orientation. (Of course, none of this negates the validity of the reverse argument, namely that divorce for couples in unhappy marriages can also be better for all individuals concerned.)

[. . .]

What role does or should government money play in helping to recreate a marriage culture? Why should an unmarried couple in their twenties pay a subsidy to a married couple of the same age, as with the married couple's tax allowance? The public health arguments for marriage are clear. But with the rise of cohabitation, it is important that the same kinds of services that are available to married couples are also open to cohabiting couples, since it is both constituencies that governments must reach if they are to foster a marriage culture.

In practice, the resources for strengthening and supporting marriage are already available to us in the form of the married couple's tax allowance; they need to be redirected in more productive ways. For example preventive initiatives such as marriage preparation classes deserve more support by comparison with reactive, palliative measures such as divorce mediation. As a new pragmatism takes hold in family policy attention will continue to shift to ways of redirecting the revenue generated from reducing this allowance, whose contribution to a marriage culture is marginal.

But we need to be clear about priorities. Children should be first in the queue for resources regardless of parents' marital status. In a study on paid parental leave I showed how a generous scheme could be financed by as little as one tenth of the value of the married couple's tax allowance, a policy measure which would do much to enhance family health and strengthen relationships. But this would still leave plenty of money left over to finance marriage-friendly initiatives such as those outlined above. The emphasis should be on investing money to promote a marriage culture wisely and where it is most needed, especially among those at risk of social exclusion.

The third trend which policy-makers should seek to reverse is the declining birth rate. The prospect of declining birth rates has raised the spectre not only of inter-generational imbalances but the prospect that there will be insufficient workers to finance the care needs of the elderly. (The UK birth rate has been declining since the 1960s and one-fifth of women born in the 1960s are predicted to remain childfree.) Reversing this trend will require a major cultural shift, what I call a 'new parentalism', and it will need to be underpinned by economic subsidies.

Experience suggests that if child-rearing is expensive it will be discouraged. If it is affordable it will be encouraged. Over the last few decades, the costs of family life have been shared unequally by individual parents (and by women). Taxpayers and governments must share the burden in recognition of the benefits created by good parenting. We should see a progressive pro-natalism take root, with other stakeholders in society (tax payers, the state and employers) bearing more costs to reduce those borne by parents.

What does this mean in practice? In policy terms, it means matching rhetoric about family values with genuine investments. Paid parental leave is one of the few policy tools with a proven track record in helping to reverse declining birth rates. Here we should look not to America, where leave is unpaid, but to Europe. Scandinavian countries have seen a dramatic return to family formation since the 1980s as a result of generous paid parental leave, and innovations in parental leave elsewhere indicate how families and ultimately the wider community can gain from integration of family-friendly policies into the world of work, and into welfare-to-work programmes for socially excluded parents.

This demands serious thinking about influencing workplace cultures and entrenched expectations about men's and women's relative engagement in paid work and family life. Involving fathers and raising the status of fatherhood will be critical. Government should also aim to bring about a healthier, more sustainable balance between work and family life. This will involve long-term debate and information campaigns to help effect a gradual culture change in our workplaces and build up a genuine commitment among employers to integrating work and family life. In this respect, the present 'family-friendly' employment agenda is not radical enough: differentiating between workers with families and those without can lead to an unhealthy tension between the two, creating more obstacles to the much-needed shift in working styles and practices in the mainstream culture of work. The challenge will be to reorganise work in such a way that as many people as possible can find ways to integrate work and home lives better, and not feel pressured by workplace demands into making choices about when or whether to have children. But a progressive pro-natalist strategy should go further. In the end our policies for family-friendliness in employment will depend how far we can foster a more child-friendly culture overall, radically affecting the design of our public spaces and our community facilities as well as our workplaces.

A key element in this programme will be to think through new ways of valuing the work of parents. This involves recognising that parents are the primary educators for their children. Community agencies could be funded to run imaginative public awareness campaigns focusing on the importance of the early years for children's healthy development. Although there are clear educational benefits from such early child development, it could be the public health benefits which will in the end prove most compelling.

Policy-makers face a particularly modern dilemma. In a fast-changing 'knowledge economy', the socialisation of children and young people as thriving workers and citizens demands much greater reserves of parental and institutional support than ever before. This comes at a time when many long-term relationships are exposed to strain, when men and women face intense demands at work and when their capacities to spend time on parenting and other family activities are being squeezed. If ever there was a time when families needed strong social support, this is it. This is why, in spite of the greying of our society, we should anticipate an inter-generational redistribution of resources in favour of children and their parents.

Ironically, it has been the parties of the centre left, not the centre right, who have led the way in thinking about ways to stabilise family life, who have been 'conservative' in recognising the need to foster strong families for the good of children and the community as a whole. That they have done so without taking the moral high ground and whilst avoiding nostalgia for the past is no mean feat. As Conservatives try to make themselves relevant to a new generation of voters, they too will have to revise their assumptions. Conservatives will have to confront head-on the tension that exists between two key strands of centre-right thinking: its economic liberalism and its socially conservative moral agenda. For the great irony is that despite Conservative rhetoric about traditional family values, globalisation combined with free market policies did much to destabilise family life and erode the traditional family values which Conservatives have claimed to defend. The lesson for the future is a simple one. Governments should focus on valuing families, strengthening and stabilising them in all shapes and sizes, not moralising about them.

16

Work or Retirement at Career's End? A Third Way Strategy for an Ageing Population

Anne-Marie Guillemard

In the last 20 years, the allocation of work and leisure over the life course has undergone major changes. For one thing, young people are entering the labour market at a later age, given longer schooling and the difficulty of finding work. They experience an increasingly long, uncertain period of joblessness before finding stable employment. In France for example, the average age of entry in the labour market has increased by three years over the last quarter century. The proportion of young people less than 25 years old in the labour force decreased by half between 1968 and 1995, and it is now under 10 per cent. This decrease cannot, in the main, be set down to population trends; it mainly has to do with the reduced labour force participation rate of young people, in France but also in many other European countries. For another thing, labour force participation after the age of 55 has fallen considerably on both shores of the Atlantic. Only Sweden and Japan have withstood this widespread trend. [. . .]

The working life is thus becoming shorter at both ends. It now mainly involves middle-aged groups. In turn, new arrangements have been made in welfare systems so as to cover the new status both of young people entering the labour market and of ageing wage earners who have left the job market early.

In brief, we have, over the last 20 years, witnessed a revolution in the way the phases of education, work and retirement spread out over the life course. A recent OECD study has documented these major changes in nearly all member-states.[1] According to it, the average number of retirement years – the time spent outside the labour market – increased rapidly from 1960 to 1995: men have gained more than 11 years. Meanwhile, the average number of years spent working decreased considerably: by seven years. [. . .]

The same study has emphasised how much time has been pared off the number of years in employment between 1960 and 1995. In 1960, the typical man in an OECD member-state devoted 50 of his 68 years of life to work. Most of the 18 others were spent at school, and a few in retirement. In 1995, a typical man lived till 76 but devoted only half his life – 38 years – to work. The other years were spent in education, unemployment and, above all, retirement. If this trend continues, men will, by about 2020, spend much more time out of, than in, employment.

This impressive trend toward a shorter work life causes concern given the quite foreseeable ageing of the population in the early part of the third millennium. It jeopardises the financial equilibrium of old-age funds everywhere. The ratio of active persons to the inactive ageing is ebbing fast because of the swelling wave of early exit from the labour force and because of demographic ageing, as baby boomers grow older while generations with fewer members will be reaching the age to start working and pay into old-age funds. [. . .] This trend toward a shorter work life also raises [. . .] questions about what kind of labour force will, in a foreseeable future, sustain national economies. The ageing of the population will, inevitably, lead to an ageing of the labour force itself as the latter is increasingly made up of wage earners between 40 and 55 years old and as the number of young people entering the labour market tapers off. In many firms, wage earners over 45 are already encountering difficulties: they are deemed too old for promotions or retraining. [. . .] Besides, early exit seems, for many ageing wage earners, the only possibility, even more so as many countries seem to think that replacing them with jobless youth can solve (un)employment problems. In the future, the question will be whether Europe can manage with such a small work force. Will firms choose to adapt the organisation of production to an older labour force, to whom they will continue giving work? Or will they recruit immigrants or even delocalise operations?

We must state forcefully that the ageing of our societies is not a catastrophe, and should not be viewed fatalistically. Let us not forget that a longer life span and lessened morbidity are, above all, evidence of social progress. There is no reason they should be catastrophic if we anticipate the consequences by reinforcing social cohesion, solidarity and equity among generations. Meeting the challenge of demographic ageing means that we must now manage an ageing labour force. This will be the major issue for the coming decades. To cope with it, we must reverse the deep trends, now under way everywhere, toward shortening the work life. This can be done only by developing effective public policies for jobs and welfare so as to maintain older wage earners' 'employability' and by stimulating firms to adjust their personnel policies accordingly. The way is hard and long, but it is one of the major challenges facing developed societies as they enter the third millennium.

Herein, I want to argue for analysing the situation by taking into account changes in how time and ages in the life course are managed. Debates about demographic ageing have, till the present, overfocused on its eventual implications for old-age pensions. This focus is much too narrow to help identify the means of action for coping with these issues.

[. . .]

Ever earlier exit from the labour market

A new risk at the end of the working life

Rising joblessness after the age of 50, as well as the reluctance of firms to promote or retrain wage earners over 40, is evidence that the sizeable drop in the economic activity rate after 55 has swollen the ranks of 'semi old' wage earners 'on the way out' in the next younger age group: 45–55-year-olds are experiencing age discrimination in the job market and at the workplace. A new age group is now at risk. The joblessness, precariousness and uncertainty that used to characterise young people is now an experience for wage earners at the other end of the work life.

A series of harmful consequences

The widespread overuse of early exit has had a serious impact, in particular on ageing wage earners' 'employability'.

Age stereotypes reinforced   Large scale recourse to preretirement schemes and other forms of early exit has thoroughly changed expectations and anticipations. Companies now have the habit of treating employees over 55 as redundant and unemployable. Hence, the latter must be pushed aside, regardless of the firm's managerial rationality. For their part, wage earners think that 55 is now the normal age for definitive withdrawal, and they make their plans in consequence thereof. In a big French automobile firm where, for 15 years, masses of employees at 55 have been pushed into preretirement via the National Employment Fund (Fonds National de l'Emploi), a worker declared: 'Retirement at 55 is the law'.

By emptying offices and workshops of those over 55, this massive early exit trend has reinforced age stereotypes. Top management, foremen and supervisors, as well as persons working on the line, will soon share the opinion that older workers: are unemployable and inefficient; lack motivation; are unable to adapt to change; and cannot be retrained. What may have been true for a generation, with a low level of initial education, is becoming a label superglued onto a whole age group, which is being declared too old to work and has lost all value in the labour market.

[. . .]

Ineffective age-related measures   Everywhere in Europe, early exit schemes have had disappointing effects on unemployment. They have, at times, disguised joblessness but at an exorbitant price. As a means of opening jobs to younger people by laying off their elders, these measures certainly have not been very efficient. Why has this myth of jobless youth being helped by the early exit of the ageing persisted, even though assessments of such job measures in Europe have constantly proven it to be false?

Esping-Andersen, in a recent study convincingly proves how inadequate the early exit schemes adopted in various countries have been in settling problems related to unemployment in general and to the unemployment of youth in particular.[2] In the countries in this study, the total number of people leaving unemployment rolls as well as the number of those in the younger age groups entering from unemployment rolls are negatively correlated with older wage earners' early exit rate. Instead of limiting joblessness, early exit tends to worsen the problem. According to these data, each 10 per cent of 55–64 year old men who have left the labour force on preretirement corresponds to two to three per cent less in the total *number* of persons leaving unemployment rolls and to four to six per cent less in the number of young people who do so. Early exit thus seems more like a means whereby firms can get rid of wage earners they no longer want than like a measure for coping with unemployment and creating job opportunities.

For firms: loss and disorder   Early exit schemes have entailed a loss for companies and also caused disorder in them. There has been a loss of experience and know-how as ageing employees have left, and, also, a negative impact on the personnel's age-pyramid. The latter looks like a rectangle, given both early exits and the limited recruitment of young people. As a consequence, the work force is made up of the middle-aged to whom it is ever harder to offer career incentives. The prospects for advancement are limited for everyone, including young recruits. This lack of reliability and visibility in career prospects offered to various age groups may entail major costs for firms and impair their ability to motivate personnel.

Unsuccessful public policies in Europe since 1990: limiting early exit

Everywhere in Europe, the expansion of early exit with its harmful con-sequences has caused public authorities to react, usually by combining measures of three sorts: reforming old-age funds and raising the retirement age; replacing early retirement with part-time retirement schemes; and implementing active job policies for keeping older workers in employment. I shall now use studies made for the Euro-pean Commission in 1998 to illustrate this policy trend. The greatest efforts in recent years to reduce the extent of early exit and keep people in the labour force longer have been made in those countries with high economic inactivity rates among men in their late 50s and early 60s. Such policies aim, independently of the effect on early exit itself, at containing the costs of welfare systems.

Increasing the retirement age

Germany will be gradually, between 2001 and 2012, increasing the retirement age to 65 for both men and women, even for those men who have paid into the Old-Age Fund for 35 years or more and who may retire once they reach 63 – as of 2002, they will see their pensions reduced by 18 per cent if they take retirement at this age. The retire-ment age has also been raised for the jobless who may draw a full pension at 60 if they have received unemployment benefits for at least 52 weeks. Although they will be allowed to retire up to three years earlier, their pensions will, in this case, be reduced by 3.6 per cent for each year taken.

In France, although the retirement age has not increased since it was set at 60 in 1982, the requisite period of contributions for a full pension has climbed six months a year since 1994: from $37\frac{1}{2}$ to 40 years. This was coupled with changing the formula for calculating pensions. Average wages during the last 10 years of the career now serve as the base, instead of average wages during the best 25 years: one year will be added on for each calendar year up till 2008.

Italy may have the pension system in Europe that tends most toward early retirement. Workers there may retire after working 35 years once they have reached 52 or else, irrespective of age, if they have accumulated 36 years of contributions to the Old-Age Fund. For civil servants, the requirements are less stringent. Although the new system being phased in since the 1995 reform will allow both men and women to retire at any time between 57 and 65, their pensions will be based more on the contributions they have paid into the Old-Age Fund than on previous wages. The transition period is, however, very long, running up to 2030. [. . .]

In Spain, the February 1995 Toledo Pact intended to improve the pension system's financial viability by increasing the retirement age. It recommended penalising early retirement and providing incentives to ageing wage earners who continue working by reducing their Social Security contributions. In July 1997, legislation was passed to rationalise the welfare system and implement many of the Pact's recommendations. It remains to be seen how effective this will be. According to a survey carried out in 1995, a large majority of Spaniards opposed raising the retirement age but favoured more flexible arrangements for combining part-time retirement with part-time employment.

[. . .]

From early to part-time retirement

A second set of policy measures has aimed at reducing the flow of older workers out of the labour market by both limiting the number who qualify for early retirement and providing incentives for those nearing the early retirement age to continue working. In a context of high unemployment, the latter sort of arrangement may be a compromise between fighting against joblessness and keeping older workers in the labour force. For many companies, this compromise has entailed the obligation to hire young people.

In Belgium, flexible retirement between 60 and 65 has been possible for all male employees since 1990, and will be open to women once their retirement age has risen to 65. Pension benefits vary depending on the person's employment record. Since 1985, employees at least 50 years old may opt for part-time work for up to three years till the age of 60, when they may retire. However, very few have taken advantage of this option: one per cent. In addition, companies are required to hire new employees to replace those opting for part-time work. A 1993 measure allows people to continue working part time once they reach 55; beneficiaries receive allowances on top of their wages from the Unemployment Fund and from employers. These measures have had no perceptible effect on the number of older workers staying in employment. By September 1997, only a few hundred people had opted for part-time early retirement.

Austria, too, has tightened eligibility requirements for early retirement, and encouraged gradual retirement since 1993, through a part-time early retirement scheme whereby women between 55 and 60 or men between 60 and 65 may either reduce the hours spent working by 50 per cent but receive 70 per cent of a full pension or else reduce the hours by 70 per cent and receive 50 per cent of a full pension. Although this option seems financially attractive, no one has taken advantage of it, partly because the eligible also qualify for full early retirement or for a full rather than partial pension.

In Finland, part-time retirement schemes were introduced in the late 1980s with the intention of smoothing the transition toward retirement and reducing the number of persons going on early retirement. According to recent studies, however, such schemes are an alternative more to full-time work than to full-time retirement: they have trimmed the number of full-time workers instead of pensioners. Subsequently, two other measures, Part-Time Work Supplementary Benefits and Job Rotation Compensation, were introduced to reduce work hours. Both programs are open to those who have worked full time for the same employer for at least a year under condition that the employer hire jobless persons. To date, these programs seem to have had little effect.

In Germany, besides tightened eligibility requirements for early retirement, a part-time retirement scheme was introduced in 1996 for a limited five-year period, enabling those over 55 to work part time, the reduction in their income being compensated by the Unemployment Insurance Fund (30 per cent for a 50 per cent reduction in the time spent working). As elsewhere, employers are required to take on either people unemployed or trainees to fill the part-time jobs thus opened up. So far, however, such jobs have been few in number.

[. . .]

Keeping older workers in employment

The third aspect of old-age policies has been to provide incentives to employers so that they keep on older wage earners. Increasing the official retirement age will be likely to miss this goal if it is not combined with measures for protecting ageing workers. No significant policy changes have occurred over the last few years. Furthermore, attempts to persuade employers to keep older wage earners in the work force have not met with much success.

Long-term unemployment has risen significantly for older workers since unification in Germany. Unlike in other countries, it is now higher for older wage earners than for youth. Under German job protection legislation, older workers are treated as a priority group to keep in employment. The most important measure of this sort provides age-dependent wage subsidies to the firms that open at least two part-time jobs for persons 50 years old or older who have been unemployed for at least 18 months. This has apparently not increased the number of older workers in employment, but it is hard to imagine what would have happened had his measure not been adopted. But such targeting, though hard to avoid, may, unfortunately, reinforce prejudices against the targeted group by giving the impression that its members are inferior or less efficient.

[. . .]

Around 1990, most European countries decided to try to reverse the long-term early exit trend. This change in public policy harbours many an ambiguity and contradiction. True, the new measures signal a determination to put an end to the golden age of early exit and to gradually shut down existing schemes in order to balance the books of old-age funds by prolonging the work life as need be. But meanwhile, most countries have not adopted coherent, comprehensive programs against age discrimination in employment. Only a few countries have launched programs with stiffer requirements for the ongoing training of wage earners during the second part of their careers. At present, given the fast pace of technological innovation, measures of this sort cannot be avoided if the aim is to maintain wage earners' skills and their ability to adapt.

[. . .]

Conclusion

For most countries [. . .] the elimination of ageing workers from the labour market is still a prevalent practice; and public policies have not affected company behaviour. Firms push wage earners over 40 onto the sidelines before pushing them all the way out after 50. These practices cannot meet tomorrow's challenge for two reasons. First of all, they cannot cope with the ageing labour force, a process already under way; nor with the slower growth in the labour force or even the predictable labour shortage as of 2006–2010, depending on the country. Secondly, they reinforce a rigid threefold organisation of ages in the life course. The ages for education and especially the time after work are becoming longer, whereas the age of work is shrinking. As we know, this threefold life course model, which is closely linked to the rise of industrial society and its time distribution, is breaking up into a slacker, flexible model.

The wage-earning relationship is less stable and less durable. New forms of employment are emerging. The concept of a lifetime job or even of a career is vanishing. Instead of successive ages of education, work, and non-work, we have overlapping periods of work, education and non-work that are dispersed over the whole life course.

Furthermore, occupational and life trajectories are diversifying. The organisation of the life course is becoming less rigid and, also less standardised. Strict chronological bounds no longer mark the ages of life. This new flexibility causes the individual's life course to be more diverse and more chaotic and unforeseeable. New social risks have thus arisen. Evidence of this is the delayed, unpredictable moment when young people enter the labour market, or the new risks cropping up at the end of the work life. Built up around the organisation of the life course in three ages, the welfare system is not capable of covering these new risks with their often serious effects. We observe a widening gap between rigid welfare arrangements and the new needs arising out of a more flexible organisation of the life course: the need for protection against the rapid obsolescence of know-how and skills, the need to change occupations several times, and the need to spread periods of 'inactivity' over the life course.

The contract between generations, which used to underlie retirement systems, must be reformulated. The accumulation of non-work oriented inactivity during the third age of life is no longer in phase with the emerging life-course model. The distribution of remunerated periods of economic activity and inactivity over the whole life course should be renegotiated for all generations. A revitalised solidarity between ages and generations could come out of this. The flexible life course model that is emerging calls for us to rethink the ways of linking the time spent working and the welfare safety net (which provides pay for periods of non-work) so as to cover these new risks, notably at the end of the work life.

Research findings suggest different courses of action. The reform of retirement systems cannot be undertaken without taking into consideration changes in work itself, in employment and in the life course. Proposals for delaying the retirement age, by simply increasing the number of years of contributions to old-age funds required for a full pension, hardly seem capable of having the desired effect of making people work longer. On the contrary, they may worsen the end-of-career risk and increase the financial burden on ageing wage earners, whose situation would be even more precarious as retirement becomes an ever more distant prospect and as pensions dwindle.

To make the work life longer calls not for a retirement policy but for an active jobs policy. The eligibility requirements for receiving an old-age pension have, nowadays, very little impact on how older wage earners are leaving the labour market. [. . .]

Working out a new contract between generations entails rethinking how remunerated periods of economic inactivity and work can be spread out more harmoniously over the life course. How unfortunate that negotiations about reducing the work week in France have been cut off from talks about the length of the work life, a topic seen only in terms of reforming retirement – as if the organisation of the life course in three ages still held. These interlinked elements should be placed at the centre of a renegotiated intergenerational contract. Only this negotiation could make all parties winners. Pensions might be paid out later but at a time chosen by the beneficiary; and the time spent working would be better spread over the life course, thanks to more possibilities for taking a sabbatical or parental leave and more flexible welfare arrangements [. . .] or 'flexible welfare provisions' for every age. [. . .] Firms could benefit from this new contract, by gaining a more flexible and motivated work force, and wage earners, by gaining protection against new risks. Public authorities would be able to move welfare systems and, especially old-age funds out of the red. It is urgent to implement an effective public policy for the second part of the work life. [. . .]

Renegotiating the distribution of periods of work and non-work over the life course is a crucial question for our societies' futures. Will public policy reforms suffice to meet the challenge of the ageing of the population with its impact on jobs and social transfers? Will it do this so as to reinforce social cohesion and intergenerational solidarity? For lack of such an overall negotiation, our societies will split up into rival generations; and 'age warfare' will break out over a dwindling and poorly distributed supply of welfare benefits and jobs.

Notes

1 The OECD calculated the average number of years by using data from 15 countries: Austria, Canada, Denmark, Finland, France, Germany, Ireland, Italy, Japan, Norway, New Zealand, Spain, Sweden, the UK and USA. OECD, *Maintaining Prosperity in an Ageing Society*. Paris, 1998.
2 G. Esping-Andersen (1999), 'Regulations and context', in *Why Deregulate Labour Markets?* Oxford University Press, Oxford [forthcoming].

PART III

Government, Democracy and Economic Power

Declining trust in government and orthodox politics is characteristic of many countries, as Joseph Nye shows. Public confidence in government has gone down in virtually all industrial countries over the past twenty years or so. We don't know for certain why this is so but the most likely theory is that such a decline is part of diminishing levels of trust in systems of authority more generally. Such trust can potentially be rebuilt, Nye suggests, by the active restructuring of government to meet the concerns that cause many to become disillusioned with politics.

Yves Mény takes a global look at the fate of democracy. Democracy is advancing round the world, but in the context of changes that are puzzling in their implications. We are moving towards what has been called the 'unknown society' – a society whose parameters are not yet properly understood. New democratic states will therefore not just be able to copy the old ones, they will have to react to the new framework of change. Vital though democracy is, as yet we do not have democratic institutions that can allow us to respond effectively to global problems.

Benjamin Barber roots democracy in civic culture – in the institutions of civil society. A healthy civil society is essential for democracy, but also for blunting the intrusion of the marketplace into areas where it does not belong. Consumer choice cannot substitute for democratic decision-making; political freedom is not the same as the capability to roam the aisles of a supermarket. To retrieve or defend civic culture we must insist upon responsible behaviour from business corporations, whether that be achieved through legal obligation or through moral persuasion. Barber draws up a charter for responsible corporate behaviour, emphasizing how essential such a charter is for the democratic rights of citizens.

Third way politics should not mean a reluctance to interfere in the nature of business activity, Michael Allen argues. In considering desirable forms of the regulation of business, the third way needs to draw upon the stakeholder point of view. A stakeholder approach doesn't mean looking to corporatist models, such as that of Germany, which seem at the moment themselves to be undergoing significant alternation. Rather it should mean spelling out the plurality of interests that modern business should protect or nurture.

The importance of social capital has been widely discussed in the third way debate. Social capital is important to democracy, argues Simon Szreter, but it is equally significant for economic success, particularly in the information economy. Social capital is not the same as community in the traditional sense. It refers to much more open relationships which are built in a deliberate fashion. Social capital can play a crucial role in an information society because the networks that it creates minimize the transaction costs of information. Most of the areas of innovation in new technology, like Silicon Valley, are home to clusters of social networks which exist in a situation of 'competitive cooperation'.

Hugh Collins takes as his subject a third way approach to labour law. Left of centre thinking in labour relations has moved away from older issues to do with trade unions and industrial conflict. Can labour law in the new environment still cope with needs for industrial partnership and the provision of security for workforces? Collins suggests that it can. Wholly deregulated labour markets would be neither economically efficient nor respect standards of social justice. The author suggests that a new agenda for labour law is both possible and necessary.

17

In Government We Don't Trust

Joseph S. Nye, Jr

[. . .] In 1964, three-quarters of the American public said that they trusted the federal government to do the right thing most of the time. In recent years, depending on the polls, only one-quarter to one-third do. The numbers are only slightly better for state and local government.

The United States is not alone. In fact, at a time when the United States and the West are celebrating victory in the Cold War, confidence in many Western governments seems to be declining. In a pair of polls taken in 11 European countries in 1981 and 1990, public confidence in government institutions declined in six (Belgium, France, Italy, Norway, Spain, and Sweden), was mixed in four (Germany, Great Britain, Iceland, and the Netherlands), and rose in Denmark. Polls in Canada show a decline similar to that in the United States. In Japan, polls show a low regard for politicians throughout the postwar period; more recently, there has been a decline in confidence in the bureaucracy as well. In a survey of 43 countries in 1981 and 1990, political scientist Ronald Inglehart found that people in low-income societies accept governmental authority more readily than do citizens of wealthier societies.

We are not experiencing the alleged "crisis of democracy" popularized in the 1970s. If you ask Americans what is the best place in the world to live, 80 per cent say the United States. If you ask them whether they like their democratic system of government, 90 per cent approve. If one looks at the Eurobarometer polls in Europe, even in those countries where there is a decline in confidence in government, 90 per cent are "satisfied with a democratic form of government." At the constitutional regime level, the current situation is not like France in 1968 –

much less 1789. Most people do not feel that the system is rotten and has to be overthrown.

Yet there is still cause for considerable concern. While there are differences of degree between loss of confidence, dissatisfaction, cynicism, and hatred, the steady devaluation of government and politics over long periods could affect the strength of democratic institutions. If people believe that government is incompetent and cannot be trusted, they are less likely to provide such crucial contributions as tax dollars and voluntary compliance with laws, and bright young people will not be willing to go into government. Without these resources, government cannot perform well, and if government cannot perform, people will become even more dissatisfied and distrustful. Such a cumulative downward spiral could erode support for democracy as a form of governance.

In the face of the information revolution and the globalization of the world economy, some argue that the best thing for governments to do is to get out of the way. Certainly governments must adapt to a world in which private and nonprofit actors are likely to play a larger role, but weak and ineffective government performance in the next century could be costly. In a global economy, for example, political stability attracts capital; education provides crucial skills; basic research in science and technology enhances competitiveness and living standards; and protection of intellectual property rights becomes more important. Each of these public goods depends upon effective government. In the defense domain, while the end of the Cold War has eased public fears of superpower conflict, the rise of transnational threats such as terrorism and the proliferation of weapons of mass destruction poses challenges that only a strong national government can meet.

Of course, the polls showing a loss of confidence in government and other institutions over the past three decades must be taken with a grain of salt. Survey research has its limits. And even if questions, data, and sampling procedures were perfect, a degree of wariness and skepticism about government is healthy for a democracy. But if the sky is not falling, neither is all well. Understanding the causes of the American loss of confidence in government is important not just for the United States, but for a world that looks to the United States as the sole remaining superpower and a harbinger of things to come. A clear assessment lies somewhere between Chicken Little and Pollyanna.

One possible explanation of the current dissatisfaction with government in the United States is that its scope has expanded too much, intruding into areas best left to private life. At first glance, responses to poll questions only partly support this view. When asked why they distrust the federal government, respondents tend to stress poor performance more than ambitious scope. Eighty-one per cent say government is wasteful and inefficient, and 79 per cent say it spends too much money on the wrong things. Only half that number say that it is interfering too much in people's lives or that the problems that it is trying to solve cannot be solved by the federal government. Of course, some complaints about poor performance may also be criticisms of scope, and if 40 per cent feel that the scope of government is too broad, that is an important fact for politicians to consider. Nonetheless, for much of the period of its greatest growth from the mid-1930s to the mid-1960s, government remained popular. Today, the areas of most rapid growth in the federal budget – Social Security and Medicare – enjoy broad support. And despite their lack of confidence in government, a majority of Americans still believe government should regulate business on matters of environment, product safety, unsafe working conditions, discriminatory hiring, and failed pension funds.

Americans say they are dissatisfied with the performance of government, and in a democracy public satisfaction with government performance is an important measure. But performance is more complicated than it first appears. To what should we compare government performance? Expectation? The past? The performance of other countries? That of other institutions such as private businesses or nonprofit organizations? Another problem with measuring performance is distinguishing general outcomes from specific outputs of government. People may be properly unhappy with poor social outcomes even though the quality of government outputs does not change. For example, American test scores in science and mathematics compare poorly with those of students in a number of other nations, but the role of schools may be less important than the role of family values and the general culture in explaining those differences. The unevenness of public knowledge poses further complications: Americans express more dissatisfaction with foreign aid than almost any other aspect of government policy, but they also think that foreign aid accounts for more than 20 per cent (rather than the actual 1 per cent) of the federal budget.

Governmental performance ratings differ by fields and by institutions. While only 10 per cent of the American public reported in 1996 that they had a great deal of confidence in Congress, 31 per cent had a great deal of confidence in the Supreme Court, and 47 per cent in the military. The latter case represents a recovery from 27 per cent during the Vietnam War and reflects the good performance during the Gulf War. It reflects the relative success of the military in dealing with the drug, race, and education issues that have plagued modern American society, but it may also reflect the fact that since the end of conscription, the military (like the post office) has been one of the few parts of government that engages in positive marketing.

A major puzzle in the relationship between public dissatisfaction and government performance is the distance people say they feel from government. For instance, while polls show a low rating for Congress, they also show a higher rating for local representatives. Although there is criticism of the school system, people express higher satisfaction with their local schools. If mistrust is not closely related to personal values and experience, then explanations may lie in generalized beliefs or moods.

This relationship between distance and perceived performance has some bearing on the issue of devolution. Some observers believe that more devolution to the state and local level will restore confidence in government; others believe that devolution will merely shift the spotlight of criticism to the local level. If the public reaction to government had a clear one-to-one relationship with performance, there would be little to explain about why attitudes have changed over the past three decades. But the ambiguities in the relationship between real and perceived performance and the decline of confidence in other major institutions besides government suggest that larger causes are also involved.

In 1965, at the peak of confidence in government, political scientist Robert Lane discerned an increase in trust since the 1930s, which he attributed to economic improvement. If so, perhaps the decline in confidence is the result of economic slowdown. Growth was higher during the two and one-half decades following World War II in all advanced economies than it was after 1974. Even though Japan's growth was high in the 1980s, it was still lower than it had been in the 1960s. As for the United States, the growth rate in the first three postwar decades was 3.5 per cent per year, and then fell to about 2.3 per cent in the period after 1975 – a 50 per cent decline in growth rate. Over 20 years that decline would represent about $2.5 trillion, enough to wipe out the government deficit or to give government the wherewithal to do some of the things that it now cannot afford to do.

The slowdown of economic growth, one might hypothesize, has led to public dissatisfaction, which in turn has led to a search for political scapegoats. From 1979 to 1995, real hourly wages in the United States rose by about 5.5 per cent, or one-third of 1 per cent per year. That contrast with wage growth in the earlier postwar period is a reason why people would say something is not as good as it used to be and blame it on government. A major problem with this hypothesis, however, is that it fits poorly with the onset of the decline in confidence. In the

United States the greatest drop in confidence occurred between 1964 and 1974, when growth was fastest, and the recession of the early 1980s was actually accompanied by a rise in confidence in government. In Europe, dissatisfaction with government is more closely related to recessions in the early 1970s, early 1980s, and 1990s.

Another related economic explanation is global competition. This argument says it is not just the economic slowdown that matters, but the popular view that the economic slowdown has been caused by global markets and competition. As some people put it, what is really at issue is the enormous rise of the East Asian economies, which provide an almost infinite source of low-priced labor that is bound to lead to a depression of wages in the advanced countries. This competition particularly depresses the wages of the unskilled and leads to increased inequality, which in turn burdens the political system.

The global competition explanation solves the timing problem of the larger "slowdown" explanation, but it faces another difficulty: Trade accounts for only about one-tenth of the American economy. And the slowdown and the depression of wages has occurred in the other 90 per cent as much as in the part that deals with traded goods. Of course, there are spillover effects from wages in traded to nontraded goods, and the fact that multinational corporations can threaten to move jobs overseas can depress wages. Still, trade may be too small a tail to wag such a large dog. In addition, 70 per cent of American trade has been with other rich countries where wages are just as high as American wages. So while global competition has an effect, it may not be sufficient to explain what is happening in the depression of wages. As economist Dani Rodrik demonstrated in his Summer 1997 FOREIGN POLICY article, the integration of markets has increased, but the level is still not very high.

Global competitiveness and interdependence, however, do produce a political dimension that is worth noting, If people feel a loss of control over their lives because of larger competition in the world, that becomes a political reality in and of itself. So when xenophobes like Pat Buchanan or Jean-Marie LePen campaign on the theme that foreigners are causing people's problems, their platform may not reflect sound economics, but it becomes a political reality.

There is something still deeper going on in the economic area – the Third Industrial Revolution. This revolution – the Information Revolution – means that computers and communications are to the end of the twentieth century what the introduction of the steam engine was to the end of the eighteenth century or the introduction of electricity to the end of the nineteenth century. We are seeing a tremendous wave of technological innovation that will take 20 to 40 years to work itself through the system. As economist Joseph Schumpeter said, capitalism is a process of "creative destruction": It has a positive and a negative effect at the same time. And while the United States may be leading this Third Industrial Revolution, other countries will be affected as well.

This creative destruction is happening in almost all the industrialized countries. Americans have responded to it by creating jobs, albeit often at low wages. Europeans have responded to it by real wage increases, but with 10 to 12 per cent unemployment – and in some countries, 20 per cent youth unemployment. The ways in which different societies respond to this economic process can take different forms, but each method creates a certain amount of turmoil, either because of the low wages or because of the high unemployment. In the long run, the country may profit from this creative destruction, but in the interim, people feel great insecurity and anxiety. People then blame the government rather than deeper economic and historical forces.

But even here the causation is complicated. If economics were the primary cause, one would expect to see the greatest decline in trust among the economic losers. Yet the decline in confidence in government is virtually the same for both winners and losers. Like the absence of a close connection between confidence and personal experience or values mentioned above, this lack of a direct connection between economics and expressed attitudes suggests the need for explanations that are more general, ideological, or reflective of the broad public mood.

One prominent sociological hypothesis about the causes behind the decline in confidence in government is the alleged decline of "social capital," a common sense concept that encompasses the ability of people to work together. Social scientists believe that such skills are developed through citizens collaborating in voluntary organizations. While not all such organizations have a positive effect, most probably do, and their decline would be a source of concern. Political scientist Robert Putnam has focused on the decline in voluntary groups such as the National Congress of Parents and Teachers (PTA), the YMCA, and the Girl Scouts since the 1960s. The decline in participatory groups would remove the kind of intermediary institution that Alexis de Tocqueville believed essential to the fabric of the civil society that undergirds our democratic government. This thesis is challenged, however, by some who believe we are seeing a transformation in types of groups rather than an absolute decline of social capital.

Another aspect of cultural change is the long-term decline of trust in authority and all institutions in developed societies. Inglehart argues that the declining respect for authority is part of postmodern values, which people adopt as they switch from preoccupation with survival to greater concern with quality of life. The youth revolts of the 1960s saw a rapid increase in challenges to authority and institutions, not only in the United States but also in Europe and Japan. If Inglehart is correct, one of the effects of development will be declining confidence in government.

In Western culture, there has probably been a change in the balance between the individual and the community in favor of greater individualism. Divorce, for example, has increased in almost all advanced societies. One aspect of divorce is that some women have been liberated from abusive and unequal marriages. Women used to be trapped economically in unhappy unions because there was virtually no way out. Men have also benefited from easier divorce. But while divorce represents a libertarian trend, it also signifies the decline of the family. It means less attention to children, less attention to the basic unit of community. Divorce illustrates two sides of the same coin, as the ratio changes in the libertarian rather than the communitarian direction.

The decline of the family has important implications for both actual and perceived performance of government. Educating children and preventing youth violence come high on the list of government tasks people care most about. Both rest heavily on the family. Government can run schools, but if parents cannot run families well, government is not going to be successful in the schools. Yet government is going to get much of the blame. People are not going to say, "I did a lousy job as a parent, so I will not blame the schools or the government." They are more likely to say, "The government is letting us down." Or many are likely to demand that government "do something" about family values – even though government may be unable to reverse the larger social causes behind the erosion of those values.

Another dimension of this cultural change is our public political philosophy and its current emphasis on rights. There used to be some basic human rights on which people broadly agreed. Now, in much of the industrialized world, there seems to be a right to everything from a pension to a vacation. We have created a society of entitlements. The net effect is extraordinarily constraining on government. Moreover, rights have costs, and some people pay a price for the expansion of the rights of others. Losers are likely to blame this cost on government. For example, the expansion of civil rights in the United States in the 1960s and 1970s benefited African Americans, but it angered many whites and helped to cause the defection of the South from the Democratic to the Republican coalition. Social changes have had large political consequences, including an erosion of confidence in government. While

the United States is a particularly litigious society, the "rights revolution" seems to be affecting other countries as well.

One political hypothesis is that the decline in confidence in government is due to the end of the Cold War. Common defense is a public
good and willingness to sacrifice is higher in wartime. A powerful
external threat, the Soviet Union was the glue that held public consensus together. The trouble with this hypothesis is that the decline in
confidence in the United States started in the mid-1960s. On the other
hand, for countries such as Italy and Japan that had one dominant
party and significant communist opposition parties, the end of the Cold
War did seem to unlock major political change and criticism of
government.

Another political hypothesis is that the decline in confidence is the
fault of poor leaders – in particular former presidents Lyndon Johnson
and Richard Nixon. The sharpest dips in confidence occurred after the
American involvement in Vietnam and the 1972 Watergate incident.
Johnson and Nixon are blamed both for misleading the public and for
becoming involved in episodes that reduced respect for government.
The more hostile tenor of press coverage dates back to these events. Yet
while Vietnam and Watergate help to explain the onset of the decline
of confidence in government, they do not explain the duration. When
President Ronald Reagan came to office, public confidence actually
made an uptick from 25 per cent to 44 per cent in the early 1980s. But
then it went down again in Reagan's second term and after. This type
of anomaly requires an explanation that goes deeper than blaming
everything on Johnson and Nixon.

A related explanation for rising mistrust is the growth of corruption
and dishonesty in American politics. Media analyst Suzanne Garment
and other close observers, however, doubt that such behavior has
increased. What has increased is media attention to scandal and the
public belief that politicians have become more corrupt. Certainly there
has been enough deceptive and dishonest behavior to fuel this belief,
but it is difficult to make the case that increased corruption is the sole
cause.

A deeper political hypothesis is that we are seeing a realignment of
political parties not only in the United States but also in Italy, Japan,
and other countries. That process of realignment and dealignment,
when the old coalitions fall apart, produces a loss of confidence, not
just in the parties, but in government more generally. The Roosevelt
coalition that governed in the United States after 1932 gradually
eroded, and with it went the faith in liberal big government that held
the coalition together. With this realignment of political parties, one

would expect a decline in the trust in government that went along with a particular view of government.

A final political hypothesis attributes the decline in confidence to the changing role of the media. Political scientist Thomas Patterson reports that since the 1960s, print and television news have become more negative, more journalist-centered, and more focused on conflict rather than substance, not just in the United States, but also in Britain, Italy, and Sweden. In its new interpretive role, the press has become an unaccountable part of the political process. In particular, television adds a special dimension because it has changed the political process. Politicians can appeal over the heads of the political parties directly to the public and that may have something to do with weakening parties. Parties are less effective in connecting politicians with the public, and the negative ads on TV and the costs of broadcast time create a greater sense of distance between politicians and the public. The combination of negative ads plus negative coverage demarkets government and contributes to a popular cultural view of bad government.

No one hypothesis explains everything, but some carry more weight than others. Many involve broad causes that suggest that the decline of confidence is not likely to be idiosyncratic to the United States. In that sense, the American experience may be prophetic. Many of these hypotheses also suggest pessimism, but the future is open. Creative destruction of the existing order may work in the polity as well as the economy. The Third Industrial Revolution may mean that the industrial countries are on the verge of a rise in productivity that will end the years of slow growth. We do not yet know. The revolution in information technology may also help government get closer to people, and when people feel a closer connection to government, confidence tends to be higher. It may be possible to have more devolution with information technology. It may also be possible to do more outsourcing and cut bureaucracy in government. Perhaps the nonprofit sector will begin to provide intermediary institutions that will work with government, both in helping to administer services and in providing the new ideas that make democracy flourish. At this stage there are more questions than answers, both about the United States and about how much one can generalize from the American experience to other developed countries.

If the era of big government is over, it is far from clear what will take its place. The answer is less likely to be more government than different governance. Major transformations of government accompanied the First and Second Industrial Revolutions. With appropriate lags, we should expect similar changes to accompany the current Information

Hypotheses About Decline in Confidence in Government

HYPOTHESIS	RELEVANCE	COMMENT
1. Scope grown too fast (as measured by size of government budget to GDP)	Low	Scope increased from 3 per cent to 20 per cent but largest growth is in programs that are popular (Social Security, Medicare). Does not explain decline in other institutions.
2. Scope grown too intrusive (measured by new subjects)	Low/Mixed	Divided views on cultural issues. Popularity of environment and safety regulation. 40 per cent say "interfering too much." Does not explain other institutions.
3. Performance has weakened	Low/Mixed	81 per cent say "wasteful and inefficient," but other researchers dispute net change; also does not explain decline in other institutions.
4. End of Cold War	Low	Largest decline is 1964–74.
5. Vietnam and Watergate	Mixed	Fits with onset, but needs auxiliary hypothesis to explain persistence. May affect all institutions.
6. "World War II effect" – high expectations not met	High	1950s seem abnormally high. May affect all institutions.
7. Political realignment and polarization of élites	High	Fits timing of onset. Explains growth of conservative coalition. Does not explain other institutions.
8. TV effects on politics (party decline, negative marketing)	High	Fits timing and persistence. Distancing of élites.

HYPOTHESIS	RELEVANCE	COMMENT
9. Changed role of media	High	Fits timing of onset and persistence. Fits other institutions.
10. Increased corruption/ dishonesty	Mixed/Low	Little evidence of increase, but perception grows, and Vietnam, Watergate had effects.
11. General economic slowdown	Mixed	Some variation with unemployment and inflation, but does not fit timing of onset.
12. Rising economic inequality	Low	Does not show variation by winners and losers.
13. Globalization and loss of control	Mixed	Affects general mood, but timing unclear and effects indirect.
14. Third Industrial Revolution	High	Explains changes in the economy and communications, but direct causal links unclear.
15. Decline of social capital (measured by voluntary groups)	Low	Evidence in dispute; causal links to government unclear.
16. Decline of social capital (measured by family cohesion)	Mixed	Timing about right regarding onset and persistence. Causal link somewhat indirect. Relation to other institutions, countries.
17. Authority patterns and "post-materialist values," particularly since 1960s	High	Fits all institutions and countries. Does not explain all variations.

Revolution. The least likely future would be a twenty-first-century public sector that looks like the twentieth-century model. The centuries-long trend of concentrating power in national capitals may be reversed in the next century. There are already signs of more collective activities taking place in the private and nonprofit sectors, as well as above and below the levels of national capitals.

This scenario of the future is often referred to as the decline of the nation-state, but that terminology can be misleading. It is likely that citizens of developed countries will continue to see the nation-state as the major source of their security, identity, and prosperity well into the next century. However, the roles of other institutions and different levels of government in providing governance of collective activities are likely to change and become more complex. We are less likely to see the end of the nation-state than we are to witness its gradual transformation, and with it, the development of a more complex type of international politics. Governments will continue to matter. They may even regain some of the popular confidence they lost. But they will share more of the processes of governance with market and nonprofit institutions. Central governments will not be home alone.

18

Five (Hypo)theses on Democracy and its Future

Yves Mény

[...]

During [the] fifty years of the second half of the twentieth century the conditions were laid down that have for ten years prevailed, and constitute the new ideological and political landscape of the nascent twenty-first century: the indisputable supremacy of the market; the ideological monopoly of the Western democratic model; the growing globalization of material, financial, human and intellectual exchanges.

The landscape is radically new, and the advance of change is exponential:

1790: Two or three so-called "democratic" systems, on which there could be much to question;
1920: A dozen incomplete, imperfect, often fragile democracies;
1950: A score of countries could claim to be democracies, on condition that the quality of that democracy was not looked at too closely;
1999: The label democracy has become so dominant that only a few countries reject the forms and the rites of the Western model. Everything happens as if there were no longer any alternatives. [...]

From this rapid summary of the evolution of the Western democratic "model", a few initial conclusions emerge that may be useful for analysing its potential development in the century to come:

• The model is becoming universalized. In any case, it has an unconcealed, sometimes indeed arrogant, pretension to universality.

- Its triumphal march goes hand in hand with the still faster and more radical expansion of the mechanisms of the market economy.
- The two phenomena are converging in a global movement of criss-cross, systematic exchanges, both international and transnational. The democratic phenomenon born in the national framework, and still rooted in it, is today developing in a radically new context, for which it is little or badly prepared.
- The democratic phenomenon is marked by its evolution, its deepening and particularly its perfectibility. The British, French and American democracies of today have little to do with what they were 50 or 100 years ago. The word remains, while the reality it denotes has changed.
- Like any political and social project, the democratic model is a mixture of reality and dreams, rules and utopias. Despite the many efforts at "disenchantment" which [. . .] have helped to give a more realistic vision of what democracy is, for much of public opinion it remains a largely mythical object, more in line with what the collective imagination believes about it than with its day-to-day functioning.

The modern world we have known since the fifties is still in place but its nature and content is changing. While entering into a new era, we do not yet know its future shape. Herman Van Gunsteren refers to it as the march towards The Unknown Society that he contrasts with the previous period along the following dichotomy:

Modern Societies	The Unknown Society
National unitary culture	Creolization within global culture
Politics of emancipation	"Lifestyle" politics
Equality	Differentiation, difference
Organization, hierarchy	Reorganization, networks
Rationality	Rationalities "we are all natives now"
Fixed identity	Fleeting and multiple identities
Guaranteed representation	Problematic, ad hoc representation
The end of ideologies	Variety of lifestyles and convictions
Pragmatism in politics	Fundamentalism in politics

The old reality is still in place and the new one is not fully born. The challenge for old as well as for new democracies will be to adjust the changing conditions of its ideological and material environment.

[. . .]

I propose to [. . .] put forward five (hypo)theses [on the future of democracy]:

Thesis 1 – The absence of any alternative to the Western political model has eliminated external threats, but enhanced internal challenges. Democratic consolidation concerns not just the new democracies, but all democracies.

When the Western model was confronted daily with the existence of counter-models in both political and economic or social terms, this situation had a twofold impact: it acted as a salutary stimulus in a competition that was not just material but also ideological; and it also enabled certain failures to be forgiven or forgotten in the name of the hierarchy of problems. Better a democracy, even imperfect, than an authoritarian or despotic régime. [. . .]

The end of any serious competition or outside danger risks arousing indifference, apathy or anomie among the citizens. In Europe there is often talk of an American syndrome in this connection, stressing that Europe, on the model of the United States, is increasingly suffering from electoral absenteeism, absence of political participation and failure to understand the issues. But this hasty equation is undoubtedly false. While the United States have always been able to reconcile a low appetite for electoral participation with a profound attachment to the constitution and the political system, most other countries, in Europe and still more in the rest of the world, have a more unstable and fragile relation with the values of the democratic system.

The main challenge lying in wait for democracy in the coming century is not an alternative still to emerge and be conceived of, but the indifference of those regarded as being its *raison d'être*, namely the citizens. Another expression of dissatisfaction with the democratic system, unfortunately experienced between the wars, is the rejection of the moderate forms of the democratic system as we know them in favour of radical popular forms: populism in its most modest expression, extremisms of right or left. Democracy might thus remain the universal reference scheme while being seriously threatened here or there during localized crises. The solidity of the whole democratic edifice would then depend on a twofold capacity: that of the international community to isolate and bring back to reason the straying country; that of the country or countries in question to take appropriate reform measures (cf. the recent examples of Greece, Argentina or Brazil, South Africa, etc.). The risk will be the greater if collective issues have been taken out of politics to be dealt with in other arenas. To sum up, democratic consolidation is not a challenge that only new democracies have to face. Old democracies have also to adjust, to reform in order to better satisfy their citizens' aspirations. In that sense democracy is "an every day referendum" as Renan used to say about nation-building.

> **Thesis 2** – Western-type democracy and the market are historically linked (even if not totally inseparable), and each claim universality. But democracies do not have suitable instruments for coping with a major economic and social crisis.

A crisis, though not foreseeable as to date and form, is nonetheless likely, failing a radical change in capitalism and economics that would allow us to contemplate a world from which crises would be banished. Since nothing at the moment justifies any such beatific optimism, it is best to take into account the blackest hypothesis. A priori, it might be claimed that democracies are in some respects better able to tackle a major economic crisis failing any credible alternative, or political or economic theory capable of replacing the existing creeds. The experience of the 1930s and the post-war Keynesian policies is also rich in lessons.

But against this optimistic interpretation one might emphasize that Western welfare state systems have exhausted their capacities and their resources. Having extended to their limit, they are unable to give any more. Let us crudely confess: in the face of an economic depression that will be all the more devastating since the planet today is in a situation of total interdependency, there is not as yet any economic or financial "safety plan", still less political remedy, except the hope that lies in the clairvoyance of the elites and the wisdom or good sense of the citizens.

It should certainly be stressed that economic science and the ability to steer the economy have made enormous progress. However, it would be naive and testify to historical ignorance to think that in this area too we have come to the "end of history". Those long-term utopias, often lasting no longer than the polemics over them in the media, are of little use in guiding us.

From past experiences one lesson can, alas, be drawn: crises catch not just political practitioners unprepared, but also theorists and experts. It is often crises that give rise not just to new economic and social conditions, but also to new paradigms, new intellectual and practical instruments. What was yesterday unthinkable and unthought of suddenly becomes possible and feasible. These democracies' weakness is however also their strength. Democratic regimes are built up to deal with uncertainty as they are concerned more about procedures and rules of the game than pre-designed policy outcomes.

Thesis 3 – The major phenomenon of contemporary pluralist democracy is its enormous geographical expansion over the last twenty years. The trend is for the democratic system to evolve towards universality, but its forms must allow a diversity of models and enable cultural particularisms to be accommodated to.

The Western model of government has become almost the sole referent, on the same basis as technology, clothing, entertainment, etc. This evolution, inspired, desired and pushed for by the Western world, has often been assessed in simplistic terms. The press and politicians have often conferred patents of democracy on the basis of the existence of a formal and institutional minimum, generally the existence of a constitution, the recognition of parties and the holding of elections. On the basis of these few indicators, following the fall of dictatorships, hasty conclusions have been drawn regarding the expansion of democracy. Much might be said as to these hasty, interested legitimations, which lead to reducing the democratic system to its elementary forms more than its substance.

But the universalization of democracy, over and above its more or less artificial nature, raises one still more formidable problem: integrating not strictly democratic elements, according to local cultures, traditions and practices. Let me explain: one does not refuse to call Britain or the Netherlands or Spain democracies, although institutionally they are monarchies; nor is the title denied to the United States, though a number of states employ the death penalty, etc. In other words, though each democratic state has features that elsewhere might be regarded as incompatible with one pillar or the other of democracy (the popular or the constitutionalist one), one does not refuse on that ground to call them democratic.

The question for the twenty-first century and for the new states in course of democratization is then the following: how can the democratic principles invented by the West – but never applied in their total purity and integrity – be reconciled with elements of local culture or tradition? Up to what point can this mixture be regarded as democratic, and where is the boundary to be drawn between the "democratically imperfect" and the "unacceptably non-democratic?" An intransigent response by the West – as is all too often the case – ignores both the specific features of nations evolving towards democracy and the residues that persist in their own systems, in both the expression of popular aspirations and the recognition and effective protection of fundamental rights. The construction of democracy is a long path, a fight on all fronts, a continuous adjustment to new aspirations.

[. . .]

Thesis 4 – Internationalization constitutes a major challenge for democratic systems, the birth and development of which went hand in hand with that of the nation state. The democracy of the future will have to be able to reconcile the contradictions between its rootedness in the nation state and the transfer of powers to universal but sectoralized authorities.

Let us say first of all that this dilemma takes various forms: first, globalization, i.e. the growing, rapid tendency to universalize problems and ways of dealing with them, in trade, the environment, transport, etc. Second, regionalization, which implies a more or less advanced integration of economies, of rules or of institutions – with the most advanced example being the European Union, whose success is arousing emulation in other parts of the world. Finally, transnationalism, resulting not just from ancient phenomena like religion, but also from emigration, the multiplication of NGOs and transnational pressure groups, or the birth of an international public opinion capable of challenging the choices or approaches of a given country (cf. the Amazon forest in Brazil, apartheid in South Africa, etc.).

The most serious challenge, in connection with which thinking is least developed, lies in the growth of a twofold phenomenon: globalization as such (which though not new is becoming a major question because of its extent), on the one hand, and technical segmentation, the sectoral specialization of the agencies of governance, on the other. This second dimension is not just concomitant with or dependent on globalization, since it is also strongly developed within the Western nation states (agencies or independent administrative authorities). But it is interesting to note that it is also emerging – and this is new – in the context of a globalization that is no longer only unilateral (conquest of the world by the colonialist countries) but multilateral, organized and institutionalized.

This twofold phenomenon leads to a considerable reduction of available policy options. The range of potential choices is reduced by external constraints but also by internal preferences for so-called non-political or apolitical organizations. It might be that the autonomous capacity of nation states to act according to their own choices was an illusion or even worse, a rationale to pursue their objectives through all means, including war. But this faith was in line with the mythical basis of state power, i.e. absolute sovereignty within its borders. National actors could pretend they were in control of decisions, free to choose among many solutions whose implications were subject to intense political debate. Today's situation is the complete opposite, as if politics, ideology, policy choices have now to be submitted to the external forces escaping the control of each nation but also of the international community itself. Past reification of actors (the state) has been substituted by a new form (the market). This loss of influence is instead benefiting new authorities not subject to the democratic principle (namely, election or control by politicians), constituted on the basis of such principles as competence, expertise and independence, and functioning on the basis of legal or technical norms that escape political manipulation or intervention.

[. . .]

The solutions to this challenge are not simple, since while there exists a national demos, a community of concerned citizens, there is no such thing for the moment at international level. The European Union is well aware of the problem – although it has not resolved it: it is itself increasingly having to face the famous "democratic deficit". To tackle this challenge, which will be the major one in the century to come, I feel we must again distinguish between the two pillars that uphold the democratic system: the popular and the constitutionalist one.

These solutions are easier to find in the second pillar, by applying at international level rules and practices already tried and tested at national level. They are called fairness, due process of law, rule of law, checks and balances, protection of rights, etc. Nothing of the constitutional pillar of Western democracy is inapplicable at international level, with some effort of imagination and good will.

Much more problematic, by contrast, is the construction at supra-national level of a demos, a community of peoples and a means of expression for these peoples that are the object of international regulations, decisions and arbitration. The "League of Society Nations" has yet to be built, over and above the forums and institutions regarded as presently representing it. Even if the ideal or the utopia of the future may be the construction of an international society (thanks to the Internet?), the times are still far off when the international community can play the same role, *mutatis mutandis*, as the national community does in democratic systems.

Yet channels of thought may well be open. Let us first say that the democratic systems would perhaps be better termed pluralist. Their objective is to govern according to a method, the majority principle, while guaranteeing that this majority is neither oppressive nor totalitarian, does not hold all the power, and offers guarantees for minorities. Moreover, their organization is territorially grounded (local/national).

If we accept that recourse to direct universal suffrage is for the moment impossible (except, with the limits and with the problems that we know, at the European Union level) in order to identify the views and opinions of the international society, we must then work at an intermediate level, that of representatives of states. For the moment we shall confine ourselves to mentioning some broad lines of thought on this point, extremely delicate and difficult as it is. Given the absence of pure democracy since the "international people" does not exist as such, the aim should be to strengthen pluralism and favour desectoralization. Strengthening pluralism means evolving from an elitist conception, the practice of a club of the "happy few", to a more universalist procedure taking the interests involved into account. Contemporary international society is something like 1789 France, when individuals and groups were not entitled to the same rights, by which I mean that this is a world where only a few countries are in a dominant position. A multitude of followers has to accept the rules of the game laid down or imposed by the leading countries.

This sort of imbalance, which is in a sense in the nature of things and cannot be corrected except by procedural, institutional, political, etc. artefacts, cannot easily be changed. Though not democratic, international society would already be on the road to progress if its pluralism were protected and guaranteed in the way it is safeguarded within national societies. This presupposes the recognition of rights the development of rules and procedures, and the acceptance of derogations and protective exceptions.

[. . .]

Thesis 5 – Globalization calls into question a number of concepts, perceptions and interests shaped by the historical merger between the nation state and the democratic area. A new definition of democratic values (liberty, equality, solidarity) is inevitable.

• The coherence laboriously established between economic space, political space and social space is increasingly threatened. How can the political frontiers inherited from history remain the same when human, commercial and financial flows no longer take them into account? The phenomenon is already explosive in North America and Western Europe, but is incomplete because the cultural, linguistic and political structures are more resistant to change, if only because of their territorialization. There is, then, a growing gap between certain types of flows that in themselves can become, and are becoming, an issue for democratic politics. Until today, a political system was typified by bringing together and combining a number of properties which are today dissociated. Political societies have changed in their nature. From closed they have become open; from sought or attained homogeneity they have moved to heterogeneity, whether accepted or not. There are only two alternatives: either this fragmented, composite character will find modes of consensus management (multiculturalism, national minorities, liberal pluralism, etc.), or else there is a great risk of the old national societies imploding in favour of more homogeneous societies, either at territorial level or at the level of specific groups and communities. If the link between groups and territories is first and foremost political, any weakening of that link is bound to bring centrifugal developments.

- In this connection, at least in Europe, the needful reform of the welfare state constitutes a challenge that is not just economic or financial. I shall not here go into the question of the weight of welfare in national economies, which does not seem to me to be a problem as such. What raises a question is the mode of financing, administering and distributing a policy that cannot any longer be called in question in principle, only in the details. A single example may serve to illustrate the point: the European governments, rightly concerned at the growth of health costs and their funding, are right to wish to reform the system. But they are wrong to forget that, for instance in the United States, expenditure per head is higher while several million people are uncovered or virtually so. The purely financial or accounting arguments obscure the debate and prevent it from advancing.

The problem in Europe is that, much more than elsewhere, welfare was used to integrate the masses into industrial societies. Granting universal suffrage was often the first step towards building a democratic society. But the realization that the ballot paper was not enough lent more attraction to the prospect of social revolution. The European democratic systems are thus at the convergence of political and social rights. Calling the latter in question again would harm the system's very legitimacy – which does not, however, mean that all the corporatisms and social egoisms are entitled to indefinite perpetuation.

The debate on welfare is, then, welcome even if it is often poorly framed. It compels the raising of fundamental questions: what is its role, what is its legitimacy? What should be the place of local, national, international or generational solidarity? What is the desirable division of labour between public and private? What redistributive policy is possible, or legitimate, and in favour of whom?

Though this debate has been going on for some thirty years in the United States and more recently in Europe, the question is far from being solved. Even if the confusion and the technical nature of the problem often obscure the debate, the question of welfare in democratic systems calls into question almost all the old certainties: the division of labour between men and women, the distribution of profit between labour and capital, the sharing of income between direct and indirect advantages, the trade-off between younger people's work and retirees' income, etc. Yet the discussions are rarely centred round these problems, tending to place the focus on the cost of welfare and the need to make serious cuts. The issue is thus reduced to a fight between pressure groups instead of a rethink about welfare as a component of democratic societies.

Other questions which are asked even less often concern the remoter but logical implications of the principle of solidarity that underlies welfare (if it is not to be reduced to a mere act of charity). First of all, if the principle of solidarity is itself called into question, then the role of democratic institutions as an arbitration body collapses: charity becomes a matter of goodwill, of kindness and of individual or collective initiative. The solidarity that entails authoritarian levies presupposes – at least in principle – a debate on the advisability and size of the transfers to be made, on the identity of the beneficiaries, etc. Solidarity implies a social locus; the family, the village, the political community as a whole. From this viewpoint it seems scarcely logical to allow the foreigner to benefit from community solidarity while refusing him access to the political community, say by granting citizenship and the right to vote.

Similarly, on the hypothesis of a democratic international community, it would be logical to strengthen the bond of solidarity within that community. For the moment, this solidarity is all too often hesitant or non-existent. There is some hypocrisy in calling, in the name of fundamental rights, for the banning of child labour or boycotting products produced by it, if we are incapable of furnishing effective aid, international solidarity to help with the problem of those children's nutritional survival. In this area more than others, international solidarity seems utopian, or reduces it to a few symbolic gestures. We can see all the difficulty of this in Europe, where no one wants to set up Europe-wide welfare for fear of giving birth to a costly bureaucratic monster. This does not, however, prevent transfer policies (notably territorial ones) from enabling poor countries or regions to be helped thanks to contributions from richer ones.

19

How to Make Society Civil and Democracy Strong

Benjamin R. Barber

[. . .] There are three obstacles to civil society as the mediating domain between the government and the private sector: government itself, when it is arrogant and overweening; market dogmas, when they presume that private individuals and groups can secure public goods; and the yearning for community, when it subordinates liberty and equality to solidarity.

As to the first, the tendency of all institutions to ossify and become distanced from their constituents (the so-called iron law of oligarchy) turns government representatives into enemies of their citizens and, eventually, makes even democratically elected governments rigid and hierarchical, with the representatives regarding themselves as the sole civic actors on the political scene, governing on behalf of citizens instead of facilitating citizen self-government. When that happens, the democratic citizenry in whose name the governments govern is actually disempowered, at once both dependent and alienated.

As to the second, the myth of the invisible hand encourages market enthusiasts to believe that privatization is a synonym for democratization and empowerment, and for civic liberty to flourish, one need only get government out of the way. But the results are quite otherwise: an eclipse of the public, a one-dimensional culture of privatism and greed, and an addictive materialism that turns autonomous citizens into dependent consumers.

As for the third, the communitarian thirst for the restoration of lost values and value communities encourages people to impose on others their own cultural values through either government or quasi-censorious institutions of civil society. In the resulting solidaristic community, insiders favor identity over equality as the most precious of all social values and everyone else is left feeling like outsiders.

Ironically, although government itself has recently been seen as part of the problem, it has an opportunity here to be part of the solution. For a disciplined, self-limiting government can behave modestly. Such modesty is characteristic of President Clinton's new Democrats [. . .], Tony Blair's New Labor Party, and Lionel Jospin's new socialists. Yet these new progressives do trust government to help ameliorate the crushing effects of monopoly corporations and counter their imposition of commercial uniformity and cultural homogenization. Through its courts and legal system government can also assure that liberty is protected against corrosive side effects of the all-too-human longing for solidarity.

The true enemy of civil society is, in fact, neither government nor corporations per se, but bureaucracy, dogmatism, unresponsiveness, totalism, bloat, unaccountability, absolutism, and inertia wherever they are found. While laissez-faire obsessives are loath to admit it, these defects are unfortunately found as much in private commerce as in the government, among firms and fraternities no less than in welfare bureaucracies. [. . .]

Where government is at fault, laws must help it move to self-limitation and reform; and where the private sector is the problem, government must be the public's ally in curbing commercial and market abuses, and in forbidding the moral encroachments that comformist communities make when they try to impose their own values and way of life on all of us. Ultimately, democratic government is but an extension of the common power of citizens, and citizens must use that common power while working to reform its susceptibility to abuse. Power corrupts, and private power, neither accountable nor, often, even visible, may be much more corrupting (and far less tractable) than the power of democratic government. We can always "throw the buggers out!" when politicians get too big for their britches or forget to whom they are accountable. But there is no recall power against managers of the marketplace when they are not accountable to the sovereign public. That is a lesson worth remembering in an age when government is so disdained and markets so widely celebrated, when the prevailing orthodoxy is so insistently laissez-faire. It is a shameful reminder of the hypocrisy of those who benefit from privatism when they pretend that government has no role in defending those whom privatism cripples.

Democracy is not a synonym for the marketplace, and the notion that by privatizing government we can establish civil society and civic goods is a dishonorable myth. The freedom to buy a Coke or a Big Mac or a video of the Lion King eating a Big Mac is not the freedom to determine how you will live and under what kind of regime. Coke and McDonald's and MTV thrive in undemocratic Singapore and China as well as they do in chaotic, semi-democratic Russia and in the genuinely democratic Czech Republic. Historically, it is not capitalism that produced democracy but democracy that produced capitalism. Capitalism needs democracy but does not know how to create or sustain it, and frequently it produces circumstances that can undermine it.

The myth of the market is our most insidious myth, not just because so many believe it, but because the market's invisible bonds slip on so easily and feel so very much like freedom. Is shopping really a synonym for choice, even when, in a hyper-consumer society, consumption is more addiction than voluntary activity? [There can be a] disastrous confusion between the moderate, mostly well-founded claim that flexibly regulated markets are the most efficient instruments of economic productivity and wealth accumulation, and the zany, overblown claim that unregulated markets are the sole means by which we can produce and distribute everything we care about – from durable goods to spiritual values, from capital development to social justice, from profitability to sustainable environments, from private wealth to the essential commonweal. This second claim has moved some people to insist that goods as diverse and obviously public as education, culture, penology, full employment, social welfare, and ecological survival should be handed over to the profit sector for arbitration and disposal, but the argument of this chapter shows how inadequate and dangerous this misapprehension is.

Markets are simply not designed to do the things democratic polities or free civil societies do. Markets give us private, not public, modes of discourse: we pay as consumers in currencies of consumption to producers of material goods, but we cannot use this currency when we deal with one another as citizens or neighbors about the social consequences of our private market choices. Markets advance individualistic, not social, goals and they encourage us to speak the language of "I want," not the language of "we need." Markets preclude "we" thinking and "we" action of any kind at all, trusting in the power of aggregated individual choices (the "invisible hand") somehow to secure the common good. In the name of diversity and private choice, markets foster a kind of consumer totalism, turning multidimensional citizens into one-dimensional, solitary shoppers. Consumers speak the divisive rhetoric of "me." Citizens invent the common language of "we."

Markets are also contractual rather than communitarian, which means they flatter our solitary egos but leave unsatisfied our yearning for community; they offer durable goods and fleeting dreams but not a common identity or a collective membership. Virulently negative expressions of communitarian solidarity are in fact often reactions to the market's desocializing features. The thinner the market's social nexus, the thicker and more bloody the response to it – and so what I have called McWorld engenders the Jihad that resists it.

Beyond our markets, then, we need the virtues of democracy and the social relations of civil society; and our markets and our ideal of civil society need democracy to survive. Markets are as likely to undermine as to sustain full employment, environmental safety, public health, social safety nets, education, cultural diversity, and real competition. These common goods are the result of common thinking, cooperation, and sharing of the kind democratic civil society makes possible. The task today, in theory no less than in practice, is to reilluminate public space for a civil society in eclipse. Making space for citizens and giving them a civil voice in their affairs must be the goal of all our practical strategies.

A government pledged to give practical support to citizenship and civil society can effectively and legitimately act through legislative initiatives and reform as a positive facilitator of civil society, as a partner of citizens in removing negative governmental obstacles to civil-society practices, and as an ally of civil society in challenging the totalizing, private commercial sector as well as overly zealous communitarian groups whose fraternal ministrations shrink the purview of citizenship.

There is no legislative domain that cannot be reframed and improved by thinking how it might promote civil society. After all, government programs, regulatory policy (or its absence), and political ideology expressed in laws helped to create our present world. The corporation, that dominating leviathan of the private sector, was itself a creature of government and in American law exists as an "artificial person" only through its status under the law. Happily, both Democrats and Republicans have shown some interest in "legislating civil society" – the Clinton Administration in its ongoing fascination with civil society and public–private partnerships, and the Republicans in the legislative agenda offered by Bill Bennett and Senator Dan Coats for government intervention to sustain civic practices. Government agencies like the United States Information Agency, private philanthropies like George Soros's Open Society Institute, and the Institute for Civil Society and Civicus (the international NGO umbrella organization) all try to strengthen civil society in transitional societies and in the international arena. Some programs are obviously more easily enacted than others. I would propose six possible areas where innovative and liberating laws could nourish civil society without incurring unreasonable new operating costs. In many cases, the new tactics would build on legislative strategies that are already in place (e.g., campaign finance reform, free TV time for candidates, using new telecommunication technologies for the public weal); in others, they could embody new initiatives. The consequences not just of an absence of government intervention but of maladroit and destructive government policy need to be addressed afresh.

In every case, the specific initiatives I suggest here aim to reorient and reconceptualize our policy goals so as to downplay government as an end in itself or as the direct solution to social problems, and to emphasize it as a facilitating instrument of citizens who want to get their own public work done. Far from disappearing, government is strengthened – but by turning it back into what it should always be in a democracy: the agent and instrument of highest resort for the highest and most general objectives of civil society and free citizens; the entity that expresses the "we" of our commonalty; civil society in its legislative mode. The aim is to remove rather than reinforce barriers between the people as a citizenry and their government as their sovereign voice.

Here are six pertinent arenas for legislative action in support of civil society:

1   Enlarging and reinforcing public spaces: specifically, retrofitting commercial malls as multi-use and thus genuinely public spaces.
2   Fostering civic uses of new telecommunications and information technologies, preventing commercialization from destroying their civic potentials: specifically, a civic Internet; public-access cable television; a check on mass-media advertising for (and the commercial exploitation of) children.
3   Domesticating and democratizing production in the global economy: protecting the labor market, challenging disemployment practices; making corporations responsible members of civil society without surrendering the government's regulatory authority.
4   Domesticating and democratizing consumption in the global economy: protecting just wage policies, workplace safety, and the environment; the labeling and/or boycotting of goods produced without regard for safety, environment, or child-labor laws.
5   National and community service, service learning programs, and citizen-nurturing voluntarism.
6   Cultivating the arts and humanities as an indispensable foundation for a free, pluralistic society; treating artists as citizens and citizens as artists in government-supported arts education and service programs.

Public spaces

In our mostly privatized, suburbanized world, there are not enough physical places where citizenship can be easily exercised and civil society's free activities can be pursued. Citizens need physical spaces where they can interact and work to solve public problems. "The trouble with socialism," Oscar Wilde once quipped, "is that it takes up too many free evenings." Civil society and its activities encroach on Wednesday afternoons and Saturday mornings, too. And they require space and place. There can be no civic activity without a palpable civic geography. Ducks, to be ducks, need their pond, and the public needs its town square.

Traditionally, town squares, village greens, general stores, city parks, community halls – even barbershops, post offices, water-coolers, and saloons – have been places for informal civic interaction: neighborly conversation, political argument, the search for shared ground. But when more than half of us now live in suburban developments that are anything but neighborhoods and that have no obvious public spaces – neither civic centers nor even sidewalks – or in inner cities where public space is often unsavory or unsafe, we have fewer and fewer of these formal and informal meeting places. In the suburbs, people go almost everywhere by car, and often bank and eat without leaving those cars. Suburbanization follows the automobile and the kinds of mobility that attend economic development; and there is good reason to think, in the absence of alternatives, that all the world may one day be New Jersey.

In New Jersey, the commonly available public spaces are commercial malls, designed to encourage and facilitate purchasing, indeed, to make material consumption a habit. Stores cater not to traditional needs (try to find a hardware store or dry cleaners or pharmacy in a mall!) but to the manufactured needs of the postmodern economy. Boutiques and novelty chains (The Nature Store, The Sharper Image, the Disney Store, Brookstone's) proliferate. Even food is proffered like fuel in "food court" pit stops that maximize caloric intake and minimize the time spent fueling up for more shopping.

Meanwhile, more traditional urban milieus have been mauled and malled by architects who think of Las Vegas (or Disneyland) as an opportunity to do a Times Square theme park, and of Times Square as an opportunity to bring Las Vegas to New York. In Washington, D.C., Union Station and the old Post Office are examples of traditional public spaces that have been recast as commercial spaces. (Ironically, the National Endowments for the Arts and the Humanities are sequestered upstairs in the commercialized old Post Office.) Might not both buildings have been refurbished to include civic and social space as well as shops? Public space means more than the accidental open areas left behind in cavernous buildings after commercialization has run its course. Even airports are coming to resemble malls with airplanes.

If our world is to be malled, is it possible to transform malls into usable civic spaces? Is an architecture geared to commerce malleable enough to permit alterations to fulfill civic needs? How might malls be designed and developers encouraged to make space for neighborhood health clinics, speakers' corners, child-care centers? for political and community meeting spaces, community theaters and art galleries, charitable organizations? for information and media groups and other civic associations? What kind of incentives might governments offer to make this happen? Could zoning regulations be used to make developers take a more civic approach? Might "curb cut" permits (which let developers have rights-of-way from public highways) do the same thing? Why not a "model" civic-mall competition sponsored by the National Endowment for the Humanities? A contest for architects to design model civic space?

[. . .]

The new moralists who applaud the containment of government like to make vigorous civic demands on pregnant children and unemployed immigrants; they might more appropriately make them on Time-Warner and Microsoft. We rightly ask whether schools adequately provide for the moral education of children. We also have the right to ask whether Disneyland and MTV and the mall do the same.

[. . .]

The current crop of progressives are critical of business, but often cast their criticism in the language of capitalist efficiency. [. . .] This inverts the progressive agenda. [. . .]

Civic responsibility, being a partnership between government, civil society, and the private market, necessarily depends on the active collaboration of political leaders, citizens, and business people. Executives have for too long suffered a kind of corporate schizophrenia in which they hived off and buried their civic identities – the small voices within that screamed "I cannot do that to my spouse, my children, my neighbors, my world!" even as their corporate hands signed orders doing exactly "that" to everyone, including their loved ones. Unless they want to live divided lives, they must accommodate their business to their human side.

It is not really so hard. The logic of the social contract enacts a set of mutual obligations among the parties who establish and benefit from democratic government. As citizens, whether of France, Germany, Russia or the United States, we have already covenanted to establish a free democratic government, although we seem to have forgotten its origin in our sovereign contract. But the wall between public and private sectors has insulated corporations and their personnel from civic responsibility and allowed this corporate schizophrenia to insulate their women and men, whether employers or employees, from their obligations as citizens. [. . .] The very citizens who otherwise might see government as an ally have as corporate managers encouraged and participated in dismantling the strong state society and the democratic regulatory institutions that enforced civic standards on them. This gives them self-imposed responsibilities they might have avoided in a strong state society (and, in a well-ordered society, *should* have avoided). In an ideal world I would prefer to have democratic government enforce public standards and leave corporations to the business of productivity and profit-taking; in the world we actually live in, the predicate for reestablishing a robust civil society is a new civic compact that specifically obligates corporations. Here is a template:

A corporate civic compact for private sector citizens

Preamble. Recognizing that democratic government is an instrument of a free society and that its elected officers and representatives are but accountable trustees of those who elect them; and

that the primary responsibility for the civic health both of government and society thus belongs to the citizens and associations that constitute civil society and the private sector; and

that the productive economy requires a free-market private sector to flourish, while civil association requires a free civil-society sector to flourish; and

that civil society occupies a space between the governmental and private sectors that can be destroyed by bloat and aggressive expansion from either side; therefore,

We the free citizens of civil society and the corporate managers, producers, shareholders, and workers of the private sector, integrating our economic and civic identities and acknowledging our primary responsibility for democracy, do therefore freely obligate ourselves to the following principles:

1   We will respect the independence and noncommercial character of civil society and actively work to prevent the privatization or commercialization of its spaces – whether those spaces are educational (no advertising in or commercial exploitation of the classroom), religious (no commercialization of religious holidays), public broadcast (no charge for civic and political use of public airwaves), or environmental (protection of parks and waterways from advertising and commercialization).

2   We will support the civic diversification of public space and support the redevelopment of what have become exclusively commercial spaces such as malls and theme parks back into true public spaces, creating a balanced social environment in which production and consumption are complemented by the cultural, religious, educational, philanthropic, and political-social activities of civil society.

3   We will work to guarantee full public and equal access by every part of civil society to the media, traditional and innovative, broadcast and cable, passive and interactive, on which information, culture, democratic discussion, and productive capacity depend; and we will support information equality and combat a gap between the information-rich and the information-poor that destroys the conditions of political and civic equality on which democracy depends.

4   We will pay special attention to diversity and independence in the information and entertainment sectors where creativity, spontaneity, and innovation, which are indispensable to a free society, are cultivated and where the heterogeneity of information and debate that is the chief object of the Bill of Rights is secured.

5   We will treat employment not only as a function of economic efficiency and the profitability of production but as a fundamental social commitment, for work, whether commercial or civic, private or public, is the measure of human dignity and civic status, and social stability and labor morale depend on private, commercial, or civic work for all.

6   We will treat fair compensation and reasonable pension plans as rights that are indispensable to workers' dignity and status as citizens as well as their efficiency as producers and their power as consumers.

7   We will make a safe workplace and a safe environment the necessary conditions of doing business in a responsible manner that honors our owners, managers, and producers in their capacity as members of civil society.

8   We will encourage worker participation and worker shareholding through employee stock-ownership plans, co-determination, worker participation in management, and other forms of active worker engagement.

9   We will establish standards for safety, health, working hours, pension plans, and child-labor regulations that will be universally applicable, whether our facilities are located within or outside our

company's headquarter nation; and we will pressure host foreign governments to accept and enforce these standards on all producers as a condition of our doing business in the host country.

10   We will establish standards for compensation that, while they may vary from country to country, offer a reasonable living wage by the measures of the host country; and we will pressure host governments to accept and enforce such standards on all producers as a condition of our doing business in the host country.

11   We will establish standards for compensation that link the salaries of all personnel to productivity, proportionally relate increases in executive salaries to those in workers' wages, and maintain a differential ratio of lowest and highest salaries, whether stockboy or CEO, of no more than twenty to one. [. . .]

12   We will nourish diversity and competition and oppose monopolies, trusts, and cartels, not only because they restrict fair trade and capitalist innovation, but because they diminish the independence, liberty, and dignity of those who work for and manage them in ways destructive to civic virtue and democratic civic culture.

13   We will not take over or merge with other firms unless we intend to maintain their work forces; we will not use the sell-off or close-down of subsidiary companies to finance the takeover of parent companies; we will not engage in mergers and acquisitions whose only product is paper profits for buyers or sellers and the lawyers, accountants, and brokers who service them.

14   We will treat the placement of our facilities and plant in particular venues as a primary social and civic commitment and will not operate or uproot them without considering the social consequences for our employees and their communities, and without adequate compensation.

15   We will treat children and their education as special priorities of a free society, and will protect them from exploitation, from advertising that might distort their capacity for critical inquiry, and from products injurious to their health or polluting to their minds.

16   We will commit the resources necessary to execute the above obligations and treat them as a necessary cost of doing business in a democratic society, where executives and workers are citizens first and economic beings afterward.

17   We will spread the cost of this commitment of resources equally among all those who are social beneficiaries of social expenditures, including executives (modestly reduced salaries), shareholders (modestly reduced profits), and customers (modestly higher prices).

18   We will encourage personnel at all levels to overcome the civic schizophrenia that forces us to regard ourselves as citizens in our social role but as corporate producers and managers in our economic role, and instead acknowledge that our civic identity is primary and must play a primary role in our economic decision-making.

I believe a commitment to this corporate civic compact will benefit the private sector no less than civil society. Rapacious capitalism that brutalizes workers and rides roughshod over the common goods of civil society in the long run only befouls its own nest. A free market undisciplined by civic concerns destroys citizens in the short term but also destroys consumers in the long term. [. . .] Capitalism needs democracy and civility, which means it needs to democratize its practices and civilize its executives. Where once we looked appropriately to the sovereign polity to bring justice and comity to an otherwise anarchic economic realm, we must now also look to the newly sovereign corporations. Either they must give us back our government and, while pursuing profits, accommodate governmental encroachments and regulation in the name of the public weal, or they themselves will have to become more civic-minded and democratic, no matter what the cost to their profits. Anything less means the end of democracy.

[. . .]

20

Stakeholding by Any Other Name: A Third Way Business Strategy

Michael Allen

Since the emergence of the third way as a distinctive approach to developing a radical centre-left politics, politicians and commentators have engaged in extensive debate – initially transatlantic, now genuinely global – about the provenance and meaning of the term. Third way politics is ambitious and radical in seeking to reconcile conventional polarities, to marry equity and efficiency, economic individualism and social solidarity, private enterprise and corporate responsibility. One way of gauging the extent to which it is able to do so is to look at the third way approach to business, which illustrates some of its underlying tensions and impulses.

To many the meaning of the concept and its political implications still seem as elusive as soap in the bath. At a recent management school conference on the implications of the third way for business, the lack of consensus on the meaning of the term was a factor in both stimulating and debilitating the debate. This is perhaps not surprising since the third way has emerged primarily from a critique of the state and traditional left notions of the political. While the limitations of neo-liberalism are also formative influences, the market *per se* emerges relatively unscathed. One consequence of these antecedents is that third way commentators have yet to develop a coherent perspective on the limitations of business, to match the healthy awareness on the modernising left of the shortcomings of the market. Third way theorists rarely engage in a discussion of business except by way of a celebration of the innovation, mutability and efficiency purportedly characteristic of private enterprise, in contrast to the conservatism, stasis and under-performance of the state. Typical of this approach, and extolling the virtues of business, is Giddens, who argues that 'many business firms have reformed themselves in recent years . . . have debureaucratised, looked for the benchmarking of standards and have accorded greater autonomy in decision-making to lower levels of the organisation. Government should seek to achieve similar results . . .'[1]

This is politically problematic; and the consequences of the lack of serious thought being given to a third way approach to the shortcomings of business has been confirmed in events [such as] the controversy surrounding BMW's decision to disengage from Rover in the UK. The prime minister was reported to have been incandescent with rage when informed of this decision. It was alleged that senior BMW executives had deceived, even 'lied' to, trade and industry minister Stephen Byers in failing to disclose longstanding plans to sell Rover to the venture capital firm Alchemy. Yet the Government remains committed to vetoing the European Commission's proposed directive extending provisions for employee information and consultation via domestic works councils, on the grounds that it would hinder corporate flexibility and constitute an additional burden on business. It is also difficult to criticise the devastating social effects of BMW's decisions from a third way perspective, since its actions seem wholly consistent with the pursuit of shareholder value, including the competitive advantage of enhanced capital mobility afforded by globalisation. Of course, a stakeholder perspective on corporate activity could reasonably criticise BMW for neglecting the interests of the employees and communities affected by its strategic decision-making. But from a consistently third way perspective, BMW can be held to have acted legitimately, especially since it was operating outside the institutional constraints of the allegedly sclerotic German 'social model'. (Giddens, for example, has criticised the 'cronyism and even corruption' of 'Rhineland capitalism' (i.e. the social model).) [. . .] This description of the European social model highlights one of the less endearing tendencies of third way commentators – the caricaturing of any alternative model to that of Anglo-American flexibility; and this is all the more regrettable since the social model remains resilient, flexible and open to considerable modernisation. [. . .]

The UK Government's plans for the biggest shake-up in company law for 150 years, published just a fortnight before the BMW affair blew up, reject a stakeholder approach, and seem set to retain shareholder value as the overriding business objective for public companies. A stakeholder approach would require companies to address the concerns of employees, suppliers, community groups and other interests alongside those of shareholders. But under the Company Law Review directors will only be required to report on social and environmental issues in a modest nod at transparency. The review explicitly rejects an equivalence of interest between shareholders and other stakeholders. Stakeholder issues may only be raised at the strategic boardroom level through a two-tier 'inclusive' approach. First, the law will specify that directors' duties must explicitly include the need to at least consider wider and more long-term issues than simply short-term shareholder value; secondly, companies must report on broad non-financial issues in an operating and financial review (OFR) in annual reports, unless directors consider them irrelevant.

Stephen Byers was conspicuously cautious about the review's suggestion that shareholders should have the right to sue company directors for damage caused to employees, the public and other stakeholders, only promising to 'reflect carefully' on the proposals. This caution came as little surprise, however, since the utilities regulation bill, introduced earlier in March, also explicitly rejected a stakeholder approach. Furthermore, Stephen Byers, in his defence of the bill, which had been criticised for excluding provision for adequate consumer protection and independent representation, told Parliament that the government would put the interests of business 'first, second and last' in such decisions.

Clearly, the third way has yet to be applied to a modernising critique of business itself, although there does exist a growing number of firms that are reconsidering and reformulating their mission statements and practices to reflect the legitimate interests and aspirations of internal and external stakeholders. This approach is clearly consonant with the third way commitment to expanding and redefining notions of citizenship, and rejuvenating the social contract on the basis of reciprocal rights and responsibilities. But the anaemic recommendations of the Department of Trade and Industry's Company Law Review suggest that there remains a prevailing deference towards business, and little has been done to challenge the narrow definition of business success as the maximisation of shareholder value.

This timidity is perhaps anomalous, since there is much in the analysis and prescriptions of the third way that can be constructively applied to many areas of business activity, from enhanced social responsibility to the reform of the opaque corporate governance regimes of US and UK companies. It is curious that New Labour should be so timid on this issue, when there is a growing consensus on both sides of the Atlantic on the shortcomings of this archaic form. [. . .]

It could be argued that third way criticisms of mainstream European social democracy seemed to be confirmed when the June 1999 launch of the Blair–Schröder manifesto – *The Way Forward for Europe's Social*

Democrats – was quickly followed by a haemorrhage of electoral support for social democrats across Europe. Less than a fifth of voters supported the socialist or social democratic parties in Belgium, Denmark, Finland, Holland, Ireland and Italy, while the French *Parti Socialiste* won only 23 per cent of the vote. These losses were, of course, duplicated in the elections for the European Parliament, when the left lost its majority for the first time in a generation. More recent developments in Austria would seem to suggest that the failings of traditional social democracy have exposed a vacuum vulnerable to exploitation by populist and authoritarian forces.

Far from representing electoral recoil from third way prescriptions, however, this collective electoral catastrophe suggests that the time is ripe for the modernisation of European social democracy. And it is open to question whether the still amorphous and elusive prescriptions of advocates of the third way represent a coherent body of thought of sufficient rigour to inform and inspire New Labour's counterparts overseas.

Modernising the business agenda

A number of the 'fundamentals of third way politics' outlined by Anthony Giddens [. . .] have clear implications for modernising the business agenda. Although Giddens's arguments are usually interpreted as being a critique of the left, they can as easily be directed towards neo-liberalism and the right. For example this could be said of Giddens's argument that Left–Right political dualism is now obsolete, diverting energies and attention from the necessary development of the radical centre of third way politics. Furthermore, citing the arguments of German sociologist Claus Offe, Giddens argues that a new equilibrium between government, economy and civil society is needed 'in the interests of social solidarity and social justice'. He also argues that the changing contours and distinctive nature of the new knowledge-driven economy demand a redefined role for the state in cultivating social and human capital. The third way seeks a new balance between regulation and liberalisation. '[D]emonising the corporations makes no sense', says Giddens, although 'corporate power certainly needs to be controlled by government and by international legislation'. (In fact, however, third way partisans have not been content with their legitimate critique of the Left's traditional hostility to business and the market; they have often embraced business and market values with a naive and wide-eyed admiration, and this at a time when even neo-liberal economists like Jeffrey Sachs and Paul Krugmann are voicing acute concerns about market failures and shortcomings.)[2]

Giddens also argues, albeit in a critique of the old Left's traditional egalitarianism, for the promotion of equal opportunities buttressed by an energetic assault on new forms of social exclusion. Finally, and ambitiously, Giddens insists that third way politics proposes a new social contract rooted in the precept 'no rights without responsibilities'. 'Those who profit from social goods', says Giddens, 'should both use them responsibly and give something back to the wider social community in return.'

Third way partisans publicly subscribe to the fundamental values of the Left. Blair and Schröder insist that social democracy 'will never sacrifice' such 'timeless' values as 'fairness and social justice; liberty and equality of opportunity; solidarity and responsibility to others'. But, inevitably, they go on to argue that notions of community, equality and solidarity must be redefined to accommodate the exigencies of modernity (or post-modernity). And the kind of adjustments put forward by advocates of the third way are usually analysed by their critics as entailing a shift to the right. Typical of this is the stinging but sophisticated critique of Jeff Faux, of the US-based Economic Policy Institute, which depicts the 'intellectually amorphous substance' of the third way as 'primarily a rationalisation for political compromise between left and right, in which the left moves closer to the right.'[3]

This interpretation is understandable in view of the modernisers' continuing failure to address the shortcomings of business. This is especially so since the principal aspects of the third way redefinition of left values have almost always involved, in one way or another, an accommodation of the market. The third way stresses the primacy and economic utility of the free market, including its globalised form; it elevates and celebrates private enterprise and entrepreneurship; and it accepts the fiscal and monetary constraints of prudent and sound finance. The emergence of the third way coincided not only with the political and ideological triumph of capital, but with the hegemony of a particular concept of capitalist enterprise. Within Anglo-American firms at least, the maximisation of shareholder value determines management practice and is held to constrain policy options.

Giddens endorses sociologist Claus Offe's caustic critique of traditional left statism, but nowhere in his recent writings do we find a similarly scathing critique of corporate activity. Yet governmental institutions are not the only agencies whose decisions and activities can constrain individual choices and life chances. The issue of corporate accountability cannot be avoided if a third way approach is to be both serious and consistent about genuine transparency and participation in social institutions. A growing number of businesses are investing considerable resources in socially responsible initiatives, from involvement in Business in the Community to incorporating corporate citizenship criteria in their balanced scorecard approach to evaluating company performance – and individual managers' rewards. But deregulation, privatisation and corporate restructuring have rendered large swathes of business decision-making immune to public scrutiny. Decisions with profound social implications – on take-overs, redundancies, closures and transfers of undertakings, for instance – are taken with minimal consultation with interested stakeholders. The lack of meaningful consultation or involvement – sanctioned in Anglo-American firms by an archaic system of corporate governance in which even institutional investors such as pension fund trustees are often left in the dark – is hardly conducive to engendering a culture of trust.

In fact, many of the Offe/Giddens criticisms of excessive statism are equally applicable to corporate institutions, an insight from which third way writers seem insulated. The opacity of corporate decision-making typified by the BMW–Rover fiasco has provoked growing demands for the reform of corporate governance. While making political capital from pre-election digs at corporate Fat Cats, New Labour has not responded to the public's legitimate concerns about questions such as executive pay excesses and incestuous inter-connecting directorships; it has not acted on these concerns by instituting policies which might secure greater transparency, for example.

Historically, it has usually been the left on whom the task has fallen of moderating the excesses of the market, often in the long-term interests of businesses otherwise driven by the imperative of short-term profit-maximisation. This task is currently necessary in relation to the knowledge economy: the rapid pace of change, and the demands for constant innovation, generate the need for different forms of business relations. These new relations must protect and enhance human resources, and cultivate productive forms of social capital – conspicuously, trust, co-operation and an element of mutual gain in pursuing innovation without engendering instability. In short, they require elements of a stakeholder approach to business, to help to foster continuity and stability and relations with customers, suppliers and employees, and to underpin flexible and consensual approaches to change.

More strategically minded business figures have recognised that the post-1989 ideological triumph of capitalism has, at least in part, had the paradoxical effect of enhancing expectations of corporate social responsibility. 'We're a customer-focused firm and it's our customers who insist that our business is ethical and socially responsible', BT's Bill Cockburn told a recent conference on *The Third Way and Business* at Cranfield School of Management. Yet there is little evidence in the Government's Company Law Review of a third way approach of balancing rights and responsibilities, or expanding notions of corporate citizenship; the Review is premised upon the antiquated notion of shareholder value as the single legitimate criterion for measuring corporate success, while accountability is seen as being ensured solely through the mechanism of the market. It may be argued that a third way approach to business must, almost by definition, be non-interventionist and accept the autonomy of business. But there seems to be no reason in principle why private companies should not be exposed to the same levels of scrutiny and demands for transparency as public bodies. Let us recall that one of Giddens's fundamental precepts of third way politics was a new social contract based on 'no rights without responsibilities'; this, he insists, applies 'to business corporations as much as the private individual'. We might expect as much, given the disparity in resources between individuals and corporations, and the disproportionate social impact of corporate decisions and actions. But there is little clarity about the reciprocal obligations that arise from the rights exercised by private property holders.

A new social contract?

Government clearly has a role in defining such obligations, even if only in promoting and generalising best practice, such as social auditing. The need for a more proactive approach also seems evident from the manifest conservatism evinced by some institutions to even modest proposals. For example, the National Association of Pension Funds is implacably hostile to the forthcoming requirement for pension funds simply to state their approach to socially responsible investment, without any actionable consequences. The application of third way prescriptions for institutional modernisation to corporate bodies would require a redefinition of shareholder value in more pluralist and inclusive terms. Its stress on individual empowerment implies a more active approach to the enhancement, and more effective utilisation, of human resources. The third way emphasis on generating social capital – particularly that elusive and economically valuable commodity, trust – requires democratic countervailing powers to the otherwise destabilising forces of capital and the market.

This is consistent with Tony Blair's own succinct synopsis of third way aspirations, for a 'dynamic knowledge-based economy founded on individual empowerment and opportunity, where governments enable, not command, and the power of the market is harnessed to serve the public interest'.[4] Of course, it is also too close to a stakeholder approach to be politically acceptable to many in the government. But New Labour fears of a Huttonesque stakeholderism are misplaced and exaggerated. A stakeholder approach encompasses a menu of options (most of which are well short of fully-fledged Rhenish capitalism) for protecting and enhancing the plurality of interests that constitute modern businesses:

- minimalist self-protection via share-holdings
- voluntary protection of stakeholder interests by long-term oriented firms
- differential statutory protection of differing stakeholder interests
- statutory protection providing an institutionally based voice or empowerment to stakeholders.

Current workplace relations and labour market bodies in Britain are still based upon attitudes, practices and institutional arrangements forged in the industrial era. Furthermore, they continue to reflect the polarised and mistrustful legacy of a Taylorist division of labour between conception and execution, creative intellect and mere implementation, power and impotence – in short, management and employee – and this has stifled employee innovation, ingenuity and commitment. One of the political weaknesses of the third way [. . .] is the absence of an accessible and popular narrative that 'tells a story' about the limitations of both neo-liberalism and statist socialism. In so far as work remains a primary source of 'personal dignity, respect, identity, and social interaction',[5] applying the prescriptions of the third way to the world of work could potentially engage constituencies hitherto marginal to – or alienated from – the modernising agenda.

But it is unlikely that the new social contract invoked by Giddens can be developed without institutional change within the corporate sector and labour market intermediary organisations. Government cannot afford to rely on voluntary initiatives, in a knowledge-based economy where social and human capital are the principal source of competitive advantage. This is particularly the case as British firms have such a lamentable record on investment in training, skills and innovation, and on adopting forms of employee involvement which most effectively utilise skills and cultivate commitment. In many of these areas, established managerial strategies and corporate practices in Britain are such as to qualify large swathes of business for inclusion in the growing army of the forces of conservatism. For example, the 1998 Workplace Employee Relations Survey (WERS) revealed that less than 20 per cent of employees reported frequent consultation about workplace change, while 75 per cent of employees were never consulted on any issue.[6] WERS also confirms the relationship between trade union presence, enhanced workplace performance and the use of 'high commitment management practices'. It also supports recent research from the US on workplace innovation in the New Economy which finds that 'employee voice has a larger positive effect on pro-ductivity when it is done in the context of unionised establishments'.[7]

A meaningful renegotiated social contract need not entail a return to the neo-corporatist arrangements of the 1970s, or to an abortive attempt to transplant continental European stakeholder practices in the UK. A modest start would be to pursue a more energetic reform of cor-porate governance than recently intimated, for example by imposing a statutory duty on directors to consult and consider a range of stake-holder interests prior to strategic decision taking. An extension of employee information and consultation rights through domestic works councils, or equivalent consultation forums, would bring British workers into line with continental European counterparts. The Government should also give serious consideration to the TUC's call for a new fair wages and competition law 'to re-establish the principle that the public sector will only do business with those who observe high employment standards', and for 'a new statutory framework to encourage high training standards through a mixture of tax incentives and levies' (*Financial Times*, 17.2.00). Both measures would help raise the floor of overall employment standards and help generalise good practice.

Such measures would be modest steps towards a richer concept of corporate responsibility, that would recognise the inherently pluralis-tic nature of the firm, and that 'employees who share residual risks by investing their human and collective human capital should have a right to participate in the governance of the firm'. Seduced by what Robert Kuttner calls the 'romance of the new economy',[8] third way commen-tators place a premium on the cultivation of trust as a morally co-hesive force in developing new workplace relations. This is consistent with calls from elsewhere on the modernising left for a 'political economy of citizenship' which would define 'what economic arrange-ments are hospitable to self-government and the civic virtues that sustain it'.[9] A concept of citizenship, based upon reciprocal acceptance of rights and responsibilities, that does not extend beyond the office door or factory gate is deeply impoverished and flawed. Just as restrictive practices have been largely consigned to the history books, so management prerogatives should no longer be invoked to legitimise disempowerment in the workplace.

There are political dangers with adopting a too manifestly deferential approach to business interests. The corporate community has considerable influence but few votes. We should be careful not to follow the trajectory of New Labour's ideological mentors in the Democratic Leadership Council in the US, which in distancing itself from traditional constituencies has, in the view of prominent US modernisers, moved on to 'champion a so-called centrist and bipartisan agenda, much of which fails to address – and some of which actually subverts – basic popular concerns', with the result that the DLC 'has grown uncomfortable with a politics centered on the lives and values of ordinary citizens'.[10] If the third way does represent a politics of 'hard choices', it remains to be seen whether there is the political will or inclination to explore a more radical and imaginative interpretation of choices which are likely to offend corporate sensibilities, question managerial prerogatives and constrain or temper market mechanisms.

Notes

1 Giddens, A. (2000) *The Third Way and its Critics*, Cambridge: Polity Press, p. 58.
2 Kuttner, R. (2000) 'The Role of Governments in the Global Economy', in Hutton and Giddens (eds), *On The Edge: Living With Global Capitalism*, London: Jonathan Cape, p. 161.
3 Faux, J. (1999) 'Lost on the Third Way', *Dissent* 46, 2 (Spring), pp. 67–76.
4 Blair, T. (1998) *The Third Way: New Politics for a New Century*, London: Fabian Society, pp. 6–7.
5 Kochan, T. (1999) *Building a New Social Contract at Work: a Call to Action*, MIT Institute for Work and Employment Research.
6 Cully, M. (1999) *Britain At Work: As Depicted by the 1998 Workplace Employee Relations Survey*, London: Routledge.
7 Black, S. E. and L. M. Lynch (1999) *What's Driving the New Economy: The Benefits of Workplace Innovation*, Federal Reserve Bank of New York and Tufts University.
8 Kuttner: 'The Role of Governments in the Global Economy', p. 151.
9 Sandel, M. J. (1997) 'The Political Economy of Citizenship', in Stanley B. Greenberg and Theda Skocpol (eds), *The New Majority: Towards a Popular Progressive Politics*, Yale University Press, p. 148.
10 Skocpol, T. and S. B. Greenberg (1997) 'A Politics for Our Time', in Greenberg and Skocpol (eds), *The New Majority: Towards a Popular Progressive Politics*, p. 11.

21

A New Political Economy: The Importance of Social Capital

Simon Szreter

[. . .]

To acquire the solid backbone necessary to become an effective and lasting new political programme which will guide the next generation, the third way will need the following three structural elements, soundly constructed and mutually articulated: moral principles and priorities (the axioms of the programme: 'what we believe in and where we are going'); a fully elaborated ideology which convincingly argues and demonstrates in more detail how these principles and priorities can be practically related to the workings of 'the real world', real people and their relationships to each other and to the economy; a specification of the practical policies and measures which are required in order to change the society and economy towards the desirable model of social and economic relationships that has been elaborated. [. . .]

The purpose of this discussion is to focus on the crucial second element in this triad, by exploring the meaning of the concept of social capital in order to show that it can offer critical assistance to the third way by providing it with its own distinctive political economy. Social capital is an exciting and controversial idea developed during the last decade or so, mainly by North American social scientists.[1] It is simultaneously an economic, sociological and political concept. This chapter attempts to offer a definition of social capital, and to argue that if third way thinking successfully integrates the concept of social capital into its understanding of the workings of the market economy, this will provide it with its own new, rigorous and *practical* analysis of the economy.

[. . .]

Social capital flows from the endowment of mutually respecting and trusting relationships which enable a group to pursue their shared goals more effectively than would otherwise be possible. Social capital therefore depends on the *quality* of the set of *relationships* of a social group. It can never be the possession or attribute of an individual. It results from the communicative capacities of a group – something shared in common, and in which all participate. The relationships among the participants must be un-coerced and set on a basis of formal equality and *mutual respect* (though the participants may freely choose to organise themselves with leaders and representatives, and endow themselves with some form of communication or authority structure).

[. . .]

From the point of view of developing the concept as a basis for a new political economy of the left [. . .] two sets of misconceptions in particular need to be corrected.

The first is the right-wing libertarian interpretation, which crudely hijacks the idea of social capital to buttress undiscriminating hostility to 'the state', by arguing that the activities of the state are intrinsically inimical to the vitality of social capital because it 'crowds out' voluntary associations.[2] This is a naive simplification: [. . .] voluntary associations are capable of damaging, as well as contributing to, social capital. In a polity actively nurturing its social capital, the state has to perform a vital partnership and facilitation role in at least two obvious ways. Firstly, it needs to deploy resources to empower disadvantaged individuals: the sick, injured, young, old, poor and poorly-educated, and other groups subject to social exclusion for reasons that are beyond their powers to alter, such as their gender or ethnic affiliation. This is to endow them with their citizenship and their liberties, and so enable them to participate with their fellow citizens on an equal status basis, in all the networks and associations through which social capital functions. Secondly, there is the importance of the locally devolved form of 'state': participatory, local self-government in active partnership and responsive negotiation with the communities and businesses whose environment it administers.

A second misconception about social capital is the idea that all that it requires is tight-knit, 'traditional' communities. It is an entirely con-

tingent matter whether or not such communities lead to effective negotiation and respectful collaboration with each other, in a form which
generates the additional social and economic benefits which comprise
social capital: the feuding and distrust of tight-knit 'Hill-Billy'
Appalachian hamlets, or the quiet, claustrophobic 'tyranny of village
vexation' – to cite Edmund Burke on pre-industrial rural England –
being equally possible outcomes. Hence Putnam's study confirmed
previous research in finding that the 'traditional' village and town communities of southern Italy were mostly characterised by hierarchical
and authoritarian social and political relations, and an 'amoral
individualism' among mutually distrustful citizens; whereas in the
'modernised' cities of the north, social and political relations were
more egalitarian, and were associated with much more voluntary
civic participation on a basis of personal freedom: only under these
circumstances did community foster liberty.[3]

   The set of relationships which generate genuine social capital should
have two key qualities, one related to the internal relations of the institution or group in question, and one to external relations: they should
entail active participation on a basis of formal equality; and they should
not contribute to forms of social exclusionism, or closure of lines of
communication and fellow-feeling with other citizens. On the contrary,
true social capital is built from practical lessons and experience in dialogue with as wide a variety of others as possible. Thus social capital
is premised on an important general principle of maximising 'communicative equality'. The leading empirical exponent of social capital,
Robert Putnam, has always emphasised that it is 'horizontal' contacts
of association between equals, rather than 'vertical' networks (which
imply inequalities of power or authority – he uses the example of the
Mafia in his studies of Italy), which produce true social capital in
human institutions.

   In recognition of these considerations Robert Putnam follows Mark
Granovetter[4] in emphasising the importance of 'weak' rather than
'strong' ties as formative of social capital. Putnam cites research on
social capital and social exclusion in the USA which has found that,
among the very poor living in inner city ghettos, those who have a relatively small number of intense family and neighbourhood gang ties
and loyalties are effectively locked into their poverty and lack of opportunities, whereas those with a wider pool of 'weaker' contacts fare
better. It has long been known that relatively 'mobile' (socially and
geographically) middle-class people benefit from their participation
in a relative abundance of networks of such 'weak' ties. An extensive
and dense range of relatively 'weak' ties, establishing multilateral lines
of communication between the maximum number of citizens, is the

key sign of well-developed social capital, rather than a set of 'strong', intensive and binding ties, dividing off whole sections of the population from each other.[5] Thus, the caste system of India, persistently one of the poorest and most unequal societies in the world, would count as a textbook example of how to minimise social capital across an economy and society. Strong, binding ties, like the caste system, tend to restrain the sphere of choice and the range of 'play' that is available in communication between diverse individuals in the population. The extent to which there are wide 'bridges' of understanding and contact between all the various associations and institutions in civil society is now coming to be seen as an important indicator of a society's capacity to sponsor social capital and counter the forces of social exclusion.

[. . .]

The issue of information is now generally recognised in economics to be a central one for understanding the way in which markets, businesses and economies work. The concept of social capital has strong affinities with this approach to the economy. Its modern intellectual roots can be traced to a seminal work within the liberal economics tradition. This was Ronald Coase's extraordinary article[6] which asked the astoundingly obvious question, 'Why do firms exist?' By providing a revolutionary and innovative answer, Coase founded the modern field of 'transaction costs', the study of the critical importance of information in the functioning of economic systems.

Social capital makes its vital contribution to a new political economy through enabling us to focus on the crucial issue of the means by which the capacities of individuals to process information are distributed across an economy. In particular it can show how the politics of a society and its institutions critically influences the information-processing capacities of its citizens, and hence, ultimately, affects the efficiency and growth potential of the economy.

Thus, James Coleman has argued that a proper understanding of the workings of a market-oriented economy requires the recognition of four analytical categories:

- financial capital (including appropriately valued industrial plant)
- bio-physical capital ('land' and the environment, more widely conceived)
- human capital
- social capital.

From a normative economics viewpoint, social capital can be briefly defined as that general set of relationships which minimises the transaction costs of information across the whole economy. Given the fundamental economic importance of transaction costs, social capital has equivalent productive significance to the other recognised forms of capital. Sustainable optimal economic growth and development requires giving approximately equal weight and attention to the deployment and reproduction of all four forms of capital together.

It is only by interpreting relevant information that we can make a judgement of the value of anything in a market economy – information about what the thing in question can do for us, and, especially, information about what other alternatives are available currently or in the near future. Anybody who has tried to buy a car knows that it is important to invest considerable time in compiling information on the range of prices from different sources for all the models which satisfy your requirements of size, age, etc, before you are in a position to judge whether you're getting a reasonable deal or not. The sellers in the market do not guarantee to offer you that fair deal. This example relates to the importance of information processing in the exchange (or 'consumption') side of the economy; but it is equally, if not more, important in the production side, the focus of Coase's work.

In his article of 1937 Coase pointed out that in fact the only economic reason why such a thing as a 'firm', the most basic element in the production side of the economy, exists at all is because of the need to minimise the 'transaction costs' of the information needed to make anything. By employing everybody within a 'firm' the owners routinise and reduce all these information costs by creating a set of 'experts' (the workers), who, in return for the security and recompense of their regular wages and salaries, all share continuously, and without having to be hired each time their input is needed, all their specialised knowledge of how best to find and process the raw materials and then sell the products at the best prices. Thus, the problem of how to manage the costs of information lies at the very heart of economic organisation into firms in a market system. Those companies which can maximise their access to and control over the relevant, high quality information for the minimum economic outlay will triumph over their competitors. Most truly successful companies – those that have become household names – have found, over the years, that one effective strategy for achieving this, and maintaining it over the long term, is ensuring the commitment and good will of an experienced and trusted workforce, by offering them a good deal.[7]

This insight has led to a number of studies which explore the reasons for economic success and failure in these terms. In particular, one phenomenon that has long puzzled economists is the existence of what Alfred Marshall called 'industrial districts' – such as, in his own time around the turn of the present century, the North Staffordshire Potteries earthenware industry, or the South Staffordshire Black Country's cluster of firms making nuts, bolts, chains and springs, or Sheffield's cutlery workshops. In each case a large number of small, medium-sized and even large firms clustered together, all manufacturing similar products for decades on end without apparently driving each other out of business but, rather, all prospering or declining together. A similar phenomenon has been noted in the 1980s and 1990s, with, for example, Silicon Valley in California, the computing and biotech 'Cambridge phenomenon' in England, and other such districts in south Germany and north-central Italy.[8] In all these areas the companies exist in clusters, enjoying the benefits of 'competitive co-operation': flexibly sharing a pool of specialist knowledge of the state of the market and technologies; sharing and subcontracting a pool of workers and their skills; and sharing the local environmental infrastructure of communications and social services which their industry and workforces require to work and live efficiently, but which any one firm or small number of firms could not provide on their own.

In the 1980s and 1990s it has often been 'the state', typically in the form of the local government administration, which has organised the environment and provided the facilities and services required by these industrial clusters (and of course, the central state also provides further facilitating support of a more general kind in terms of the wider infrastructure supporting the locality in its relations with the rest of society and in maintaining confidence in the rules of the market). This is an example of what is called 'co-production' in the social capital literature, a partnership across the public–private divide, showing that success in the global market often depends on 'the state' nurturing its industries and companies – and vice-versa, in that the productivity of the companies then nourishes the state and society.[9] The companies are embedded in a long-term mutually beneficial relationship with state agencies; and the long-term interdependence of all the companies means that there is little sense in a naked commercial opportunism on the part of any one company, trying to profit unduly at the expense of the others, because such a company would risk subsequent ostracism, and the breakdown of high quality communications with the other companies in the industrial community. There are many incentives for co-operation, and there is often also in these industrial districts a rich shared associational life outside work, among the employers and among the employees. Together, the firms in the industrial district, with their joint resources and high quality shared information, can compete on price and quality against anything else in the rest of the world.

[. . .]

In long industrialised economies such as Britain's, services already account for almost two-thirds of the value produced. The economy is ever-increasingly knowledge and information driven, and much manufacturing is highly knowledge and information-driven (much of what you're paying for when buying a car is the salaries of the research teams who perfected its design, not the metal, glass and plastic it's made from). Creative ideas, cultural diversity, and path-breaking science are linked ever more directly to the productivity of the economy (even more than 'technology', that great buzz word of the 1960s). It has become uncontentious among economists that this means that a key issue for the future success of industrialised economies will be developing and nurturing human capital, whether funded by the state or by employing private companies, or by some combination of the two.

However, there is also the critical question of the most effective means through which – once it has been 'produced' through the education and training systems – human capital (skills and expertise) can be combined in the market economy into creative and productive commercial partnerships and teams. This is where social capital is of crucial significance. Social capital is the result of the maximum diversity and density of positive social relationships between individuals in the market place of work and production. This, in turn, permits human capital to achieve its most productive combinations and outcome for the economy. As efficiency in the simple physical processing of the material content of products becomes less central to the productivity of long industrialised economies, while the commercial value of the creative content of goods and services steadily grows, we must develop an economic analysis which gives correct weighting to this economic fact of life: the ever-increasing importance of information sharing and manipulation. That means a political economy focused around the promotion of effective social relationships as the critical accelerator of information around the economy, thereby enhancing the value of human capital investment.

It follows from this that it is a crucial goal to maximise and equalise the social and cultural scope of information exchange among the economy's workers. Through generating the capacity to process information effectively – the promotion of communicative competence – on the part of the greatest proportion and diversity of citizens, social capital will provide a dynamic primary driving force for a knowledge-processing, creative economy of the future – just as the cheap and accessible supply of coal, oil and electricity have each successively driven, at a basic level, the material-processing economies of the recent past.

[. . .]

One of the most significant and powerful sources of disruption of the possibility that citizens might enjoy a state of equality of communicative competence with each other is a dramatically unequal distribution of wealth and income in society. The national education system is the other principal general influence, after income and wealth distribution, upon the formation of social capital, and the possibilities for equality of communicative competence. This is because it is simultaneously producing not just one economic product, as previously understood by economists, but two: both human capital and social capital. And it is only a good *overall* education system, in which all can have pride in their schools and from which all can derive a sense of personal achievement and worth, which can lay the necessary foundations for the proliferation of social capital all across the economy, by providing its basis in common communicative competence and mutual respect. This argument from social capital holds in principle for a range of other important social policies which affect the equality of citizens' capacities, such as health, housing and social security.

[. . .]

It would, of course, be impractical in both political and economic terms, to implement policies promoting equality of income and wealth in too literal and rigid a fashion. All liberal, market societies will have to continue to get by with a certain degree of inequality, an inevitability in the real world. However, what the social capital insight demonstrates is that there are very significant economic efficiency costs being incurred, in terms of a liberal economic understanding of the functioning of the market economy, in polities which tolerate extreme inequalities of income and wealth distribution among their citizens. In simple terms, there is an important efficiency trade-off, therefore, between socio-economic inequality and a society's endowment in social capital. This leads to the radical and highly distinctive policy conclusion that, in order to promote the economic efficiency of the market and the productivity of its economy, governments should act systematically to correct the tendency towards income, wealth and power inequality which the liberal market's functioning produces. Previously it has typically been argued that liberal economic theory offers a primary presumption in favour of inequality; and that separate, social justice, arguments are required to provide any significant reasons for countenancing the moderation of economic inequality in a market-oriented society. But a polity which permits too much accumulation of capital in the hands of too few of its citizens will be paying a high price in terms of social capital; and, consequently, over the long term, its overall economic performance will be significantly poorer than would otherwise have been achieved.

[. . .]

A full-length version of this chapter is published as: S. Szreter, 'Social capital, the economy and education in historical perspective' in S. Bason and T. Schuller (eds) Social Capital: Critical Perspectives *(Oxford University Press, 2000).*

Notes

1   On this contested concept's brief history, see M. Woolcock, 1998; A. Portes, 1998.
2   Green, 1994; 1995.
3   Putnam, 1993, pp. 109–15.
4   1985.
5   Putnam, 1998.
6   1937.
7   Collins and Porras, 1994; Kay, 1993.
8   Putnam, 1993, p. 160; Granovetter, 1994.
9   Evans, 1995.

References

Coase, R. H. (1937), 'The nature of the firm', *Economica* 4 (November), pp. 386–405.
Coleman, J. S. (1988), 'Social capital in the creation of human capital', *American Journal of Sociology* 94, S95–120.
Coleman, J. S. (1990), *Foundations of social theory.*
Collins, J. C. and Porras, J. I. (1994), *Built to last. Successful habits of visionary companies,* London, Century.
Evans, P. (1995), *Embedded Autonomy. States and industrial transformation,* Princeton, New Jersey, Princeton U.P.
Granovetter, M. (1985), 'Economic action and social structure: the problem of embeddedness', *American Journal of Sociology* 91, 3 (November), pp. 481–510.

Granovetter, M. (1994), 'Business groups', ch. 18 in N. J. Smelser and R. Swedberg (eds), *The handbook of economic sociology*, pp. 453–75, Princeton, New Jersey, Princeton U.P.

Green, D. (1994), 'Re-inventing Civil Society', London, Institute of Economic Affairs.

Green, D. (1995), 'Community without politics', London, Institute of Economic Affairs.

Kay, J. A. (1993), *Foundations of Corporate Success: how business strategies add value*, Oxford, O.U.P.

Portes, A. (1998), 'Social capital: its origins and applications in contemporary sociology', *Annual Review of Sociology* 24, 1, 1–24.

Putnam, R. D. (1993), *Making social democracy work. Civic traditions in modern Italy*, Princeton, New Jersey, Princeton U.P.

Putnam, R. D. (1998), Plenary Address, 'The distribution of social capital in contemporary America', Michigan State University International Conference on Social Capital, 20–22 April 1998.

Woolcock, M. (1998), 'Social capital and economic development: toward a theoretical synthesis and policy framework', *Theory and Society*, 27, 1, 151–208.

22

Is there a Third Way in Labour Law?

Hugh Collins

The third way is attractive to politicians. As a slogan to describe a set of political values, it exhibits many desirable properties: it is brief and unspecific, yet it implies that it is at once new, radical, but centrist. The third way can be presented as a global movement in politics, yet at the same time it professes a local resonance by claiming to disentangle itself from established party politics and traditional ideological divisions, whatever that politics has been in the past. Above all, the third way movement presents itself as a practical political programme, a way to cope with modern problems rather than a fixed set of beliefs. These modern problems that need to be addressed also have a special character: they are new, big, hard to define, and cannot be permanently solved. These problems include the effects of the forces of globalisation of the economy, the incalculable risks to the ecology of the planet of continued population and economic growth, the need to provide legitimacy for government in mass societies, and the challenges presented by radical changes in personal and family life.[1] Politics becomes defined by the practical ways in which to tackle these problems, not by grand ideological schemes.

Issues surrounding work have been peripheral, though not absent, in discussions of third way politics. Because the third way does not propose any change to the basic arrangement of capitalist societies that most people earn their wealth by selling their work through the labour market, the perennial issues presented by this market mechanism still need to be addressed. As ever, work can be hard, stressful, dangerous, denigrating, unrewarding, poorly paid, insecure, and alienating. This essay describes and analyses how the themes of third way politics have been interpreted in relation to legal regulation of employment issues in the United Kingdom. Since many aspects of labour law fall within the competence of the European Community, we also consider aspects of European legal regulation that fit into a third way agenda. But the significance of these developments in the employment law of the United Kingdom extends far beyond these borders if they contain the seeds of [a] radically new approach to labour law. For the new standards of employment regulation proposed by the third way appear to conflict with some aspects of accepted international norms as embodied in the Conventions of the International Labour Organisation.

It is a characteristic of new political movements that they focus on fresh problems and tend to ignore the old agendas. The third way regards the old problems of labour law as those concerning trade unions, collective bargaining, and industrial conflict. A key division in the old politics concerned attitudes towards the legitimacy of trade unions, the desirability of collective bargaining, and restrictions on industrial conflict. But the third way no longer regards these issues as especially pertinent. As Tony Blair said in the principal policy statement of his government in respect of labour law: 'The White Paper ... seeks to draw a line under the issue of industrial relations law.'[2] The old solutions to the old problems can be left alone, largely because they are no longer a pressing political problem – there are no strikes these days – and partly because in any case the established solutions more or less accord with third way philosophy. The crucial task is rather to address the new problems confronting employment relations.

More controversially, I suggest that the third way also diminishes concern about distributive issues in the workplace. Many established political agendas regard the regulation of the workplace for distributive purposes as a key ingredient of labour law. This regulation aims to redistribute power and wealth within the organisation by giving workers, either individually or collectively, legal rights to control or influence the decisions of management. Under this agenda, for instance, laws may promote collective bargaining in order to give workers the right to influence management decisions by making collective agreements, or laws may award individual workers rights to be protected against unfair treatment such as discrimination or the provision of unsafe working conditions. Within traditional social democratic political agendas, these redistributive aims were described as achieving industrial democracy and fairness in the workplace.[3] Although the third way leaves much of this regulation in place, and indeed may strengthen some aspects of it, the justifications for this regulation become subtly modified in response to a new agenda.

From the perspective of the third way, the number one problem is to improve the competitiveness of businesses. To survive and prosper in the new context of a global economy, businesses constantly have to improve the quality and design of their products, invest in new technologies, and reduce costs. A key ingredient of competitiveness is to use the workforce efficiently and effectively. For this purpose the workforce has to be properly trained, to be prepared to work flexibly, and to co-operate with all innovations. The third way believes that labour law, together with other branches of law such as company law, can assist through its regulation of the workplace in the improvement of the competitiveness of businesses. This regulation for the purpose of promoting competitiveness establishes a radically new agenda for labour law. It can justify regulation about old topics such as collective bargaining and individual employment rights, but the objective of this regulation shifts decisively. Instead of regulation of collective bargaining representing either the expression of ideals of industrial democracy, or distributive fairness, or a pragmatic way for resolving fundamental conflicts of interest in an industrial society, the dominant purpose of the regulation becomes the improvement of the competitiveness of the business. Similarly, instead of individual legal rights for employees being justified as representing a fair distributive pattern or recognition of fundamental rights to dignity and respect, the dominant purpose of the regulation is characterised as the promotion of competitiveness of the business.

[. . .]

Regulating for competitiveness

[. . .] This agenda rejects the simplistic view that competitiveness is best achieved through deregulation. At the same time, however, the third way politics diminishes the importance attached to distributive values and ideals of workers' rights. Regulation seeks to improve the operation of the market, not to replace it or impede it. Regulation may protect workers' rights and establish institutional arrangements in the workplace, but the purpose of the regulation is conceived rather differently. The purpose is instrumental: to improve the competitiveness of the business. The rights are not accorded to workers out of respect for basic values or to ensure compliance with ideal standards of fairness and justice. Instead, the legal rights are justified primarily because it is believed that they will contribute to the enhancement of efficient business methods, innovation, improvements in design, more successful marketing, and so forth.

The implications of regulating for competitiveness extend to all aspects of employment law. I will illustrate some of these implications through two examples. The first explains how the third way leads to an endorsement of the style of worker participation known as partnership at work. The second examines how legal regulation that provides individual workers with detailed rights against their employer becomes modified to accord with the goal of regulating for competitiveness.

Partnership

A legal right for workers to participate collectively in management decisions respecting the workplace and the business can be justified on many different grounds. Traditional justifications have tended to emphasise either the need for consultation out of respect for the individual rights of workers to be treated with dignity and respect, or the need for participatory institutions in the workplace as a dimension of democracy in an industrial society. The third way agenda has adopted the metaphor of partnership to express its objective in regulating worker participation. The idea of partnership can be viewed cynically as being sufficiently vacuous that it appeals to a wide range of political opinion without tying the government to any specific regulatory proposals. I shall argue, however, that once partnership is understood within the context of regulating for competitiveness, its objectives, if not all the details of its institutional arrangements, become sufficiently clear to signal an innovative political agenda. We can grasp the principal elements of the institutional arrangements envisaged by the objective of partnership through a comparison with traditional justifications for worker participation.

The model of partnership

One model of social democracy regards the right of workers to join and participate in trade unions as an aspect of freedom of association, a basic individual right that deserves strong legal protection as a part of the constitutional arrangements of society.[4] Legal regulation guards against discrimination and victimisation by employers against union members. The right to freedom of association also applies to employers in the form of freedom of contract; employers should not be forced to enter into contracts with individuals or trade unions. The *Wilson* case[5] illustrates this individual rights framework: employees have the right to join a trade union of their choice, but, as part of freedom of association, the employer also has the right to prefer to enter contracts with workers who do not use the trade union as their representative for the purpose of collective bargaining over terms and conditions of employment.

A second model of social democracy views collective bargaining as the best mechanism for achieving simultaneously social justice and the extension of democracy throughout society. It becomes public policy to promote collective bargaining, which can be supported, where necessary, by legal measures. Collective bargaining is perceived as the only realistic way of achieving distributively fairer outcomes in the firm given the employer's strong bargaining position *vis à vis* individual workers. Similarly, the collective voice of organised trade unions is perceived to be much more effective than other mechanisms such as individual consultation or consultation with works councils. Under this second model, as well as protection of the right to organise, the law can also force employers to enter into bargaining relations where this represents the democratic wishes of the workforce. Thus under this model the right to freedom of association gives way to more powerful collective values of social justice and democracy. A closed shop can be tolerated as a necessary instrument of public policy (thus interfering with the freedom of association of workers) and union recognition can be imposed upon employers (thus interfering with the freedom of association of employers).

In the third way, there is continuing respect for the individual right of freedom of association, but it becomes public policy to promote mechanisms at work that facilitate co-operative work relations on the ground that these are necessary to achieve efficient and more competitive production. These mechanisms for achieving co-operative work relations are described as partnership. The essential elements of partnership institutions comprise the exchange of information between employers and workers together with a commitment to use this information in order co-operatively to improve the efficiency of the relations of production. Collective bargaining might serve this purpose in some instances. As collective bargaining is traditionally conceived, however, in the form of an antagonistic bargaining mechanism to set the price of labour, it is inappropriate and redolent of an old culture that partnership is designed to supersede. Partnership supports consultation about the details and objectives of production, and the business strategy of the firm, but is not particularly interested in collective discussions about the price of labour except in so far as these may be part of productivity-enhancing agreements. This sharing of information and consultation can be achieved by many mechanisms including work groups such as quality circles, works councils, committees of many kinds. It is for each business or each workplace to consider how best to forge effective partnerships.

This third way differs from the first model by placing constraints on freedom of association for the sake of promoting partnerships. At the same time it differs from the second model by promoting institutions other than collective bargaining for the purpose of consultation on the ground that partnership arrangements promote competitiveness. These differences set up a tension between the regulatory proposals of the third way and international conventions that embody the values of the earlier models. For example, the third way can tolerate interference with the employer's freedom of association by imposing models of works councils or other partnership arrangements on businesses. But the third way distances itself from the second model, for it has no reason to compel employers to enter into collective bargaining agreements that fix the price of labour, so it rejects any general right of workers to insist upon collective bargaining.

The efficiency of partnership

Why is partnership necessary for improving the competitiveness of firms, or more briefly, for efficiency? One effect of increasing global competition in product markets (and I include services in this as well) is that countries which pay high wages have to compete increasingly on the basis of quality, design, responsiveness to changes in the market, and technological superiority. To meet this need, many major manufacturing companies have altered their relations with their suppliers or subcontractors. Instead of components being purchased according to the manufacturer's design on the basis of competitive tendering from a pool of potential suppliers, manufacturers entered into long-term partnership arrangements with suppliers. These long-term relations involved the introduction of TQM (Total Quality Management) principles into the suppliers, the use of JIT (Just-in-Time) ordering systems, and the sharing of design, technological, and production expertise. Despite increased management costs for the manufacturer and the component supplier, the competitive advantage of these supplier partnerships lies in the potential for permanent innovation in design, continuous improvements in quality, responsiveness to changes in consumer taste, and technological superiority.[6]

The model of supplier partnerships has been translated by Human Resources Management (HRM) into a theory of how to conduct labour–management relations. In order to achieve innovations in design, continuous improvements in quality and efficiency, and technological superiority, it is argued that employers needed to treat their workforce in a similar way, like partners. Employers need to tap into the potential represented by the human capital (the knowledge and expertise) of the workforce. Quality circles were an early sign of this style of personnel management, but HRM theory quickly expanded this practice into a more general theory of the need to establish partnership arrangements with the workforce. The purpose of partnerships is to enhance competitiveness through improvements in quality and efficiency. This purpose requires the exchange of information: management needs to explain their product and marketing plans to the workforce, and the workers need to use their human capital in order to suggest how production and products can be improved. Instead of the old model of an authority relation in which the workers were told by management what to do, the partnership concept insists that the workforce needs to help management to devise methods of production and to create improvements in the product.

This link between partnership and efficiency is supported by theoretical work in institutional economics.[7] Employers can acquire labour power through diverse contractual arrangements ranging from a brief contract to perform a particular job to a contract of indefinite duration with indeterminate obligations. The choice between contractual forms is important, because it can reduce costs (including transaction costs), and can enable the parties to maximise their wealth derived from the transaction. Most contracts of employment are incomplete by design,[8] because the employer cannot specify in advance what tasks will have to be performed by the worker. The contract obtains specificity by granting the employer the discretion to direct labour to its most profitable use. This transactional model of an incomplete contract with a unilateral governance structure achieves superior outcomes in terms of efficiency whenever the parties to the transaction anticipate that variations in the details of performance will be required and where it is hard to specify in advance adequate measures of work effort. This model provides the conceptual foundation for the traditional (or 'master and servant') legal analysis of the contract of employment of indefinite duration based upon the obligation of obedience to management. This model can also be criticised, however, for having certain inefficient properties. In particular, this traditional model (a) may not encourage active co-operation by employees beyond obedience to orders, and (b) provides little incentive for workers to use human capital to improve the employer's business. To redress these sources of inefficiency, and by analogy with supplier partnerships, another contractual model can be proposed.

In this model, which is sometimes described as a symbiotic contract, the basic framework of incentives is designed as two simultaneous principal and agent relations. We are not using the language of principal/agent in the technical legal sense here; the terms merely describe a type of business relation where one person (the agent) acts according to the instructions and in the interests of another (the principal), and where the principal obtains the residual profits (after costs) of any transaction. Symbiotic contracts have the puzzling feature that both parties act simultaneously as not only principals in their own right but also as agents for the other. In order to make this symbiotic model of transactions function efficiently, both parties have to share the profits of the enterprise by having the incentive of being residual owners, and, crucially, the parties have to co-operate by extensive sharing of knowledge and expertise. This analysis has been applied, for instance, to business format franchises.[9] The franchisor is both a principal who uses agents to market the business format, and at the same time an agent of the franchisees in the promotion and development of the reputation of the business format.

Applying this principal and agent idea to an employment relation, the symbiotic contract model suggests that at the same time as the employee is the agent for the employer in carrying out the work (as under the master and servant model), the employer is acting in part as the agent of the employee in creating work to be performed and in enhancing the worker's employability.[10] The potential competitive advantage of this model over traditional employment forms is that it creates an incentive for the employees to use their human capital to co-operate by maximising the joint product in return for the employer undertaking various obligations as their agents. It is important to note that the symbiotic model does not assume that management and workers share a common interest. On the contrary, the idea that both parties are principals in their own right explicitly denies any 'unitary frame of reference'.[11] The interests of management and workers conflict, as in the simple complete contract model, but in order to maximise their self-interest they have to engage in extensive co-operation with each other. The important point about symbiosis is that it is a two-way street: employees have to co-operate, but so too do management. It is this symbiotic quality that the metaphor of partnership tries to express and for which the law must provide an institutional embodiment.

[. . .]

Flexibility and security

In pursuing the goal of regulating for competitiveness, the third way adopts a particular stance with respect of legal rights granted to individual workers. In traditional social democratic and liberal political agendas, the principal justification for conferring rights upon individuals has been either to accord respect to basic human rights, such as the right to be treated with dignity and respect, or to establish a fair distributive pattern in the workplace. Those justifications usually lead to the establishment of a mandatory minimum set of rights for all workers, and those rights are protected because they are regarded as valuable in themselves. In this vein, for instance, legal regulation may provide standards with respect to maximum hours of work, minimum hourly wage, minimum safety standards, and minimum standards of fairness in discipline and dismissal. In the third way agenda of regulating for competitiveness, however, a different approach to employment rights emerges.

The third way addresses the following paradox. Fixed legal rights might impede co-operation and flexibility on the part of the workforce, which in turn would harm competitiveness. Yet without some reliable promises of fair treatment, job security, and fair rewards, the workforce is unlikely to co-operate in the flexible way envisaged in the model of symbiotic contracts. Fair treatment is required primarily, not because it is a good in itself, but for instrumental reasons: without fair treatment, employees will not co-operate and will be unwilling to agree to flexible working arrangements, with the consequence of damaging the efficiency and competitiveness of the firm.[12] Thus legal regulation needs to avoid rigid entitlements, whilst at the same time buttressing the confidence of employees that they will be treated fairly in the workplace. Legislation needs to induce employers to make credible commitments about fair treatment at work, to support those commitments, but not to determine the precise content of those commitments in order to avoid the risk that fixed legal rights might obstruct flexibility in work.

How can an employer best make a credible commitment to treat the workforce fairly whilst insisting at the same time upon flexibility in all working practices? Can the law serve a useful purpose here? The most credible promises by employers result from voluntary actions rather than coerced legal obligations. If the employer structures its procedures and rules that comprise the organisation around respect for fairness, the bureaucracy is likely to carry out these standing orders. In contrast, reliance upon background legal rights enforceable in an employment tribunal is likely to produce little sense of commitment on the part of the employer. In crude terms, an employee who is concerned about job security is likely to be rather more impressed by an employer's staff handbook that describes fair disciplinary procedures and transparent disciplinary standards than by the employer's legally coerced commitment to pay compensation for unfair dismissal if ordered to do so by a tribunal. In order to enhance the credibility of the employer's commitment, the task of legal regulation is not primarily to grant employees legal entitlements that may be enforced by way of compensation in tribunals, but rather to re-engineer the internal rules of organisations so that they present credible commitments towards fairness. How can such an ambitious agenda be achieved through law?

A crude strategy, but nevertheless sometimes effective, is simply to raise the stakes for employers. If breach of the legal rights of employees leads to sufficiently high levels of compensation, it will be cheaper for employers to introduce fail-safe procedures into the workplace to avoid this potential liability. This is one of the justifications put forward by the government for raising the upper limits on compensation for unfair dismissal: the low limit provided insufficient incentive for employers to adopt fair internal disciplinary procedures.[13] The same effect may be anticipated from the general revision of levels of compensation for breach of legal rights and their future linking to price indexes.

A more subtle strategy for inducing employers to revise the internal rules of their organisation is to describe explicitly the kinds of procedures required, though leaving the detail to employers to determine, and to provide incentives to adopt these procedures. For example, the legislation on public interest disclosure is designed to provoke employers to create internal procedures for disclosure, with the incentive that the presence of such procedures prevents employees from 'going public' except as a matter of last resort.[14] The legislation is not about creating a right to blow the whistle, but about giving employers the right to deter such action by adopting certain procedures. A similar justification was also advanced by the government for supporting the arbitration option in unfair dismissal: disputes are more likely to be settled by voluntary private procedures.[15] In this case, however, I think that the legislation misses the mark, for what is really required is an opt-out procedure. By adopting internal fair disciplinary rules and procedures, the employer could prevent employees disciplined under such rules from bringing any legal claim at all except for an order to enforce observance of such procedures. But the arbitration alternative to employment tribunals does not achieve that objective at all; it merely provides a cheap alternative forum for adjudication, one which is likely to be stacked against employees, and is therefore unlikely to be used. Another example of this method of regulation designed to re-engineer the internal rules of organisations is the European Works Councils Directive.[16] In that Directive, the objective was to induce multinational corporations to adopt some kind of representative consultation procedure with the entire workforce, and this was achieved by enabling companies to opt out of the legislative model by introducing their own bespoke system earlier.

A third regulatory strategy for achieving the objective of altering the internal rules of organisations has not, I think, been used yet in an employment context in the United Kingdom, but my guess is that it will appear on the agenda. This technique involves the certification of rules in order to enhance their credibility. For example, most employers claim these days to be 'equal opportunity employers'. But this claim has (or should have) no credibility whatsoever, because it is merely an assertion by the employer. It would be very different, however, if such a claim could only be advanced if the employer's internal rules, practices, and procedures had been inspected by a neutral and expert third party and then certified as complying with the requisite standards. This technique is used widely in consumer protection, as in the case of 'kitemarks' and British Standards, with good effect. The same technique of certification is also central to the European Commission's strategy for ensuring quality and safety of consumer goods in the Single Market.[17] In my view this technique is very powerful, and it will not be long before the government perceives that Codes of Practice can be turned into certification standards. For example, in my view a certification procedure for equal opportunities in the workplace would do more than any legal measures to achieve a change in the culture of management practices and a reduction in discrimination, and it has the great attraction that it need not cost the government a penny.

[. . .]

These regulatory strategies do not rule out the possibility of establishing a set of basic legal entitlements for employees. But the concern to promote competitiveness through flexibility discourages the adoption of mandatory and inalienable rights. Fixed rights might either conflict with the optimal arrangement of work from the point of view of efficiency and competitiveness, or they might grant either party the legal right to obstruct alterations to working practices designed to promote co-operation. In many business contexts such as commercial transactions, legal regulation eschews fixed rights in favour of default rules such as implied terms which the parties are free to modify. This style of regulation of commercial contracts is likely to be conducive to efficient outcomes between parties of equal sophistication and bargaining power. But private agreements between employer and employee are likely to be flawed due to asymmetries of information. The crucial problem is that the employee cannot be sure whether the employer's commitments to fairness are credible.[18] In addition, the employee is often like a consumer in being willing to sign written contracts of employment that replace the default rules with terms that heavily favour the employer. These 'market failure' considerations tend to lead to the conclusion that a legal framework based merely on default rules such as implied terms is unlikely to create the necessary credible commitments to fairness at work.

The objective of regulating for competitiveness in the context of employment points to a more complex strategy that adds to the options of fixed entitlements and default rules. Some employment rights might be alienable or modifiable only as a result of a collective agreement with the workforce. Other legal rights might be alienable only after the event as a result of a settlement that conforms to a fair procedure. The possibilities can be illustrated by the Working Time Regulations 1998,[19] which classifies the rights conferred upon employees according to the conditions under which they can be modified or alienated. The maximum hours standard of the 48 hour week is alienable by individuals,[20] thus representing a default rule. The rights in relation to night work (limited to 8 hours per 24), daily rest (11 consecutive hours in 24), the weekly day of rest, and short rest breaks are alienable only by contrary collective agreements through collective bargaining or 'workforce agreements'.[21] The right to paid four weeks of holiday is inalienable. The timing of the holiday is, however, subject to individual agreement or managerial direction,[22] which leaves the timing to be fixed by express agreement. My explanation for this varied pattern in the legislation is that in order to support the instrumental goals behind the rights, which in this case include improvements in health and safety as well as wealth maximisation, it is believed that alienable rights are more likely to achieve efficient outcomes than fixed entitlements. The differentiation between rights that require collective negotiation for alienation or modification and those that permit individual alienation depends upon an assessment of whether individual employees will have the bargaining strength to achieve the optimal outcome. For example collective negotiation is required where the employer is likely to be able to use its bargaining power to chip away at the right opportunistically, such as making occasional demands for work without rest breaks or a day off.

The issue of alienability has obviously been considered carefully in relation to the Working Time Regulations, but under the agenda of regulating for competitiveness, it has equal application to other employment rights. For example, the issue applies to legal rights in relation to dismissal. In its legislation, the government eventually favoured the ability of individuals on fixed term contracts to contract out of redundancy payments, but removed this possibility in relation to the right to claim unfair dismissal. The objective here was to facilitate the flexible working arrangement of fixed term contracts, but to keep the legal sanction against unfair dismissal in order to buttress the credibility of the employer's commitment to treat short-term workers fairly. But the third way agenda could lead to further developments that permit easier exclusion of legal rights in the event of dismissal, provided that the employer has established alternative, binding commitments, perhaps at a collective level, to comply with high standards of fairness in the workplace.

Conclusions

In construing the agenda of a third way in labour law, I have no doubt attributed to it a greater coherence than is appropriate for an evolving set of ideas. By stressing the novelty of some of the ideas, I have also downplayed significant continuities, especially the fidelity to civil liberties inherited from traditional strands of social democracy and reinforced by the Human Rights Act 1998. Nor have I sufficiently challenged the assumption of the third way that the forces of globalisation will permanently reduce some of the previous major sources of industrial conflict. Despite these reservations, I hope that I have offered a persuasive interpretation of some of the key elements in an evolving new agenda for labour law.

The agenda of the third way for labour law is set by the political goals of combating the origins of social exclusion and improving the competitiveness of business. These goals lead towards new tasks for legal regulation, such as family friendly policies to permit equal access to the labour market and to the promotion of credible partnership arrangements. I have also stressed that the achievement of these goals requires more complex and responsive regulatory techniques than the traditional pattern of mandatory employment rights. The regulatory method becomes more subtle and indirect, seeking to provoke the parties themselves to re-engineer their own economic and social relations through partnerships and contractual agreements.

This third way agenda presents a wide range of difficult issues that will need to be addressed seriously in the future. The challenge to structural obstacles to equality of opportunity, or if you like, citizenship, presents an enormous and shifting agenda for action by government. One can foresee, for instance, that the position of older workers in the labour market will become a crucial concern from the perspective of social exclusion. Government intervention can sometimes itself be part of the problem to be addressed, as in the case of poverty traps, so we must expect a constant process of regulation and re-regulation. At the same time, we are only just beginning the strategy of regulating for competitiveness, and the way in which the law can promote partnerships and assist employers to make credible commitments to treat the workforce fairly will benefit from the experience of trial and error. Regulatory techniques used in labour law remain relatively crude outside the field of health and safety at work, so we can expect to see much more experimentation. In particular, the possibility of using incentives to induce employers to adopt competitive institutions and fair employment standards has not been explored fully. For example, to promote partnership arrangements in the workplace, the employer could be offered tax incentives or potential exclusion of legal liabilities.

These regulatory techniques may be unfamiliar to labour lawyers. But there is no reason to think that the employment relation will not continue to present a vital area of interest for lawyers, even if the problems to be addressed change radically from those that dominated the twentieth century. Legal regulation of employment and the labour market remains in the third way an important dimension of state activity.

Notes

1   A. Giddens, *The Third Way: The Renewal of Social Democracy* (Cambridge: Polity Press, 1998).
2   Foreword to *Fairness at Work*, Cm 3968 (London: HMSO, 1998).
3   K. D. Ewing, 'Democratic Socialism and Labour Law' (1995) 24 *Industrial Law Journal* 103.
4   This right to freedom of association as a basic principle of labour law is expressed in e.g. European Community Charter of the Fundamental Social

Rights of Workers (1989) art. 11; International Labour Organisation Convention (No 87) on Freedom of Association and Protection of the Right to Organise (1948).

5   *Associated Newspapers Ltd* v. *Wilson*; *Associated British Ports* v. *Palmer* [1995] IRLR 258, HL.

6   For more detailed explanations see: M. Sako, *Prices, Quality, Trust: Inter-Firm Relations in Britain and Japan* (Cambridge: Cambridge University Press, 1992); C. R. Taylor and S. N. Wiggins, 'Competition or Compensation: Supplier Incentives Under the American and Japanese Subcontracting Systems' (1997) 87 *American Economic Review* 598; H. Collins, 'Quality Assurance in Subcontracting', in S. Deakin and J. Mitchie (eds.) *Contracts, Co-operation, and Competition* (Oxford: Oxford University Press, 1997) 285.

7   For example, see Oliver E. Williamson, *The Economic Institutions of Capitalism* (New York/London: Free Press, 1985), especially Chapter 9.

8   H. Collins, *Regulating Contracts* (Oxford: Oxford University Press) 161.

9   E. Schanze, 'Symbiotic Contracts: Exploring Long-Term Agency Structures between Contract and Corporation', in C. Joerges (ed.), *Franchising and the Law* (Baden Baden: Nomos, 1991).

10 H. Collins, *Regulating Contracts* (Oxford: Oxford University Press, 1999) 239.

11 A. Fox, *Beyond Contract: Work, Power and Trust Relations* (London: Faber, 1974) 248.

12 *Fairness at Work*, Cm 3968 (London: HMSO, 1998) para. 1.9.

13 Ibid. para. 3.5.

14 Ibid. para. 3.3 (justifying Public Interest Disclosure Act 1998).

15 Ibid. para. 3.4 (justifying Employment Rights (Dispute Resolution) Act 1998).

16 Directive 94/45/EC, OJ L 254, 30.9.94, p. 64.

17 European Council Resolution on a Global Approach to Conformity Assessment OJ C10, 16/01/90, p. 1.

18 H. Collins, 'Justifications and Techniques of Legal Regulation of the Employment Relation', in H. Collins, P. L. Davies, R. Rideout (eds.), *Legal Regulation of the Employment Relation* (Kluwer, 2000).

19 SI 1998/1833.

20 Reg. 5.

21 Reg. 23.

22 Reg. 15 (2), (5).

PART IV

A Global Third Way

Intensifying globalization, Michael Jacobs points out, has fundamental consequences for environmental management. The existing ecological literature, he says, stands at some distance from the rapid changes going on in the world. In fact, a sound ecological framework can only be developed if we situate it directly in the context of these changes. This means developing a sophisticated analysis of risk, but also recognizing that environmental decay affects poorer people much more directly than the more affluent, within nations but also in the world community at large.

Although he doesn't use the term, Joseph Stiglitz in effect argues for a third way approach to development. Two approaches to development have been dominant over the past several decades. One sees the state as the prime medium of development, while the other turns to markets. Both approaches have failed. A new perspective is needed. The new perspective stresses partnerships between government and the private sector, based upon a pragmatic assessment of what a specific economy needs at a particular time. Governments can be improved in their effectiveness, while markets need the hand of government to flourish.

Luiz Bresser Pereira assesses the third way debate from the point of view of the Southern countries. What relevance does the third way have in a developing country like Brazil? A great deal, is his answer. Globalization and the new technologies are important no matter where one is in the world. To the third way or the 'new left' globalization is an opportunity, not just a destructive force. The competitiveness of a country depends upon in some part its own motivation to undergo political and economic reform. Bresser Pereira agrees with Stiglitz that the role of the state needs to be endorsed rather than minimized. A decline in the effectiveness of government in the Southern countries was not the result of globalization, but of the over-extension and bureaucratization of state institutions. Investment in government is necessary both to develop market exchange and to maintain macro-economic stability.

Ethan Kapstein argues that globalization must be responded to at world level, not just locally or nationally. In order to promote economic development, and protect the global poor, regulation of the flow of mobile capital is required. There is an imbalance in the international system, since while investors can express their demands quite readily workers cannot. The poor need to be given more voice in international organizations. They might then be one force pushing for the development of taxation on mobile capital, which at the moment mostly escapes tax completely. We must focus upon global inequalities, which could be massively reduced if the richer countries collaborated to ensure that investment goes to the needy countries of the world.

Michael Edwards takes an optimistic attitude to global problems and divisions. The idea that there is some alternative to a global market economy, he points out, must be discarded. Capitalism produces many problems, but no one knows of an alternative system that works. Capitalism needs to be rehumanized now that trade unions, welfare systems and national governments are less effective in doing so. Nations – or left of centre governments – should act in concert to help develop new rules and networks on a global level. This need not be just the imposition of policy from above. Economic transactions based around the local community, the author points out, make up fully 25 per cent of global transactions. It should be possible to reinvigorate local power and local regulation while still networking such groups into larger global contexts.

David Held points out that the relationship between globalization and the power of nation states is complex. It isn't the case simply that nations are becoming less important with the advance of global interdependence. Globalization in some respects promotes more activist forms of state and government rather than less. States now interact with a wider range of agencies than before in the international arena – NGOs, international agencies and other interest groups. These developments provide for possibilities of democracy above the level of the nation that were not previously available. The deepening of democracy within nations can go along with the expansion of 'cosmopolitan democracy' operating across national boundaries.

23

The Environment, Modernity and the Third Way

Michael Jacobs

One of the striking features of environmentalism – and this is true as much of the discourse of sustainable development as of its utopian forebears – is its value-driven nature. Environmental literature tends to start with an analysis of present and predicted environmental degradation; but the next move is nearly always to a normative – that is to say, value-based – description of what the world should instead be like. We should care more about future generations; we should live in harmony with other species; we should consume less; we should share resources more fairly with poorer nations; we should produce more efficiently. There is of course nothing wrong with such expressions of idealism; but what frequently seems to be missing is the sense of *movement* which might take us from the present world to the desired better one.

This is not because environmentalists have no policies to get us from here to there. The sustainable development literature is full of them. But they do not often seem very closely connected to what is actually happening in the world. Modern societies are going through a period of rapid social and economic change – through globalisation, the growth of information technologies, increasing individualism in society, rising inequalities, and so on. Much of the time governments and individual businesses are rather desperately trying to cope in the face of these trends. But the environmental movement's prescriptions rarely seem to recognise them at all. Driven by its values rather than by analysis of the world as it is, environmentalism often gives the impression of standing apart from these dynamic processes; indeed of wishing to institute quite different ones going in other directions. But then it is not surprising that it struggles to make headway in the political mainstream. If environmentalism looks and sounds as if it is ignoring, let alone trying to reverse, the trends of the modern world, even its most pragmatic advocates are in danger of appearing (however they would wish) utopian.

Of course this is exactly where many greens stand. Contemporary economic and social change *is* basically going in the wrong direction, they believe, leading to ever greater environmental degradation and human misery. In this sense, for them, environmentalism cannot help but be an oppositional movement; and if this makes it seem utopian, so be it.

But this is not a necessary perspective. It rests on a simplistic view of change: that current trends have just a single dynamic, one possible future path which cannot be shaped or redirected, only (perhaps) over-turned. In fact the future is always open. Yes, there are powerful forces, some of them almost certainly too strong to turn back. But this does not mean that the currents can flow only down a single channel. They can be steered in different directions, given different forms, prevented from having certain effects, pushed into having others. Political action is therefore not about halting the present dynamic, but of shaping and moulding it: neither simply accepting the present order, nor wishing to reverse it, but of finding the limits of its possible forms.

It is this kind of analysis that environmentalism now needs, one which connects its idealism in some way to the trends of the contemporary world. Of course, such connections must exist: there must be plausible ways of shaping current social and economic dynamics to environmental ends. But happily, as we shall show below, there are.

What makes this exercise particularly interesting is that it is just the kind of approach which underpins Tony Blair's third way. [. . .] The third way is at root a response to a changing world – to the particular trends which society and economy are currently experiencing. [. . .]

For industrial societies change is a constant. But many writers and commentators argue today that modern life is undergoing a particu-larly radical shift in its character. A combination of deep-seated trends and forces, in the economy, in technology, in social relations and in culture is altering the very nature of 'modernity'.

Different authors writing in this field highlight different elements of change, and the nature of the overall shift which they claim is occur-ring varies too. As in any academic field, there are some profound disagreements between them. But taken as a group the analysts of modernity are important, for they have begun to influence political thinking. In Britain, and indeed more widely, the best known of them is the sociologist Anthony Giddens. [. . .] Giddens is particularly significant because he has tried to apply his theories of modernity to current British politics. [. . .]

There is insufficient space or need in this chapter to examine the new theories of modernity in detail. Our purpose will be served here simply by describing some of the main socio-economic trends which underpin them. (These are in any case in less dispute than the overarching frameworks.) With a cavalier disregard for their complexities, brief sketches will be offered of three combined trends in particular. These are: globalisation and the emergence of the 'knowledge-driven' economy; 'individualisation' and the rise of 'reflexivity'; and the growth of inequality. [. . .]

The first and probably most important trend is globalisation. This has become something of a portmanteau term in recent years, covering a wide range of phenomena, with both economic and 'cultural' dimensions. We are most concerned here with its economic aspects, the broad outlines of which are now familiar. The world economy is becoming more integrated, with liberalised trade flows and greater mobility of capital exposing both domestic and export markets to fiercer competitive pressures. [. . .]

Globalisation is now intertwined with a related trend, the growth of the so-called 'knowledge economy'. For advanced industrial societies like the UK economic success is increasingly dependent on human rather than physical capital: on skills, intelligence and creativity. The rapid growth of new information and communication technologies and of electronic commerce is changing the way businesses operate in fundamental ways, from the nature of their products through the size, location and composition of their workforces to the forms in which commercial transactions are made. With microchip and related product prices still falling and diffusion throughout society rapidly increasing – particularly with the imminent merging of internet and television services – the cultural and economic impact of the new technologies looks difficult to overestimate.

[. . .]

The second key trend of concern to us is what some sociologists have described as 'individualisation'. Over the last three decades, as class, religious and geographic identities have gradually broken down, people in industrialised societies have come to have an increasingly individualised outlook on life. Individuals – now women as well as men – feel they can make their own identity and their own way in the world. They perceive themselves to be largely autonomous in what they can be and do. Their attachment to other people and to society at large becomes more instrumental. People make their own friends and networks rather than relying on those in the local community; there is an increasing rate of divorce.

This is tied up with the phenomenon of 'de-traditionalisation', the declining purchase of traditional authorities, customs and belief systems. In Giddens' terms, societies and individuals are becoming more 'reflexive', forced to make active choices and to rethink their responses in each new circumstance they face; unwilling (and unable) to rely on tradition and habit. Information and knowledge are central to this, as both societies and individuals become more aware of, and reflective upon, themselves and their environments. In politics, for example, voting behaviour is no longer based on tradition. As voters have become less deferent to political authority, judging parties and governments on performance, the electorate has become more volatile – and many people may not vote at all.

[. . .]

The third trend relates to this, and indeed to globalisation. One of globalisation's most marked effects is an increase in inequality. As economic activity is internationalised, particular areas of the world are favoured for production and employment while others are not. This leaves huge disparities between regions, both domestically [. . .] and internationally (for instance, between East Asia and Africa). At the bottom end of the labour market, increasing competition holds wages down, while at the top huge rewards become available to those with scarce and marketable skills. The result is that the divergence between those on middle to higher incomes and those on very low incomes grows wider. While in Britain these effects were exacerbated by particular policies introduced under the Conservative Government, the trend towards inequality arises from deeper global economic forces which the advent of a new Government has not changed.

[. . .]

Modernisation

[. . .]

To explore this in a little more detail, we can examine the environmental aspects of each of the key trends.

Environmental degradation is one of the features of globalisation. This is true in two different senses. At its simplest, it is evident that pollution does not recognise national boundaries. Phenomena such as global warming and the depletion of the ozone layer are truly global in nature, occurring outside the territorial boundaries of nation states and caused by economic activities in every part of the world. Other environmental issues cross boundaries and require international cooperation to tackle: pollution of rivers and seas, fish stock depletion, acid rain, nuclear radiation, chemical releases. (The range over which chemicals can be dispersed is large: toxic PCBs have been found in Antarctica, emitted by industrial plants located thousands of miles away.)

But there is a stronger sense in which the environment and globalisation are tied together. The new global economy has simultaneously increased the range and extent of environmental degradation; *and* begun to develop responses to it.

All industrial economic activity causes environmental damage: resources must be extracted, wastes produced. But globalisation is massively increasing the scale. The simple growth of demand for consumer and industrial goods in newly industrialising countries is placing huge new pressures on global resources, with carbon dioxide emissions alone due to double over the next thirty years. Rising international trade in goods inevitably requires more transport, a major source of carbon emissions and other forms of pollution. Just-in-time production and distribution systems cut down on stocks by increasing the total transport distances covered by goods. As production is consolidated the geographical scale of environmental risks expands.

Yet at the same time there are counter trends. First, environmental degradation creates its own reaction, opposite if not yet equal. Resource depletion, pollution and transport congestion undermine the continued profitability of global production. They increase costs and raise risks. So environmental regulation – the attempt to reduce environmental damage – becomes an essential part of the global economic process. Interestingly, this takes both private and public forms. Pollution controls, environmental taxes, international environmental agreements: these are the familiar governmental means of constraining environmental damage, and there has been a huge increase in their number over the last two decades as the effects of environmental damage have become clear.

But at the same time environmental controls have started to be imposed autonomously within the private sector. Where resource use and waste production are inefficient, they represent costs which can be cut. Environmental risks incur higher insurance premiums and investor concern about environmental liabilities. Increased public concern about environmental damage affects consumer demand and corporate image. As a result the last few years have seen the near-universal adoption among major firms of environmental programmes, including capital investment, new staff, new management systems and audits. As any business leader will acknowledge, no company of significant size can now afford to ignore environmental factors in its decision making.

But there is a second trend here too. Production is becoming less materially intensive. This is partly because the increasing competitiveness of markets is forcing firms constantly to improve their productivity. Energy and resource efficiency in industry is improving; unnecessary wastes are gradually being reduced. But demand is changing too. Products are getting smaller and lighter. In many cases the economic value of a product lies in its design (or its designer label) rather than in its simple mass. Many of the fastest expanding sectors of modern economies produce immaterial things: computer software, television programmes, financial services, gene research, internet services. Services now comprise much the largest part of the economy; but these include not just the traditional personal services (restaurants, hairdressers and so on) but new kinds of high-value products altogether. At the same time new communications technologies have the potential to cut both transport and paper demand, as commerce is transacted electronically. Various forms of 'teleworking' and 'teleshopping' could reduce both household and business travel. As some analysts have put it, we seem to have entered an increasingly 'weightless world'.

In this way the new global economy encompasses trends which are at the same time increasing and reducing environmental pressures. The problem is that the former are still largely winning.

The overall environmental impact of any kind of economic activity is the product of two competing forces. Economic growth increases the level of environmental damage, as higher output demands more resources and produces more waste. But at the same time productivity gains – improvements in the efficiency with which resources are used, including the 'dematerialisation' of output – help damage to be reduced. If the rate of growth exceeds the rate of productivity improvement, environmental damage increases over time; and vice versa.

Over the last decade the OECD has been measuring environmental impacts. The results are instructive. Between 1985 and 1995 the average rate of economic growth in industrialised countries was around 2.5 per cent pa. In the same period some environmental impacts declined: air pollution from heavy metals, sulphur dioxide emissions and phosphate fertilisers. (In the UK the same is true of river pollution.) In these cases economic growth has been outweighed by efficiency gains. But for a whole set of environmental impacts the reverse is the case. For example, although the efficiency of energy use has been increasing, it has not been increasing fast enough to counter growth: carbon emissions have been rising at around 1 per cent pa. The same is true of total material flows and water supply. Meanwhile transport energy use and the volume of municipal waste have risen at almost exactly the same pace as overall output: there's been no net efficiency gains at all.

There's an important reason for the differences between these different overall impacts. Heavy metals, sulphur dioxide and phosphates are by and large not required by the economic processes which generate them. They are by-products. Given technical application it is therefore relatively easy to eliminate or reduce them from the production process. But the things which have risen – carbon emissions, transport energy use, total materials and waste – are not by-products at all. They are the very resources from which production and consumption are generated. They are therefore much more difficult to reduce. It is not impossible, but it will take a deeper shift in the technologies and production processes of the economy.

And this is in simple terms a good description of where the environmental agenda stands today. (In fact it is rather more serious than this, since in the newly emerging economies of the South rates of economic growth are higher and efficiency improvement lower.) To begin to reduce the overall level of damage a significant change is needed in the 'eco-efficiency' of industrial production; and this must inevitably occur first in the industrialised countries.

If one of the symptoms of the trend towards individualisation is the heightened significance of personal consumption, environmental degradation must be counted among the consequences. It is ultimately rising consumer demand which drives environmental impact. But there are counter trends too. For the environment is a good in itself.

At first sight it might look difficult to associate environmental protection with the trends towards a more individualised society. The environment is after all a quintessentially collective good, shared between fellow human beings. The air you breathe is the same air I breathe; countryside and open spaces are (mostly) public, not private; the entire population of the world may be affected by ozone depletion. Many environmental goods, such as biodiversity (the variety and interdependence of living things), are barely experienced by individuals at all.

Yet this emphasis on the collective character of the environment can be over-exaggerated. Many aspects of the environment are very much individually experienced. As air quality has declined, its impacts have affected many people very directly, with a significant growth in respiratory diseases, including asthma (and asthmatic symptoms) among children. Increasing traffic congestion may be a collective problem, but it is certainly experienced by individuals, both those in cars and those not. Indeed, distasteful though it may sound to some, parts of the environment are effectively aspects of consumption. As leisure activities and tourism expand, people are spending more and more money to experience the particular qualities of 'nature' provided by the countryside and national parks, beaches and other 'natural' places, both at home and abroad. (And if nature is thus in a sense 'consumed', it must also be actively 'produced': specifically protected and managed in certain ways in order to maintain it in the form we value. Most people would be surprised at how much human effort goes into maintaining the apparently 'wild' landscapes of places like the Lake District or Dartmoor.)

The fact that much of the environment *is* individually experienced does not mean that collective action to protect and improve it is somehow unnecessary. On the contrary, it gives such collective action much greater political weight. If (as social surveys show and as rising incomes would lead us to expect) people are becoming more concerned about environmental quality, and this can only be improved through government action – whether through regulation, planning policy, taxes, spending or whatever – public political pressure will rise. And this is exactly what is happening. Individualisation does not diminish the need for collective responses.

But there is a more intriguing twist to this. For the area where public pressure is strongest is one where the sociological trends associated with individualisation have not merely heightened but practically created the issue. This is the field of food and health.

Personal health and diet have become obsessions in modern society. The evidence is all around, from the proliferation of food programmes on television to the emergence of men's health magazines; from the explosion of anorexia and other food disorders among young girls to the rapidly growing market in organic produce. An apparently unending succession of food-health scares in recent years have both indicated and fed public concern: BSE, pesticide residues in foods, phthalates in baby milk, dioxins in Belgian dairy products, GM foods.

In many ways the growth of public anxiety in this area is paradoxical, since as a society we are healthier than ever before. But as Anthony Giddens has pointed out, this is in fact a predictable symptom of greater individualisation. Our bodies are us. As individuals take more control over their lives, it is unsurprising that we take more interest in our own health and wellbeing. As globalisation makes an almost infinite variety of foods available on the supermarket shelves, we are forced to make active choices about what we eat. In this sense, as Giddens' 'reflexive' individuals, we are all on a diet.

But then in turn we cannot help but feel concern about the effects of our food choices on our health. The very processes of industrialised, global food production which have required and allowed us to choose dietary 'lifestyles' are also increasing their apparent dangers. The use of pesticides, artificial fertilisers, growth hormones and now genetic engineering have created new types of *risk*.

The concept of risk is one of the most discussed in the debates about the nature of modernity. It is a central theme in Giddens' work, and is the subject of a now famous analysis by the German sociologist Ulrich Beck, that of so-called 'risk society'.[1] [. . .]

The concept of a risk society has two different dimensions. At one level, the claim that we are living in a 'risk society' is simply an extension of the analysis of individualisation. Increasing personal autonomy goes hand in hand with insecurity. Where previously personal identity was simply a given – people were born into particular social classes, with more or less fixed value systems, family structures, communities and life-trajectories – now these dimensions of life are subject to uncertainty and choice. Labour markets no longer offer stable, lifetime employment. Gender relations are in flux. Rapid technological change brings ethical and environmental uncertainties. Life in modern society has become more open-ended; there are more possibilities, but also more risks.

The second dimension to risk society is one of the key sources of this sense of insecurity. This is the increasing scale and pervasiveness of environmental risks arising from industrial production. For Giddens, Beck and others, environmental impacts are the prime source of risk in the modern world. In earlier industrial periods pollution was localised, reasonably well understood, and relatively easily controlled. But, they argue, the new environmental risks are of a qualitatively different scale. They arise both from relatively recent technologies – such as nuclear power, the production of synthetic chemicals and now particularly genetic engineering – and from the continuing expansion of old ones, such as fossil fuel combustion with its consequences in global warming. The risks society faces now are both global (respecting neither national boundaries nor class divisions) and pervasive, arising in the midst of everyday life, in foods, plastics and other materials. Many will have long-term effects; and some will be irreversible, potentially altering the life-conditions of future generations. Perhaps most importantly, though generated by scientific advance, scientific knowledge barely understands some of these risks at all.

It is the latter point which has become the crucial one for environmental politics. It is important to distinguish between different meanings of 'risk' here. To the individual most environmental hazards are risks in the sense that there is only a possibility that one may be affected. Everyone breathes polluted air; but only some people get respiratory disease. So as individuals we face a risk; but the environmental impact itself is now reasonably well understood. This is true of many environmental problems: scientific advance has made us reasonably confident of what the impacts are, and both individuals and society can take preventative action on this basis.

But the new risks we face today are not like this. In the cases of (for example) BSE, genetically modified crops and foods, apparently hormone-mimicking chemicals ('endocrine disrupters') and growth hormones in livestock, *we simply do not know what the potential impacts might be*. There is insufficient scientific knowledge. So the risk is not a calculable probability of damage, but an unknown – and for long term effects, potentially unknowable – possibility. In these fields, at least at present, the science here is better characterised as one of ignorance than of mere uncertainty.

But then there should be no surprise that people feel anxious. Individuals are urged to make up their own minds up as consumers whether or not to eat GM foods or beef fed on growth hormones. But they have almost no basis on which to do so. If the scientists do not know, but have grounds for some concern, anxiety is an understandable response. In the circumstances, and contrary to the claims of hysterical over-reaction, consumer boycotts of BSE-tainted beef and GM foods – neither of them a necessity of life – can be considered rather rational behaviours.

Of course, in any of these fields, as with previous environmental issues, new scientific research may generate more confident understandings. These issues may then return to a 'simpler' form of environmental problem, where reasonably known impacts can be assessed against the costs of preventing and ameloriating them. But the rapid development of new technologies, particularly in the genetic field and in synthetic chemicals, will surely bring forth new issues in the future where scientific ignorance confronts possible hazard. Modernity and the politics of environmental risk appear to be inextricably linked.

One of the most frequently heard environmental arguments is that environmental degradation affects everyone. Pollution is no respecter of class or income; we all breathe the same air; everyone will go down together if global warming occurs or a chemical plant blows up. This 'universalist' claim has had a powerful effect in galvanising public concern (spawning various metaphors of collective responsibility, such as that of 'Spaceship Earth' and 'planetary stewardship') and emphasising the central role of government in tackling environmental problems. But in fact it's only partially true.

Poorer people almost always experience worse environments than richer ones. Air pollution and traffic congestion are worse in inner city areas than leafy suburbs; there's less green space and more litter. Rich people can buy sufficient energy to give their cars air conditioning; poor people cannot afford to heat their homes properly. [. . .]

The reason is obvious. These areas have *become* low-income because they are next to polluting factories; no-one with enough money to get out would choose to live there. In a market society, richer people can buy better environments. *Within* neighbourhoods, most environmental goods are public goods, meaning that they are collectively rather than individually consumed. Middle class and poor people living in the inner city have a common interest in cleaner air and more green space. But the middle classes have the option of buying their way out to pleasanter neighbourhoods where the environment is better. Most of them have taken it.

The general trend towards inequality in society is therefore manifested partly through increased environmental inequality. In Britain today there are an estimated 4.3 million people living in conditions of 'fuel poverty', unable to afford to heat their poorly insulated homes to an adequate level of warmth. Consequent damp contributes to respiratory disease, and in winter, among elderly people, an intolerable level of deaths from cold – over 30,000 extra deaths on one estimate.

Similarly, there is now a phenomenon of 'food poverty'. On many of the most deprived housing estates there are almost no shops – certainly none selling fresh food and vegetables or other nutritious foods. The supermarkets have all decamped to out-of-town locations (rarely located close to out-of-town estates) accessible only by car. The result is the creation of so-called 'food deserts', whole areas where people on low incomes simply cannot get hold of decent and reasonably priced foods.

And accompanying this there is increasing inequality too in travel opportunities. In the last twenty years the physical landscape has become increasingly determined by car use, with not just retail sites locating out of city centres but also cinemas, leisure centres, hospitals and workplaces. As incomes have risen, the majority of people, those with cars, have been able to travel further, for employment, to visit friends and family, at weekends and on holiday. But for the 30 per cent of households without access to a car, life has become more difficult. Public transport services have declined, fares have risen: things have become less accessible, not more.

These trends suggest an interesting parallel. Just as we now speak of those unable to take part in the social mainstream of employment, education and consumption as experiencing social exclusion, so those who do not enjoy the environmental benefits of warmth, nutritious food and easy travel opportunity can be said to experience a kind of 'environmental exclusion'. Unfortunately, this too looks like one of the features of the new modernity.

The argument here, then, is that environmental issues are bound up with the central trends of contemporary society. The environmental impacts of these trends are complex. Globalisation simultaneously embodies forces tending towards environmental degradation and away from it. A highly developed consumer society heightens environmental impacts; but it also increases the demand for environmental protection. Rapid technological development is expanding the scope and character of environmental risks; but the trend towards individualisation helps force those risks onto the business and political agendas. Increasing inequality in society is manifested in environmental inequality; but the widely perceived 'universality' of environmental degradation encourages a collectivist politics potentially capable of tackling this.

The appropriate political response to this analysis follows what has been said before. The new modernity cannot be wished away. But it needs to be shaped as far as possible to reduce environmental impacts. Those forces within it which tend towards increased degradation need to be slowed and controlled, and the environment protected against them. Those forces tending towards protection need to be strengthened. The trend towards inequality needs to be countered.

The parallels here with the general approach of the third way is apparent. Indeed the argument is essentially that an extension of the third way into the environmental arena is what is required. We can call this project 'environmental modernisation'.

Environmental modernisation is thus a new political discourse. It sees the environment through the prism of modernity, placing environmental issues in the context of the changes now occurring in contemporary societies. It shares with existing forms of environmentalism the aim of reducing environmental impacts to sustainable levels. But it seeks to escape the value-driven basis of existing environmental discourses.

From this analysis we can suggest five key features of environmental modernisation. First, it is intended to 'go with the grain' of globalisation. It seeks to pick up and promote the trend towards higher environmental productivity, and to adapt the new knowledge-based economy towards environmental ends. Second, it acknowledges the trend towards individualisation and understands the role of consumption in modern life, but seeks to encourage consumption towards environmentally benign forms. It argues that collective consumption can contribute as much to the overall quality of life as individual. Third, environmental modernisation gives a central place to the perception of risk and scientific uncertainty, and makes risk management a key policy field. Fourth, it seeks to counter the trend towards greater environmental inequality or exclusion. Fifth, it is firmly a modernist project, accepting the central role of science and technology in tackling as well as contributing towards environmental problems. It sees the future as essentially optimistic, and environmental problems as soluble. [. . .]

A new policy agenda

The discourse of environmental modernisation offers the Government new ways of approaching the environment as a political subject. In some areas this means introducing new policies, or at least developing them from existing positions. But in others it is more to do with new ways of 'framing' policy: of arguing for it, of connecting it to other issues, and of making it a central part of the New Labour project.

Building on such an analysis, we can suggest four key policy areas which flow from the environmental modernisation discourse.

Economic and industrial policy

From the perspective of environmental modernisation the central field of policy is not the environment *per se*, but the economy and industry. The key objective is to raise environmental productivity: to get more out of the economy from less.

As we have seen, the global economy already contains trends in this direction. But they are going to have to be speeded up. The targets for productivity improvement must be not just a few per cent, but something like 5–10 per cent a year. At normal rates of economic growth environmental efficiency gains of around 2.5 per cent are required simply to keep environmental impacts at present levels. To reduce them, we will have to make significantly larger efficiency improvements.

The parallels here with the Government's existing priorities in economic policy are very striking. There is in effect a second 'productivity gap' which needs to be closed: not just the difference in labour productivity between the UK and its competitors, but the gap between present environmental productivity levels and those needed to sustain absolute reductions in environmental impact. As the Government constantly emphasises, to close the labour productivity gap British firms must raise their rates of investment and of technological innovation. To close the environmental productivity gap exactly the same is true. It is through new, cleaner production technologies, the development of new products and services, and the use of information and communications technologies (ICT) that environmental productivity will be raised. In most cases the technological possibilities are already clear; it is the investment in their development and application that is lacking.[2]

For Government this requires an active industrial policy. It is sometimes said that Labour has abandoned this field; and in the sense of industrial planning on the 1960s model this is certainly true. But the Government's Competitiveness White Paper in fact sets out a rather profound approach to industrial policy.[3] Its central themes are that business must embrace technological and knowledge-driven change much more quickly and more widely than it is currently doing, and that the Government's role is to promote this. The Government makes clear that it eschews the old idea of 'picking winners'; but it has clearly selected the new knowledge-based industries – both in themselves and as applied to other sectors – as the keys to Britain's economic prosperity. (Indeed one particular industry, biotechnology, is singled out for special treatment.) The rationale for the Government's approach is that there are market failures and institutional or 'cultural' obstacles among firms to the take-up of new technologies and practices. Government intervention in various ways can help to reduce these.

Based as it if on an analysis of trends in the global economy, and on the research evidence of firm behaviour, this approach is surely correct. And for the same reasons, it is just what is required in the environmental field. Oddly, however – or perhaps symptomatically – the link here has not been recognised. The White Paper has one paragraph acknowledging the congruence of environmental objectives with those of the Government's industrial policy as a whole; but fails entirely to develop these into policy initiatives.

This is what environmental modernisation would seek to do. In exactly the same way that the Government is promoting knowledge-based sectors and the more general diffusion of ICT and electronic commerce, so it needs to support the development and diffusion of environmentally clean technologies and practices. An environmental-industrial strategy of this kind would have four key elements.

Developing environmental technologies and industries First, greater funding needs to be provided for research and development into cleaner technologies and products. The Government has created a new Sustainable Technologies Initiative for exactly this purpose, but its funding, at £7.8m over three years, is inadequate, and needs to be significantly increased. One way then of encouraging the uptake of such technologies would be to introduce an 'accelerated depreciation allowance' allowing firms to depreciate selected investments in innovative technologies faster than normal, say in one year. The Netherlands has a very successful scheme of this kind covering around 500 new technologies, which are removed from the list once they reach a significant market share: over 10,000 companies have taken advantage of it.[4] A UK Treasury scheme could be a similarly powerful tool.

An important recognition here is that such measures would help to support the environmental technology and services sector – the firms which manufacture and supply environmental systems. The aim should be to ensure that environmental improvements in the UK economy as far as possible create jobs and income for the UK too. Though clearly not as significant as the knowledge-based sectors of the economy, the environmental technology and services industry already employs around 100,000 people in the UK. It also has considerable export potential. The worldwide market in this sector is currently $400bn a year, and is predicted to grow by 50 per cent over the next decade as environmental pressures increase. The UK has a trade surplus in this field, but in terms of market share falls well behind the US, Japan and Germany.[5] There are clearly significant employment creation possibilities in this field.

The Competitiveness White Paper proposes a range of measures to promote technological development in new industries. The new English Regional Development Agencies, Scottish Enterprise and the Welsh Development Agency are being encouraged to support regional 'clusters' in particular sectors, linking higher education institutions and venture capital funds with emerging firms. (Particular support is to be given to biotechnology clusters, including the creation of several 'genome valleys'.) There is obvious potential here to provide parallel support to various environmental technology and service sectors. In some fields Government itself may have the key role, for example in renewable energy and waste recycling, where infrastructures and regulatory frameworks will determine the growth of the industry.[6]

Promoting environmental performance   Second, support needs to be provided to firms to enable them to improve their environmental efficiency not just through highly innovative technologies but in more basic ways. It is widely recognised that small and medium sized enterprises (SMEs), in particular, find it difficult to learn about and to invest in new technologies and operational practices, even where these are profitable. Grant and loan schemes to assist them are almost certainly required if take-up is to be spread. The Government has accepted the principle that such financial support should be available to firms in its proposal for an energy efficiency fund (of £50m) to be paid for from the proceeds of the Climate Change Levy. It would be appropriate for this to be made part of a wider Environmental Modernisation Fund aimed at assisting businesses to improve their environmental performance more generally.

Alongside this the information and advice available to firms in this area must be much improved. As part of its programme to encourage the take-up of ICT the Government is putting considerable effort into improving business advice and support services, through local Business Links, specialist centres, the University for Industry, collaborative networks and the internet itself. Exactly the same should be done in the environmental field. A Special Representative for the Digital Economy, the 'e-Envoy', has been appointed by the Prime Minister to help publicise ICT. There would seem ample scope for an Environmental Business Envoy too.

Sectoral strategies   Third, the Government should take an active role in developing sectoral environmental modernisation strategies with key industries. Such strategies would aim to accelerate improvement in environmental productivity across a range of impacts over a five to ten year period. Targets and methods of meeting them would be negotiated with the industry trade associations. They could cover energy consumption, materials use, air and water emissions, solid waste, transport and product design; and would seek to develop strategies not just for the leading edge firms but throughout the supply chain.

The idea of such sectoral strategies has in fact already emerged from the Government's consultations on its Sustainable Development Strategy, and a number of sectors have expressed an interest in them. But the early proposals on these are extremely limited, and progress has been minimal.[7] More interesting work in this area is actually going on under the aegis of the climate change levy proposals, where the Government has offered a reduced tax rate to sectors which negotiate energy efficiency agreements. The DETR is now engaged in detailed design of such agreements with a wide range of sectors. Once these have been completed, they will offer a useful model for wider sustainability strategy agreements. A similar carrot of tax reductions or other fiscal incentives could be offered to support them.

Environmental taxation Fourth, and following on from this, these measures to support improved environmental productivity need to be backed up by regulatory regimes which ensure that environmental *in*efficiency is not an attractive option. The new field of environmental taxation provides the key here. By raising the prices faced for environmentally damaging activities, taxation provides firms with a continuing incentive to improve their productivity. The more efficient and innovative they become, the lower their costs.

The principle of environmental taxation was first accepted by the Conservative Government with the introduction of the landfill tax (on the disposal of waste) and the annual petrol duty escalator. But it has been the Labour Government's proposal for a 'climate change levy' on the use of energy by industry and commerce which has brought this issue fully into the political domain. Unfortunately, the vociferous rearguard action mounted by the CBI and the energy intensive industries against the Government's proposals has obscured the underlying principles involved.

The obvious objection to any taxation of business is that it increases company costs and reduces competitiveness. This is what the industrial lobby is now arguing. But the Government's proposals embody two key principles which act to counter this, and which as such are central to the environmental modernisation agenda. They concern, not the tax *per se*, but the use of the revenues.

First, the revenues from environmental taxation can be recycled to reduce other business taxes. This is what is proposed for the climate change levy, which will be accompanied by an equivalent reduction in employers' National Insurance contributions. The principle here is far-reaching. It is that the price system, the central mechanism of a market system, should reinforce rather than resist the key objectives of policy. By shifting the burden of taxation within the economy away from desirable 'goods' such as employment and towards undesirable 'bads' such as energy use, powerful incentives are created: both to reduce environmental damage and to create jobs. (The incidental benefits to the Government's employment strategy should not be underestimated:

reducing employers' National Insurance contributions is an important way of reducing labour costs, particularly at the lower end of the market, and thereby stimulating the creation of jobs.)

Second, environmental tax revenues can be 'hypothecated' or earmarked for environmental spending. The various funding schemes suggested above, for example, could be resourced from environmental tax revenues – as the climate change levy is proposed partly to do. The key idea here is that such hypothecation can act to improve the effectiveness of the tax, assisting firms to make the efficiency gains which will cut environmental damage and reduce their tax burden. In turn, hypothecation may help win public support for the tax measure. Taxes which in this way are clearly aimed at improving the environment are likely to be more popular (or at least less unpopular) than those which appear simply to raise money for the Exchequer.

Using the revenues in these ways means that environmental taxation need not increase the overall burden on business. But of course it will mean that some firms lose out – those with very high and/or inefficient energy use – while others, the more labour intensive and the highly energy efficient, benefit. But this is inevitable, and it is desirable. The point of environmental taxation is to engineer the long-term restructuring of the economy on environmentally efficient lines. As with any structural change – not least, the digital revolution itself – this will involve shifts in the distribution of production between firms and between sectors. But the net outcome for the economy as a whole will be positive: a more productive economy, with higher employment and lower environmental damage.[8]

It is in this context that the present dispute over the climate change levy must be seen. It is inevitable that some industries and firms will face higher costs. But others will gain. The evidence is that the net effect on Britain's competitiveness will be positive.[9] There is certainly room for some concessions in the proposals to help those industries worse affected to adapt; the rates of taxation, the timescale for implementation, the use of negotiated environmental efficiency agreements can all no doubt be modified. In the longer term it may be necessary to get concerted European and international action if more deep-seated environmental taxation is to be pursued. (Most EU countries have now introduced or announced such taxes.) But on the central principle the Government must not concede. If the British economy is to modernise environmentally as well as in other ways, the price system must be part of the solution.

The Government's agenda   There are other elements of policy which could be added to this discussion, particularly in the international field.

There is an important opportunity to create an 'environmental Europe' to accompany the 'social Europe' to which Britain has now signed up. The new round of World Trade Organisation negotiations should ensure that environmental factors are allowed in trade agreements. There are opportunities to encourage environmental issues into corporate boardrooms in the Government's current reviews of company law and of the banking system. But the central argument – the need and the opportunity to raise the environmental productivity of the British economy – should be clear.

Two conclusions follow. One is that the lead department of government in this area is not going to be the Department of the Environment, Transport and the Regions, but that of Trade and Industry, with the Treasury close behind. The environmental agenda goes to the heart of economic and industrial policy, and must become part of it.

The second is that all this looks much less difficult for New Labour than might have been thought. There is indeed a rather remarkable fit between the environmental modernisation agenda and the Government's existing economic and industrial policy. Labour's vision is of a 21st century economy based on high productivity, high levels of investment in both technological innovation and human capital, and the widespread diffusion of digital technologies and knowledge-based sectors. But environmental modernisation makes exactly the same demands. It adds to them simply that part of the investment and technological development – including development of ICT – should take the form of raising environmental productivity. It is inevitable that the 21st century will see environmental pressures grow – both directly as environmental damage rebounds on firm costs, and then as this is manifested in higher regulatory demands. What is required now, perhaps, is for the Secretary of State for Trade and Industry and the Chancellor of the Exchequer to acknowledge this in their vision of the future British economy.

Health, food and the management of risk

If the development of an environmentally-based economic and industrial policy is environmental modernisation's response to the challenges of globalisation, how does it respond to the second of the trends we identified in the last two chapters, towards greater individualisation?

We can say at once how it does not. It does not seek to place responsibility for dealing with environmental problems in the hands of individuals. There is always a temptation to do this, one curiously felt by the green movement as well as by mainstream politicians. The former wielding the notion of personal responsibility, the latter trusting in 'consumer sovereignty', both greens and Conservatives have tended to argue that it is up to individuals to reduce their consumption if they wish to do so. But this is a strategy doomed to failure. The expectation that consumers will, *en masse*, spend extra for environmentally friendly products which have no additional direct benefits to themselves is simply unrealistic. There is a niche market for green consumerism and a greener lifestyle, but this is not, and cannot be, the driver of significant market change. However well-intentioned, publicity campaigns such as the Government's current 'Are You Doing Your Bit?' initiative are therefore of limited value. Indeed there is a danger, by associating environmentally friendly behaviour with altruism or public-spiritedness, that such behaviour will be seen as exceptional, rather than the expected norm.

Consumption patterns do have to change, but in most cases this will be driven from the supply side rather than by demand. (Though in some cases consumption may well need to be taxed more highly itself.) Under the pressure of environmental taxation or regulation, or through the kinds of industrial policy initiatives discussed above, firms will start supplying new goods and services which are not just environmentally more efficient but improved all round. Manufacturers will start organising the disposal and recycling of consumer goods they have previously supplied. Utilities will provide cost-saving insulation services and water efficiency measures, paid for on future (reduced) bills. Kerbside collection will make recycling convenient to the average, pressed-for-time household. Home shopping and delivery will cut travel demand – with the motivation for most consumers being simply convenience and time saving.

In these ways focusing environmental policy on the producer rather than on the consumer will help to ensure that environmental modernisation does not involve a reduction in the perceived standard of living. If take-up is to be widepread, greener goods and services must appeal to consumers whose primary motivation is not environmental. But to do this suppliers have to ensure that their products are generally better performing and of higher quality. Market competition will support the environmental agenda here.

But there is one important exception to the general rule that consumption *per se* is not the driver of environmental change. This is that of food, and to a lesser extent other products with direct health impacts on their purchasers. Here consumers do wield considerable power: the withdrawal of supermarkets and major food manufacturers from GM foods under pressure of consumer boycotts is testament to this. And there is a simple reason. Most environmental problems are 'external-ities', their impacts mainly borne by other people. Food by contrast is an 'internality' – literally, since its direct impacts on the consumer arise from the act of eating it. It is therefore unsurprising that the market for healthy foods is much greater than that for, say, recycled paper or phosphate-free detergents.

Given (as we have seen) their importance to a more individualistic culture, the issues of food and health are central to the environmental modernisation agenda. This has two implications for policy. The first is that agriculture is more significant than is generally thought. Part of the Government's problem over GM foods has been the lack of an overall strategic context in terms of food and agricultural policy. It is important now that a clear strategy for this sector is set out, based on the primary objective of improving food quality and safety. This is not the place for a review of proposals for agricultural reform: suffice to say that far more support could be given to organic and less chemically intensive production. What does seem likely, however, is that consid-erable public support will be won by the political party which seeks to restructure the agricultural industry as the champion of the consumer's food and health concerns. Exactly the same might be true in other risk fields. It is noticeable how the DTI has recently come to pose as the consumer's rather than industry's champion in respect of prices, for example in the car sector. There would seem ample opportunity to take up the same stance in relation, say, to potentially toxic chemicals, consumers and the chemical industry.

Managing risk   The second policy implication is of course a new approach to GM crops and foods themselves. The Government can hardly be said to have handled this issue well, with public opinion turning against not just this particular application of biotechnology but the wider industry – as well as the Government itself.

What is perhaps most striking is the failure to learn from previous episodes of this kind. Put simply, governments cannot rely on science and scientists when making decisions about environmental risks. Nuclear power, Brent Spar and the BSE crisis have all revealed the fragility of public confidence in scientific advice. And for good reason: as we have already seen, scientists are often operating in these fields in conditions of uncertainty and ignorance. For the lay public, the key issue is not the balance of scientific opinion, on which it is impossible for the non-expert to make a judgement; but their trust in the institu-tions in whose responsibility the issue lies. In the end, without inde-pendent access to scientific knowledge, such trust is all they have. Unfortunately, public trust in the Government is extremely low. Following a whole series of cases where governments' reassurances about potential risks were subsequently disproved – the BSE saga being the most powerful of these – people simply don't believe that the advice they are offered is sound. (This explains, incidentally, why the public boycotted beef when told it was safe, and clamoured to eat beef on the bone when told it was not.)

In these circumstances governments need to do three things. First, they need to ensure that they are not regarded as partial or biased on risk issues. There is considerable public scepticism about the role of large businesses in issues of these kinds: the suspicion that corporate profit, rather than public safety, is driving the agenda.[10] To retain their own credibility, governments need to ensure that they are not identified with such interests – a test which the present Government, given the apparent support for GM foods of some of its members, is in danger of failing.

There is an important principle here. If governments are genuinely to represent their publics on risk issues, they have to be prepared to reject certain applications of new technologies. This has already occurred in the field of reproductive technology, where certain cloning techniques and some uses of human embryos are illegal. When and if research programmes have generated reliable results, this possibility has to remain open in other fields, including that of GM crops and foods. The rules of the World Trade Organisation and EU which assume that new products are safe until proven otherwise, and cannot be held back from the market by governments while research is conducted, may well in the long term prove untenable in this respect. It is notable that they conflict with the precautionary principle established at the Earth Summit in 1992.

Second, the Government needs to establish independent mechanisms for providing political and scientific advice on risk issues. If public trust is to be restored, the independence of the institutions pronouncing in these fields is essential. This is not simply about scientific judgements. The Government needs an advisory body which will also look at the social and ethical concerns which new technologies raise – as already occurs, for example, in the field of reproductive technology. A new body should be created to do this, called perhaps the Commission on Environmental Risk. Its members should be drawn from a variety of fields, including scientists, social scientists and philosophers, and representatives from business and non-governmental organisations. Its composition must be broad enough to attract maximum public support.

Perhaps most importantly, third, the role of this Commission should not simply be to report on risk issues, but actively to promote public debate about them. Innovative methods might be used to do this. These might include open public meetings and exhibitions in different places around the country; short, accessible publications, television and radio programmes and internet sites; the use of citizens' juries and consensus conferences to explore issues in detail with lay members of the public; focus group and opinion surveys; and national conferences bringing together industry and interest groups. There is some experience of these in this country and elsewhere in Europe already. The need is to raise the level of public information and discussion above the hysteria generated by much of the press (not least on genetic modification), and thereby create the context in which more considered decisions can be made.

These are not panaceas. Risk decisions are hard, and will always be so. Caution can prevail, but knowledge can never be complete, and uncertainty is inescapable. In the GM field, however, the importance of shifting the public perception of the issue could hardly be greater. Most of the biotechnology sector, particularly in Britain, has nothing to do with GM crops or foods. Its field is mainly health care, and certain other applications such as waste management. The real danger now is that these applications – which are in themselves fields of risk, but of different kinds – will be tainted by the public reaction to GM foods, with firms seeking to locate elsewhere or investors frightened off altogether. Careful public management of risk is therefore crucial to the health of the industry itself.

Notes

1 Ulrich Beck, *Risk Society*, Sage, 1992.
2 See for example Ernst von Weiszacker *et al*, *Factor Four*, Earthscan, 1997; Paul Hawken *et al*, *Natural Capitalism*, Little, Brown, 1999.
3 *Our Competitive Future: Building the Knowledge Driven Economy*, Cm 4176, The Stationery Office, 1998.
4 Environmental Industries Commission, 'Fiscal Incentives to Overcome Barriers to Investment in Environmental Technology', 1998.
5 *Ibid*.
6 Robin Murray, *Creating Wealth From Waste*, Demos, 1999.
7 DETR and DTI, 'Sectoral Sustainability Strategies: A Discussion Document', 1998. A much better account is in DETR, *Consumer Products and the Environment: A Consultation Paper*, 1998.
8 Paul Ekins, *Ecological Tax Reform, Environmental Policy and the Competitiveness of British Industry*, Forum for the Future and Friends of the Earth, 1998.
9 *Ibid*.
10 Robin Grove-White *et al*, *Uncertain World: Genetically Modified Organisms, Food and Public Attitudes in Britain*, Centre for the Study of Environmental Change, Lancaster University, 1997.

24

An Agenda for Development for the Twenty-First Century

Joseph Stiglitz

This is an exciting time for those committed to advancing economic growth, reducing poverty and sustaining policy reform in developing countries and countries that are making the transition to a market economy. The success, not just of one but of several countries in breaking out of the poverty in which they had been mired for centuries, shows that development is possible. In Latin America, the debt crisis and the growth stagnation to which it gave rise seem to be behind us, and the latest data show that developing countries are growing faster than industrial countries. In fact, between 1991 and 1995 the growth rate of high-income countries was 2.5 per cent, while that of low- and middle-income countries was 4.5 per cent. Although the financial crises in East Asia have attracted much attention lately, they should not obscure the amazing achievements of the East Asian countries. Per capita income in the Republic of Korea increased tenfold in just over three decades. There is almost no one in Korea, Malaysia or Thailand living on less than US$1 a day, and Indonesia is within reach of that goal. Even Africa, where many countries experienced negative growth in the 1970s and 1980s, has at last started to experience growth, and countries such as Uganda that have sustained reforms over several years are showing consistent growth averaging 6 per cent – still not in the league of China, but far better than was the case a few years ago.

It is now clear that countries that pursue appropriate policies have a better chance of economic success than those that do not. And there is mounting evidence that economic assistance, when combined with good policies, promotes economic growth, especially among the poorest countries. That is, of course, good news not only for the countries involved, but also for those who offer advice and dispense aid: They can make a difference. The challenge is to understand which policies are appropriate and how to target assistance to promote growth and reduce poverty most effectively. There is clearly no magic formula: If there were, the number of successes would be far higher than it is. And the fact that the messages that have been emphasized have changed over time – and that many of the countries that were successful did not take the particular medicine that was then being dispensed by the development community – should, at the very least, induce a modicum of humility as future directions are considered.

Changed perspective

It is an exciting time too because of the fast pace of change in the world and the concomitant changes in the world of ideas – changes that inevitably would have necessitated modifying the development strategy, even if there was one that had worked unfailingly in the past. Over the past decade, three changes in particular have influenced thinking about effective development strategies.

Collapse of the socialist economies

This event provided an immediate lesson. For almost a hundred years, two theories had competed for the hearts and minds of people struggling to break free of poverty – one focusing on markets, and the other on government. The failure of the socialist economies appeared to demonstrate that the second model was not viable. But another conclusion sometimes drawn, that markets by themselves would provide the answer, also has not been justified by economic theory or by historical experience. [. . .] Historical experience [has not] been kind to the view that by themselves markets would have generated development: Almost all the major successes – the economies of East Asia, the United States, many countries in Europe – involved heavy doses of government involvement. There is a remarkable similarity between the government activities undertaken by the East Asian tigers and those undertaken by the United States in a comparable period of its development. There are few examples on the other side, of success without government involvement.

One of the striking lessons that emerged from the post-Cold War era is how difficult it is for markets to get established. Those in the more advanced industrial economies take for granted a rich institutional infrastructure, much of which requires government action to establish and maintain.

Success of the East Asian economies

This experience has had an intellectual impact, by teaching that development is possible and that successful development requires (or at least is enhanced by) governments undertaking appropriate policies that go well beyond simply getting out of the way of the market. While there remains an active debate about the precise lessons to be learned and the extent to which the experiences of East Asia are replicable elsewhere, there remains little doubt that government played a critical, catalytic role.

But East Asia's success has had another consequence: These economies have been an engine of growth for much of the rest of the world. US merchandise exports to East Asia, for instance, more than doubled between 1990 and 1996, and exports to developing countries were responsible for roughly one-sixth of US GDP growth in this period. China, while still a developing country in terms of GDP per capita, could soon become the second largest economy in the world. Developing countries have become an economic force to be reckoned with.

Globalization of the world economy

This development is partly attributable to the tremendous drop in transport and communication costs in recent decades. Globalization has increased trade and capital flows, and developing countries that have opened their economies have especially benefited. Since 1990, private capital flows to developing countries have increased more than sixfold. And East Asia's success was driven by exports: Production was not limited by the size of domestic economies, competition in exporting raised standards and increased efficiency, and exports helped transfer advanced technology and management practices. Increasing integration of the world economy has meant that a factory in Indonesia can be closely linked with markets in the United States and Europe, with changes in preferences and demands there being quickly translated into changes in what is produced. Computer programmers in India can be linked with programmers in California's Silicon Valley. Distances have been shrunk, and geographical isolation has been reduced. These trends are just beginning, and they open up a host of new opportunities and challenges for all countries – and for developing countries, the hope of narrowing the knowledge and resource gap that has separated them from more developed countries, but also the challenge that the target they are chasing may be moving that much faster as well.

These changes in the global economy must guide development strategies in the coming decades.

Changed objectives

Another set of changes was equally important in affecting thinking about development strategies – a change in objectives. It used to be that development was seen as simply increasing GDP. Today, there is a broader set of objectives, including democratic development, egalitarian development, sustainable development, and higher living standards.

It is recognized that there is more to living standards than is typically captured in GDP accounting. Improvements in education or health are not just means to an end of increased output, but are ends in themselves. Growth by itself does not ensure that the fruits will be equitably shared. It is recognized that there are costs, both to individuals and to society, of economic insecurity. Finally, the environment can no longer be taken for granted – in the struggle to increase GDP, the air in many developing country cities became so polluted as to make them almost unlivable. Moreover, it is now clear that cutting down an irreplaceable hardwood forest provides an increase in measured GDP that is probably not sustainable.

Fifty years ago, the common wisdom was that there was a tradeoff between rapid growth and democracy – Russia could grow faster, but at the cost of basic liberties. In retrospect, it is clear that people living under totalitarian regimes gave up their freedoms and sacrificed economic growth. In a regime without a free press, millions of people can starve, even starve to death, without public outrage mobilizing efforts to save them. And within developing countries, there is a growing recognition of the virtues of democratic development as an end in itself.

This broadened set of objectives leads to quite different development strategies: For instance, democratic development leads to increased emphasis on participation and the development of political institutions and education.

As always, perspective must be maintained: While increasing GDP is not an end in itself, or not the only end, increasing GDP is essential to achieving the other objectives. Raising education levels and improving the health status in a country require resources, and resources are scarce. The fact that some countries have not used their increased resources in ways that comport with these broader development objectives should not be confused with the fact that increased resources expand a country's opportunities.

Similarly, while greater participation is essential to democratic development, the actions to achieve it must be constantly scrutinized: How representative, for instance, are those whose voices are being expressed? This is a concern even with respect to democratically elected leadership when voter turnout is small: extreme groups may be more likely to express their views. [. . .] There is concern, too, about the influence of money in electoral processes. But electoral processes in which there is a simple rule of "one person, one vote" still provide the most systematic way of ensuring representativeness.

In some cases, participation can improve other outcomes (for instance, the amount of learning that occurs). But in other cases, the effect on outcomes may be less certain. Some studies have found no correlation between rankings of perceived health impacts of various environmental hazards by scientists and rankings by nonscientists. Those who want to ensure that funds are spent on improving the environment to reduce overall health risks would surely want to rely more on the informed judgments of scientists than on a broader set of participatory views – while at the same time recognizing the importance of educating people more broadly about the scientific evidence on actual health risks associated with various hazards.

Reflections on the past

Given the changes in the world, in our ideas, and in our views of development objectives, it is not surprising that development strategies have changed markedly over the past half century. When I was a graduate student, development planning was all the rage, and development economics was a mechanistic exercise. A country had a certain amount of resources that had to be allocated efficiently. Development strategies consisted of increasing those resources – in particular, the amount of physical capital – and ensuring, through development planning, that those resources were optimally used and that the various investments were coordinated. Government was required because markets were not sufficiently developed to provide the signals for resource allocation or to perform the coordination role that they were supposed to perform. Even when behavior was introduced into these models, it was done in a mechanistic manner. Savings rates were fixed, and they were lower among workers than among capitalists. Increasing the savings rate thus required shifting the distribution of income toward capitalists and away from workers.

Throughout this period, however, another strand of thought argued that government was part of the problem, not the solution; that more private initiative and entrepreneurship was required; and that government was inhibiting that private initiative. In the academic literature, this perspective was reinforced by data showing the responsiveness of peasants to price signals: Peasants in developing countries were just as rational as their urban cousins in the developed world. From here it was an easy step to suggest that the government should simply get out of the way, liberalize trade, and get the prices right. Development would follow.

This simplistic advice ignored the background from which the development planning literature had emerged: Many developing countries lacked markets for many commodities, and there was little reason to believe that markets would develop on their own. Market imperfections – imperfections that imply that the resource allocation that the market would provide on its own will not be (Pareto) efficient – while common in industrial countries, are rife in developing countries. Not only were more markets absent, but competition was often more limited and information more imperfect.

There was a curious incongruity: Economic practitioners were preaching the free market gospel just as economic theorists began to realize its lack of robustness. One of the central theoretical results of the 1950s was to establish rigorously the conditions under which Adam Smith's insight about the invisible hand guiding the efficiency of markets is valid. Yet one of the central theoretical results of the 1980s was to show that whenever information is imperfect and markets are incomplete – which is essentially always – markets are not even *constrained* Pareto optimal. In other words, taking into account the costs of acquiring information and establishing markets, there are interventions that *in principle* could make some individuals better off without making anyone else worse off.

To be sure, another strand of thought emphasized not the perfections of markets but the imperfections of government. These were taken to be inevitable – or at least a judgment was made that it was better to ignore market imperfections than either to attempt to improve the performance of government or to use imperfect governments to correct the market imperfections.

The debt crisis of the 1980s shifted the focus to macroeconomics: Countries could not grow if governments did not provide a stable macroeconomic environment. Governments needed to hold their expenditures to their revenues and to limit the expansion of the money supply.

Many governments began following what came to be called the Washington consensus: They liberalized trade, achieved macroeconomic stability, and got the prices right – yet growth did not follow as quickly or as strongly as envisaged. By contrast, the governments of East Asia took a less dogmatic approach: While they achieved macroeconomic stability, they intervened extensively in the market. They helped create and regulate markets, and used them to achieve their development objectives. They also experienced the most rapid growth. Since 1997 many East Asian countries have experienced serious financial turmoil. In my view, far from a refutation of the East Asian miracle, this turmoil may, in part, be the result of departing from the strategies that have served these countries so well, including well-regulated financial markets. In part, too, it may be the result of the failure to adapt quickly enough to changing circumstances, especially in the international financial system.

The new perspective

The new agenda is informed by these experiences and is responsive to the changes in the economic environment and the broadened set of objectives noted above. It sees government and markets as complements rather than substitutes. It takes as dogma neither that markets by themselves will ensure desirable outcomes nor that the absence of a market, or some related market failure, requires government to assume responsibility for the activity. It often does not even ask whether a particular activity should be in the public or the private sector. Rather, in some circumstances the new agenda sees government as helping to create markets – as many of the East Asian governments did in key components of the financial market. In other areas (such as education), it sees the government and the private sector working together as partners, each with its own responsibilities. And in still others (such as banking), it sees government as providing the essential regulation without which markets cannot function.

And behind all of this lies a special responsibility for government: to create the institutional infrastructure that markets require in order to work effectively. At a minimum, this institutional infrastructure includes effective laws and the legal institutions to implement them. If markets are to work effectively, there must be well-established and clearly defined property rights; there must be effective competition, which requires antitrust enforcement; and there must be confidence in the markets, which means that contracts must be enforced and that antifraud laws must be effective, reflecting widely accepted codes of behavior. Laws that ensure a level playing field (for example, that restrict insider trading in securities markets) are not just matters of consumer protection: Without such laws investors will be reluctant to invest their funds in securities markets lest they be cheated.

The partnership between the government and the private sector has other dimensions.

Financial regulations that ensure the safety and soundness of banking institutions not only help mobilize capital, by giving depositors more confidence in the banking system, they also help ensure the efficient allocation of investment. (The dangers from excessive risk taking or looting that occur when banks are undercapitalized have been widely discussed in the aftermath of the banking crises of the 1980s and 1990s.)

Government support for education helps ensure a supply of well-trained workers.

Government either helps provide infrastructure or provides a regulatory structure that ensures the private provision of infrastructure at reasonable prices.

Government often plays a vital role in developing and transmitting technology, such as through agricultural extension services.

Government can help promote equality and alleviate poverty, policies that in East Asia contributed to overall growth.

In each of these areas, the rationale for government action can be found in the theory of market failure. For instance, knowledge (especially its production) is a public good, and like other public goods it will be undersupplied. But the rationale for government action in these areas can also be found in the historical record: Economies in which government performed these roles well also performed better.

The exact role of government will change over time. It used to be thought that telecommunications and electricity were natural monopolies in which competition was not viable. Government would either have to regulate these industries closely or take charge of production. Today, partly because of changes in technology and partly because of changes in thinking, it is known that competition is viable in large parts of these sectors if an appropriate regulatory structure is in place. What is required is not deregulation, the naive stripping away of regulations, but regulatory redesign, that is, the changing of the regulatory structure in ways that promote competition where it is viable and that ensure that monopoly power is not too badly exploited where it is not.

Improving government performance

Once the vital role that government plays in a development strategy is recognized, the next step is to determine how the performance of government can be improved. There is a great deal that is known about markets and market failures, but far less understanding about governments and government failures. Still, a few things are known.

Governments can become more effective if they use market and market-like mechanisms. Auctions (both for procurement and for the disposition of government assets) can increase transparency (and thus confidence in government), improve the allocation of resources, and bolster the government's budgetary position. Rather than addressing specific actions or transactions, government regulations may be designed to establish incentives for private firms to act appropriately – for example, by ensuring that banks have adequate net worth. Similarly, government may require commercial firms to have fire insurance, leaving it to the insurance company to ensure that appropriate precautions are taken (such as installing sprinklers), knowing that the insurance company has appropriate incentives.

Governments that are less frequently subjected to temptation are less likely to give in to it. Discretionary actions, such as the allocation of quota rights, provide opportunities for corruption. Corruption has adverse effects on economic growth (partly by raising the costs of doing business and thereby discouraging investment) and undermines confidence in government. Thus using transparent, market-like mechanisms has a double set of advantages.

Governments should constantly reexamine the rationale for the regulations they have imposed. Historical processes often lead to regulations that are not appropriate to today's circumstances: The objectives of the regulations could be achieved at far less cost. For instance, before there were devices that could measure the pollution being emitted by a smokestack, it might have been appropriate to require technologies that met environmental standards. But once reliable monitoring devices are available, regulations should focus on outputs (here, the level of emissions) rather than inputs (technology standards.)

The quality of a government's bureaucracy depends on the composition and quality of its workforce. Those in turn depend in part on its internal systems for hiring, training, and promotion and, as with any enterprise, in part on wages. Low wages and a mismatch between rewards and results discourage output and result in low performance.

Governments can help stimulate and can use competition: It can create competing public agencies, and it can allow private agents to compete with public agencies. The success of market economies is based on deep institutions that support incentives built around private property and competition. While there is ongoing debate about the relative importance of private property and competition, a plausible case can be made in a variety of settings that competition is what is essential. (Some view the success of China as bearing witness to this proposition. More narrowly, studies of government-run enterprises that are subjected to competition suggest that they can perform as effectively as private firms. In large organizations, whether public or private, principal–agent problems arise; the scope for putting in place *individual* incentives may differ little between public and private organizations.) One of the central themes of the World Bank's report on the East Asian miracle is that competition played a crucial role (especially competition for exports).

Sequencing of reforms

The simple lesson that emerges from this discussion is that incentives matter: that they matter in both the public and the private sector, that government should make more extensive use of incentives to guide its behavior, and that government should take actions to improve incentives in the private sector. (The variety of restrictions within the banking sector are examples of actions taken to improve the incentives of banks.)

By the way it sequences reforms, government can affect not only the performance of the economy in the short run but also the momentum for the continuation of reforms. Consider, for instance, the consequences of privatization in a large, closed economy before trade is liberalized and before an effective competition law is in place. Under these conditions, privatization would convert a government monopoly into a private monopoly. Consumers (or firms who use the privatized firm's output as input) probably would not see any benefits (real prices might actually increase), overall economic performance probably would fail to improve (increased efficiency within the privatized firm is offset by loss of systemic efficiency from higher prices), and a vested interest might be created that would have the incentive and the resources to work against efforts to implement an effective competition law. A regulatory structure might evolve, but it would arrive already compromised, captured by those whom it should regulate.

Or consider the consequences of the privatization of a utility before an effective regulatory law is put in place. Uncertainty about the future regulatory structure could cause the government to receive less from the sale of the assets than it should. There is also the possibility that users, both consumers and firms, will face higher prices and that a vested interest will be created that has the incentive and the resources to resist effective regulatory reform. Moreover, in the absence of an effective regulatory structure, other public objectives that had been pursued by the industry before privatization – such as universal service – may be abandoned. High profits, low sales price, and decreased service will all undermine public support for the continuation of reform.

A regulatory structure can be created to ensure that some of the efficiency gains from privatization are shared by consumers and other users and that other social objectives, such as universal service, are enhanced. But the proposition that privatization can, in principle, increase the efficiency of the economy and achieve other social objectives should never be confused with the proposition that, in the absence of effective regulatory structures, privatization may do neither in practice.

Neither economic theory nor historical experience gives clear guidance in these complicated matters. (Even in the case of privatization the principal theoretical proposition, the fundamental privatization theorem, shows how restrictive the conditions are under which privatization can guarantee a welfare improvement.) Theory may predicate that under certain idealized circumstances market economies are efficient. But theory provides less clear prescriptions for the inevitable second best situations in which many of the idealized circumstances underlying the pure theory are not satisfied. And theory gives even less clear guidance on sequencing: how to get from here to there. For these decisions, experience and judgment – as well as perhaps the guidance that comes from a careful consideration of cross-country experiences – must be relied on.

The role of high-income countries

Most of this discussion has focused on what developing countries must do to succeed in enhancing their economic growth. But there is much that high-income countries can do as well.

The enormous increase in private capital flows to low- and middle-income countries has been a boon to countries that have created a welcoming investment environment. But the magnitude of these flows should not conceal the fact that they have been very concentrated: Ten countries, representing half of the developing world's GDP, have received 75 per cent of the funds, and only a handful of low-income countries have received any significant amounts relative to the size of their economies. Moreover, these private flows have not gone to all sectors of the economy – health and education, for instance, remain largely within the public sector.

That is the reason why the decline in official development assistance is so disturbing. In 1996, such aid, measured as a percentage of high-income countries' GDP, reached an almost fifty-year low. It is ironic that such cutbacks are occurring just as evidence of the effectiveness of aid is mounting.

Development assistance promotes economic growth, especially among low-income countries, if they have put in place good economic policies. True, aid cannot buy reform, and it works best for countries that can help themselves. But as a complement to local initiatives, aid can enlarge and precipitate the positive effects of reforms, and by helping to build political momentum it can make the reforms sustainable. More important, aid may be an effective instrument for transferring knowledge and, as pointed out below, the diffusion of appropriate and well deployed knowledge can greatly enhance development prospects even in the poorest countries.

Some of the high-income countries that have been least forthcoming with aid have emphasized the importance of trade. But here too there is a gap between rhetoric and reality. For instance, while preaching the virtues of a market economy, Western producers accused Russian firms that were selling their excess aluminum at international prices of engaging in dumping, and encouraged their governments to impose trade restrictions. As an alternative, they proposed establishing what in effect would be an international cartel to restrict worldwide production and raise prices – which is what was done.

How can the advanced economies preach the gospel of competition and free markets, yet turn to managed trade and restricted markets when their own interests are in jeopardy? There are many, many more examples, but the point is clear: The advanced economies should be the role models. They are far more able to absorb the shocks that inevitably occur as a result of changing trade patterns. Why is it that they seemingly find it so acceptable to refer to "political pressures" forcing their deviations from policies of openness while finding such excuses so hard to take from developing countries?

The World Bank's role in the development agenda

Some analysts claim that the huge flows of private capital to developing countries have made the World Bank unnecessary. I disagree. The rationale for the World Bank and for development banks more generally can be summarized as follows.

Private capital flows are targeted. Most low-income countries receive very little of this capital, and little of the money goes to vital sectors, such as health and education, that are complementary to the private flows.

The World Bank and the other international financial institutions have an important role in helping developing countries establish the institutional infrastructure (regulations and laws) that is required to attract capital. This infrastructure is a public good; thus the private sector cannot be expected to provide adequate assistance in its establishment. Moreover, in a world where competing private interests are always looking for the establishment of rules and regulations that favor themselves, the World Bank can serve as an honest broker.

While private capital flows are much more varied in form than they were in the past – there are now substantial equity flows – there are still important gaps.

The World Bank has a distinct advantage in gathering information and producing knowledge about successful development practices and policies. Knowledge is an international public good that will be undersupplied if left to the market.

In some cases, the World Bank and other multilateral development banks may signal that a developing country has embraced sound policies and hence boost its credibility, providing an additional incentive for maintaining these policies in the future.

World Bank staff have a special responsibility not only to produce knowledge that will enable developing countries to grow more effectively, but also to ensure that that knowledge translates itself into appropriate action – including in its lending practices. A reference was made above to research showing the effectiveness of aid when good economic policies are in place. The flip side of that research suggests that when good economic policies are not in place, aid may have no effect on economic growth. This finding poses a moral dilemma: If a loan does not increase an economy's resources, unless it is explicitly aimed at achieving other social objectives, it leaves future generations more impoverished, since they inherit the indebtedness. And even if it does achieve some other social objective, the tradeoffs need to be considered.

The issue of the fungibility of funds adds further complications: To the extent that funds are fungible, the issue is not the quality of the project being funded, but what happens as a result of the additional flow of funds. Evidence on the extent of fungibility (or the circumstances under which funds are more fungible) remains somewhat ambiguous. Yet recent studies indicate that, with the exception of sectors such as transport and communications, aid funds are largely fungible and foreign finance does significantly substitute for (rather than complement) domestic spending. But people living in the poorest countries that also do not have good economic policies cannot be ignored. They need help in putting in place good policies by providing advice and technical assistance. In addition, investments should be made in areas such as human capital that will be ready to support growth once good policies are adopted. And effective delivery mechanisms must be found when governments have demonstrated their lack of capability.

Conclusion

The development agenda for the twenty-first century outlined in this discussion includes a wider set of objectives than those of the past. It includes a changing role for the state – with a partnership between government and the private sector   that involves a catalytic function for government in helping to create markets. In some areas, it includes a more enduring role for government in regulating markets. And it requires governments to improve their own performance, partly by making more extensive use of market-like mechanisms through using and helping to create competition wherever it can.

For both developing and industrial countries, the new agenda requires an openness that both groups have often resisted. The mutual benefits are clear: Developing countries will continue to be an engine of growth for industrial countries, providing a broader variety of products at lower prices to their consumers and offering higher returns to their investors. For developing countries, the transfer of resources and knowledge will enable a continuation of growth.

As mentioned above, there is an important role in this agenda for the World Bank and other international financial institutions. But what that role is and how it can best be performed must undergo a continuing process of reexamination.

There is no room in this agenda for dogma or for doctrinaire approaches. The general consensus on basic economic reforms – keep inflation to a moderate level, limit the size of the fiscal deficit, avoid introducing large distortions in the economy, open the economy to foreign competition – addresses issues of fundamental importance and has made substantial contributions to stabilization in several countries. There is a danger that this consensus has become dogma and, as dogma, it may sometimes be applied inappropriately.

One of the principal advantages of this consensus is its simplicity. But the policy agenda of the coming decade will not be as amenable to such a cookie-cutter approach. Regulatory regimes and legal and other institutional structures should be better adapted to country circumstances. And in many cases, reforms are far more technically complex than the consensus suggests. For instance, designing regulations that promote competition in telecommunications and electricity is extremely difficult, as the experience of the United States and other countries have shown.

There is a need to learn from theory and history, from best practices, and from what has worked. But care must be taken in extracting the appropriate lessons.

- The world today is different from the world thirty, twenty, or even ten years ago. Private capital flows are more important today than they were then; this opens up new opportunities – and new challenges. The fact that some East Asian economies made relatively little use of foreign capital may have little bearing on whether a developing country today should make more extensive use of these flows.
- Some of the most successful economies did not follow all the key prescriptions that are commonly given today. Much of the growth in GDP among all low-income countries can be accounted for by the growth in China. China focused on creating new enterprises and engendering competition rather than on privatizing state enterprises. Would these successful enterprises have grown even faster had China followed the alternative strategy? Most observers are doubtful. The Republic of Korea has been widely criticized during its 1997 financial crisis for its failed economic system – yet that system somehow increased per capita incomes tenfold in three decades, a record unmatched by any large country following the prescriptions now commonly proffered.
- What works in one set of circumstances may not work in others. Analysis is required to identify the factors that determine success and to establish the counterfactuals (what would have happened in

the absence of a particular project or policy). Examples of best practices may provide useful and persuasive anecdotes, but they are no substitute for analysis.

- Care should be taken not to confuse means with ends. Macroeconomic stability, deficit reduction, and even enterprise reform are not ends in themselves, but means to the broader development objectives described above. If a government reduces its fiscal deficit by cutting back vital investments in infrastructure or in human capital, growth may actually suffer. If a government reduces its fiscal deficit by cutting back on food subsidies and that leads to rioting that undermines the country's political stability, is that likely to make the country more or less attractive to foreign investors?

- Ends also must not be confused with means: Improved education and health are essential means of increasing GDP, but they are also ends in themselves.

- The broadened set of objectives is an essential aspect of the new development agenda. But while it is recognized that there is a richer set of objectives, the constraints provided by limited resources are no less binding. In the words of one of my colleagues, these issues must be approached with soft hearts and hard heads. There is a difficult tradeoff: It might be possible to reduce poverty more today, but only at the expense of fewer resources – and therefore more poverty – in the future.

- One of the lessons of East Asia's experience is that there are important instances of policies that increase economic growth, promote equality, and ameliorate poverty. The search for such policies – and their implementation – must be at the center of the development agenda of the future.

- If one truly believes in democratic development, the limited role of technical advisers must be recognized. They can offer judgments about the consequences of alternative policies. But an essential part of the new development strategies involves the creation of institutions and the changing of cultures – the movement to a culture of change and science, where existing practices are questioned and alternatives are constantly explored. (These cultural changes were, of course, the subject of considerable discussion in the development literature a half century ago.) Deciding how best to effect such changes requires a great deal of local knowledge, and it is not obvious that development advisers have either that local knowledge or the corresponding technical expertise. Moreover, democratically elected governments must, in the end, make the judgments about both the tradeoffs and the political consequences. These are principles that apply to advisers in advanced as well as in

developing economies. Having said that, it is important to emphasize that there are vast areas in which technical expertise is highly
relevant. For example, certain fundamentals in establishing effective banking regulations apply to all countries.

Today, development is recognized as more than the accretion of
physical capital and even more than the accretion of human capital. It
includes closing the knowledge gap between rich and poor economies.
And it includes other transformations, such as those that result in lower
population growth rates and changes in economic organization.

I am confident that the coming decade will certainly see enormous
growth in the developing world and a reduction of poverty. It will be
a struggle. The challenges are great, but the opportunities are many.

The challenge for those who advise governments will be to strike
hard-to-find balances between the roles of the state and the roles of the
private sector, and between the doctrinaire positions that have often
characterized the policy advice of the past and the agnosticism that
gives little guidance to those struggling to make the hard choices that
will affect millions of lives.

Further reading

Arnott, Richard, Bruce Greenwald, and Joseph E. Stiglitz. 1994. "Information and
    Economic Efficiency." *Information Economics and Policy* 6 (1): 77–88.
Burnside, Craig, and David Dollar. 1997. "Aid, Policies, and Growth." Policy
    Research Working Paper 1777. World Bank, Policy Research Department,
    Washington, D.C.
Daves, D. W., and L. R. Christensen. 1980. "The Relative Efficiency of Public and
    Private Firms in a Competitive Environment: The Case of Canadian Railroads."
    Journal of Political Economy 88 (4): 958–76.
Dreze, Jean, Amartya Sen, and Athar Hussain, eds. 1995. *The Political Economy of
    Hunger: Selected Essays.* New York: Oxford University Press.
Feyzioglu, Tarhan, Vinaya Swaroop, and Min Zhu. 1997. "Foreign Aid's Impact on
    Public Spending." Policy Research Working Paper 1610. World Bank, Policy
    Research Department, Public Economics Division, Washington, D.C.
Greenwald, Bruce, and Joseph E. Stiglitz. 1986. "Externalities in Economies with
    Imperfect Information and Incomplete Markets." *Quarterly Journal of Economics*
    101 (3): 229–64.
——. 1988. "Pareto Inefficiency of Market Economies: Search and Efficiency
    Wage Models." *American Economic Association Papers and Proceedings* 78: 351–5.
Hellman, Thomas, Kevin Murdock, and Joseph Stiglitz. 1997. "Financial Restraint:
    Towards a New Paradigm." Stanford Graduate School of Business Research
    Paper, Stanford, California.

Pack, H., and J. R. Pack. 1990. "Is Foreign Aid Fungible? The Case of Indonesia." *Economic Journal* 100 (March): 188–94.

———. 1993. "Foreign Aid and the Question of Fungibility." *Review of Economics and Statistics* 75 (May): 258–65.

Sappington, David, and Joseph E. Stiglitz. 1987. "Privatization, Information, and Incentives." *Journal of Policy Analysis and Management* 6: 567–82.

Slovic, Paul, Mark Layman, and James H. Flynn. 1993. *Perceived Risk, Trust, and Nuclear Waste: Lessons from Yucca Mountain.* Durham, N.C.: Duke University Press.

Stiglitz, Joseph E. 1990. "The Economic Role of the State: Efficiency and Effectiveness." In Thomas P. Hardiman and Michael Mulreany, eds., *Efficiency and Effectiveness.* Dublin: Institute of Public Administration.

———. 1994. *Whither Socialism.* Cambridge, Mass.: MIT Press.

———. 1996. "Some Lessons from the East Asian Miracle." *The World Bank Research Observer* 11 (2): 151–78.

Stiglitz, Joseph E. 1997. "An Agenda for Development for the Twenty-First Century." In Pleskovic, Boris, and Joseph E. Stiglitz, eds. *Annual Bank Conference on Development Economics 1997.* The World Bank, Washington, D.C.

Stiglitz, Joseph E., and Marilou Uy. 1996. "Financial Markets, Public Policy, and the East Asian Miracle." *The World Bank Research Observer* 11 (2): 249–76.

Taylor, Lance. 1979. *Macro Models for Developing Countries.* New York: McGraw-Hill.

USEPA (US Environmental Protection Agency). 1987. *Unfinished Business: A Comparative Assessment of Environmental Problems.* Washington, D.C.

World Bank. 1993. *The East Asian Miracle: Economic Growth and Public Policy.* A Policy Research Report. New York: Oxford University Press.

———. 1994. *Adjustment in Africa: Reforms, Results, and the Road Ahead.* A Policy Research Report. New York: Oxford University Press.

———. 1997a. *Global Development Finance 1997.* Washington, D.C.

———. 1997b. *Global Economic Prospects and the Developing Countries.* Washington, D.C.

———. 1997c. *World Development Report 1997: The State in a Changing World.* New York: Oxford University Press.

25

The New Left Viewed from the South

Luiz Carlos Bresser-Pereira

[. . .]

In this discussion I shall primarily discuss ideas, not governments or administrations. I will examine the historic form the left assumes in current times – how the new social democrats have been able, through these ideas, to distinguish themselves from the old social democrats and from the conservative new right, to conquer the center, and to win elections. The first country where this clearly happened was in Spain, in the early 1980s. It was, however, in Britain, with the third way, that the new left gained a more precise conceptual character. I will focus upon the differences between the new and old left, and the new right, in relation to the globalization issue. I will give special attention to what is or should be the new left in a developing country like Brazil. And, in conclusion, I will ask if these ideas will tend to produce good outcomes or not, if they will foster better government and better states, or will be ineffective.

Historical perspectives

Starting in the early 1970s we witnessed a crisis that was marked by reduction of the growth rates and concentration of income in practically all countries except the well-known cases of East and South-East Asia. This crisis was essentially a crisis of the state – as the 1930s crisis was a crisis of markets. Its most evident political outcome was the shift of the political center to the right, which caused a crisis in the left, while a neo-liberal or libertarian right advanced in all fields. In the 1990s, when the failure of the neoliberal proposals in stimulating growth and redistribution of income became apparent, the pendulum again started to move, now towards the left. Probably never before has such a great number of governments been social democratic as today. [. . .]

This 20-year-old crisis allowed for the emergence of a new center-left: the new democrats in the United States, the third way in Britain, the new center in Germany, the new left in France and Italy, modern social democracy in Brazil. This change was possible, first, because the neo-liberal new right failed in fulfilling its vows. Uncontrolled markets produced unprecedented levels of social insecurity and of income concentration, without having economic growth as a trade-off. The old right's conservatism was based upon respect for order, for traditional institutions and professions; the new right's conservatism is essentially contradictory to this. Actually, it is a strange conservatism, which, as a well-known political theorist, John Gray, asserts, had the effect of undermining real conservatism as a political project.[1] Neo-liberal policies brought about social problems that new right politicians do not know how to face. In his words, "the hegemony, within conservative thought and practice, of neo-liberal ideology had the effect of destroying conservatism as a viable political project in our time."

Second, the new left won elections, defeating the right in most developed countries, because it was able successfully to criticize both the neo-liberal right and the old left, while presenting new and pragmatic programs in the respective countries. The fall of the Berlin wall in 1989 produced an enormous literature on the "crisis of the left." Actually, its outcome was a crisis of the old left, while the new left was strengthened given the decades-old critique it had been directing toward the Soviet system. In its turn, the new right, which assumed a triumphalist attitude, commemorating "the definitive victory of markets over state," soon realized that its reforms, although necessary, were not being well received by voters, given their unnecessary radicalism and poor results – and got into its own crisis.

[. . .]

The new left politicians are only favored by the left's intellectuals while they are out of government. The moment a given social-democratic party uses the new ideas to win elections, and comes to the challenge of transforming them into effective public policies, intellectuals feel uneasy. This recently happened with New Labour in Britain. In Brazil, this is a permanent phenomenon. In Britain the new ideas were developed by party members and intellectuals, but soon after the

Labour Party won the 1997 election, intellectuals started to be critical.
[. . .]

Why? Because governments, in order to govern, are supposed to
deal with practical issues, and to make compromises in order to
address them, while intellectuals do not need to compromise; because
politicians' legitimate objective is getting and exerting political power,
while academics are concerned with the advancement of knowledge.
And, third, because politicians are more pragmatic than average intellectuals are.

Thus, when a social democratic party gets to power, its fate will soon
be to be accused of betraying the "left's ideals," or "socialist ideals."
Censure of this kind always existed. Before, the communists accused
the social democrats of betrayal; now the old left and idealistic academics do the same in relation to the new left. There are, however,
major differences between the two movements. Divergent views
between the new and the old left are less pronounced than they were
when the divide was between social democrats and communists. And,
second, the new left is a more viable political alternative to the right
than the old social democracy was.

[. . .]

There are, however, similarities between the new left and the new
right. They may be attributable to the fact that both dispute the center.
Besides, the precedence gained by markets over the state in resource
allocation is a lasting one. The political pendulum may already have
started to move in the direction of more equality and to some industrial policy, but it will not return to the state planning the whole
economy. It will plan its own expenditures, and it will regulate markets,
instead of being a substitute for markets. These facts make people say
that the new left in government follows the lead of the new right. As
a matter of fact, the new left learned with the new right, and now, in
power, it is transforming what it learned into its own terms, while the
pendulum again starts to move to the left. A similar phenomenon took
place in the 1930s. Then the crisis was of the market. The lead was taken
by the left, or by the progressives, like Keynes and Roosevelt. The right,
in order to be able to win elections and recover power, was constrained
to learn with the left, and adopted many of the policies the left parties
originally implemented when in government.

Two factors limit the decision making of the new left when it
becomes a viable power alternative. First, the new left is supposed to
conquer the political center. It already counts upon its supporters in the

left. Its problem is to take over the center from the right. To do that, it has to moderate its proposals, it has to have rather a discourse of consensus than a discourse of conflict. This always was true, but it is even truer in our times, when the middle class has become so large and pervasive.

Second, the new left is supposed to abide by economic constraints. There is an ingrained propensity among critics as well as patrons of the left in identifying it with state expenditure and budget deficits – an identification that has some historical support but makes little sense. Macroeconomic fundamentals are there to be respected. One may respect them in a dumb way, as if they were articles of faith, or in a smart and creative way. The really good economists and policymakers are the ones able to do the second thing, but this has nothing to do with left and right: there are competent and incompetent economists on the right and on the left.

Among the macroeconomic fundamentals, one with which the left is supposed to be especially careful is the security and profitability of investments. The veto power capitalists have on economic policies derives from the fact that they will invest or not depending on their confidence in the institutions and in the administration. Capitalists will only invest if they can expect reasonable and relatively secure rates of return on their investments. As the new left has learned well, there is no viable government if capitalists are not investing.

[. . .]

[In the new perspective] the individual has a major role. Equality is not any longer seen by the new left as equality of income and wealth, but as equality of opportunity. [. . .]

Yet the equality of opportunity to which the new left refers should not be confused with the "American dream." In this case, equality of opportunity is seen as intrinsic to American society, something that market forces and democracy, just corrected for racial discrimination, automatically provides. In new left terms, equality of opportunity is to be pursued by public policy in a deliberate form, in all areas of society. Equality of opportunity starts with offering effectively equal opportunities of access to education and health. It obviously involves the active elimination of all kinds of discrimination – gender, ethnic, racial, religious – but it is supposed to go further than that.

[. . .]

To be achieved, these values require adequate means. They require a strong civil society and a strong state, active and free markets, and good governments, i.e., governments that are able to take the right decisions at the right moment, and that are able to manage the state apparatuses in an efficient and effective way. Thus, when the new left demands efforts towards deepening democracy and citizens' rights, in rebuilding state capacity, in freeing while regulating markets, and in creating an adequate technical and political environment for competent policymaking, it is being consistent with its major political objectives.

New left and globalization

Globalization is a central problem for the new left. A usual assertion of the new right is that globalization made social democracy a phenomenon of the past, because the social and economic policies it proposed rested on the capacity of sovereign states to limit the free movement of capitals. Since the state, according to this vision, lost capacity in relation to this, it follows that active macroeconomic policies and welfare policies, both intended to limit the scope of markets, have no role any longer in a contemporary world. And the new right concludes (in this case fully in agreement with the old left): if the new left acknowledges these new realities and dutifully adopts monetarist macroeconomic policies and opts for flexible markets, it ceases to be left; it is a watered down new right, disguised neo-liberalism.

To this allegation the new left has two answers. First, it strongly rejects the "new realities," the unfettered dominion of markets that globalization is said to have brought about. The new social democratic parties may have different views in relation to globalization, but they all accept Lionel Jospin's recent statement, that globalization does not make the state powerless: "We fully recognize globalization. But we don't see its manifestations as inevitable."[2] [. . .] The state indeed has lost some macroeconomic autonomy due to globalization in exchange rate policy matters. Given that in the global economy capital flows are huge and fast, the exchange rate will either float, or will be firmly pegged to a strong currency, leaving national economic authorities with little room for active policymaking in this area. In other areas, however, national states conserve a substantial autonomy. The state has many and major roles to perform. If well-governed, state institutions and policies may have a substantial positive impact on the economy and society.

Second, the new left rejects the proposed substitution of "flexible markets" – the euphemism for unfettered markets – for the welfare state. It is not opposed to markets, the spirit of enterprise, profits, and individual incentives. It is hostile to dogmatic pro-market views. It affirms the permanent possibility of regulating markets, including the labor market. It asserts that a well regulated market will, in the long run, produce a kind of social solidarity that more than compensates for some shirking on the part of workers. There is a trade-off here, but this trade-off proved, till now, favorable to the Continental model of social democracy, when compared with the more individualist Anglo-American liberalism.

The new social democratic parties do not fully agree about the social and economic consequences of globalization. On this subject, France and Germany are more critical, United States and Britain, less, if not supportive. Giddens, for instance, says that the new left "takes a positive attitude towards globalization, although not an uncritical one. Globalization is not the prime source of new inequalities."[3] Giddens' last phrase is correct: the acceleration of technological progress, increasing the demand for skilled people and decreasing the demand for non-skilled labor, the rise in the number of single mothers, and the rise in the number of economically successful childless people are, as Giddens himself emphasizes, the prime causes. But if one understands globalization as the dominion of uncontrolled markets, there is little doubt that markets are usually prone to promote insecurity at all levels of society, and concentrate rather than redistribute income within each nation and among nations. [. . .]

For the new right globalization is an opportunity; for the old left, a threat; for the new left, a challenge. The new right sees globalization as an opportunity for further international integration of the dominant elites in each country. For the new left the challenge involved in globalization is clear. It will not refuse competition, as the old left wants, but it will try to increase the national industries' capacity to compete. [. . .]

Globalization severely limits the autonomy of highly indebted countries. Capital flow volatility is a major concern for these countries, particularly when they insist upon accumulating trade and current account deficits to be financed by foreign savings. The best way to confront the globalization challenge is to reduce foreign indebtedness by achieving substantial trade surpluses. But this will only be possible if developing countries are committed to increase state capacity, to achieve fiscal balance, to create stable institutions. The loss of state capacity that has taken place in the last twenty years is not, primarily, a consequence of globalization, but of the endogenous crisis of the state. Thus, it is not a permanent deprivation, as globalization apologists affirm, but a transitional one that will be overcome as the crisis of the state is overcome.

[. . .]

The social contract that emerged from World War II is not exhausted, contrary to what the new right insistently claims. It is being challenged by technological progress, by the crisis of the state, and by globalization. Now, the response to the challenge is change: social change, institutional change. Thus, labor contracts are being restructured and other institutions reformed. Given the overall high levels of productivity, coupled with a relatively even distribution of social goods, that the social democratic compact achieved in Europe, there is no reason for the advanced social democracies to acquiesce in the radical changes neo-liberals propose.

Neo-liberals are not any more able to sell their ideas in the advanced countries. But, with the support of local elites, they remain relatively dominant in the developing countries, particularly in Latin America. They have been successful in leading most countries to privatize and liberalize their economies to an extent developed countries did not follow. They are not being so successful in making labor contracts much more flexible, nor in dismantling the poorly established, already existing welfare systems. But they still represent a threat, which only a new left, emerging or about to emerge in these countries, will be able to neutralize.

Development reconsidered

The distinction between left and right, besides having a historical character, left and right changing over time, depends on the stage of economic growth of each country. There are substantial differences between what a new left may be in Latin America, when compared with the one existing in, for instance, Europe.

First, the left and the right, in order to conquer the political center, are usually supposed to be more nationalist than the advanced countries, since they have yet to build a nation and a state – a task that has already been achieved by the developed nations. How nationalist should the left be? The old left has a negative view of nationalism, assuming that the country is surrounded by imperialist powers. It has a general attitude "against" advanced countries, viewed as "imperial-ist states," and wants to close the country to foreign influence rather than negotiate mutual and conflicting interests. The new left, on its part, rejects the view that the national interests of developed and devel-oping countries are always contradictory, but does not believe – as the new right usually does – that they are always the same. Instead of a general attitude "against" or "in favor" of advanced countries, the national interest is to be assessed in each case.

Again, it will be easy for the old left out of power (and also for the intellectual left which is by definition out of power) to criticize – a cri-tique that only can be made by those who do not hold office. If a politi-cal party with old nationalist ideas wins national elections, it will have to live with international capitalism; and it will soon realize that the existing constraints in running a developing country are greater than it could imagine. The constraints will be particularly strong if the country is highly indebted, but even for the developing countries that have comfortable international balances, the global economy's con-straints will always be there.

If the country is highly indebted, the confidence of international markets will be required. This is an objective constraint that govern-ments in developing countries face. But it is a constraint that can be faced in three different ways. It can be faced as the right does: affirm-ing that globalization has reduced substantially the autonomy of the national states, rejoicing in that, and happily engaging in the "confi-dence building game." It can be approached like the old left, which ineffectually denounces the fact when it is out of government, or engages in populist politics when it transitorily achieves political power. And, third, globalization may be lived with, but not overesti-mated or accepted as the will of God.

For the new left in developing countries, globalization as a real phenomenon should be clearly distinguished from globalization as ideology – the ideology of definitive loss of state autonomy. The new left sees the loss of state autonomy as a transitory phenomenon. The fiscal crisis of the state, the crisis of strategies of state intervention, and the crisis of the bureaucratic form of managing the state, reduces state capacity. As soon as this crisis is overcome, state autonomy will be recaptured. When someone explains the loss of state autonomy in terms of globalization, he or she is suggesting a permanent change. Wherever the explanation is based on the idea of a crisis, the alleged constraints to state autonomy are transitory. The state will always face constraints, as everything does, but not new or overwhelming con-straints, as neo-liberals claim. This kind of interpretation supplies the left with a major assignment: to rebuild the state institutions, to overcome the state's crisis.

Acceptance of globalization as the unfettered dominance of markets leads the right, in the developing countries, to engage in the "confidence building game." By this I mean the uncritical adoption of the economic policies that officials in Washington (i.e., the G-7 governments), and in New York (the international financial markets) believe the country should adopt. It is a game that will most likely be headed for disaster, unless we assume that Washington and New York have a monopoly of universal economic policy wisdom . . . If they don't, if they often recommend mistaken policies, given, on one side, their interests and ideological constraints, and, on the other, their limited knowledge of local conditions, which are permanently changing, the only alternative for developing countries' governments will be to decide according to their own judgment.

Is it possible to achieve confidence in this way, not always accepting Washington's and New York's advice? The new right and the old left say "no," for different reasons: the new right, because it believes the elites in developed countries are almost always correct; the old left, because it believes that Washington and New York control the fate of developing countries. In fact, the new left argues, it is possible to achieve confidence without necessarily following the "Washington consensus." It is not an easy task, as it is not simple to govern capitalism in a more competent way than capitalists do. But one should remember that elites – particularly politicians, officials, and financial agencies – in the advanced countries are rational and pragmatic people. They may offer some resistance to initiatives which do not meet with their initial approval, but eventually what is important to them are results.

A final difference. New social democratic parties in Europe are already looking for effective equality of opportunity at all levels, starting with the educational one. Equality is not achieved, but it is not a dream. In contrast, in Latin America economic inequality still looms large. Social democrats in the region are far from being able to speak in realistic terms about equality of opportunity.

Some distinctions

The policies that the new left is adopting [. . .] go ahead with [. . .] necessary market-oriented reforms (for instance, trade liberalization, privatization of competitive industries, introduction of managerial public administration). The new left believes more in the market than the state as a coordinating agent of the economy, but it is not dogmatically pro-market as is the new right. And it still attributes to the state a major role. The state exists not to replace markets and entrepreneurs, but to regulate markets and protect property rights, maintain macroeconomic stability, create an appropriate climate for investment and growth, promote science and technology, foster national competitiveness, guarantee a minimum income, provide basic education, health and culture for all and protect the environmental and the cultural inheritance of the country. Yet, these roles will be differently performed in a developed as compared with a developing country.

In Latin America, and particularly in Brazil, it is possible to discern clear distinctions between the new and the old left, and between the new left and new right. I will ignore the old right, not because it has fully disappeared, but for the sake of simplicity. In synthesis, the old left in Brazil is corporatist and statist, while the new left is pro-market and is committed to reform and to rebuild the state. The new right is radically pro-market, and involved in the confidence building game.

I shall specify some of these differences in the form of questions: Who controls the new left political parties? Does the state have a central role or not? What is needed to reform the state apparatus? Which organizations are supposed to provide the social and scientific services financed by the state? How to reform social security? Which kind of macroeconomic policy is to be adopted?

The criteria and the differences are portrayed in Table 1 on page 368. I will not go over all of them. Some have already been referred to. To a certain extent they are self-explanatory. I will emphasize rather arbitrarily some that I have not yet discussed or that are worthy of some additional explanation.

Party control. It remains restricted to elites. The old left was never able to change this. Only recently there have been signals in this direction, as civil society assumes an increasing role. The left just added to the existing elites – capitalist and bureaucratic elites – two kinds of bureaucratic elite: unions leaders in the private sector and in the civil service, and apparatchiks in the political parties. In Brazil the old left parties remain in control of sizable sectors of the state bureaucracy, of the new professional middle class, and of union leaders. The new left parties are mostly supported by the new professional middle class, associated with progressive capitalists – a concept that is quite elastic. The new right parties are supported mainly by big business. All, obviously, strive to involve the workers and the poor.

State reform. The old left is not interested in reforming the state. It would like to have it large and bureaucratic. The new right under-

Table I   Old and New Left and New Right in Developing Countries

Criteria	Old left	New left	New right
Party control	Bureaucrats	New middle class	Business elites
Role of the state	Central	Complementary	Secondary
State reform	Remain bureaucratic and large	Change to managerial	Downsize
Execution of basic social services	Directly by the state	By public non-state organizations	By private business firms
Financing of basic social services	By the state	By the state	Private
Social security (basic and complementary)	State assured	State assured basic social security	Privately assured
Macroeconomic policy	Populist	neo Keynesian	Neoclassical
Globalization	Threat	Challenge	Benefit

stands reform as liberalization and privatization, or just as downsizing. For the new left to reform the state means to rebuild it, to increase state capacity, to recover public savings as a means of overcoming its financial crisis, and to promote managerial reform. It means also to redefine the role of the state, giving to organizations of civil society a larger role, be it in the production of social and scientific services, or in exerting social control.

Managerial reform means devolving authority to decentralized units to be directed by a new kind of official: people with managerial skills. It means controlling decentralized units through agreed outcomes rather than through detailed procedures. But the new left is not just concerned with reforming institutions, it is convinced that improvement of day-to-day public services is vital. Tony Blair, for instance, often says that the emphasis of his administration is on delivering real progress in public services. [. . .]

Managerial reform is only possible in democratic regimes when civil society plays a double role. It supplies social services on a competitive basis, and it exerts social control. The state should transfer to the public non-state sector (or non-profit sector) a good deal of responsibility for the provision of services, such as those involving many schools, hospitals, or research institutes, but keep its social democratic role as main provider of funds for these activities. The assumption is that, being competitive, such agencies will be more efficient than state agencies, and being public (oriented to public ends) they will be more reliable than private enterprises in providing services in which information is limited, and trust is important, given the core human values involved. Basic education, health, and a minimum income should remain financed by the state, since they presuppose or express universal citizenship rights. In other words, if managerial reform means decentralization and devolution, it means also control of outcomes by officials and politicians in the strategic core of the state, and social control by civil society.

Third, state reform means strengthening democratic institutions. Efforts should not be limited to representative democracy, but include direct forms of democracy, particularly the ones that involve social control by NGOs and other forms of active social capital. In this regard, committees and associations formed with the aim of providing social services in the areas of education, health, crime protection, public transportation and poverty alleviation are particularly important.

Fourth, state reform means creating institutions able to protect what might be called "republican rights," i.e., the right every citizen has that public resources, be they the historical-cultural, environmental, or economic, be used for public ends. For a long time we have been defending civil rights against a powerful state; more recently it became important to defend the state against powerful citizens. Since state revenues became high as a proportion of GDP in all countries, rent-seeking, the capture of the state for private objectives, became increasingly dangerous, and the need to protect republican rights pressing.

Social security. Here the distinction between the old left, which wants pensions state-guaranteed, and the new right, which favors privatization, is simple. More complex is the new left view, which favors state guarantees for a basic income in old age, while the complementary pension system would be private. The left, old and new, wants the basic pension system financed according to a cash system, while the

right, repeating wise economists' counseling, favors a complete capi-
talization system, Chilean style. Finally the old left, given its corporatism, defends the special (and privileged) pension system for civil
servants, while the new left and the new right aim at making it more
similar to the pension system of private workers. A significant point is
the fact that the only countries that have fully adopted the right's prescription are developing countries: Chile and Bolivia. The developed
countries have not adopted these prescriptions, and almost certainly
will not do so in the future. First, because they know that, in the end,
the state should guarantee a basic pension system. Second, because,
when the state is involved, it makes little sense to develop capitaliza-
tion systems, since the state is not a competent agent in managing the
financial assets backing pension funds.

This "anomaly," however, is not at all restricted to social security
systems. In some Southern countries, privatization or trade liberalization went much farther than in the North. I already referred to the confidence building game. It is consistent with an old saying: subjects are
often more royalist than the king.

Economic policy. The old left imagines itself to be Keynesian, but
actually it is populist and interventionist. Often in the past it got
involved in the "populist cycle," that starts with the over-evaluation of
the currency, leading to higher inflation and higher salaries, and eventually ending in a balance of payment crisis and devaluation. The new
right hopes to be modern, but in fact is *laissez-faire* and engaged in
the confidence building game, which also easily leads to balance of
payment crises. The new left is supposed to think independently, but
is not always successful. It is essentially Keynesian when macroeconomic policy is in hand, but it is ready to use mainstream microeconomic tools to understand how a market economy works or should
work. It assumes that markets are imperfect, that asymmetry of information is pervasive, that negative and positive externalities are
everywhere, but still believes that the market is a more efficient
resource-allocating mechanism than the state. Only in limited cases is
the state supposed to intervene in resource allocation. But it believes
that markets are ineffective in distributing income. Thus, in this area,
and in science and technology, it reserves a major role for the state. It
does not believe, as the old left does, that increasing taxes is always a
good solution, but rejects the tax reduction or tax flattening that the
dogmatic right proposes.

The new right proposes tax cuts, but, when in power in Latin
America, it will not reduce taxes. In the North there is a lot of fuss about
reducing taxes, but, with a few exceptions, the right is not able to put
into practice what it preaches. Eventually taxes are maintained at exist-

ing levels. What does happen, when tax reform is achieved by the new right, is that taxes turn less and less progressive, a greater emphasis being put on indirect taxes. This happened in the developed countries, but soon found a limit and taxes remain progressive. In some developing countries, although direct taxes are dismally small and inheritance taxes absent, tax reforms tend often to follow the neo-liberal model. Again, subjects are more royalist than the king.

Can the new left make a difference?

I hope the distinctions are clear. Old left intellectuals remain uncomfortable with new left policies, given the fact that the new left ideas are connected with real government. Moreover, governments will never fit the model as outlined here. They will follow these prescriptions only in broad terms. In practice they will make mistakes and compromises, or their policies will be the outcome of political coalitions. My discussion concentrates not on actual governments but on political ideas. There are major questions I have not discussed. Is a new left government more prone to be a good government? Can it make a difference? Some are pessimistic about the capabilities of governments in both of these respects. I think they are wrong. If properly applied, the ideas of the new left can both renew state power and help use it to achieve core social and economic goals.

Notes

1   John Gray, 'The Undoing of Conservatism,' in John Gray and David Willetts, *Is Conservatism Dead?* (London: Profile Books), p. 3.
2   Quoted in Bresser-Pereira, 'Modern Socialism,' in *Lionel Jospin* (London: Fabian Society, 1999), p. 9.
3   Anthony Giddens, 'Why the Old Left is Wrong on Equality,' *New Statesman*, 25 October 1999, pp. 25–7 (p. 27).

26

The Third Way and the International Order

Ethan B. Kapstein

In a world of increasing trade flows and capital mobility, even good policymaking aimed at improving the lives of working people is constrained by external economic forces. This naturally leads us to a consideration of the role that international institutions can play in shaping labor-market outcomes. Organizations such as the World Bank and the International Monetary Fund loom large in the economies of several of their member countries, and their effect on the international economic system goes way beyond their capital base. Through the policy advice they articulate, and the signals they send about national economic performance, their influence ripples broadly throughout the world's capital markets, and in turn throughout labor markets.

It is ironic that these same organizations often make the claim that responsibility for social welfare rests squarely with the nation-state and its capacity for "good governance." Thus, the IMF states that a country's long-term per capita income levels are determined by its "own policies and resources." Yet at the same time, the Fund tells us that "globalization may be expected to increasingly constrain governments' choices of tax structures and tax rates. . . ."[1] If governments lack the power to shape tax policy, it is hard to see what sorts of powers they have over economic performance. These contradictions do not instill much confidence in its capacity for providing sound advice.

To claim that states alone are responsible for their fate in a global economy is disingenuous on several counts. First, it begs the question that if good national policy were enough to ensure good economic outcomes, why were international organizations ever needed, and why are they still needed today? Second, to the extent globalization undermines national policymaking capacity – as the IMF and the World Bank admit it does to some degree – then alternative methods obviously must be found for making good governance a reality. Third, since the benefits of globalization are not evenly distributed among nations, international mechanisms are needed to ensure that all players gain sufficiently to keep them in the game. Finally, since globalization requires international policy coordination and information-sharing with respect to the activities of both state and nonstate actors, efforts at international governance are needed by definition.

These points are not made in defense of an argument that what we need is world government. International institutions, including the most advanced among them, such as the European Union, are fundamentally creatures of their member states. But member states can use these organizations in any number of ways. In some cases, state elites exploit international organizations as a way of escaping domestic political confrontations, claiming that the government's hands are tied on this or that issue. European leaders frequently make this argument with respect to Brussels, and of course they will use it about monetary policy as the European Central Bank and single currency become operational. Similarly, the International Monetary Fund serves this purpose for developing-country leaders who seek to make economic-policy reforms in the face of domestic opposition. In these cases, the international organization in question seems to be serving the policy goals of mobile capital rather than of immobile labor. For this reason, critics of international institutions frequently point to a democratic deficit between them and the citizens of their member countries.

It would be incorrect, however, to take the extreme position that international financial organizations have no concern with the fate of working people and only serve, say, the interests of multinational corporations and banks. If for nothing more than Real-politik concerns with political stability, organizations such as the IMF can go only so far in pushing for policy reform. Russia comes to mind as a good case study of a country that continued to receive significant IMF assistance largely because of its geostrategic importance – despite its failure to adopt economic reforms. In the European Union, too, the bureaucrats in Brussels can only adopt communitywide directives in light of what the political traffic will bear.

Still, the question remains as to whose interests are being served at the international level, and what the distribution of costs and benefits from given policy decisions looks like. The evidence suggests that mobile capital is the big winner to date from policies aimed at promoting globalization, while unskilled workers are the losers. These economic outcomes are a reflection of relative political power, and the simple politics is that working people face a serious problem of collective action at the international level. This means that as policies are determined in arenas beyond the nation-state, it becomes increasingly difficult for workers to make their voices heard. As mentioned earlier, transnational union activity has been relatively weak during the postwar era, and international competition has been successfully used as a tool for dividing and conquering workers. This inability of labor to articulate common international goals means that it is harder for multilateral organizations to understand and respond to its concerns. Contrast this with the case of mobile capital, which can state with great clarity its demand for macroeconomic stability, balanced budgets, free-trade policies, and so forth.

[We should] therefore seek to provide policy recommendations that give voice to the least advantaged. In a phrase, international organizations should play a more positive and active role in ensuring that fairness, no less than efficiency considerations, shapes global economic policies.[2] Such policies are in the long-run interests of all those who seek to advance the globalization experiment and believe in its contributions to world peace and prosperity. By helping the world's unskilled workers realize their talents and live in dignity, we all promote the causes of productivity, of stability, and of justice.

As the allies began the liberation of Western Europe from Nazi terror in the summer of 1944, a group of international financial bureaucrats from the victorious powers met in Bretton Woods, New Hampshire, to shape the postwar economic order. While their grand design of free trade and financial stability would never be fully realized in a battle-scarred world that would soon enter the Cold War, they nonetheless gave the global economy its basic shape and vision. Simply put, that economy would combine the utilitarian, wealth-producing benefits of free multilateralism with the social benefits of the welfare state. It is a model that served industrial-world labor reasonably well for much of the postwar era, although we may question how well it has done by workers in the developing countries.

Today, the foundations of that structure are beginning to show their age. The world has learned to live with flexible exchange rates, but whether or not that has improved or impaired its health is a matter of some debate. While correlation is not causation, the shift from fixed to flexible rates that occurred in the 1970s also saw the beginning of much slower rates of industrial-world investment and growth, and higher unemployment and inequality, which have remained with us to the present day.[3] Tremendous capital mobility (threatened and real), never anticipated to such an extent by the postwar architects, is now emerging. Increasing trade flows are raising the specter of zero-sum international labor competition. With these developments, unskilled workers are becoming fearful of their futures – as well they might in the midst of unemployment, poverty, inequality, and insecurity.

If the great powers wish to restore confidence in the global economy, they would do well to consider a new Bretton Woods conference. The purpose of the meeting would be to address the sorts of questions [following]: How are workers doing, and what can be done to improve their lot? Is the current financial system consistent with growth and stability, or must a new order be contemplated? This latter issue would seem especially pertinent as Western Europe introduces its new common currency.

Among the most significant issues that a labor-oriented Bretton Woods conference would have to address is migration policy. As even the World Bank admits, while myriad international agreements have aimed at promoting capital mobility and free trade, "international migration of people in search of work is the laggard in this story."[4] People are no more free to migrate than they were a generation ago, and much less so in many cases than their grandparents. The role of labor mobility and migration in the global economy is an issue of the first order, and it must be treated in the interest of assuring working people the greatest possible set of opportunities. Again it must be emphasized that there is little point for an individual to invest in education, training, and self-improvement if no jobs are available. At the same time, he must recognize that societies may have legitimate reasons for limiting immigration.

Yet a second issue on which a new Bretton Woods should seek agreement is how to give workers a voice in existing international institutions. In the original postwar order, the planners had contemplated the creation of an International Trade Organization that would concern itself with both commercial and employment policies. With the failure to establish such an entity, trade and labor concerns went on separate paths, but workers have unfortunately stumbled into a dead end. Mechanisms for ensuring labor representation at the International Monetary Fund, the World Bank, and other such institutions would be one way to promote a more equitable global order, and a possible model might be found at the Organization for Economic Cooperation and Development, which has done perhaps the most of any multilateral organization to solicit labor input in its deliberations.

A third item for this meeting's agenda should be consideration of an international social minimum. This does not mean that we can expect agreement on a global minimum wage or anything of the sort. Instead, it means that each country should be responsible for defining what constitutes a decent standard of living for *all* citizens, including their access to education and health care, their working wages, and their entitlement to social safety nets. An international organization, perhaps the World Bank, should be charged with producing an annual "social policy report," just as the International Monetary Fund produces studies of macroeconomic performance in its member countries. Gaps in providing the social minimum should be highlighted, to become targets for national economic reform efforts and international assistance. [. . .]

In thinking about a future Bretton Woods, we should recall that the last one only occurred following a generation of world conflict and depression that enveloped the major powers. Today, war and economic deprivation have, in large measure, been removed from the global economy's core countries, and instead they fester in the developing-world periphery, where, tragically, they draw less attention. What this means is that a sense of crisis is lacking in world capitals, making it unlikely that any bold initiatives will be forthcoming anytime soon. In the interests of political reality, then, the following paragraphs offer some recommendations that fall between a full-scale Bretton Woods-type conference on the one hand and the sort of marginal fixes now popular on the other.

Trade and labor policy have been on separate tracks since the end of World War II. The General Agreement on Tariffs and Trade, and its successor World Trade Organization, focused narrowly on reducing trade barriers, while the International Labor Organization was responsible for advancing the cause of core labor standards. That dualistic approach has now run its course, and it is time to join the issues.

The great fear that policymakers and economists usually express on this matter is that tying trade agreements to core labor standards (i.e., freedom of association, collective bargaining, removal of hiring discrimination, and the prohibition on using child and forced labor) will lead world trade down the slippery slope of trade protection. The failure of countries to achieve international labor standards, it is claimed, could be used as an excuse to halt trade with them, or it could raise their labor costs to the point where they are no longer competitive.

But these arguments are absurd for several reasons. First, a set of core international labor standards, promulgated by the International Labor Organization, *does* exist. Second, international trade is not a right but a privilege, and countries that seek to barter and truck with the community of nations should accept the common standards that exist. Third, the possibility of free trade and membership in the World Trade Organization *should* be held out as a carrot to those states that currently violate core labor standards; if it is not, what incentives can be offered?

The international system has often responded with sanctions to countries exhibiting "bad behavior" of various kinds. India and Pakistan were slapped with trade sanctions by the United States following their nuclear tests in 1998. Iraq has been the target of a United Nations embargo since 1990, and Iran has enjoyed only limited access to world markets since its Islamic Revolution. Other countries that remain ostracized include Cuba, North Korea, and Libya. In short, sanctions are widely used but for some reason have not been applied to states that violate core labor standards.

The world trading system can put great pressure on countries that fail to adopt these standards. Countries such as China would find their economic opportunities severely limited. But China is a case where the trading system seems to be basically operated by and for the large multinational corporations, which consistently reject tying trade agreements to labor rights.

We should note that the vigorous pursuit of core labor standards by the international community implies the acceptance of new, associated responsibilities. A country that is willing to abolish child labor, for example, may need foreign assistance to expand its school system. That is the sort of collective response that a world community bent on a just form of globalization should be willing and able to make.

At the same time that countries pursue free-trade agreements, they must also be sensitive to how trade will affect working people, and they will need to establish programs that assist displaced workers. Indeed, compensation should be another core labor standard. Traditionally, such compensation programs have been solely a national responsibility. But with a growing number of developing countries and transition economies entering the trading system, international assistance on this issue could be of tremendous value, and could help maintain political support for continued globalization. Again, it is important to emphasize that if the benefits of trade are so great, why not be generous to those on the losing end of this policy change?

Trade and finance cross borders with relative ease, workers less so, and governments not at all. That tension is at the heart of all efforts aimed at greater international supervision over multinational activities. International policy coordination over multinational business has traditionally been an information-sharing exercise, but increasingly it is becoming a supervisory activity seeking to prevent international competition from sparking a destructive race to the bottom in which countries end up relieving themselves of all tax and regulatory authority. With the recent financial crisis in East Asia, the calls for tightened control over cross-border capital flows have grown in intensity and volume.

378   Ethan B. Kapstein

Already there is a significant amount of activity in this area. Banks and investment firms face the common standards set by the Basle Committee of Bank Supervisors and the International Organization of Securities Commissions with respect to capital adequacy, and the European Union is responsible for regional regulation over such areas as competition and antitrust policy.[5] The Organization for Economic Cooperation and Development (OECD) and the United Nations Conference on Trade and Development (UNCTAD) have also established codes of conduct for multinational enterprises regarding consumer protection and the like. Three issues of rising international importance, however, concern worker rights, capital controls, and international taxation. [. . .]

In the absence of international agreements linking trade and labor standards, an alternative or complementary path would be to establish minimum codes of conduct regarding how multinationals treat their workers. These codes would include the core ILO labor standards and, it can be argued, provisions regarding a living wage and compensation in the event of worker displacement. Efforts have already been made along these lines by minority shareholders of some major corporations – almost always over the objections of the boards of directors – but they have generally failed to win the needed votes at shareholder meetings. Governments, nongovernmental organizations, and international organizations could thus play a useful role in shaping these standards, publicizing them, and monitoring enterprise performance. Indeed, in the absence of positive government action in this direction at the national level, code-setting could provide an interesting case of how NGOs and international organizations might form transnational alliances for the benefit of labor interests.

With respect to portfolio investment or "hot money" flows, it appears that governments and international organizations are again giving serious thought to capital controls of some type, through either tax policy or quantitative restrictions on inflows. With respect to tax policy, perhaps the most prominent idea is that of economist James Tobin, who suggests a tax on all cross-border financial transactions, in the hope of decreasing such flows and making them more manageable. Other approaches include graduated taxes according to the length of time in which an investor keeps his money inside a given country. The purpose of such graduated policies, which have been adopted with perhaps the greatest success in Chile, is to penalize short-term portfolio investors and reward long-term direct investment.

The national orientation of these measures, however, may mean that they will lose their effectiveness over time. States will be tempted to use differing policies on capital controls, including taxation, to the advantage of their domestic economies and financial institutions. Since large banks and investment firms tend to have significant voice in domestic policymaking, given their prominent role in economic activity and money creation, officials are sensitive to their competitive concerns and will develop regulatory policies that are in their interests.[6] In addition, monetary and financial policies tend to be obscure to many voters, and labor often has failed to understand how such policies will affect workers. Decisions over capital and labor markets thus become dissociated, often to labor's disadvantage.

These comments suggest that several problems associated with capital mobility must now be dealt with at the international level. One of the most prominent in light of the East Asian crisis concerns its destabilizing effects on national economies. And there is increasing discussion of international financial cooperation aimed at, for example, supervising or even limiting the cross-border loans made by banks and other financial institutions.[7] Since labor has been hit so hard by these destabilizing effects, its representatives should have a seat at the policy table while any decisions in this area are made. Unfortunately, the center of action in this debate has been the International Monetary Fund, which to date has hardly shown itself to be sensitive to workers' concerns or open to their participation in its deliberations.

A second and potentially more significant issue in terms of reshaping the international political economy concerns international taxation of mobile capital. As the public-finance literature shows, the effective tax rate on mobile capital is zero. And the data demonstrate that tax rates on mobile capital are falling. While tax competition has been used by states in the interest of attracting direct investment, it has had many negative effects as well, including declining revenues for government coffers. Tax competition can easily lead to a race to the bottom among states in which mobile capital gets away with paying virtually nothing to any government; that suggests a possible role for international coordination in this area.[8]

[. . .]

If we know one thing about the aftermath of an economic crisis, it is that the rich usually get richer and the poor get poorer. In the interests of macroeconomic stability, states often end up cutting those programs that benefit working people and the least advantaged. Further, it seems that interventions by such international organizations as the IMF and the World Bank do little to alter that outcome. To the contrary, the IMF has traditionally only suggested overall targets for budgetary spending; it generally avoids making recommendations with respect to which items should be cut or saved.

Given the economic and moral arguments made in this analysis, it follows that the Bank and the Fund should give greater thought to the distributional consequences of their policy-based lending. They should place more emphasis on the needs of the least advantaged and ensure that spending on education and social welfare programs receive adequate levels of funding. In this regard, the World Bank's announcement that it would seek to create seventy-five million jobs in East Asia through its post-financial-crisis project loans is welcome news indeed.[9] The Bank also said it would give significant attention to poverty alleviation in its program of lending to this troubled region.

Similarly, the International Monetary Fund could take a more aggressive line in advocating for the poor and disadvantaged in its macroeconomic stabilization programs. Slowly, that recognition is dawning on policymakers. U.S. Deputy Secretary of the Treasury Lawrence Summers has said, "If most now agree that macroeconomic reforms took precedence over microeconomic . . . and reducing the size of government took precedence over improving its quality – then it is fair to say that education and other basic social investments were especially ill-served by these biases." He and others are now calling on the IMF and the World Bank to bolster their social-sector lending.[10] In so doing, they should consult with labor, nongovernmental organizations, and other interest groups.

Normally, when we think of international cooperation in health care, it is in terms of humanitarian assistance. That is all to the good, but in fact, good health care is a major contributor to economic performance as well. In the words of World Health Organization Director-General Gro Harlem Brundtland, new research "is making it increasingly clear that ill health leads to poverty in individuals, populations, and nations."[11] By recognizing its contributions to worker productivity and well-being, we can see that health care should be given significant attention by those who would promote the cause of globalization.

Unfortunately, that does not seem to be the case. Around the world, millions of people die each year from a variety of infectious diseases. More than one billion people do not have access to clean water, and nearly two billion lack proper sanitation facilities. At least 840 million people face the anguish of going hungry each day. As a result, in the developing world, nearly one-third of the population is not expected to reach the age of forty.[12] It is hard to develop an economy when large numbers of workers are dying in what should be the prime of life.

These facts seem far removed from the industrial countries, which have made great strides in disease and famine control, environmental protection, and in the provision of basic human needs. But even here, the gap between the haves and the have-nots is dramatic. In the United States, nearly fifty million people have no health insurance. Some urban slums are once again seeing the reemergence of diseases such as tuberculosis, stumping health-care experts who thought these particular enemies had been defeated. Indeed, many American slums have health-care statistics more typical of the third world than the first world.

In most of the post-communist transition economies, the health-care situation verges on the catastrophic. Soviet-style planning left a legacy of environmental devastation that has poisoned two generations, and it will take at least that long to clean up. Alcoholism, drug use, and poor nutrition further contribute to the deadly toll. On top of these problems, poorly paid doctors face a terrible shortage of medical equipment and drugs in outdated hospitals and clinics. Simply stated, living in Eastern Europe and the former Soviet Union is not good for one's health.

These public-health issues should be treated as economic problems for several reasons. First, an unsanitary and polluted environment is a major barrier to one's life chances. People living under these conditions are more likely to become ill and thus less capable of realizing their talents. The result is a waste of human resources. The more that people lose work or education days to illness, the more society as a whole suffers. Work and education represent important investments, and if people are incapacitated, that investment goes to waste.

Second, people and companies are more likely to invest in countries where the health risks are manageable. Where the threat of illness, epidemic, or famine looms large, investors understandably will wish to go elsewhere. Not surprisingly, a strong correlation exists between wealth and health.

Creating a healthy environment, then, would seem to make good economic sense, and this means it ought to receive greater consideration in debates over economic reform, alongside such standard measures as macroeconomic stabilization, privatization, and liberalization. Again, making this case could be the job for new transnational coalitions that join labor unions with health-care experts and environmentalists. Traditionally, health care has been the exclusive province of medical experts and their various national and international institutions, but [. . .] the time may be ripe for new initiatives in this issue-area.

Few public expenditures seem to be more unpopular than foreign aid.[13] In a recent poll, some 66 per cent of Americans responded that "foreign aid spending is too high."[14] They may be right, as even the IMF has concluded that "development aid has not had a significant impact on growth in recipient countries." This is because it had little or no effect on a country's propensity to invest.[15]

Today, foreign aid occupies only a small fraction of both industrial-world and recipient-country budgets. According to the Paris-based Organization for Economic Cooperation and Development, official foreign aid in 1996 totaled just $59.9 billion, down nearly 6 per cent from the previous year. Aid totaled no more than 0.25 per cent of the combined gross domestic product of OECD member states. According to the OECD, this is "the lowest ratio recorded over the nearly thirty years since the United Nations established a goal of 0.70 per cent." While it is true that private-sector investment flows to the developing world have increased during this time, these are not a direct substitute for foreign aid, which has poverty reduction as its focus.

The question then arises: What do governments do with the money they receive? In principle, they could do one of two things: invest it in projects of various kinds (these could range from education to health care to infrastructure), or transfer it to citizens through tax policy or cash payments. Since the IMF and other organizations have found no correlation between aid and investment, this suggests they transfer it. Then we must ask, to whom?

In a recent study, economist Peter Boone raised this very question. He found that, rather than transfer money to the poor, governments instead gave it to the regime's wealthy supporters. He found no evidence that aid was used in support of such human-development initiatives as health care or schooling; instead, it went to consumption by elites. This suggests that the problem with aid is that the donor institutions in practice do little to ensure that their funds are being used to help the neediest in target countries.[16]

Rather than abandon aid altogether, however, we should seek to improve its effectiveness. This means working closely with recipient countries to ensure that funds go to education, health care, and development of the social safety net. Contrary to the conventional wisdom, donor and recipient countries are capable of structuring assistance programs that make a material difference to the poor and the least advantaged.

Notes

1   International Monetary Fund, *World Economic Outlook: May 1997* (Washington, DC: IMF, 1997), pp. 70, 80.

2   For a similar argument in the European context, see Fritz Scharpf, "Economic Integration, Democracy and the Welfare State," unpublished manuscript, 1996.

3   Paul Davidson, "Post Keynesian Employment Analysis and the Macroeconomics of OECD Unemployment," *The Economic Journal* 108 (May 1998): 817–31, at 819.

4   World Bank, *World Development Report: 1997*, p. 134.

5   See Ethan B. Kapstein, *Governing the Global Economy: International Finance and the State* (Cambridge, MA: Harvard University Press, 1994).

6   See Kapstein, *Governing the Global Economy*.

7   For an overview, see Barry Eichengreen, "International Financial Cooperation: Lessons and Questions from the Asian Crisis," paper presented at the Meeting on Global Public Goods, United Nations Development Program, 22 June 1998.

8   Vito Tanzi, "Is There a Need for a World Tax Organization?" paper presented at the International Institute of Public Finance, Tel Aviv, Israel, 26–29 August 1996.

9   Jay Solomon, "World Bank Says It Was Wrong on Indonesia," *Wall Street Journal*, 5 February 1998, A17.

10 Lawrence Summers, "Equity in a Global Economy," *Treasury News*, 8 June 1998.

11 Lawrence K. Altman, "Next WHO Chief Will Brave Politics in Name of Science," *New York Times*, 3 February 1998, B10.

12 UNDP, *HDR 1997*, p. 5.

13 This section is drawn from World Bank, *World Development Report: 1997*, p. 140.

14 Robert J. Blendon, et al., "Bridging the Gap Between the Public's and Economists' Views of the Economy," *Journal of Economic Perspectives* 11 (Summer 1997): 105–18, at 113.

15 Tsidi Tsikata, "Aid Effectiveness: A Survey of the Recent Empirical Literature," IMF Paper on Policy Analysis and Assessment, March 1998, p. 1.

16 For an elaboration of this approach to foreign aid, see Peter Boone, "Politics and the Effectiveness of Foreign Aid," *European Economic Review* 40 (1996): 290–329.

27

Humanising Global Capitalism: Which Way Forward?

Michael Edwards

People everywhere dream of better days to come, when poverty is no more, discrimination and violence have been banished for good, the air is clean and all are free to enjoy life to the full. Of course, we all wake up to a very different reality, but that has never stopped us from trying to change it for the better. Utopians apart, we know that we can never have a perfect world, but why can't we find a better balance between economic growth, political freedom, social cohesion and the preservation of what we care for in ourselves and the world around us? In theory this is an easy question to answer, but in practice we have not been able to demonstrate a viable non-capitalist route to sustained economic growth. There is nothing in history to suggest that capitalism is anything but disruptive, dirty and unequal, however many material and technological advances it brings. Yet the alternatives we have tried have turned out even worse (like centrally-planned economies), and the others we still talk about (like co-operative self-reliance) lack a constituency to put them into practice. So we are left with the task of humanising capitalism, that is, preserving the dynamism of markets, trade and entrepreneurial energy while finding better ways to distribute the surplus they create and reshape the processes that produce it.

Economic growth is not sufficient for development, but development needs growth, growth needs markets, and markets always impose costs and inequalities. Does that mean, however, that basketball player Michael Jordan has to earn 31,000 times more for advertising Nike sports shoes than the workers who produce them, despite the fact that should the wages be doubled the cost of production would still fall below US$1 a pair?[1] – or that all the hydroelectricity in Laos has to be produced from large dams and exported to Thailand instead of from a range of large and small ones that do less damage to the environment and bring more benefits to local industry? Of course not! There is plenty of room to manoeuvre in the market economy, and if in exploring it we find more radical alternatives that people will vote for, so much the better. Inequalities result from political decisions about the distribution of gains from economic activity. What is allocated to private consumption, public spending, and social responsibilities is never fixed, and it is democracy's job – not the role of markets – to determine our collective goals and common interests. The journalist Matthew Parris once observed that *'our morality does not mesh with our economic system, but because we need both they cohabit in an awkward marriage based on silence'.*[2] Why settle for silence when an active conversation could make the marriage happier and more fulfilling?

There are three reasons why international co-operation is central to a 'conversation' of this kind. The first is that integrated markets dictate a co-ordinated response to social and environmental questions. Few governments will impose eco-taxation or insist on improved labour standards unless other countries agree to do the same. Second, there is no consensus on how to humanise capitalism, now that the traditional ways of doing so through trade unions, welfare states, a large public sector with extensive market regulation, and expanding, progressive taxation have been eroded. The measures recommended to replace these things, like better education and training or partnerships between the public and private sectors, seem inadequate when set against the inequality-producing power of real markets and the systematic discrimination that is built into current economic models on grounds of gender and age, especially in the global context. There is unlikely to be any universal answer to these questions across so many different national contexts, but we can support each other to find some answers. [. . .] Third, it is hard to have a dialogue when you are starving, and difficult to innovate without a basic level of security, voice and equality of rights. The preconditions for successful 'conversation' have not yet been established in most poor countries. Humanising capitalism is not just a matter of market reform; it means tackling the interlocking structures of social, economic and political power that exclude particular groups of people. As security and voice increase, the possibility of meaningful dialogue grows, and with it the likelihood that people will find solutions that distribute the costs and benefits of change more equally across society. In such a situation, 'short cuts to progress' may still be possible.

'Empowering the poor' is well-worn territory in development debates. [. . .] However, any serious attempt to humanise capitalism depends on changing the ways people use the power they gain, not just for themselves, but also in the service of the common good. [. . .] It is not just a case of regulating systems of power, but transforming them to reproduce a different set of power relations and a new kind of individual: competitive where that makes sense but co-operative where it does not, protective of the environment, committed to an equal sharing of paid and household work, and willing to defend the rights of strangers as fiercely as their own. And that is a much deeper challenge, especially in societies which have yet to reach a minimum level of economic security.

The importance of redistribution

Countries that reduce poverty and inequality while maintaining a high economic growth rate and a reasonable level of peace and social cohesion always make redistribution a priority – by spreading the ownership of assets and opportunities widely through the population. This is especially important in the high-risk economies that are emerging under globalisation, since individuals who do not possess an increasing portfolio of marketable skills will be excluded from higher-wage jobs and the rewards that go with them. The minimum required to make the market economy more inclusive is to guarantee equal access to the opportunities it provides, and that cannot be done where the majority of the population lack the basic wherewithal to participate. Third World countries (especially the agrarian economies of Africa and South Asia) are still characterised by extreme inequalities in the distribution of land, work and other assets, and these inequalities reinforce other forms of oppression based around gender and ethnicity. Without land reform and more equal access to other productive assets there is no possibility of eradicating absolute poverty, broadening the base of market-led growth, or promoting sustainable resource management, since ownership is a precondition for conservation. High levels of inequality make intergroup conflict inevitable and deny people the basic security they need to participate in governance and civic life, so redistribution is much more than an economic measure.

Just under one billion absolutely poor people live in the rural areas of the developing world, and poverty of assets is the prime reason for their condition. Landlessness is actually increasing in countries like Bangladesh, up from 35 per cent of rural households in 1960 to 45 per cent 25 years later, and is especially acute among women. [. . .] In countries that have a large labour surplus, land reform is insufficient; they need activities that expand productivity and the demand for labour simultaneously. Although 'green revolution' techniques can do this, they are often outperformed by low-input farming practices which have the added benefit of conserving soil, water and forests. In cities, access to jobs is the most important requirement, along with a secure claim on property, such as titles registered in a woman's name, not just her husband's.

Equally important are less tangible assets that enable people to bargain, negotiate, and advance their interests. [. . .] Collective action is vital in attacking exclusion, since *'power and privilege do not willingly submit to popular control or market discipline'.*[3] If poor people's voices are excluded from decision making, their interests will be ignored. That is why community organisations and other civic groups are so important. Trade unions are currently out of favour with aid agencies, but they were vital to success in Kerala and East Asia. The Landless Movement in Brazil and the Union of Rubber Tappers led by the murdered activist Chico Mendes achieved huge gains for their members, and there is no reason why unions cannot reinvent themselves to suit a changing world, perhaps as members of wider civil-society alliances which mediate between business and workers. Underlying the ability to organise in any group are the most basic assets of all, such as self-belief, human ingenuity, and independence of thought. *'If people feel good about themselves they can start to create change'* and participate in the fundamental task of defining alternatives – perhaps the *'supreme instrument of power'* as some have called it. Building these less tangible possessions is vital because inequalities based on gender or race can withstand the effects of education, training and even the redistribution of material assets like land and jobs.

At the national level, governments need to prioritise agrarian reform, public intervention to guarantee basic food security and employment on public works, and investment in essential services like health care, education and agricultural extension. These are tried and tested strategies, but they are difficult to sustain in weak economies without international support, and that implies redistribution at the global level through foreign aid. A full-scale attack on inequality is a necessary condition for poverty eradication, but it is far from sufficient. Rising economic participation stimulates competitive behaviour as well as co-operation; increased political participation brings more disagreement as well as consensus; and empowerment strategies may reinforce anti-developmental notions of power over others if they neglect the need for inner transformation. The fact that poor people share in decision making does not mean that the outcome will always be better, even for them. [. . .] We cannot assume that more participation will generate the best results, since people's access to information may be imperfect and the views of one group might have to be overridden in favour of others, as for example when natural resources of value to the broader common interest must be given up by those who own the land on which they sit. As a right, participation is incontestable; as a practice, it is essential in generating more sustainable solutions; but as an alternative paradigm it is unconvincing.

Transforming systems of power

If redistribution is not a sufficient condition for humanising capitalism, how do we make material advancement the handmaiden of much broader social, environmental and personal goals? The answer lies through measures that increase security while encouraging people to surrender at least some of their ambitions to the concerns of others, whether they be present or future generations. Many commentators have observed that co-operation declines as people grow in wealth and status. This produces a *'culture of contentment'* as J. K. Galbraith describes it, and the ebbing away of the *'habits of the heart'*. In these circumstances, rising incomes do not lead to sustainable development; they reinforce competition, exclusion and pollution instead. Addressing this problem requires all systems of power to be regulated and reconstructed in ways which encourage three things: a better distribution of what they deliver, less costly ways of producing it, and more co-operative attitudes which encourage people to set some limits to their self-interest.

Put like this it sounds an impossible task, but lots of experiments are already underway: new forms of business which compete effectively but distribute work and profits more equally; social policies that provide what children need but place less of a burden on women; and formulae for decision making that achieve a less damaging set of trade-offs between growth and the environment. In an era of integrated markets and increasing cross-border influences, mainstreaming these experiments implies co-ordinated action from the local to the global level, but it is the grassroots that provides the foundation for sustainable change. It is here that we can see the impact of decisions in our own lives, and that acts as a powerful incentive to personal responsibility. The UN cannot prevent global warming unless people judge that their own environment has to be protected from their own actions. So the transformations we are searching for should be easier to find in neighbourhoods, local authorities and firms. Humanising capitalism is partly a matter of localising more activity so that we enjoy a new level of intimacy in our jobs, decision making and relations with each other: a connectedness that shows us the destructive consequences of our uncooperative actions. There can be no escape into blaming anonymous corporations or governments if firms, schools and communities have the wherewithal to govern themselves. That does not mean limiting our horizons to the local, which would be a recipe for stagnation, but self-reliance need not reject outside resources or contacts unless they actively erode autonomy and choice. However, since these are threatened by unaccountable power in a globalising economy, grassroots action must be strongly connected to a supportive framework at the national and international levels if it is to thrive. What does this mean for the way we practice economics, politics, and social policy?

Do we mean business?

In economic terms, the most importance structures of power are markets and firms, and if we are serious about humanising capitalism that is where we should begin. Complex societies are best governed by feedback from individuals to decision makers through prices – which means markets – and votes. But prices must reflect social and environmental costs if the common interest is to be protected, and markets must be tied down to their signalling role and not extended into governance or social life. At present, some resources (like air) are not priced at all, and others (like oil) are priced without regard to their scarcity, so markets will not necessarily correct destructive practices over time. Labour rights (like all human rights) are too important to be left to the price mechanisms, especially when – as is universal – markets are permeated by power relations of various kinds.

Fortunately, markets can be influenced to work in different ways. At one extreme that means attacking monopolies and oligopolies so that the price mechanism can operate more efficiently. At the other it means a completely different set of market principles, like Islamic economics in which interest is outlawed. The most likely situation lies between these two extremes, when social and environmental goals are inserted into the mechanisms of the market as we know them. That can happen in a number of ways.

First, access to information among consumers and producers on how things are made and what they really cost can be increased – the foundation for ethical consumption, investment and trading. Good citizens do not switch off their citizenship when they go shopping or arrive at work, and few people are *'interested in wearing clothes made by exploited workers'* as the US Labor Committee put it in 1997. Consumers cannot make these judgements unless they know how goods are produced, so that means more labelling systems like the 'Fairtrade mark' and footballs that are certified free of exploitative child labour. The information revolution makes fair trade much easier, since purchasers can deal direct with producers over the Internet. Artisans in Guatemala, for example, are already using it to get feedback from consumers in North America on their designs.

This process raises much wider questions about business accountability, though criticisms of corporations are nothing new. As far back as 1909, reformers in the USA demanded that all firms be regulated toward 'constructive goals', with everyone affected by their operations having a say in company decisions (including consumers and employees). Ninety years later this remains a challenge to a system of corporate governance dominated by shareholders, especially large institutions like investment funds which may care little for non-economic goals. An increasing number of businesses are recognising that they must establish decent working conditions for their employees, contribute to the life of the communities in which they operate, and hold themselves accountable on social and environmental criteria as well as profitability. In the USA the Social Accountability 8000 standard developed by the Council on Economic Priorities provides one way of doing this, though its compliance procedures are weaker than the independent verification measures that are being piloted in coffee production, clothing, footballs, and timber supplies. Accountability implies specific commitments that few large companies are prepared to make. As pioneers like the Body Shop have discovered, this is risky because claims to fairness must be publicly tested, and that requires a degree of transparency that goes against the grain in competitive institutions that guard information jealously. The commercial benefit is that consumers will repay adherence to standards with their loyalty in the marketplace, but that requires a huge expansion of 'ethical demand'. In the meantime even small victories are valuable, like the gains made in Sri Lankan clothing factories under pressure from local NGOs: the reinstatement of a worker sacked for writing poems that lamented her life; increased compensation for another who put a needle through her eye; and the formation of a support group for a colleague raped on her way to work on Christmas Day.

Second, markets can be made to work to the benefit of smaller consumers and producers by reducing the benefits that are siphoned off
by intermediaries. In South India, over 90 per cent of crop storage
capacity and 80 per cent of credit disbursements are controlled by the
richest ten per cent of merchants – the *'masters of the countryside'* as
economist Barbara Harriss-White calls them. International NGOs have
helped peasant foresters in Mexico to negotiate higher prices directly
with the timber companies, just as rubber tappers in Brazil have
been able to retain a higher proportion of the surplus they create by
clubbing together to sell their produce at a main depot. The Inter-
American Foundation finances a joint marketing organisation for small
producers in MERCOSUR which increases their bargaining power in
negotiations over prices and conditions of sale. Collective action like
this stimulates both equity and efficiency, and builds a sense of solidarity among people who are sharing risks as well as benefits. That
reverses the normal position in markets whereby the rich protect themselves against exposure by purchasing insurance or taking expensive
legal action, while the poor bear the costs of market failure.

Third, it is possible to change the structure of business so that goods
and services are produced in ways which build co-operation, and
profits are distributed with a social purpose. Community-based economic activities are nearly always excluded from national accounts, but
according to futurist Hazel Henderson they already make up 25 per
cent of global transactions. [. . .] Some economists think that low-
income countries can bypass the sweatshop stage of production
altogether by concentrating on micro-economic reforms that boost
productivity and raise living standards, while adhering to Northern
standards of social protection and environmental sensitivity. However,
many 'social enterprises' find that they must be less social and more
commercial over time as markets become increasingly competitive, just
as a highly-responsible company like Levi Strauss still has to close
plants when cost pressures increase in the global marketplace. Co-
operative production requires an unusual set of circumstances to be
successful in open markets, especially as the scale of the enterprise
increases. But it can work if it builds on pre-existing collective work
arrangements that still meet market standards of cost and quality, like
the firms in Papua New Guinea that work on both commercial and
community tasks together, or the Native American businesses in
Canada which are owned collectively but work in partnership with
large corporations who offer them access to global markets.

Experiments like these need support from macro-economic policies
that integrate social and environmental criteria into decisions over
prices, interest rates, industrial policy and labour markets; rewarding

behaviour that is beneficial, like labour-intensive production; and penalising what is undesirable, like pollution. In Latin American cities, infrastructure is now routinely provided through labour-intensive works co-managed by communities, NGOs and private companies, which makes design more relevant and keeps more of the economic surplus local. Decision makers must assess the impact of fiscal measures on vulnerable people, protect public expenditure for the poor, stabilise the prices of key consumption goods, and integrate gender considerations into decision making so that the hidden costs of public-expenditure reform on women and children can be addressed.

Since resources are obviously limited in low-income countries, most of these measures will need temporary support in the form of foreign aid, along with graduated agreements to level up working conditions and environmental standards around the world. This must be done carefully. For example, in Bangladesh an estimated 55,000 children lost their jobs in the garment industry as a result of a US trade boycott during 1996. None of the children went back to school, and at least half ended up in much lower-paid jobs or prostitution. It is better to work with local producers on codes of conduct, and provide additional support for factory inspections and compensation if children lose their jobs. Although it is multinational companies that are usually criticised for exploitation, conditions are often worse among small local firms. This poses problems for global regulation, but research in Asia shows that even small firms can improve their standards if they get enough support to improve production processes and submit themselves to local regulation more sensitive to the need for flexibility. Encouraging corporations to adopt some minimum standards and enforce them along their supply chains is a sensible strategy so long as it is applied fairly, as sportswear giant Nike did when it severed ties with four Indonesian contractors in 1997 for gross abuses of labour rights. Most governments already support the principle of core standards, though they argue about how big the core should be. An irreducible minimum (already protected in the International Bill of Human Rights) should include the right of workers to organise and bargain (since that provides the basis for locally-appropriate standards in other areas) and a ban on forced labour, slave labour, and exploitative child labour, defined – as in the Bangladesh example – following a dialogue with parents and their children.

Finally, changing the way economic decisions are made requires a new framework for national accounting which reflects the real costs of production and exchange (not just the level of economic activity). The current system is based on GNP, which as Senator Robert Kennedy once noted, *'measures everything except that which makes life worthwhile'*.

There can't be much sense in a system that confuses goods with bads and addictions with cures; counts weapons production on a par with investment in schools; treats child care as valueless, and discounts the costs of pollution. When these costs are revealed and quantified there will be stronger incentives to steer clear of decisions which damage the things we want to protect, like our human and natural resources. And that will stimulate the transition to an economy which grows without increasing the throughput of non-renewable resources or placing an unfair social burden on women. There are many possibilities on offer, like 'green GDP' and the index of sustainable economic welfare. All have problems of methodology, but most can be handled by developing a system of 'satellite accounts' to run alongside the normal ones. The more we can change the language of economics and the measurement of prices in this way, the easier it will be to use the market to advance social and environmental objectives. And that will take us closer to a win-win future where economic efficiency does not have to be traded off against long-term common interests.

[. . .]

Notes

1   Jordan's fee in 1993 was US$20 million, compared to wages of $1.75/day: Wiseman, J (1997) *Alternatives to Globalisation: an Asia–Pacific Perspective*, Community Aid Abroad, Melbourne, p. 39.
2   Cited in Brittan, S (1995) *Capitalism With a Human Face*, Edward Elgar, London, p. 50.
3   Chomsky, N (1994) *World Orders, Old and New*, Pluto Press, London, p. 271; Mann, M (1986) *The Sources of Social Power*, 3 vols, Cambridge University Press, Cambridge.

28

Regulating Globalization?
The Reinvention of Politics

David Held

[. . .]

Contemporary globalization is transforming state power and the nature of political community, but any description of this as a simple loss or diminution of national powers distorts what has happened. For although globalization is changing the relationship between states and markets, this is not straightforwardly at the expense of states. States and public authorities initiated many of the fundamental changes – for example, the deregulation of capital in the 1980s and early 1990s. In other spheres of activity as well, states have become central in initiating new kinds of transnational collaboration, from the emergence of different forms of military alliances to the advancement of human rights regimes.

The fact of the matter is that on many fundamental measures of state power – from the capacity to raise taxes and revenue to the ability to hurl concentrated force at enemies – states are, at least throughout most of the OECD world, as powerful if not more powerful than their predecessors.[1] On the other hand, the pressures upon them have grown massively as well. In this context, it makes more sense to talk about the transformation of state power in the context of globalization – rather than simply to refer to what has happened as a decline.[2] The power, authority and operations of national governments are changing but not all in one direction. The entitlement of states to rule within circumscribed territories (sovereignty) is far from on the edge of collapse, although the practical nature of this entitlement – the actual capacity of states to rule – is changing its shape. A new regime of government and governance is emerging and displacing traditional conceptions of state power as an indivisible, territorially exclusive form of public power. Far from globalization leading to 'the end of the state', it is stimulating a range of government and governance strategies and, in some fundamental respects, a more activist state.

Nowhere is this better seen than in the political context of economic globalization. Alongside global economic change there has been a parallel but distinct set of political changes, shifting the reach of political power and the forms of rule. Although governments and states remain powerful actors, they have helped create, and now share the global arena with, an array of other agencies and organizations. The state is confronted by an enormous number of intergovernmental organizations, international agencies and regimes that operate across different spatial reaches, and by quasi-supranational institutions like the European Union.[3] Non-state actors or transnational bodies also participate intensively in global politics. These developments challenge the conventional, state-based accounts of world order and generate a much more complex picture of regional and global governance. In this more complex world, states deploy their sovereignty and autonomy as bargaining chips in negotiations involving coordination and collaboration across shifting transnational and international networks.[4]

What developments in such domains as politics, law and the economy suggest is that globalization is far from being a singular phenomenon. While it is [in effect] a multidimensional phenomenon that depicts a general shift in the organization of human activity and the deployment of power towards transcontinental or interregional patterns, this shift can take different forms and follow different types of trajectory across economic, political and other domains. It can also generate conflicting as well as complementary tendencies in the determination of relations of power and authority.

For example, the global economy is more open, fluid and volatile than ever before; economies are less protected and international markets react rapidly to changing political and economic signals.[5] It is harder to buck international economic trends than it was in the earlier decades of the postwar years. Because markets are more liquid, they are an enhanced source of instability. Financial and industrial capital enjoy increased exit options from political communities, altering the economic context of national labour markets. Moreover, in a 'wired world' disturbances rapidly transfer across markets and societies, ramifying the effects of change. Accordingly, the costs and benefits of pursuing certain policies become fuzzier, and this encourages political caution, 'adaptive politics', and precautionary supply-side economic measures.

Nonetheless, there has been massive growth in regional and global governance which increasingly surveys, mediates and manages these developments. Moreover, demands for increased levels of international regulation are growing – from George Soros to the World Trade Organization (WTO) and the UN. More and more people recognize the need for enhanced political accountability and for transparency and openness of decision-making in international, social and economic, domains; although the proper form and place for such initiatives, it has to be said, is far from clear.

The transformation of democracy

Contemporary globalization has contributed to the transformation of the nature and prospects of democratic political community in a number of distinctive ways. It is worth dwelling on these for a moment. First, the locus of effective political power can no longer be assumed to be national governments – effective power is shared and bartered by diverse forces and agencies at national, regional and international levels. Second, the idea of a political community of fate – of a self-determining collectivity – can no longer be meaningfully located within the boundaries of a single nation-state alone, as it could more reasonably be when nation-states were being forged. Some of the most fundamental forces and processes that determine the nature of life chances within and across political communities are now beyond the reach of individual nation-states. The system of national political communities remains, of course, but it is articulated today with complex economic, organizational, administrative, legal and cultural networks and processes that limit and check its efficacy. If these processes and structures are not acknowledged and brought into the political process themselves, they may bypass or circumvent the democratic state system.[6]

Third, national sovereignty today, even in regions with intensive overlapping and divided political structures, has not been wholly undermined – far from it. However, the operation of states in increasingly complex global and regional systems affects both their autonomy (by changing the balance between the costs and benefits of policies) and aspects of their sovereignty (by altering the balance between national, regional and international legal frameworks and administrative practices). While massive concentrations of power remain features of many states, these are frequently embedded in, and articulated with, other domains of political authority – regional, international and transnational.

Fourth, the present period is marked by a significant series of new types of 'boundary problems', which challenge the distinctions between domestic and foreign affairs, internal political issues and external questions, and the sovereign concerns of the nation-state and international considerations. States and governments face issues like BSE (bovine spongiform encephalopathy), the spread of malaria, the use of non-renewable resources, the management of nuclear waste and the proliferation of weapons of mass destruction, which cannot easily be categorized in traditional political terms as domestic or international. Moreover, issues like the location and investment strategy of multinational corporations, the regulation of global financial markets, the development of European Monetary Union, the threat to the tax base of individual countries which arises from the global division of labour and the absence of capital controls, all pose questions about the continued effectiveness of some of the traditional instruments of national economic policy. In fact, in all major areas of government policy, the enmeshment of national political communities in regional and global processes involves them in intensive issues of transboundary coordination and control. Political space for the development and pursuit of effective government and the accountability of political power is no longer coterminous with a delimited national territory.

The growth of transboundary problems creates what I like to refer to as 'overlapping communities of fate'; that is, a state of affairs in which the fortunes and prospects of individual political communities are increasingly bound together.[7] Political communities are locked into a diversity of processes and structures that range in and through them, linking and fragmenting them into complex constellations. Moreover, national communities themselves certainly do not make and determine decisions and policies exclusively for themselves when they decide such issues as the regulation of sexuality, health and the environment; national governments by no means simply determine what is right or appropriate exclusively for their own citizens.

The assumption that one can understand the nature and possibilities of political community merely by referring to national structures and mechanisms of political power is clearly anachronistic. Accordingly, questions are raised both about the fate of the idea of the political community and about the appropriate locus for the articulation of the political good. If the agent at the heart of modern political discourse, be it a person, group or government, is locked into a variety of overlapping communities and jurisdictions, then the proper 'home' of politics and democracy becomes difficult to locate.

This matter is most apparent in Europe, where the development of the EU has created intensive discussion about the future of sovereignty and autonomy within individual nation-states. But the issues are important not just for Europe and the West, but for countries in other parts of the world, for example, in East Asia. The countries of East Asia must recognize emerging problems – for instance, problems concerning AIDS, migration and new challenges to peace, security and economic prosperity – that spill over the boundaries of nation-states. Moreover, they are developing within the context of growing interconnectedness across the world's major regions, with few better illustrations than the economic crisis of 1997–8.[8] This interconnectedness is marked in a whole range of areas, from the environment and human rights to issues of international crime. In other words, East Asia is necessarily part of a more global order and is locked into a diversity of sites of power which shape and determine its collective fortunes.

Global transformations have affected our concept of the political community and, in particular, our concept of the democratic political community. It is too rarely acknowledged that the proper nature and form of political communities are clouded by the multiplying interconnections among them. How so, exactly?

Electoral politics and the ballot box are at the heart of the process whereby consent and legitimacy are bestowed upon government in liberal democracies. However, the notions that consent legitimates government and that the national vote is the appropriate mechanism by which authority is periodically conferred on government become problematic as soon as the nature of a 'relevant community' is examined.[9] What is the proper constituency and realm of jurisdiction for developing and carrying out policy in relation to issues such as the policing and prosecution of paedophilia, the maintenance of military security, the harvesting of rain forests, the use of non-renewable resources, the instability of global financial markets, the pursuit of those who have committed crimes against humanity and the management and control of genetic engineering in animals and humans? It has been taken for granted for the best part of the last 200 years that national boundaries are the proper bases to demarcate which individuals are included and excluded from participation in decisions affecting their lives; but if many socioeconomic processes and the outcomes of decisions about them stretch beyond national frontiers, then the implications of this are serious, not only for the categories of consent and legitimacy but for all the key ideas of democracy. At issue is the nature of a political community and how the boundaries of a political community might be drawn, as well as the meaning of representation and the problem of who should represent whom and on what basis and the proper form of political participation – who should participate in which domains and in what ways. As fundamental processes of governance escape the categories of the nation-state, the traditional national resolutions of the key questions of democratic theory and practice look increasingly threadbare.

The idea of government by or of the state, democratic or otherwise, can no longer be simply defended as an idea suitable to a particular closed political community or nation-state. The idea of a political community of fate – of a self-determining collectivity – can no longer meaningfully be located within the boundaries of a single nation-state alone. We are compelled to recognize that the extensity, intensity and impact of economic, political and environmental processes raise questions about where they are most appropriately addressed. If the most powerful geopolitical and economic forces are not to settle many pressing matters simply in terms of their own objectives and by virtue of their power, then the current institutions and mechanisms of accountability need to be reconsidered. In my writings over the last few years, I have sought to offer such a reconsideration by setting out a cosmopolitan conception of democratic governance.

The cosmopolitan project

In essence, the cosmopolitan project attempts to specify the principles and the institutional arrangements for making accountable those sites and forms of power which presently operate beyond the scope of democratic control.[10] It argues that in the millennium ahead each citizen of a state will have to learn to become a 'cosmopolitan citizen' as well: that is, a person capable of mediating between national traditions, communities of fate and alternative styles of life. Citizenship in a democratic polity of the future is likely to involve a growing mediating role: a role which encompasses dialogue with the traditions and discourses of others with the aim of expanding the horizons of one's own framework of meaning and prejudice. Political agents who can 'reason from the point-of-view of others' might be better equipped to resolve, and resolve fairly, the new and challenging transboundary issues and processes that create overlapping communities of fate. In addition, the cosmopolitan project contends that, if many contemporary forms of power are to become accountable and if many of the complex issues that affect us all – locally, nationally, regionally and globally – are to be democratically regulated, people will have to have access to and membership in diverse political communities. Put differently, a democratic political community for the new millennium necessarily describes a world where citizens enjoy multiple citizenships. Faced with overlapping communities of fate they need to be not only citizens of their own communities, but also of the wider regions in which they live and of the wider global order. Institutions will certainly need to develop that reflect the multiple issues, questions and problems that link people together regardless of the particular nation-states in which they were born or brought up.

With this in mind, the cosmopolitan position maintains that democracy needs to be rethought as a 'double-sided process'. By a double-sided process – or process of double democratization – is meant the deepening of democracy within a national community, involving the democratization of states and civil societies over time, combined with the extension of democratic forms and processes across territorial borders.[11] Democracy for the new millennium must allow cosmopolitan citizens to gain access to, mediate between and render accountable the social, economic and political processes and flows that cut across and transform their traditional community boundaries. The core of this project involves reconceiving legitimate political authority in a manner that disconnects it from its traditional anchor in fixed borders and delimited territories and, instead, articulates it as an attribute of basic democratic arrangements or basic democratic law which can, in principle, be entrenched and drawn upon in diverse self-regulating associations – from cities and subnational regions to nation-states, regions and wider global networks. It is clear that the process of disconnection has already begun as political authority and legitimate forms of governance are diffused 'below', 'above' and 'alongside' the nation-state.

The 20th century embraces many different forms of globalization. There is the rise of neoliberal deregulation so much emphasized from the mid-1970s. But there is also the growth of major global and regional institutions, from the UN to the EU. The latter are remarkable political innovations in the context of state history. The UN remains a creature of the inter-state system; however, it has, despite all its limitations, developed an innovative system of global governance which delivers significant international public goods – from air-traffic control and the management of telecommunications to the control of contagious diseases, humanitarian relief for refugees and some protection of the environmental commons. The EU, in remarkably little time, has taken Europe from the disarray of the post-Second World War era to a world in which sovereignty is pooled across a growing number of areas of common concern. Again, despite its many limitations, the EU represents a highly innovative form of governance which creates a framework of collaboration for addressing transborder issues.

In addition, it is important to reflect upon the growth in this century of the scope and content of international law. Twentieth century forms of international law – from the law governing war to that concerning crimes against humanity, environmental issues and human rights – have created the basis of what can be thought of as an emerging framework of cosmopolitan law, law which circumscribes and delimits the political power of individual states. In principle, states are no longer able to treat their citizens as they think fit; for the values embedded in these laws qualify in fundamental ways the nature and form of political power, and they set down basic standards and boundaries which no agent (political or economic) should be able to cross.

Moreover, the 20th century has seen the beginning of significant efforts to reframe markets – to use legislation to alter the background conditions and operations of firms in the marketplace. While efforts in this direction failed in respect to the NAFTA agreement, the 'Social Chapter' of the Maastricht Agreement, for instance, embodies principles and rules which are compatible with the idea of restructuring aspects of markets. If implemented, the 'Social Chapter' could, in principle, alter working conditions – for example, with respect to the provision of information and patterns of employee consultation – in a number of distinctive ways. While the provisions of the Maastricht Agreement fall far short of what is ultimately necessary if judged by the standards of a cosmopolitan conception of democracy, they set down new forms of regulation which can be built upon.[12]

These examples of changes in global politics and regulation suggest that, while globalization is a highly contested phenomenon, it has embraced important collaborative initiatives in politics, law and the economy in the 20th century. Together, these create an anchor on which to build a more accountable form of globalization. The cosmopolitan project is in favour of a radical extension of this development so long as it is circumscribed by democratic public law, that is, by the entrenchment of a far-reaching cluster of democratic rights and duties. Democratic public law sets down standards – entitlements and constraints – that specify an equality of status with respect to the basic institutions and organizations of a community and of overlapping communities of fate. The cosmopolitan project advocates its entrenchment *via* a series of short- and long-term measures in the conviction that, through a process of progressive, incremental change, geopolitical forces will come to be embedded in and socialized into democratic rules and practices.[13]

What does this vision mean in the context of the kind of economic crisis which engulfed Indonesia, Russia and many other countries in 1997–8? I would like to address this briefly by considering some of the underlying economic and political issues involved in the crisis and some of the questions they raise about political regulation and the proper site of democratic accountability. The aim of this is to show that cosmopolitanism, as I understand it, has policy implications – in the here and now, and not just in the there and then!

The explosive growth of global financial activity and the expansion of global financial markets since the 1980s has transformed the context of national economies. Contemporary global finance is, as already noted, marked by high extensity, intensity and volatility in exchange rates, interest rates and other financial asset prices. As a result, national macro-economic policy becomes vulnerable to changes in global financial conditions. Speculative flows can have rapid and dramatic domestic economic consequences; and financial difficulties faced by a single institution or sector in one country can have major implications for the rest of the global financial sphere. The collapse of the Thai currency in 1997 contributed to dramatic falls in currency values across East Asia and affected currency values in other emerging markets. The rapid flow of short-term capital out of these economies also affected stock markets around the world. Given the volatile nature of financial markets and the instantaneous diffusion of financial information between the world's major financial centres risks were generated with implications for the entire global financial system, and which no government alone could either diffuse or insulate itself from.[14]

A cosmopolitan political approach to economic and financial crises distinguishes itself from both liberal market solutions, with their constant emphasis on unburdening or deregulating markets in the hope that they might better function in the future, and national interventionist strategies, which champion the primacy of national economic management without giving due attention to regional and global policy options and initiatives. What are the targets that a cosmopolitan approach could pursue?

First, the extension of legislation to reframe markets is necessary in order to counter their indeterminacy and the massive social and environmental costs they sometimes generate. The ground rules of the free market and trade system have to be altered in subtle and less subtle ways. Ultimately, this necessitates entrenching new regulatory terms – about child labour, trade union activity, social matters (such as childcare and parental leave) and environmental protection – into the articles of association and terms of reference of economic organizations and trading agencies. Only by introducing new terms of empowerment and accountability throughout the global economic system, as a supplement and complement to collective agreements and welfare measures in national and regional contexts, can a new settlement be created between economic power and democracy.

Second, new forms of economic coordination are indispensable. Organizations like the IMF, the World Bank, the OECD and G-7 all operate with separate agendas. Policy-making is fragmented. A new coordinating economic agency, working at both regional and global levels, needs to be created. This is not as fanciful as it might at first seem, especially in the light of the establishment of new multilateral bodies after the Second World War and, most recently, the WTO. Where exactly a new economic coordinating agency should be located (at the UN, or elsewhere?) is a matter for debate. But the primary issue is to recognize the need for a new transnational economic authority that is capable of deliberating about emergency economic situations, the dynamics of international capital markets and the broad balance of public investment priorities and expenditure patterns. The brief of such a body would be to fill a vacuum; that is, to become a coordinator for economic policy that is set at global or regional levels or is not set at all, at least not by public authorities.

Third, it is important to develop measures to regulate the volatility of international financial markets and their speculative pursuit of short-term gains. Taxes on turnover in foreign exchange markets, the retention of capital controls as a policy option and a substantial increase in the regulation and transparency of bank accounting and of other financial institutions are necessary measures if international short-term capital markets are to be amenable to democratic intervention.

Such initiatives must be thought of as steps towards a new 'Bretton Woods' system – a system that would introduce accountability and regulation into institutional mechanisms for the coordination of investment, production and trade. If linked, fourth, to measures aimed at alleviating the most pressing cases of avoidable economic suffering – by radically reducing the debt of many developing countries, by generating new economic facilities at organizations like the IMF and World Bank for development purposes and, perhaps (as George Soros has suggested), by creating new international credit insurance funds – then the basis would be created for entrenching capitalism in a set of democratic mechanisms and procedures.

But none of these developments alone will create the foundations for adequate democratic regulation unless they are, fifth, firmly linked to measures to extend democratic forms and processes across territorial borders. Such a positive policy of democratization might begin in key regions by creating greater transparency and accountability in leading decision-making centres. In Europe this would involve enhancing the power of the European Parliament and reducing the democratic deficit across all EU institutions. Elsewhere it would include restructuring the UN Security Council to give developing countries a significant voice in decision-making; deepening the mechanisms of accountability of the leading international and transnational public agencies; strengthening the enforcement capacity of human rights regimes (socioeconomic as well as political), and creating, in due course, a new democratic UN second chamber. Such targets point the way towards laying the foundations for forms of accountability at the global level. In short, they are necessary elements of what I earlier referred to as a cosmopolitan conception of democracy. Faced with overlapping communities of fate citizens in the future must become not just active citizens of their own communities, but also of the regions in which they live and of the wider global order.

If globalization refers to those processes that underpin a transformation in the organization of human affairs, linking together and expanding human activity such that it encompasses frameworks of interregional and intercontinental change and development, then many of our most cherished political ideas – which formerly centred on nation-states – need to be recast. It is beyond the brief of this discussion to pursue these issues at any length. But if we live in a world that is marked by enhanced forms of global politics and multilayered governance, then the efficacy of national democratic traditions and national legal traditions is challenged fundamentally. However this challenge is specified precisely, it is based upon the recognition that the nature and quality of democracy within a particular community and the nature and quality of democratic relations among communities are interconnected, and that new legal and organizational mechanisms must be created if democracy and political communities themselves are to prosper.

It would be wholly fallacious to conclude from this that the politics of local communities or national democratic communities will be (or should be) wholly eclipsed by the new forces of political globalization. To assume this would be to misunderstand the very complex, variable and uneven impact of regional and global processes on political life. Of course, certain problems and policies will properly remain the responsibility of local governments and national states; but others will be recognized as appropriate for specific regions, and still others – such as elements of the environment, global security concerns, world health questions and economic regulation – will be seen to need new institutional arrangements to address them. Tests of extensiveness, intensity and comparative efficiency can be used to help filter and guide policy issues to different levels of governance.[15] But however such issues are precisely filtered, the agenda facing political theory in the face of regional and global shifts is now clearly defined.

The history of democratic political thought and practice has been marked by two great transitions. The first led to the establishment of greater participation and accountability in cities during antiquity and, again, in Renaissance Italy; and the second led to the entrenchment of democracy over great territories and time spans through the invention of representative democracy. From the early modern period to the late 19th century geography could, in principle, be neatly meshed with sites of political power and authority. Today, we are on the cusp of a third great transition.[16] Democracy could become entrenched in cities, nation-states and wider regional and global forums, or else it might come to be thought of as that form of national government which became progressively more anachronistic in the 21st century. Fortunately, the choice remains ours.

Notes

1 M. Mann, 'Has Globalisation Ended the Rise and Rise of the Nation-State?', *Review of International Political Economy*, 1987, 4 (3): 472–96.

2 D. Held, A. G. McGrew, D. Goldblatt and J. Perraton, *Global Transformations: Politics, Economics and Culture* (Cambridge: Polity, 1999).

3 D. Held, *Democracy and the Global Order: From the Modern State to Cosmopolitan Governance* (Cambridge: Polity, 1995, Chs. 5 and 6).

4 R. Keohane, 'Hobbes's Dilemma and Institutional Change in World Politics: Sovereignty in International Society', in H. H. Holm and G. Sorensen (eds), *Whose World Order?*, (Boulder, CO: Westview Press, 1995).

5 J. Perraton, D. Goldblatt, D. Held and A. McGrew, 'The Globalisation of Economic Activity', in *New Political Economy*, 1997, 2 (2): 257–77.

6 S. Sassen, *Globalisation and its Discontents* (New York: The New Press, 1998).

7 D. Held, *Democracy and the Global Order*; D. Held, *Models of Democracy*, 2nd edn, (Cambridge: Polity, 1995); D. Archibugi, D. Held, M. Köhler (eds), *Re-Imagining Political Community: Studies in Cosmopolitan Democracy* (Cambridge: Polity, 1998).

8 D. Held and A. G. McGrew, 'The End of the Old Order?', *Review of International Studies*, Special Issue, 1998: 219–52.

9 D. Held, *Democracy and the Global Order*.

10 D. Held, *Democracy and the Global Order*; D. Archibugi, D. Held, M. Köhler (eds), *Re-Imagining Political Community*; A. Linklater, *The Transformation of Political Community*, (Cambridge: Cambridge University Press, 1986).

11 David Held, *Models of Democracy*.

12 D. Held, *Democracy and the Global Order*, pp. 239 66.

13 D. Held, *Democracy and the Global Order*, Pt. III.

14 D. Held, A. G. McGrew, 'The End of the Old Order?', op. cit., pp. 229–30.

15 D. Held, *Democracy and the Global Order*, pp. 236–7.

16 R. A. Dahl, *Democracy and Its Critics*, (New Haven, CT: Yale University Press, 1989).

Index

Index compiled by Ann Kingdom